Testimonials

"With the publication of *Redeeming Sex: The Battle for the Body*, Dr. Eduardo Echeverria launches *Creation Redeemed*, the first of a three-volume set that promises to be an undertaking of critical importance in the recovery an integral vision of the human person and of our culture. He tells us that at the heart of the entire series is a conviction that the new evangelization called for by Pope St. John Paul II must overcome the divide between faith and culture such that the whole of human thought and action is permeated by the Gospel. In this first installment, Dr. Echeverria offers us a profoundly insightful approach to engaging in the confrontation between orthodoxy and modernity by taking up several vexed questions: the existence of a normative account of human sexuality and marriage, the intrinsic importance of the body to human personhood, and – perhaps most significantly in light of contemporary discourse – a realist account of the place of experience in arriving at the truth, both of reality and of oneself. The volume illustrates one of the author's own key points: that the aggiornamento called for by the Second Vatican Council is not the starting place but a consequence of the creative retrieval of the wisdom of our tradition."

– Dr. Deborah Savage
Franciscan University of Steubenville
and co-editor of *Lived Experience and the Search for Truth: Revisiting Catholic Sexual Morality*

"St. Pope John Paul II preached at his inaugural mass: 22 oct. 1978: 'Do not be afraid. Open wide the doors for Christ. To his saving power open the boundaries of States, economic and political systems, the vast fields of culture, civilization and development. Do not be afraid. Christ knows 'what is in man'. He alone knows it.' This book does just that: by intellectually bringing Christ in the realm of sexuality, it opens our minds, hearts and bodies for His redeeming power!"

+ Everard de Jong
auxiliary bishop of Roermond, Netherlands
and apostolic administrator of the Military Ordinariate of Netherlands

"With his customary incisiveness, carefulness, and depth, Eduardo Echeverria has produced an essential study of one of the most neuralgic moral and theological subjects in our time. Current discussions of sex, the body, and human nature have too often descended into sterile polemics and mutual anathemas. Echeverria brings a bracing breath of fresh air to the discussion which, simultaneously, reserves a proper place for justice, truth, and mercy amid many difficult questions."

– Robert Royal
Faith & Reason Institute

"This work by Dr. Echeverria is a testimony to the continued luminosity that can and must be drawn from the pontificate of Pope St. John Paul II regarding truly chaste sexuality and sound Christian anthropology."

– Matthew K. Minerd
Professor of Philosophy and Moral Theology
Byzantine Catholic Seminary of Ss. Cyril and Methodius
Pittsburgh PA

Vol. 1
Creation Redeemed

Redeeming Sex

The Battle for the Body

En Route Books and Media, LLC
Saint Louis, MO

En Route Books and Media, LLC
5705 Rhodes Avenue
St. Louis, MO 63109

Contact us at contactus@enroutebooksandmedia.com

Cover art by Sebastian Mahfood using a wall mural from Saint Vincent de Paul Church in Paris

Copyright 2025 Eduardo J. Echeverria

ISBN: 979-8-88870-298-7
Library of Congress Control Number: 2024952694

All rights reserved. No part of this book may be reproduced, stored in a retrieval system, or transmitted in any form, or by any means, electronic, mechanical, photocopying, or otherwise, without the prior written permission of the author.

Amici

Robin Beck

Philip Blosser

Mary Boersen

Oana Gotia

Thomas G. Guarino

Stephanie and Lawrence Toth

Further let me ask of my reader, wherever, alike with myself, he is certain, there to go on with me; wherever, alike with myself, he hesitates, there to join with me in inquiring; wherever he recognizes himself to be in <u>error</u>, there to return to me; wherever he recognizes me to be so, there to call me back: so that we may enter together upon the path of charity, and advance towards Him of whom it is said, "Seek His face evermore" [Ps 105:4].

St. Augustine, De Trinitate, I, 3, 5

Acknowledgments

Since 2003 when I first came to Sacred Heart Major Seminary, Detroit, MI, I continue to be immensely grateful for the ongoing support of the administrators and staff of this theological university, and for my many friends among staff, and colleagues, especially for their deep commitment to the Second Vatican Council, the Catholic faith, and the truth of the Catholic Church's teachings. To them all who provide me with a sanctuary, indeed, a home for teaching and writing, I owe a debt of gratitude.

I am especially grateful to Matthew Wright for copyediting, Nelson Kloosterman for translating from untranslated Dutch works as well as doing the bibliography, and Sebastian Mahfood, publisher and indexer of this book.

I am also grateful to a network of friends for their support in the current circumstances of my daily life: Robin Beck, Philip Blosser, Mary Boersen, Oana Gotia, Msgr. Thomas G. Guarino, and Stephanie and Lawrence Toth.

I am additionally grateful for the testimonials from Robert Royal, Bishop Everard de Jong, Matthew K. Minerd, and Deborah Savage.

Last, but certainly not least, I am grateful beyond words to my wife, Donna Rose, especially now, for her wonderful and enduring support in all things, making it possible for me to do my work. Indeed, she is *sine qua non*.

May God grant that I speak with judgment and have thoughts worthy of what I have received, for He is the guide even of wisdom and the corrector of the wise. For both we and our words are in His hand, with all our understanding, too (Wis 7:15–16).

Table of Contents

Preface...v

Introduction..1

Chapter 1: Hermeneutical Considerations on Meaning and Truth......93
    The Idea of Doctrinal Development...93

Chapter 2: Christian Anthropology, the Unity of Human Nature, and
    the Bodily Subjectivity of the Human Person............................129
    Dualism, Duality, and Unity 133
    Individuality Structure That is Man 155
    Dooyeweerd's Critique of the Substance-Concept in Thomist
        Anthropology..169
    What Is Christian Personalism? 175
    Cosmological and Personalist 187

Chapter 3: Culture Wars, The Sexual Revolution, Ethics, and
    Hermeneutics 205
    The Pathos of Liberal Theology...205
    Erotic Wars..212
    Hermeneutics of Continuity...225
    False Dilemma: Permanence and Change 228
    Moral Authority?...238
    Teleological Approach to the Moral Life..................................244
    Ethics and Hermeneutics..253
    Again, Hermeneutics of Continuity 268
    The Law of Gradualism and the Gradualism of the Law............275
    No, the Sexual Revolution is not a Renewal Movement.............283

Materialistic Anthropology, Sexual Disenchantment, and Its Implications 288
The Love Commandment and the Personalistic Norm 291
The Roots of Sexual Promiscuity, Hedonism, and Self-transcendence 296
Creation, Sexual Difference, and its Eschatological Significance 309
Four Foundational Presuppositions to Sexual Ethics 318

Chapter 4: Ethics in Search of Its Experiential Point of Departure 345
The Philosophical Ethics and Moral Theology of Margaret A. Farley and Karol Wojtyla/John Paul II 345
Meaning of Divine Revelation 356
A Thin versus a Thick Idea of Revelation 356
A Thick Idea of Revelation 358
Doctrinal Development 361
Special Divine Revelation 363
Sources of Christian Ethics 369
Ethics as a Philosophical Theory of the Experience of Morality . 383
What are Science and Experience? 383
Different Aspects and Layers of the Moral Life: axiology, praxeology, and deontology 386
The Necessity of Metaphysics: the normative order of Natural Law 389
What is Just Love? 392

Chapter 5: Mercy and Truth—Pastoral Care of Individuals in Spiritually and Morally Problematic Relationships 397

Chapter 6: The Triumph of the Therapeutic Mentality 431
Experience, Dialogue, and Respect 434
Christianity is Life-Affirming 443

Table of Contents

- Defeating the "maladie catholique" 446
- Teaching Authority? 448
- Homosexual "Love" a Gift? 451
- "The Spirit of Truth" 470
- Call to Conversion and Holiness 478

Afterword: The Project of Redeeming Sex: The Battle for the Body .. 487
- Six Theses 488

Bibliography 507

Index 545

Preface

True spirituality cannot be abstracted from truth at one end, nor from the whole man and the whole culture at the other. If there is a true spirituality, it must encompass all.[1]

—Francis A. Schaeffer

The new evangelization that can make the twenty-first century a springtime of the Gospel is a task for the entire People of God, but will depend in a decisive way on the lay faithful being fully aware of their baptismal vocation and their responsibility for bringing the good news of Jesus Christ to their culture and society.[2]

—John Paul II

The Church's saving mission takes priority over its public and cultural tasks, thanks to the very essence of what the Church is: "The mystery of the holy Church is manifested in its very foundation" (*Lumen Gentium* 5). The meaning of the imitation of Christ becomes clear when we look at the Incarnation, through which "God send his Son in the likeness of sinful flesh" (Rom 8:3), God's self-abasement even to the death of his Son on the Cross (Phil 2:6-11), and the redemption of [man] through the "stumbling block and folly of the crucified Christ" (1 Cor 1:23). "Just as Christ carried out the work of redemption in poverty and persecution, so the Church is called to follow the same route that it might

---

[1] Francis A. Schaeffer, *The God Who Is There*, 30th anniversary edition (Downers Grove: InterVarsity Press, 1988), 177.

[2] John Paul II, *Springtime of Evangelization*, The Complete Texts of the Holy Father's 1998 ad Limina Addresses to the Bishops of the United States, ed. and intro. Fr. Thomas D. Williams, L.C. (San Francisco: Ignatius Press, 1999), 89.

communicate the fruits of redemption to men. [...] Thus the Church, although it needs human resources to carry out its mission, is not set up to seek earthly glory, but to proclaim, even by its own example, humility and self-sacrifice" (*Lumen Gentium* 8).³

—Gerhard Cardinal Müller

The number of specialist journals of theology is gradually becoming incalculable. The result is that essays which "appear" in them tend rather to be hidden than to be published. Naturally it is not the business of the author to judge whether the obscurity into which these essays fall is a just fate or a regrettable misfortune. But if he has the right to make any- thing appear at all, he cannot be reproached for trying to publish his work in some other form which will make it more probable that some- one will read it. And so we have at tempted here to disinter a few essays from periodicals.⁴

—Karl Rahner, SJ

---

³ *The Pope: His Mission and His Task,* Translated by Brian McNeil (Washington, DC: Catholic University of America Press, 2021), 88-9.

⁴ Karl Rahner, SJ, *Theological Investigations,* vol. 1, *God, Christ, Mary and Grace,* trans. Cornelius Ernst (Baltimore: Helicon Press, 1961 [1954]), xxi. Msgr. Thomas Guarino of Seton Hall University referred me to this passage of Karl Rahner found in the 1954 Preface of *Theological Investigations,* Volume I, reminding me of the context of my own book. My three-volume work, *Creation Redeemed,* too, is a collection of published essays from 2009–2024.

Introduction

This chapter introduces the book, *Creation Redeemed*, which consists of three volumes: one, *Redeeming Sex: The Battle for the Body*; two, *Redeeming Reason: Parts 1 and 2: Faith, Rationality, and Truth*; and three, *Redeeming Culture: Christ the Sign of Contradiction*.

Now, the doctrine of creation is an integral part of Christian revelation, but so too is a doctrine of sin. Man, savagely wounded by the Fall into sin, original sin (see Genesis 3), bears within himself this wound, which, as John Paul says, "constantly draws him towards evil and puts him in need of redemption."[1] The doctrine of sin, he adds, "has great hermeneutical value insofar as it helps one to understand human reality."[2] Yet, the deepest foundation of created reality is still what God made it despite the Fall.[3] The creation order continues to be upheld by God's common grace, which is a non-saving grace that limits the damaging effects of sin from having its full way with reality. Dutch Reformational philosopher, Herman Dooyeweerd (1894-1977), is right:

> Relegating creation to the background is not scriptural. Just read the Psalms, where the devout poet rejoices in the ordinances that God decreed for creation. Read the book of Job, where God himself speaks to his intensely suffering servant of the richness and depth of the laws which he established for his creatures. Read

---

[1] John Paul II, *Centesimus Annus*, §25. See also, "The Church's wisdom has always pointed to the presence of original sin in social conditions and in the structure of society: 'Ignorance of the fact that man has a wounded nature inclined to evil gives rise to serious errors in the areas of education, politics, social action, and morals' [*Catechism of the Catholic Church*, §407]" (Benedict XVI, *Caritas in Veritate*, § 34).

[2] John Paul II, *Centesimus Annus*, §25.

[3] Aidan Nichols, O.P., *The Shape of Catholic Theology*, 45.

the Gospels, where Christ appeals to the creational ordinance for marriage [Mark 10: 2-9; Matt 19-3-9] in order to counter those aimed at trapping him. Finally, read Romans 1: 19-20, where the creational ordinances are explicitly included in the general revelation to the human race.[4]

What is the consequence of denying the centrality of creation? Dooyeweerd explains, "A denial of this leads to the unscriptural conclusion that the fall is as broad as creation; i.e., that the fall destroyed the very nature of creation. This would mean that sin plays a self-determining, autonomous role over against God, the creator of all. Whoever maintains such a position robs God of his sovereignty and grants Satan a power equal to that of the origin of all things."[5] Furthermore, the wounds affecting creation are healed through the saving work of Jesus Christ, redeeming and restoring creation from within this fallen world. The Catholic tradition presupposes a theology of nature and grace in which its key theme is grace restoring and renewing nature. This theology is, however briefly, well expressed by Etienne Gilson, "The work of creation is shattered, but the fragments remain good, and, with the grace of God, they may be reconstituted and restored."[6] Elsewhere he writes, "The true Catholic position consists in maintaining that nature was created good, that it has been wounded, but that it can be at least partially healed by grace if God so wishes. This *instauration*, that is to say, this renewal, this re-establishment, this restoration of nature to its primitive

---

[4] Herman Dooyeweerd, *Roots of Western Culture*, trans. John Kraay, and edited by Mark Vander Vennen and Bernard Zylstra (Toronto: Wedge, 1979), 59.

[5] Dooyeweerd, *Roots of Western Culture*, 60.

[6] Etienne Gilson, *The Spirit of Mediaeval Philosophy*, 127.

goodness by grace, is on this point the program of authentic Catholicism."⁷ This understanding of the redemption of creation shapes the three volumes of this book.

Integral Evangelization: Christ and Culture, Nature and Grace

Perhaps the most central theme in the almost twenty-seven-year pontificate of the philosopher-Pope John Paul II is the call to the *new evangelization*, that is, to the revitalization of the Christian faith at the heart of Western culture.⁸ This vital call for renewal is, in truth, an expression of the permanent validity of the Church's missionary mandate⁹ to preaching the gospel throughout the world, bringing the gospel to the whole spectrum of human life, and transforming creation from within and making it new—the plan of creation, fall, redemption, and the consummation of all creation in Christ. I believe that John Paul urged us to carry out the new evangelization as *integral evangelization*—to use a term of Aidan Nichols that nicely captures the full scope of this call.¹⁰ As

---

⁷ Etienne Gilson, *Christianity and Philosophy*, 21-22.

⁸ Adapted from my monograph, *Slitting the Sycamore: Christ and Culture in the New Evangelization* §12, Christian Social Thought Series (Grand Rapids, MI: Acton Institute, 2008; 2013). See the *Compendium on the New Evangelization*, Pontifical Council for the Promotion of the New Evangelization 1939-2012 (United States Catholic Conference, 2015), which documents the history of this conception from the early parts of the 20th century popes, beginning with Pius XII, John XXIII, Vatican II, Paul VI, continuing with John Paul II, and Benedict XVI. The writings of John Paul II receive extensive coverage in this compendium, 113-880, next to Benedict XVI, 881-1018.

⁹ John Paul II, *Redemptoris Missio*, "On the Permanent Validity of the Church's Missionary Mandate," December 7, 1990.

¹⁰ Fr. Aidan Nichols, O.P., "Integral Evangelization," *Josephinum Journal of Theology* 13, §1 (2006): 66–80.

Nichols describes his understanding of integral evangelization, "I understand an evangelization that addresses all the dimensions of the person-in-society that Christian wisdom can help to flourish."[11] John Paul adds to this: "The men and women of today, like those of every time and place, are yearning for salvation. They wish to *rediscover the truth of God's dominion over creation and history, to encounter his self-revelation, and to experience his merciful love in all the dimensions of their lives.* The great truth to be proclaimed to this and every age is that God has entered human history so that men and women can truly become children of God."[12] Furthermore, John Paul calls for a new evangelization, for integral evangelization, because Western culture has become missionary territory as it increasingly is more estranged from its Christian roots.[13] Moreover, the new evangelization includes not only a call to conversion, to respond to the gospel, but also to the renewal of contemporary civilization and culture, society, politics, and economics—indeed to the whole spectrum of life. John Paul was convinced that, as he put it, "A faith that does not become culture is a faith not fully accepted, not entirely thought out, not faithfully lived."[14]

In particular, integral evangelization includes, according to John Paul, "*a proclamation of the Church's social doctrine.*" "There can be *no genuine solution of the 'social question',*" he adds, "*apart from the Gospel.*"[15] That is,

---

[11] Nichols, "Integral Evangelization," 68.

[12] John Paul II, *Springtime of Evangelization*, 39. Emphasis added.

[13] John Paul II, Apostolic Letter, November 10, 1994, *Tertio Millennio Adveniente*, §57.

[14] John Paul II, Letter instituting the Pontifical Council for Culture, May 20, 1982, AAS LXXIV (1982), 683–88, as cited in *Towards a Pastoral Approach to Culture*, Pontifical Council for Culture, 1999, §1.

[15] John Paul II, Encyclical Letter, May 1, 1991, *Centesimus Annus*, §5.

the Church's social teaching is itself a *valid instrument of evangelization*. As such, it proclaims God and his mystery of salvation in Christ to every human being, and for that very reason reveals man to himself. In this light, and only in this light, does it concern itself with everything else: the human rights of the individual, and in particular of the "working class," the family and education, the duties of the state, the ordering of national and international society, economic life, culture, war and peace, and respect for life from the moment of conception until death.[16]

Now, one fundamental component of Catholic social teaching is the doctrine of natural law, which is a theonomic principle because it is grounded in the order of creation and, hence, of God's general moral revelation (cf. Rom. 2:13–15).[17] God is the source of this law, given to man in the very act of being created and in principle open to being known by human reason.[18] Significantly, natural law is essential to the evangelization of the power of the state. How so? Nichols explains,

---

[16] John Paul II, *Centesimus Annus*, §54.

[17] On the relationship between natural law and general revelation, see J. Budziszewski, *Evangelicals in the Public Square* (Grand Rapids: Baker Academic, 2006), 15–37. See also, Russell Hittinger, *The First Grace: Rediscovering the Natural Law in a Post-Christian World* (Wilmington, Del.: ISI Books, 2003), esp. xi–xlvi, 3–37. For an important study of natural law in the Reformed tradition, see Stephen J. Grabill, *Rediscovering the Natural Law in Reformed Theological Ethics* (Grand Rapids: Eerdmans, 2006).

[18] For this definition of natural law, see *A Concise Dictionary of Theology*, ed. Gerald O'Collins, S.J. and Edward G. Farrugia, S.J. (New York: Paulist Press, 1991), 153.

Evangelization of the State power means its confrontation with the abiding objectivity of the natural moral law, itself an expression of the divine Wisdom and the measure of all positive law on earth. Human beings govern—whether as law-makers or legislators, law-enforcers or rulers, or law-adjudicators or judges—only by participation in a higher law, by sharing in the care of divine providence for the common good, as by reference to moral truth people build characters that can fit them for life everlasting. No State is excused from the worship of God and obedience to a moral law both integral to that worship and the only stable foundation for human rights. Woe to that State that accepts the seduction of the serpent in the garden, "Ye shall be as gods," and seeks to establish the "natural measures of good and evil." The State's recognition of a higher norm—something implied in different ways in the founding documents of the American Republic and in the coronation of English monarchs—prepares the way for an acknowledgment of Christian revelation, of which the coronation ceremony indeed is a quasi-sacramental expression. This brings us to the distinctively Christian aspect in the evangelization of civil society.[19]

In the latter part of this introduction, I shall consider briefly the contributions of John Paul II and Benedict XVI to the evangelization of civil society. For now, I want to make clear how it is that, in a Catholic theology of culture, the question of the relationship between nature, sin and grace—or among the orders of creation, fall into sin, redemption, and fulfillment—becomes the problem of faith and culture (and thus Christ and culture, Church and world).

---

[19] Nichols, "Integral Evangelization," 76–77. Similarly, see Pius XI, *Mit Brennender Sorge*, Encyclical March 14, 1937, §29.

Introduction

At a 2006 national conference held at Sacred Heart Major Seminary on the new evangelization, the Archbishop of Chicago, the late Francis Cardinal George, who holds that the faith and culture relationship presupposes a truly Catholic theology of nature and grace, expressed the particular importance of this question.[20] He says, "Grace builds on nature, for human nature wounded by sin is not hopelessly corrupt. As grace builds on nature, so faith builds on culture, which is second nature. Culture is terribly damaged by human sinfulness, but seldom is it hopelessly corrupt. A culture is a field which offers plants from native seeds for grafting on to the tree of universal faith." "Faith transforms everything that is human," the Cardinal adds, "including culture."[21] In other words, as the French Catholic philosopher Jacques Maritain had already said in the first half of the last century, "the grace of the Incarnation draws to itself all that is human."[22]

Three quarters of a century past, Jacques Maritain significantly remarked regarding the question of the relationship of nature and grace

---

[20] Francis Cardinal George, "The Culture in Which We Evangelize" (paper presented at Sacred Heart Major Seminary, St. John Conference Center, Plymouth, Mich., March 24–26, 2006).

[21] For a more developed understanding of Cardinal George's views on the relationship of faith and culture, see "Catholic Faith and the Secular Academy," *Logos* 4, no. 4 (Fall 2001), 73–81; "One Lord and One Church for One World," *Origins* 30, no. 34 (February 8, 2001): 541, 543–49; "The Promotion of Missiological Studies in Seminaries," http://www.sedos.org/english/george_e.htm; "Law and Culture," *Ave Maria Law Review* 1, no. 1 (Spring 2003): 1–17; "A New Apologetics for a New Evangelization," *Theology Digest* 47, no. 4 (Winter 2000), 341–59; and "Public Morality in a Global Society: Catholics and Muslims in Dialogue," *Theology Digest* 49, no. 4 (Winter 2002): 319–33.

[22] Jacques Maritain, "The Conquest of Freedom," in *The Education of Man: The Educational Philosophy of Jacques Maritain*, ed. Donald and Idella Gallagher (Garden City, N.Y.: Doubleday, 1962), 159–79, and here at 179.

that it is erroneous to ignore both the distinction between nature and grace as well as their union.[23]

Although Maritain firmly maintains the distinction between nature and grace, he nonetheless rejects a dualism of both a "hard" and a "soft" sort.[24] Hard dualism, which Maritain rejects, conceives of nature first in terms of its own end, to which is then "superadded" a second, supernatural end. Yet, Maritain also rejects a softer dualism in which a harmony between nature and grace is conceived, but there is still an *extrinsic* relationship between them. This more subtle form of dualism accepts that there is only one ultimate end for nature, a supernatural one, but it nonetheless fails to consider that this end directs and orders nature and all its intermediate ends, *from within* rather than alongside of or above nature. By contrast to both forms of dualism, Maritain emphasizes that grace restores or transforms nature from within:

> It is clear that the order of redemption, or of the spiritual, or of the things that are God's, should vivify to its most intimate depths the order of terrestrial civilization, or of the temporal, or of the things that are Caesar's; but these two orders remain

---

[23] Maritain states, "There is one error that consists in ignoring [the] distinction between nature and grace. There is another that consists in ignoring their union," *Clairvoyance de Rome* (Paris, 1929), 222. Cited in Henri de Lubac, "Apologetics and Theology," *Theological Fragments* (San Francisco: Ignatius Press, 1989), 91–104, and for this citation at 103n28. For an extensive discussion of Maritain's theology of nature and grace, see my essay, "Nature and Grace: The Theological Foundations of Jacques Maritain's Public Philosophy," *Journal of Markets & Morality* 4, no. 2 (2001): 240–68.

[24] For the conceptual distinction between hard and soft dualism, I am indebted to David L. Schindler, "Christology, Public Theology, and Thomism: de Lubac, Balthasar, and Murray," in *The Future of Thomism*, ed. Deal W. Hudson and Dennis William Moran (Minneapolis: American Maritain Association, 1992), 247–64.

clearly distinct. They are distinct, [but] they are not separate. To abstract from Christianity, to put God and Christ aside when I work at the things of the world, to cut myself into two halves: A Christian half for the things of eternal life—and for the things of time, a pagan or diminished Christian, or ashamedly Christian, or neutral half...—such a splitting is only too frequent in practice.... In reality, the justice of the Gospel and the life of Christ within us want the whole of us, they want to take possession of everything, to impregnate all that we are and all that we do, in the secular as well as in the sacred. If grace takes hold of us and remakes us [in] the depths of our being, it is so that our whole action should feel its effects and be illuminated by it.[25]

For our purposes here, then, the *leitmotif* regarding a truly Catholic theology of the relationship of nature and grace can be formulated in the phrase: "grace restores or transforms nature." Now, this way of formulating the relationship between nature and grace will undoubtedly strike some neo-Calvinists such as Abraham Kuyper, Herman Bavinck, and Herman Dooyeweerd as decidedly un-Catholic.[26] For more than a century, neo-Calvinists have contrasted their own "organic way of relating nature and grace," as Bavinck puts it, with "the mechanical juxtaposition and dualistic worldview of the Catholic Church."[27] On this "two-tier"

---

[25] Jacques Maritain, *Integral Humanism: Temporal and Spiritual Problems of a New Christendom*, trans. Joseph Evans (1936; repr., New York: Scribner's, 1968), 292–93.

[26] Abraham Kuyper, *Lectures on Calvinism*, Stone Lectures (Grand Rapids: Eerdmans, 1931), 122–23.

[27] Herman Bavinck, *Reformed Dogmatics*, vol. 1: *Prolegomena*, ed. John Bolt, trans. John Vriend (1895; repr., Grand Rapids: Baker Academic, 2003), 303–5; 353–61. See also, Herman Bavinck, "Common Grace," trans. R. C. van

relationship between nature and grace, they say, the latter is merely added (the *donum superadditim*) to a nature that has not been integrally affected by sin, and hence human nature requires little or no internal healing. I agree with Dooyeweerd that the mechanical juxtaposition and dualistic relationship of nature and grace is unquestionably found in both Protestant and Catholic traditions.[28] Furthermore, Catholic criticisms of this dualism have not been in short supply. Besides Etienne Gilson, they may also be found in the works of Karl Rahner, Henri de Lubac, Jacques Maritain, and Hans Urs von Balthasar, to name just several of the most illustrious but very different Catholic thinkers of the twentieth century.[29] Where I strongly disagree with Bavinck and, by implication with Dooyeweerd as well as Kuyper, is with the thesis that dualism is, in short, the defining view of the Catholic tradition over against the "ineluctable unity of nature, sin, and grace" (in the words of the American neo-Calvinist Henry Stob)[30] posited in the biblical revelation and as

---

Leeuwen, *Calvin Theological Journal* 24, no.1 (1989): 45–47, and for this quote, 60. "Common Grace" is a translation of Bavinck's rectorial address at Kampen Theological Seminary, Netherlands, in December 1894, entitled "De Algemeene Genade" (https://www.neocalvinisme.nl.hb/broch/hbag.html).

[28] Herman Dooyeweerd, *In the Twilight of Western Thought: Studies in the Pretended Autonomy of Philosophical Thought* (Nutley, N.J.: Craig Press, 1968), 44.

[29] Here is a sample of important criticisms of the nature-grace dualism from a Catholic standpoint. Henri De Lubac, *The Mystery of the Supernatural*, trans. Rosemary Sheed (1965; repr., New York: Crossroad, 1998). See also, De Lubac's *A Brief Catechesis on Nature and Grace*, trans. Richard Arnandez, F.S.C. (San Francisco: Ignatius Press, 1984); Karl Rahner, *Nature and Grace and Other Essays*, trans. Dinah Wharton (New York: Sheed and Ward, 1963); Hans Urs von Balthasar, *Love Alone* (New York: Sheed and Ward, 1969) and *The Theology of Karl Barth* (San Francisco: Ignatius Press, 1992); Maritain, *Integral Humanism*.

[30] Henry Stob, "Calvin and Aquinas," in *Theological Reflections: Essays on Related Themes* (Grand Rapids: Eerdmans, 1981), 126–30, and for this quote,

grasped by neo-Calvinism. Although I, too, reject a "two-story" relationship between nature and grace, I share the view of Henri de Lubac, Jacques Maritain, Louis Dupre, Alasdair MacIntyre, Nicholas Wolterstorff, Arvin Vos, Dewey Hoitenga, and others that, to quote Calvinist Hoitenga: "This objection is directed against a later (sixteenth- and seventeenth-century) corruption within Catholic thought, which entered it under the spell of the new humanist, Cartesian, and later Enlightenment views of an autonomous conception of reason and will."[31] It would not be an exaggeration to say that this study of mine on the relationship of nature and grace, and the corresponding understanding of Christ and culture, is a defense of the thesis that the teaching of the Catholic Church on the biblical unity of nature, sin, and grace is remarkably similar to the teaching of the neo-Calvinist tradition.[32]

I think that this is true not only in Maritain's case but also in that of John Paul II's. Indeed, this is how the late philosopher-pope describes the Church's mission of evangelization and, indeed, "the purpose of the

---

130. Stob shares the standard neo-Calvinist view that "Roman Catholic thinkers tend to regard created nature, both human and nonhuman, as integrally exempt from the ravages of sin, and to restrict the effect of sin to the loss of supernatural endowments (the *superadditum*) with which the human head of the created cosmos was originally engraced" ("Observations on the Concept of the Antithesis," in *Perspectives on the Christian Reformed Church: Studies in Its History, Theology, and Ecumenicity*, ed. Peter De Klerk and Richard R. De Ridder [Grand Rapids: Baker, 1983], 241–58).

[31] Dewey J. Hoitenga, Jr., *John Calvin and the Will: A Critique and Corrective* (Grand Rapids: Baker, 1997), 113.

[32] For an ecumenical Catholic dialogue, especially with respect to the tradition of Dutch neo-Calvinism, on the question of nature and grace, see my book, *Dialogue of Love: Confessions of an Evangelical Catholic Ecumenist* (Eugene, OR: Wipf and Stock, 2010). For a more recent study, see my book, *Roman Catholicism and Neo-Calvinism: Ecumenical and Polemical Engagements* (New York: Peter Lang, 2024).

Gospel," namely, "'to transform humanity from within and to make it new. 'Like the yeast which leavens the whole measure of dough (cf. Matt. 13:33), the Gospel is meant to permeate all cultures and give them life from within, so that they may express the full truth about the human person and about human life."[33]

This means that the redemption accomplished through Jesus Christ's saving work—his life, passion, death, resurrection, and ascension, in short, the Christ event—does not (1) stand opposed to, and hence replace altogether created reality because the latter is hopelessly corrupt as a consequence of the fall into sin. Nor does it merely (2) supplement or (3) parallel that reality, which would leave nature untouched by grace, and thus nature and grace would have only an *extrinsic relationship* to each other. Furthermore, nor does it merely involve (4) acceptance of created reality of one's humanity *as it is*, for that would deny created reality's fallen state, which would, as Msgr. Thomas Guarino puts it, "overlook God's judgment on the world rendered dramatically in the cross of Christ."[34] Rather, reality stands in need of being reconsecrated to its Maker, and hence Christ's redemption (5) seeks to penetrate

---

[33] John Paul II, *Evangelium Vitae*, March 25, 1995 Encyclical Letter, §95. The quote within this quote is from Paul VI, 1975 Apostolic Exhortation, *Evangelii Nuntiandi*, §18. Paul VI adds, "The purpose of evangelization is therefore precisely this interior change, and if it had to be expressed in one sentence the best way of stating it would be to say that the Church evangelizes when she seeks to convert, solely through the divine power of the message she proclaims, both the personal and collective consciences of people, the activities in which they engage, and the lives and concrete milieu which are theirs."

[34] Thomas G. Guarino, *Foundations of Systematic Theology* (New York: T&T Clark, 2005), 20.

and restore from within the fallen order of creation,[35] "bringing it to fullness of expression," as Francis Cardinal George says elsewhere.[36]

Against the background of the theology of nature and grace adumbrated above, I would like to revisit the enduring question of the relationship between Christ and culture. Deeply embedded in the Roman Catholic and Reformed traditions of historic Christianity is the conviction that Christians as such have a *normative cultural vocation* that God gave to man at creation. By exercising this vocation, man is realizing the design, or obeying the cultural mandate or commandment, given to him

---

[35] I owe this succinct way of formulating the various possibilities of relating nature and grace to my friend and colleague Albert Wolters, "What Is To Be Done? Toward a Neo-Calvinist Agenda," at http://www.wrf.ca/comment/article.cfm?ID=142. Especially influential not only in my own thinking but also that of Wolter's on the relationship between nature and grace are the writings of Dutch neo-Calvinist philosopher Herman Dooyeweerd (1894–1977). For a brief introduction to his thinking, see *In the Twilight of Western Thought*. Also instructive is James M. Gustafson "Theological Bases," in *Protestant and Roman Catholic Ethics* (Chicago: University of Chicago Press, 1978), 95–37. On nature and grace in the early history of the Church, see Jaroslav Pelikan, "Nature and Grace," in *The Christian Tradition: A History of the Development of Doctrine, vol. 1, The Emergence of the Catholic Tradition (100–600)* (Chicago: University of Chicago Press, 1971), 278–331.

[36] Regarding the relationship between faith and the world, Cardinal George asks, "What does the faith say to the world? To my mind, it says two things: first, the world is good, it was created good and therefore we are at home in it, and our faith is at home in it; second, the world is fallen. Because of sin, the world is estranged from God and therefore faith is something that makes us strangers in a strange land. These two questions and these two responses are both true, and people of faith live out their lives in the world in a dialectic between those two moments." Yet, there is more: "At the heart of the Incarnation, therefore, is God's loving embrace, in Christ, of the whole cosmos, that is to say the world of nature and the realm of human culture.... God's presence ... far from threatening or overwhelming the worldly, *raises it up and enhances it, bringing it to fullness of expression*" ("Catholic Faith and the Secular Academy," 75, 77, respectively; italics added).

at creation to "Be fruitful and multiply, subdue the earth and have dominion over it" (Gen. 1:28).[37] As John Paul II explains in his last book: "These words are the earliest and most complete definition of human culture. To subdue and have dominion over the earth means to discover and confirm the truth about being human.... To us and to our humanity, God has entrusted the visible world as a gift and also as a task. In other words, he has assigned us a particular mission: to accomplish the truth about ourselves and about the world." "We must be guided by the truth about ourselves," John Paul adds, "so as to be able to structure the visible world according to truth, correctly using it to serve our purposes, without abusing it. In other words, this twofold truth about the world and about ourselves provides the basis for every intervention by us upon creation."[38]

Although the foundation of this cultural mandate is in the order of creation, we must not lose sight of the basic truth that "cultures, like the

---

[37] Both Catholic and Reformed thinkers regard this passage as the biblical warrant for the cultural mandate. On the Catholic tradition, see *Gaudium et Spes* (Pastoral Constitution on the Church in the Modern World), Vatican Council II, 7 December 1965, §§34, 57. Subsequent references to *Gaudium et Spes* (hereafter *GS*) will be made parenthetically in the text. See also the *Catechism of the Catholic Church*, §§307, 373, 1604, and 2427. On the theological foundation of the cultural mandate, see the work of the great Italian-German Catholic priest, philosopher, and theologian, Romano Guardini (1885–1968) *The End of the Modern World* [*Das Ende der Neuzei*] (1950; repr., Wilmington, Del.: ISI Books, 2001). For the Reformed tradition, see Klaas Schilder, *Christ and Culture*, trans. G. van Rongen and W. Helder (1932; repr., Winnipeg: Premier, 1977), 37-41. For an insightful study of the Calvinist tradition on the enduring question, see Henry R. Van Til, *The Calvinistic Concept of Culture* (1951; repr., Grand Rapids: Baker Academic, 2001). See my essay, "Does one have to be a Calvinist in order to be a Kuyperian?" *Pro Rege*, 49, no. 3, (March 2021): 1-18.

[38] John Paul II, *Memory and Identity, Conversations at the Dawn of a Millennium* (New York: Rizzoli, 2005), 81.

people who give rise to them," says John Paul, "are marked by the 'mystery of evil 'at work in human history."[39] Most importantly, still, "The good news of Christ continually renews the life and culture of fallen man."[40] This view "gives Christ, the Redeemer of man, center of the universe and of history, the scope of completely renewing the lives of men 'by opening the vast fields of culture to His saving power.'"[41] Moreover, from the Christian standpoint, this normative cultural vocation has eternal meaning and value and hence is tied to eschatology because we will find the fruits of our labor, the subjection of the earth and mastery over it, "once again, cleansed this time from the stain of sin, illuminated and transfigured, when Christ presents to his Father an eternal and universal kingdom." "Here on earth the kingdom is mysteriously present; when the Lord comes it will enter into its perfection." (GS, §39). In short, culture, indeed all of fallen creation, belongs to God's culminating renewal in the kingdom of Jesus Christ.

---

[39] John Paul II, "Dialogue between Cultures for a Civilization of Love and Peace," *Origins* 30, §8 (January 4, 2001). See also, John Paul II, *Evangelium Vitae*, §104: "*life is always at the center of a great struggle* between good and evil, between light and darkness." Similarly, see *Centesimus Annus*, §25: "Through Christ's sacrifice on the Cross, the victory of the Kingdom of God has been achieved once and for all. Nevertheless," adds John Paul, "the Christian life involves a struggle against temptation and the forces of evil. Only at the end of history will the Lord return in glory for the final judgment (cf. Mt 25:31) with the establishment of a new heaven and a new earth (cf. 2 PT 3:13; Rev 21:1); but as long as time lasts the struggle between good and evil continues even in the human heart itself."

[40] *Gaudium et spes*, §58. Hereafter reference to this Vatican II document will be cited parenthetically in the text as GS.

[41] The Pontifical Council for Culture, May 23, 1999, *Towards a Pastoral Approach to Culture*, §6. The quote within the quote is from John Paul II, *Homily of the Enthronement Mass*, October 22, 1978, *L Osservatore Romano*.

In this Preface to this three-volume work, I will develop an understanding of that vocation, drawing both on confessional Catholicism with its roots in the Augustinian and Thomist traditions and confessional Protestantism with its own roots in the Augustinian and more recent Reformed or neo-Calvinist tradition.[42] I write, however, primarily as a committed Roman Catholic who has been philosophically and theologically formed by both traditions. I am persuaded that the cross-fertilization of these great traditions has borne much fruit in my own reflections, not only on the relationship among *creation, fall into sin, redemption, and consummation/fulfillment*, as I have sketched these four basic Christian themes in the previous paragraph, but also on Tertullian's enduring question regarding the relationships between the gospel of Jesus Christ and cultures.

This Preface is organized as follows. In the first place, I expand in some depth on the indivisible unity of *creation, fall into sin, redemption*, and *consummation*. I follow this up in with five sections, each of which con-siders the following five typical answers to the enduring question of how Christ and culture are related and whether the emphasis should be on *opposition* (Christ *against* culture) or *accommodation* (Christ *of* cul-

---

[42] By *Reformed* I mean that version of Protestant Christianity arising from the Calvinist Reformation in sixteenth-century Europe. The term *Neo-Calvinist* refers to a movement within Reformed Christianity that stems from the nineteenth-century Dutch educator, theologian, church leader, and politician Abraham Kuyper (1837– 1920). Besides Kuyper, other genial spirits within this intellectual milieu include Herman Bavinck (1845–1921), Klaas Schilder (1890–1952), Gerrit C. Berkouwer (1904–1996), and Herman Dooyeweerd (1894–1977).

ture) or *fulfillment* (Christ *fulfiller* of culture) or *duality* (Christ *and* culture) or *transformation* (Christ the transformer of culture).⁴³ My aim is to describe such typical answers but also to argue that not one of these emphases by itself is sufficient in answering the enduring question. To that end, I will sketch, in a concluding section, the outline of a Catholic answer in which both Christ and culture are properly distinguished and affirmed in order to understand better the scope of John Paul II's call to the *new evangelization*.

Theological Foundations: Creation/Fall/Redemption/Consummation

God reveals himself in nature, history, culture, society, and human existence; indeed his omnipotence and wisdom; his goodness and justice; his blessings and judgments; and in short, his creation, maintenance, and governance embrace the totality of relationships within cosmic reality.⁴⁴ As the *Catechism of the Catholic Church* states, "The totality of what exists ... depends on the One who gives it being."⁴⁵ Yet, although creation is good and perfect in its own right, God did not make creation complete from the beginning. "The universe was created 'in a state of journeying '(*in statu viae*) toward an ultimate perfection yet to

---

⁴³ H. Richard Niebuhr's classic book, *Christ and Culture* (New York: Harper & Row, 1951), is the source of this typology of Christian answers to the enduring question of Christ and culture. I take my cue from Niebuhr's study of these types, but in general I do not follow his discussion of these types closely. Also helpful to me for a study of this question is Nicholas Wolterstorff, "Tertullian's Enduring Question," *The Cresset* (June/July 1999): 1–14.

⁴⁴ Bavinck, *Reformed Dogmatics*, 1:310–11. G. C. Berkouwer, *General Revelation* (Grand Rapids: Eerdmans, 1955), 290–92.

⁴⁵ *Catechism of the Catholic Church*, §290. Subsequent references to the *Catechism* (hereafter *CCC*) will be made parenthetically in the text.

be attained, to which God has destined it. We call 'divine providence' the dispositions by which God guides his creation toward this perfection" (*CCC*, §302; italics added).

God is the sovereign Lord of creation, yet, he carries out his maintenance and governance of this creation in and through secondary causes, that is, "creatures 'cooperation" (*CCC*, §306). In other words, "God grants his creatures not only their existence, but also the dignity of acting on their own, of being causes and principles for each other, and thus of cooperating in the accomplishment of his plan" (*CCC*, §306). Cultural activity, then, which involves mastery, belongs to our very humanity, indeed our creatureliness, and because God operates in and through secondary causes, we are his coworkers, cooperating in his plan.

> To human beings God even gives the power of freely sharing in his providence by entrusting them with the responsibility of "sub-duing" the earth and having dominion over it. God thus enables men to be intelligent and free causes in order to complete the work of creation, to perfect its harmony for their own good and that of their neighbors. Though often unconscious collaborators with God's will, they can also enter deliberately into the divine plan by their actions, their prayers, and their sufferings. *They then fully become "God's fellow workers" and coworkers for his kingdom* (*CCC*, §307).

In particular, God has given man the mandate to be cultivator and custodian of the goods of creation, attaining mastery over nature, the social, and the cultural world; for example, establishing laws and legal institutions, developing science, the arts, family life, the whole civic community, and the free-market system. (cf. *GS*, §§ 53, 57).⁴⁶ Central to Catholic social teaching is the principle that in carrying out this mandate, man is perfecting the work of creation by bringing to fulfillment creation's potentialities for the sustenance of human life. Indeed, says John Paul II, "God gave the earth to the whole human race for the sustenance of all its members, without excluding or favoring anyone." He adds: "This is *the foundation of the universal destination of the earth's goods.*"⁴⁷ John Paul explains:

> The earth, by reason of its fruitfulness and its capacity to satisfy human needs, is God's first gift for the sustenance of human life. But the earth does not yield its fruits without a particular human response to God's gifts, that is to say, without work. It is through work that man using his intelligence and exercising his freedom, succeeds in dominating the earth and making it a fitting home. In this way, he makes part of the earth his own, precisely the part

---

⁴⁶ See also, Wolterstorff, *Until Justice and Peace Embrace* (Grand Rapids: Eerdmans, 1983), 54–57. Herman Dooyeweerd explains admirably well the relationship among the cultural activity of attaining mastery over the natural world, social world, and oneself as well. He writes: "The cultural mode of formation reveals itself in two directions, which are closely connected with each other. On the one hand, it is a formative power over persons and unfolding itself by giving cultural form to their social existence; on the other, it appears as a controlling manner of shaping natural materials, things, or forces to cultural ends. The Germans speak of *Personkultur* and *Sachkultur*. Since all cultural phenomena are bound to human society in its historical development, the development of *Sachkultur* is in principle dependent on that of *Personkultur*. For the cultural formation of natural materials or forces can only occur by human persons, who must learn it by socio-cultural education, given in a socio-cultural form to their minds" (*In the Twilight of Western Thought*, 91–92).

⁴⁷ John Paul II, *Centesimus Annus*, §31. Subsequent references to this encyclical (hereafter *CA*) will be made parenthetically in the text.

which he has acquired through work; this is *the origin of individual [private] property*. Obviously, he also has the responsibility not to hinder others from having their own part of God's gift; indeed, he must cooperate with others so that together all can dominate the earth.... This process, which throws practical light on a truth about the person which Christianity has constantly affirmed, should be viewed carefully and favorably. Indeed, besides the earth, man's principle resource is *man himself*. His intelligence enables him to discover the earth's productive potential and the many different ways in which human needs can be satisfied (*CA*, §31).[48]

Significantly, cultural activity, such as science, politics, and economics, cannot be considered only in the light of the order of creation because the influence of sin, of the presence and universality of sin in man's history, in short, of the historic fall into sin central in the historical-redemptive narrative of Genesis 3, also manifests itself in such activity (cf. *CCC*, §§397–406). As Henri de Lubac once wrote, "No culture is really neutral."[49] I take de Lubac to mean that the world cannot be neu-

---

[48] For a fuller treatment of the principle regarding the universal destination of the earth's goods and its relationship to private property, see *Compendium of the Social Doctrine of the Church*, Pontifical Council for Justice and Peace (Libreria Editrice Vaticana, 2004), Chapter 4, Part 3. section b, §§171–84. Online: http://www.vatican.va/roman_curia/pontifical_councils/justpeace/documents/rc_pc_justpeace_doc_20060526_compendio-dott-soc_en.html #Theuniversaldestination of goods and private property.

[49] De Lubac, *A Brief Catechesis on Nature and Grace*, 92.

tral with respect to the spiritual battle that is being waged in world history between the *civitas Dei* and the *civitas terrena*—to speak with Saint Augustine in a manner that is deeply biblical (cf. Eph. 6:10ff.).[50]

Indeed, if I understand John Paul II correctly, no cultural activity is neutral in that sense, not even the economic activity of the market economy. By the market economy, he means "an economic system which [rightly] recognizes the fundamental and positive role of business, the market, private property and the resulting responsibility for the means of production, as well as free human creativity in the economic sector" (*CA*, §42). This understanding of the market economy stands in contrast, he says, to an economic "system in which freedom in the economic sector is not circumscribed within a strong juridical framework which places it at the service of human freedom in its totality, and which sees it as a particular aspect of that freedom, the core of which is ethical and

---

[50] Jacques Maritain agrees. In his own words, the battle is between *"the World as the Antagonist"* and *"the World as redeemed and reconciled."* He explains this antithesis admirably well: "The Gospel considers the world *in its concrete and existential connections with the Kingdom of God*, already present in our midst. The world cannot be neutral with respect to the Kingdom of God. Either it is vivified by it, or it struggles against it. In other words, the relation of the world with the universe of grace is either a relation of union and inclusion, or a relation of separation and conflict" (*On the Philosophy of History*, ed. Joseph W. Evans [New York: Scribner's, 1957], 133). On this, see also John Paul II's 1986 encyclical, *Dominum et Vivificantem*, "[T]he history of salvation shows that God's coming close and making himself present to man and the world, that marvelous 'condescension' of the Spirit, *meets with resistance and opposition* in our human reality.... Unfortunately, the resistance to the Holy Spirit which St. Paul emphasizes in the *interior and subjective dimension* as tension, struggle and rebellion taking place in the human heart [cf. Galatians 5:16-25], finds in every period of history and especially in the modern era its *external dimension*, which takes concrete form as the content of culture and civilization, as a *philosophical system*, an *ideology*, a *program* for action and for the shaping of human behavior" (§§55–56).

religious" (*CA*, §42).⁵¹ Of course, John Paul regards economic activity to be only "one dimension of the whole of human activity," and hence "economic freedom [to be] only one element of human freedom" (*CA*, §39). Thus, he opposes any view of the market economy that takes the economic aspect as absolute, in short, as man's highest good, taking it as the interpretative key for understanding the whole of reality, of man's social and cultural life. There are some serious consequences that follow from taking the economic aspect as absolute, according to John Paul II. This happens in the worldview of consumerism with its commercialization or commodification of the goods of human existence (cf. *CA*, §§36, 40–41).⁵² For one thing, man is seen as nothing but a producer or consumer of goods rather than as a "subject who produces and consumes in order to live." Because the relationship between the human person and production or consumption of goods is, on this view, reversed, says John Paul, "economic freedom loses its necessary relationship to the human person and ends up by alienating and oppressing him." At the root of

---

[51] Of course, John Paul II also rejects the Marxist socialist system, or what he also calls "State capitalism." "Marxism criticized capitalist bourgeois societies, blaming them for the commercialization and alienation of human existence. This rebuke is of course based on a mistaken and inadequate idea of alienation, derived solely from the sphere of relationships of production and ownership, that is, giving them a materialistic foundation and moreover denying the legitimacy and positive value of market relationships even in their own sphere. Marxism thus ends up by affirming that only in a collective society can alienation be eliminated." "The historical experience of socialist countries has," John Paul adds, "sadly demonstrated that collectivism does not do away with alienation but rather increases it, adding to it a lack of basic necessities and economic inefficiency" (*Centesimus Annus*, §41).

[52] For a critique of the worldview of consumerism, see Gregory R. Beabout and Eduardo J. Echeverria, "The Culture of Consumerism: A Catholic and Personalist Critique," *Journal of Markets & Morality* 5, no. 2 (Fall 2002): 339–83.

this reversal and, in consequence, self-alienation is a reductionist anthropology: reducing the totality of man's being to the sphere of economics and the satisfaction of material needs. Against this background, we can well understand John Paul's critical points that (1) an economic system as such does not possess criteria for distinguishing basic human needs ("real goods") from artificial needs ("apparent goods"), and (2) there are qualitative human needs and their corresponding goods that escape the logic of market mechanisms. Real human goods satisfy these human needs, says John Paul, and such goods "by their very nature cannot and must not be bought or sold" (*CA*, §40). Friendship, intimacy, human sexuality, community, love, pride, happiness, virtue, solidarity, health, human life, children, goodness, truth, knowledge, and last but not least, the reality and vocation of man's final end, namely, having been created by God and for God, man is called to share in the truth and highest good that is God himself—the nature of these goods is such that they are not and cannot be mere commodities.[53] When we make the eco-

---

[53] Of course, the worldview of consumerism has left its mark on religion. As Craig M. Gay astutely notes, "The rise of denominational, and now religious, plurality in modern societies has led to a situation in which we are increasingly encouraged to 'shop for, 'and so to be consumers of, religion itself. The consumption of religion, furthermore, suggests a fundamental change in the meaning of religious belief such that it has increasingly less to do with conviction [and truth] and more and more to do with personal preference. Many churches and religious organizations have responded to the changing meaning of belief by obligingly repackaging religion to make it conveniently and easily consumable. Such trends have contributed to the emergence of a kind of religious marketplace in which modern consumers are faced with a veritable smorgasbord of religious options" *The Complete Book of Everyday Christianity: An A-to-Z Guide to Following Christ in Every Aspect of Life*, ed. Robert Banks and R. Paul Stevens (Downers Grove: InterVarsity Press, 1997), 220–22), s.v. "Consumerism."

nomic aspect an absolute, we render the market an idol whereby the dignity and irreplaceable worth of the human person is undermined, given that human beings are treated as a commodity. The idolatry[54] of the market is one of the causes of man's self-alienation in contemporary culture.

> The concept of alienation needs to be led back to the Christian vision of reality, by recognizing in alienation a reversal of means and ends. When man does not recognize in himself and in others the value and grandeur of the human person, he effectively deprives himself of the possibility of benefiting from his humanity and of entering into that relationship of solidarity and communion with others for which God created him. Indeed, it is through the free gift of self that man truly finds himself. This gift is made possible by the human person's essential 'capacity for transcendence'... As a person, he can give himself to another person or to other persons, and ultimately to God, who is the author of his being and who alone can fully accept his gift. A man is alienated if he refuses to transcend himself and to live the experience of self-giving and of the formation of an authentic human community oriented towards his final destiny, which is God. A society is alienated if its forms of social organization, production and consumption make it more difficult to offer this

---

[54] On idolatry, see the *Catechism of the Catholic Church*, "Idolatry not only refers to false pagan worship. It remains a constant temptation to faith. Idolatry consists in divinizing what is not God. Man commits idolatry whenever he honors and reveres a creature in place of God, whether this be gods or demons (e.g., Satanism), power, pleasure, race, ancestors, the State, money, et cetera. Jesus says, 'You cannot serve God and mammon '[Matthew 6:24].... Idolatry rejects the unique Lordship of God; it is therefore incompatible with communion with God" (§2113).

gift of self and to establish this solidarity between people (*CA*, §41).

John Paul II's analysis of consumerism brings us back to the religious dynamics of our culture. In sum, then, "A monumental struggle [of the Kingdom of God] against the powers of evil pervades the whole history of man" (*GS*, §37). Thus, the drama of man's life is a spiritual battle throughout the whole of the temporal creation (cf. *CCC*, §409). "Finding himself in the midst of the battlefield man has to struggle to do what is right, and it is at great cost to himself, and aided by God's grace, that he succeeds in achieving his own inner integrity. Hence, the church of Christ, trusting in the design of the creator (to be cultivator and custodian of the goods of creation) and admitting that progress can contribute to man's true happiness, still feels called upon to echo the words of the apostle: 'Do not be conformed to this world '(Rom. 12:2). " "'World 'here means," the Council Fathers add, "a spirit of vanity and malice whereby human activity from being ordered to the service of God and man is distorted to an instrument of sin" (*GS*, §37).

This means, in particular, that Christians may not embrace an *optimistic* view of cultural progress. Alternatively, they may not embrace the radical *pessimism* entailed by the cultural judgment that our culture is *slouching toward Gomorrah* (read: cultural decline), or, as Herman Dooyeweerd has put it, "resign to an abandonment of culture to the power of apostasy." "In the light of the Christian basic motive of Redemption," adds Dooyeweerd, "culture belongs to the Kingdom of Jesus Christ. And the task set to mankind in the cultural commandment of creation should be fulfilled in a continuous contest with the historical development of the power of sin, a contest to be waged through the spiritual power of the Redeemer."[55] This spiritual power has its source in the finished work of Jesus Christ the Redeemer, the Incarnate Word, the Eternal Son of God become man—his life, passion, death on the cross, bodily resurrection from the dead, and ascension into heaven— and renews the life and culture of fallen man. "It combats and removes the error and evil which flow from the ever-present attraction of sin. It never ceases to purify and elevate the morality of peoples. It takes the spiritual qualities and endowments of every age and nation, and with supernatural riches it causes [man's life and culture] to blossom, as it were, *from within; it fortifies, completes and restores them in Christ*" (*GS*, §58; italics added).

This evangelical Catholic and reforming view of culture is, as Nicholas Wolterstorff rightly says, "gripped by the Colossian's vision of cosmic redemption."[56] Basic to this vision is the truth that *the whole creation*

---

[55] Herman Dooyeweerd, *A New Critique of Theoretical Thought*, trans. David H. Freeman and H. de Jongste (1936; repr., Philadelphia: Presbyterian & Reformed, 1955), 2:262.

[56] On this, see Wolterstorff's "Keeping Faith: Talks for the New Faculty at Calvin College," *Occasional Papers from Calvin College* 7, no. 1 (February 1989): 13. See also John Paul II's 1986 encyclical, *Dominum et Vivificantem* "The Incarnation of God the Son signifies the taking up into unity with God not only of human nature, but in *this human nature, in a sense, of everything that is flesh* : the whole of humanity, the entire visible and material world. The Incarnation, then, also has a cosmic significance, a cosmic dimension. The 'first-born of all creation, 'becoming incarnate in the individual humanity of Christ, unites himself in some way with the entire reality of man, which is also 'flesh,' and in this reality with all 'flesh, 'with the whole of creation.... He who in the mystery of creation *gives life* to man and the cosmos in its many different forms, visible and invisible, again *renews* this life through the mystery of the Incarnation. Creation is thus completed by the Incarnation and since that moment is permeated by the powers of the Redemption, powers which fill humanity and all creation" (§§50, 52).

is recapitulated in Christ (*GS*, §38). In the written Word of God, the lordship of Jesus Christ over creation and redemption is revealed (Phil. 2:11). Thus, "The Lord is the goal of human history, the focal point of the desires of history and civilization, the center of mankind, the joy of all hearts, and the fulfillment of all aspirations" (*GS*, §45). It follows from this vision of cosmic redemption that Christians are called to engage in the sanctification of culture by transforming it through God's grace in Christ. In short, they are called to the work of restoring all areas of culture, indeed, all dimensions of human existence, all of creation itself, to Christ, so that "in everything he might be preeminent" (Col. 1:18), and of making them share in the redemption he accomplished, and in this way to be his agents, coworkers, for exercising his lordship in creation.[57]

As the Pontifical Council for Culture states in a passage I cited above: "[A] Christian cultural project ... gives Christ, the Redeemer of man, center of the universe and of history, the scope of completely renewing the lives of men 'by opening the vast fields of culture to His saving power.'"[58] In sum, the Pontifical Council explains, "the primary objective of [this] approach to culture is to inject the lifeblood of the Gospel into cultures to renew from within and transform in the light of Revelation the visions of men and society that shape cultures, the concepts of men and women, of the family and of education, of school and of university, of freedom and of truth, of labor and of leisure, of the economy and of society, of the sciences and of the arts."[59]

---

[57] On this, see *Lumen Gentium* [Dogmatic Constitution on the Church], Second Vatican Council, November 21, 1964, §§30–38, 57–59; and also *Apostolicam Actuositatem* [Decree on the Apostolate of Lay People], November 18, 1965, especially §§5–7.

[58] Pontifical Council for Culture, *Towards a Pastoral Approach to Culture*, §§3, 6.

[59] Pontifical Council for Culture, *Towards a Pastoral Approach to Culture*, §25.

God created everything good, but this whole creation has suffered the radical fall into sin. Requiring divine recreation, renewal, and restoration, creation is thus redeemed in Jesus Christ, made a new creation at its very root, and "is in principle again directed toward God and thereby wrested free from the power of Satan."[60] God continues, even now, until the return of Christ, to work for the consummation of his plan in the renewal of the entire creation. In this restoration, we are his coworkers, agents in the struggle that God's kingdom continues to wage against the kingdom of darkness until his consummating total recreation—the new heavens and the new earth (cf. Rev. 21:1–4). "The good things—such as human dignity, brotherhood and freedom, all the good fruits of nature and of human enterprise—that in the Lord's Spirit and according to his command have spread throughout the earth, having been purified of every stain [of sin], illuminated and transfigured, belong to the Kingdom of truth and life, of holiness and grace, of justice, of love and of peace that Christ will present to the father, and *it is there that we shall once again find them* (italics added)."[61] Not only is culture, then, eschatologically oriented, but also the whole creation ever looks forward to its consummation in Christ: "to unite all things in him, things in heaven and things on earth" (Eph. 1:10).

Finally, the redemptive purpose of the Kingdom of God, as far as humanity is concerned, is the Church. As Aloys Grillmeier states in his commentary on Chapter 1 of *Lumen Gentium*:

> Those who are members of the Church of Christ are enabled to enter into the most intimate union with God and into a deeper fellowship with men, one not founded merely on the usual basis of human relationships but also on the unifying force of the self-

---

[60] Dooyeweerd, *A New Critique of Theoretical Thought*, 1:175.
[61] *Compendium of the Social Doctrine of the Church*, §57.

communication of God in Christ and the Spirit. And here we can see at once an essential characteristic of the salvation bestowed in Christ. To enter the Church is to be accepted really, though for the present only initially and invisibly, into the eschatological family of the children of God, of which the centre is God and Christ, the unifying bond the Holy Spirit. *Since mankind has no other goal than this Church in which all is fulfilled,* the Council must bring out as clearly as possible the universal significance of this sign of salvation [italics added].[62]

But the italicized portion of the concluding sentence is true only when we are speaking of the Kingdom's redemptive goal for humanity. Yes, the Church is "the seed and beginning of that kingdom on earth," indeed; it is "the kingdom of Christ already present in mystery."[63] There are several points to make here. First, severing the Kingdom of God from its concentration point in the institutional Church has resulted in much contemporary theology in a reductive sense of the mission of that Kingdom, says John Paul II, "inasmuch as [ideas about salvation and mission] are focused on man's earthly needs." "In this view, the pope adds, "the Kingdom tends to become something completely human and secularized; what counts are programs and struggles for a liberation which is socio-economic, political and even cultural, but within a horizon that is closed to the transcendent.... Such a view easily translates into one more

---

[62] Aloys Grillmeier, Dogmatic Constitution on the Church, Chapter 1, Mystery of the Church," in *Commentary on the Documents of Vatican II*, Volume 1. Translated from the German by Lalit Adolphus, et al. (New York: Herder and Herder, 1967), 140.

[63] *Lumen Gentium*, §§5, 3, respectively.

ideology of purely earthly progress."[64] There is a second point to make: the Kingdom of God is broader than the Church. It is the plan of God that is realized in and through Christ, encompassing the whole of creation. Indeed, as Romana Guardini writes, "the purpose of Christ [is] to win reality, with all that the word implies, for the Kingdom of God."[65] Herman Ridderbos explains, "[The Kingdom of God] has a much more comprehensive content. It represents the all-embracing perspective, it denotes the consummation of all history, brings both grace and judgment, has cosmic dimensions, [and] fills time and eternity."[66] In my view, and arguably the view of the Second Vatican Council, the Kingdom of God is not identical with the Church because the realization of that Kingdom is an enactment of the great divine work of redemption in its recapitulation—fulfillment and consummation—of all the fallen creation in Christ. "In a word," as John Paul II wrote, "the Kingdom of God is the manifestation and the realization of God's plan of salvation in all its fullness."[67] In all its fullness, I would say, refers to the restoration or renewal of creation "in the redemptive plan and in the redemptive power

---

[64] John Paul II, *Redemptoris Missio*, §17. Pope Benedict XVI makes the same point in his widely praised, *Jesus of Nazareth*, 53-54: "A secularist reinterpretation of the idea has gained considerable ground, particularly, though not exclusively, in Catholic theology.... 'Kingdom', on this interpretation, is simply the name for a world governed by peace, justice, and the conservation of creation. It means no more than this. This 'Kingdom' is said to be the goal of history that has to be attained. This is supposedly the real task of religions: to work together for the coming of the 'Kingdom'."

[65] *Vom Sinn der Kirche* (Mainz: Matthias Grünewald Verlag, 1922), 39. English translation by Ada Lane as *The Church and the Catholic* (New York: Sheed & Ward, Inc., 1935), 54.

[66] Herman Ridderbos, *The Coming of the Kingdom*, translated by H. de Jongste, Raymond Zorn, ed. (Philadelphia, PA: Presbyterian and Reformed Publishing Co., 1962 [195]), 354.

[67] John Paul II, *Redemptoris Missio*, §15.

of Jesus Christ."⁶⁸ That this, too, is the teaching of the Council is clear from the following passages. For instance, regarding the vocation of the laity:

> But the laity, by their very vocation, seek the kingdom of God by engaging in temporal affairs and by ordering them according to the plan of God. . . . . They are called there by God so that by exercising their proper function and being led by the spirit of the gospel they can work for the sanctification of the world from within. . . . It is therefore his [layman] special task to illumine and organize [temporal] affairs in such a way that they may always start out, develop, and persist according to Christ's mind, to the praise of the Creator and the Redeemer.⁶⁹

Furthermore, regarding the relation between Christ and culture:

> The good news of Christ constantly renews the life and culture of fallen man. It combats and removes the errors and evils resulting from sinful allurements which are a perpetual threat. It never ceases to purify and elevate the morality of peoples. By riches coming from above, it makes fruitful, as it were from within, the spiritual qualities and gifts of every people and of every age. It strengthens, perfects, and restores them in Christ.

---

⁶⁸ Yves Congar, OP, *Jesus Christ*, translated by Luke O'Neill (New York: Herder and Herder, 1966), 176, but see also the entire chapter, The Lordship of Christ over the Church and the World, 167-219.

⁶⁹ *Lumen Gentium*, §31, but see also §36. For a fuller development of the Church's teaching on the mission of the Laity, see *Apostolicam Actuositatem* . See also, the insightful 1881 essay of Herman Bavinck on the all-encompassing character of the Kingdom of God, "Het Rijk Gods, Het Hoogste Goed," in *Kennis en Leven* (Kampen: J.H. Kok, 1992), 28-56.

Thus by the very fulfillment of own mission the Church stimulates and advances *the human and civic culture*. (*GS* 58; italics added).

More generally, the Council makes crystal clear the cosmic significance of Christ in creation and redemption:

[T]he Church has a single intention: that God's kingdom may come, and that the salvation of the whole human race may come to pass. For every benefit which the People of God during its earthly pilgrimage can offer to the human family stems from the fact that the Church is "universal sacrament of salvation," simultaneously manifesting and exercising the mystery of God's love for man. For God's Word, by whom all things were made, was Himself made flesh so that as a perfect man He might save all men and sum up all things in Himself. The Lord is the goal of human history, the focal point of the longings of history and civilization, the center of the human race, the joy of every heart, and the answer to all its yearnings. He it is whom the Father raised from the dead, lifted on high, and stationed at His right hand, making Him judge of the living and the dead. Enlivened and united in His Spirit, we journey toward the consummation of human history, one which fully accords with the counsel of God's love: "To re-establish all things in Christ, both those in the heavens and those on the earth (Eph 1:10)." (*GS* §45).

Introduction 33

Toward a Theology of Christ and Culture

Christ *Against* Culture

Is life in this world *only* a means of reaching the end of forever enjoying God in heaven? If so, then life here and now seemingly would have merely instrumental value, extrinsic to the Christian life, rather than essential to living that life in Jesus Christ. Of course, what is right about this view is that communion with God is the supreme good and that the cultivation and enjoyment of all created human goods should be pursued in a rightly ordered relationship with God. Pushed to the extreme, however, this view may encourage us to think of life here and now as a mere waiting room with "the only task that [does] matter [being] the contemplation of heavenly things." "Only the making of a soul [is] the true human value," adds John Courtney Murray. "For the rest, what [does] it matter whether one [weaves] baskets or wrought[s] whole civilizations?"[70] Put differently, this view may encourage us to think of participating in the life of culture as a necessary evil rather than as a normative cultural vocation essential to serving God.

Furthermore, this conclusion has led some Christians to the view that the *natural realm*, that is, the created world, society, history, indeed the entire human cultural enterprise—the cultivation of, for example, the arts, sciences, laws, and juridical institutions—is radically corrupt, evil, threatening, or inferior such that, as Christians, we must turn away

---

[70] John Courtney Murray, S.J., *We Hold These Truths: Catholic Reflections on the American Proposition* (New York: Sheed and Ward, 1960), esp. 175–96, and for these quotes, 187.

from it toward an entire *otherworldly, supernatural* goal.[71] Abraham Kuyper rightly rejects this view, which posits an antithesis between the Christian faith and the created world. He writes,

> The world after the fall is no lost planet, only destined now to afford the Church a place in which to continue her combats; and humanity is no aimless mass of people which only serves the purpose of giving birth to the elect. On the contrary, the world now, as well as in the beginning, is the theater for the mighty works of God, and humanity remains a creation of His hand, which, apart, from salvation, completes under this present dispensation, here on earth a mighty process, and in its historical development is to glorify the name of Almighty God.[72]

---

[71] I am indebted to the late German Grisez for this way of posing the sacred-secular, supernatural-natural, grace-nature problematic. On this, see his master work, *The Way of the Lord Jesus*, 1, *Christian Moral Principles* (Chicago: Franciscan Herald Press, 1983), 16–17, 807–30, and for this citation at 811. Also helpful to me was Wolterstorff, *Until Justice and Peace Embrace*, 3–22.

[72] Kuyper, *Lectures on Calvinism*, 162. This, too, is the view of John Henry Cardinal Newman in his famous autobiography, *Apologia Pro Vita Sua* (1864; repr., New York: Random House, 1950). The Catholic Church "does not teach that human nature is irreclaimable, else wherefore should she be sent? Not that it is to be shattered and reversed, but to be extricated, purified, and restored; not that it is a mere mass of evil, but that it has the promise of great things, and even now has a virtue and a praise proper to itself. But in the next place she knows and she preaches that such a restoration, as she aims at effecting in it, must be brought about, not simply through any outward provision of preaching and teaching, even though it be her own, but from a certain inward spiritual power or grace imparted directly from above, and which is in her keeping. She has it in charge to rescue human nature from its misery, but not simply by raising it upon its own level, but by lifting it up to a higher level than its own," 245.

No doubt, this view threatens not only the Christian belief in the inherent goodness of creation, devaluing all the this-worldly goods of the human enterprise but also the radical and integral nature of redemption in Jesus Christ through which the entire fallen creation is renewed, including a Christian transformation of culture.[73] Put differently, the Christ *against* culture view has led some Christians—both Protestant and Catholic—to accept a false dichotomy within the Christian life between the sacred and secular, the supernatural and merely natural, and grace and nature. Ironically, this contempt for the world that stems from *opposing* Christ and culture, which results in withdrawing from the world and its corollary, a "citadel mentality,"[74] also has the unintended consequence of fostering the "wholesale secularization of culture."[75] Maritain rightly traces this consequence back to an incorrect theology of

---

[73] Pushed to the extreme, the supporters of the Christ against culture position convert the spiritual dualism "into an ontological bifurcation of reality." Their rejection of culture leads to "the problem of the relation of Jesus Christ to the Creator of nature and Governor of history ... ultimately they are tempted to divide the world into the material realm governed by a principle opposed to Christ and a spiritual realm guided by the spiritual God." Niebuhr, *Christ and Culture*, 80–81.

[74] By citadel mentality I mean, as Schaeffer put it more than forty years ago: "living in a castle with the drawbridge up and occasionally tossing a stone over the walls ... [A] Citadel mentality—sitting inside [the castle] and saying, 'You cannot reach me here.'" *The God Who Is There*, 172.

[75] Tracey Rowland, *Culture and the Thomist Tradition After Vatican II* (New York: Routledge, 2003), 29. Regarding the dualism between nature and grace and its implication of "total secularization," see De Lubac, *The Mystery of the Supernatural*, 35. See also, Henri De Lubac, *Catholicism: Christ and the Common Destiny of Man*, trans. Lancelot C. Sheppard and Sister Elizabeth Englund, O.C.D. (1938; repr., San Francisco: Ignatius Press, 1988), 313–14: "the supernatural, deprived of its organic links with nature, tended to be understood by some as a mere "super- nature," a "double" of nature. Furthermore, after such

nature and grace. He writes: "[A]s a result of the achievement of grace, as a result of grace [penetrating and] perfecting [and transforming] nature, nature is superelevated in its own order.... If we do not admit it, we are led willy-nilly to a kind of separatism between nature and grace, to a kind of naturalism—nature will have its own course separately from any contact with grace."[76]

Of course, there is also something right in an anticultural position that recognizes a necessity in "the movement of withdrawal and renunciation," as Niebuhr puts it.

> The relation of the authority of Jesus Christ to the authority of culture is such that every Christian must often feel himself claimed by the Lord to reject the world and its kingdoms [e.g., "the culture of death"] with their pluralism [e.g., "all religions are the same" or "right and wrong, truth and falsity, are relative to the individual"] and temporalism [this-worldliness], their makeshift compromises of many interests [resulting in the betrayal of orthodoxy], their hypnotic obsession by the love of [this] life [rather than the love of God] and the fear of death [rather than trusting in Christ's death and resurrection that defeated the power of death and frees us from the fear of our mortality].[77]

---

a complete separation what misgivings could the supernatural cause to naturalism? ... Such a dualism, just when it imagined that it was most successfully opposing the negations of naturalism, was most strongly influenced by it, and the transcendence in which it hoped to preserve the supernatural with such jealous care was, in fact, a banishment. The most confirmed secularists found in it, in spite of itself, an ally."

[76] Maritain, *On the Philosophy of History*, 130.

[77] Niebuhr, *Christ and Culture*, 68.

Notwithstanding the necessity of this *ad hoc* strategy of withdrawal and renunciation, it must "*be followed by an equally necessary movement of responsible engagement in cultural tasks,*" as Niebuhr correctly adds.[78] However, "withdrawal Christianity" is unable to make that move because it wrongly takes sanctification in Jesus Christ to mean renouncing creation as if creation itself were evil. Rejecting this withdrawal from the world as unbiblical, Dooyeweerd correctly remarks: "We have nothing to avoid in the world but *sin*. The war that the Christian wages in God's power in this temporal life against the Kingdom of darkness, is a joyful struggle, not only for his own salvation, but for God's creation as a whole, which we do not hate, but love for Christ's sake. We must not hate anything in the world but *sin*."[79] Thus, making this movement of responsibly engaging in cultural tasks requires a theological affirmation of the world: "For everything created by God is good, and nothing is to be rejected if it is received with thanksgiving" (1 Tim. 4:4).

Christ *of* Culture

There is another typical answer, a highly influential one, which Christians— both Protestants and Catholics—have given to the question of how Christ is related to culture, and I know of no better word to describe its strategy than with the word *conformism*. The *leitmotif* of this strategy is accommodation, adaptation, updating, and inculturation of the Christian faith in order to *reconcile* it with some of the truth-claims, values, and basic orientation of modern secular culture. The assumption here is that the Church is somehow lagging behind modern cultural and intellectual developments and so it needs to catch up with them by updating its teaching. The result of this kind of adaptation is best called

---

[78] Niebuhr, *Christ and Culture*, 68, italics added.
[79] Dooyeweerd, *A New Critique of Theoretical Thought*, 2:34.

"cultural Protestantism" or "cultural Catholicism."[80] For cultural Christianity of either sort, however, the relationship between the Christian tradition and the modern secular consciousness is not one-sided. Rather, it is a two-sided relationship, a mutually critical correlation between faith and world, Christ and culture. As Niebuhr describes the two-sided relationship of cultural Christians:

> They feel no great tension between church and world, the social laws and the Gospel, the workings of divine grace and human effort, the ethics of salvation and the ethics of social conservation or progress. *On the one hand* they interpret culture through Christ, regarding those elements in it as most important which are most accordant with his work and person; *on the other hand* they understood Christ through culture, selecting from his teaching and action as well as from the Christian doctrine about him such points as seem *to agree with what is best in civilization*. So they harmonize Christ and culture, not without excision, of course, from New Testament and social custom, of stubbornly discordant features. They do not necessarily seek Christian sanction for the whole of prevailing culture, but only for what they regard as real in the actual.[81]

Although I cannot argue fully the point here, I think there are three reasons why the accommodationist interpretation of inculturation is fundamentally flawed. *First*, regarding the question of how Christ

---

[80] For a defense of "cultural Catholicism," see Dolan, *In Search of an American Catholicism*. For a similar defense, see also John T. McGreevy, *Catholicism and American Freedom: A History* (New York: W. W. Norton, 2003).

[81] Niebuhr, *Christ and Culture*, 83–84 (italics added).

should relate to culture, the cultural Christian is confronted by an answer of his own making in which Christianity increasingly loses its "transcendent" standpoint, that is, critical distance *over* culture because it seems to conceive of faith primarily as a religious experience of God without any determinate content, and as if beliefs were always generated only as a result of positive dialogue with the culture.[82] In other words, cultural Christianity seems to have abandoned the "dogmatical principle," as John Henry Newman called it, in which *revealed truth* about God, human beings, and the world is received, defended, and transmitted by Christians as something "definite, and formal, and independent of ourselves." This principle states that revealed truths have been "irrevocably committed to human language." This propositional revelation in verbalized form is at once *true* though *not exhaustive*,[83] "imperfect because it is human," adds Newman, "but definitive and necessary because

---

[82] Pushed to its extreme, this view leads to a cultural Catholicism that is radically pluralistic, indeed, relativistic. It is represented by contemporary lay Catholics who say, "'I'm afraid the church as a whole is coming to the point where it isn't one size fits all any more, 'said Jack Scalione, 66, a turnpike inspector who was watching the papal funeral [of John Paul II] on television at Our Lady of Mount Carmel church in East Boston. 'What's good in Europe isn't necessarily good in America, and what's good in America isn't necessarily what's good in Latin America. You have to fit to the wishes of the people because the people are the church'" (*New York Times*, April 11, 2005, A16).

[83] John Paul II, *Fides et Ratio*, 1998 Encyclical Letter, "For faith clearly requires that human speech should in some universal way give expression—even though voiced analogically, but no less meaningfully—to divine, transcendent reality. Deprived of this assumption, the Word of God, which despite its use of human language remains divine, *could signify nothing of God*. The interpretation of this Word cannot merely keep tossing us from one interpretation to another, never directing us to a statement that is simple and true: were that the case there could be no revelation of God, but instead only the expression of human concepts about God and of the things it is presumed he thinks about us"

given from above."[84] Furthermore, this classical view of revelation holds that revelation is at once God's self-revelation and the communication of divinely authorized truths. "And so," as Aidan Nichols correctly notes, "revelation has at one and the same time existential, cognitive, and ontological dimensions. In other words, it changes the human situation, our awareness of it, and our very being itself."[85]

My trouble with and hence resistance to the strategy of cultural Christianity does not stem from emphasizing the unchangeableness of our *understanding* of Christian truth and looking upon a restatement of Catholic teaching as a sign of apostasy. Not at all. Put positively, "The Church learned early in its history to express the Christian message in the concepts and language of different peoples and tried to clarify it in the light of the wisdom of their philosophies. It was an attempt to adapt the Gospel to the understanding of all men and the requirements of the learned, insofar as this could be done. Indeed, this kind of adaptation and preaching of the revealed Word must ever be the law of all evangelization."[86] Indeed, John XXIII's opening address at Vatican II points

---

(John Paul II, §84; italics added). The former Joseph Ratzinger, now Benedict XVI, remarks on John Paul II's very point: "Man is not caught in a hall of mirrors of interpretation; he can and must look for the way out to the reality that stands behind the words and manifests itself to him in and through the words." *Truth and Tolerance: Christian Belief and World Religions*, trans. Henry Taylor (San Francisco: Ignatius Press, 2003), 189. Further references to this work will be cited parenthetically in the text as *TT*.

[84] John Henry Cardinal Newman, *An Essay on the Development of Christian Doctrine*, 6th ed. (1845; repr., Notre Dame: University of Notre Dame Press, 1989), chap. 7, sec. 5, par. 3, and sec. 1, par. 4, 348 and 325, respectively.

[85] Aidan Nichols, O.P. *Epiphany: A Theological Introduction to Catholicism* (Collegeville, Minn.: Liturgical Press, 1996), 32.

[86] *Gaudium et Spes*, §44. When considered alone, without context, passages such as these have led some to misinterpret the meaning of inculturation as

out that we can deepen our understanding of Catholic teaching by taking "a step forward toward a doctrinal penetration and a formation of [doctrinal] consciousness in faithful and perfect conformity to the authentic doctrine." The understanding of the faith can only be deepened without threatening its unchangeable truth if we hold to the following distinction made by John XXIII: "the deposit or the truths of faith, contained in our sacred teaching, are one thing, while the mode in which they are enunciated, keeping the same meaning and the same judgment, [*eodem sensu eademque sententia*] is another."[87] In other words, "the propositional truths of faith are distinct from their linguistic expressions." The former are, if true, always and everywhere true; the latter may vary in our attempts to more clearly and accurately communicate revealed truths, but do not affect the truth of the propositions. Of course, this understanding of the relationship between the truths of faith and their linguistic expression allows for doctrinal development. As Germain Grisez puts it,

---

taught by the Second Vatican Council. Representative of such misinterpretations is that of Jay P. Dolan who suggests, as I understand him, that inculturation, in the sense of the Church's adapting and accommodating to the times, was John XXIII's major reason, if not the only reason, "for the council. He wanted to bring the church up to date, and to gain this goal he sought to establish a dialogue with people of other religions, with fellow Catholics, and with the world beyond the Church" (*In Search of An American Catholicism* [Oxford: Oxford University Press, 2002], 193). One of the major problems with this interpretation of inculturation is that it undervalues the critical and transformative dimensions of the Second Vatican Council's understanding of inculturation, as I will show in the text.

[87] Ioannes XXIII, "Allocutio habita d. 11 oct. 1962, in initio Concilii," 54 *Acta Apostolicae Sedis* (1962), 796, and for this quote, 792. This translation from the Latin of the opening address is from Germain Grisez, *The Way of the Lord Jesus*, 1:502.

The fact is that truths of faith need nothing added to them to be true, but always need further truths of faith added to them to develop God's relationship to his people as he wishes it to develop.... [T]he Church always can bring such fresh truths from the riches of revelation. Since every such new truth is an aspect of the one truth revealed by God in the Lord Jesus, no authentic development of doctrine ever can contradict what the Church believed and taught in earlier times and other places.[88]

Second, the concept of inculturation is understood differently and, I think, more theologically correct, in the perspective of an "incarnational humanism," borrowing John Courtney Murray's phrase, where the "one overarching Christian endeavor [is] the bringing of all things under the headship of Christ."[89] This perspective includes but goes beyond the em-

---

[88] Grisez, *The Way of the Lord Jesus*, 1:496. See also, Vatican I, Dogmatic Constitution *Dei Filius* on the Catholic Faith (1870): "For the doctrine of faith which God has revealed has not been proposed like a philosophical system to be perfected by human ingenuity, but has been committed to the spouse of Christ as divine trust to be faithfully kept and infallibly declared. Hence also that same meaning of the sacred dogmas is to be retained which our Holy Mother Church has once declared, and there must never be a deviation from that meaning on the specious ground and title of a more profound understanding.' Therefore, let there be growth and abundant progress in understanding, knowledge and wisdom, in each and all, in individuals and in the whole Church, at all times and in the succession of the ages, but only in its proper kind, i.e., in the same dogma, the same meaning, the same understanding'" (c. 4).

[89] Murray, *We Hold These Truths*, 190. For a similar account linking inculturation to the lordship of Jesus Christ, see "Select Themes of Ecclesiology on the Occasion of the Eighth Anniversary of the Closing of the Second Vatican Council" in *International Theological Commission: Texts and Documents 1969–1985* (San Francisco, Ignatius, 1989), 267–316, and for the following quote, 281:

phasis of enjoining Christians to engage modern secular culture and enter into a positive dialogue with it. By contrast, the over-arching endeavor of inculturation in the Christ *of* culture type is accommodation, updating, and adapting, which at best *undervalues*, or at worst *neglects*, the *transformationist* dynamic, or *conversionist* motif, of inculturation that is theologically rooted in the transcendent truth of the Incarnate Word, which is the objective self- revelation of the eternal Son of God, the second Person of the Holy Trinity, becoming man. As John Paul II explains, "Inculturation includes two dimensions: on the one hand, 'the intimate transformation of authentic cultural values through their integration in Christianity 'and, on the other, 'the insertion of Christianity in the various human cultures. 'The theological justification for inculturation is: "Just as 'the Word became flesh and dwelt among us '(John 1:14), so too the Good News, the Word of Jesus Christ proclaimed to the nations, *must take root* in the life-situation of the hearers of the Word. Inculturation is precisely this insertion of the Gospel message into cultures. For the Incarnation of the Son of God, precisely because it was complete and concrete, was also an incarnation in a particular culture. 'Every culture needs to be transformed by Gospel values in the light of the Paschal Mystery.'" Therefore, inculturation is both critical and transformative: "It is by looking at the Mystery of the Incarnation and of the Redemption that the values and countervalues of cultures are to be discerned. Just as the Word of God became like us in everything but sin, so too the inculturation of the Good News takes on all authentic human

---

"In the evangelization of cultures and the inculturation of the Gospel, a wondrous exchange is brought about: on the one hand, the Gospel reveals to each culture and sets free within it the final truth of the values which that culture carries. On the other hand, each and every culture expresses the Gospel in an original fashion and manifests new aspects of it. *This inculturation is an aspect of the recapitulation of all things in Christ* (Ephesians 1:10) and of the catholicity of the Church" (italics added).

values, purifying them from sin and restoring to them their full meaning."[90]

Third, the insurmountable dilemma that the cultural Christian now faces is one of his own making. As Niebuhr explains:

> In so far as part of its purposes is always that of recommend-ing the gospel to an unbelieving society, or to some special group, such as the intelligentsia, or political liberals or conservatives, or workingmen, it often fails to achieve its end because *it does not go far enough, or because it is suspected of introducing an element that will weaken the cultural movement. It seems impossible to remove the offense of Christ and his cross even by means of these accommodations*; and cultural Christians share in the general limitation all Christianity encounters whether it fights or allies itself with the "world." *If the evangelists of the Christ of culture do not go far enough to meet the demands of men whose loyalty is primarily to the values of civilization, they go too far in the judgment of their fellow believers of other schools.* These point out that the cultural answers to the Christ-culture problem show

---

[90] John Paul II, *Ecclesia in Africa*, 1995 Post-Synodal Apostolic Exhortation, §§59–61. See also the document prepared by the International Theological Commission, October 1988, "Faith and Inculturation," in *Catholicism and Secularization in America*, ed. David L. Schindler (Huntington, Ind.: Our Sunday Visitor, 1990), "Scandal for the Jews, the mystery of the Cross is foolishness to the pagans. Here the inculturation of the faith clashes with the radical sin of *idolatry* which keeps 'captive 'the truth of a culture which is not assumed by Christ. As long as man is 'deprived of the glory of God 'all that he 'cultivates 'is nothing more than the opaque image of himself. The Pauline kerygma begins therefore with creation and the call to the covenant, denounces the moral perversions of blinded humanity, and announces salvation in the crucified and risen Christ" (224).

a consistent tendency to distort the figure of the New Testament Jesus.[91]

Rather than making Christianity culturally relevant, this strategy *culturally marginalizes* Christianity precisely because in its accommodationist interpretation the cultural Christian offers the secular humanist "less and less in which to disbelieve."[92] Now, his fellow Christians will then protest not only that this is going too far in adapting Christianity to the times "where the faith so easily disappears into cultural dialogue"[93] but also, indeed chiefly, that this strategy has the opposite effect it set out to achieve, namely, it makes Christianity culturally irrelevant by no longer being distinctive enough to be needed in a dialogue. It is interesting to note here that it is often the critics of Christianity who wish that Christians would be more orthodox in their beliefs. Why do these critics insist upon this? They believe, rightly, I think, that there can be no serious dialogue with Christians beyond a certain point if they are not *integrally* Christian. As Jeffrey Stout once upon a time incisively put it, "One wants one's conversation partners to remain distinctive enough to

---

[91] Niebuhr, *Christ and Culture*, 108–9 (italics added).

[92] Alasdair MacIntyre, "The Fate of Theism," in *The Religious Significance of Atheism* (New York: Columbia University, 1969), 24. Similarly, Niebuhr says, "The cultural Christian ... makes common cause with the nonbeliever to an extent which deprives him of distinctively Christian principles" (*Christ and Culture*, 143). Also helpful in understanding this dilemma was Van A. Harvey, "The Pathos of Liberal Theology," *Journal of Religion* 56 (1976): 382–91. This is Harvey's article review of David Tracy's book, *The Blessed Rage for Order: The New Pluralism in Theology*.

[93] Aidan Nichols, O.P., "Rerelating Faith and Culture," in *Christendom Awake: On Reenergizing the Church in Culture* (Grand Rapids: Eerdmans, 1999), 17.

be identified, to be needed."[94] This view suffers the fate of the pathos of liberal theology. As the late American liberal theologian, Van A. Harvey (1923-2021) succinctly describes that pathos:

> The pathos of the liberal is that, by adopting modernity and accommodating Christianity to it, he is confronted by a solution of his own making in which Christianity has lost its 'transcendence' over common experience and is simply a re-presentation of its own self-understanding. On the other hand, if the theologian identifies himself with a faith that transcends and judges modernity, he must appear to that modernity and to himself, perhaps, as out of joint with the times.[95]

"Consequently," as Aidan Nichols rightly notes, "it is of the first importance to evangelization that the minds of the Church's members be not only alert to contemporary culture but also well-stocked with maturely reflected and apologetically honed dogmatic truth."[96]

Christ *Fulfiller* of Culture

The third typical answer that Christians have given to the enduring question of how Christ relates to culture is, I believe, an advance on the second specifically where it affirms that culture is, unqualifiedly, neither good nor evil but rather is something that may be transformed and hence fulfilled through the critical and transformative truth of the

---

[94] Jeffrey Stout, "The Voice of Theology in Contemporary Culture," in *Religion and America: Spirituality in a Secular Age*, ed. Mary Douglas and Steven M. Tipton (Boston: Beacon Press, 1983), 249–61, and for this quote, 260.

[95] Van A. Harvey, "The Pathos of Liberal Theology." 391.

[96] Nichols, "Integral Evangelization," 70.

Christian faith. Saint Thomas Aquinas 'teaching that grace perfects nature, neither abolishing nor leaving it untouched, is a basic presupposition of this answer.[97]

What is the theological basis for claiming that culture is, unqualifiedly, neither good nor evil? Interestingly, neo-Calvinist Herman Dooyeweerd and John Paul II both take the gospel parable of the good grain and the weeds (cf. Matt. 13:24–30) growing together until the harvest as a "key to the entire history of mankind." This history, John Paul says, "is the 'theater 'of the coexistence of good and evil" until the eschaton. "So even if evil exists alongside good," he adds, "good perseveres beside evil and grows, so to speak, from the same soil, namely human nature."[98] Significantly, both Dooyeweerd and John Paul affirm that God himself has imposed a definitive limit upon evil in light of the Redeemer, Jesus Christ. "The limit imposed upon evil by divine good has entered human history ... through the work of Christ. So it is impossible to separate Christ from human history." That is, "it is impossible to think of the limit placed by God himself upon ... evil without reference to the mystery of Redemption." This is so only for this reason, says John Paul: "The Paschal Mystery confirms that good is ultimately victorious, that life conquers death and that love triumphs over hate."[99]

Now, Dooyeweerd takes the idea that Christ limits evil, given that "the antithesis between sin and creation is *really* abrogated by his redemptive work," and develops it by being more specific than John Paul

---

[97] On this, see St. Thomas Aquinas, *Summa Theologiae*, I, q. 1, art. 8, resp. 2, "Grace does not abolish nature, but perfects it." See also, *De veritate*, q. 14, art. 10, ad 9. For a brief discussion of Aquinas on nature and grace, see W. D. Hughes, O.P., "The Infusion of Virtues," Appendix 3, in St. Thomas Aquinas, *Summa Theologiae*, vol. 23, *Virtue* (New York: McGraw-Hill, 1975), 247–48.

[98] John Paul II, *Memory and Identity*, 4. See also, Herman Dooyeweerd, *A New Critique of Theoretical Thought*, 1:523.

[99] John Paul II, *Memory and Identity*, 15, 19, 21, and for this quote, 55.

II regarding the sense in which Christ limits, checks, or restrains the operation and power of sin. He does so by appealing to Abraham Kuyper's notion of common grace.[100] Kuyper distinguishes between common grace and particular (or special) grace: The former is a "temporal restraining grace, which holds back and blocks the effect of sin"; the latter is a "saving grace, which in the end abolishes sin and completely undoes its consequences."[101] These two forms of grace, special and common, have a common origin in Christ, which Kuyper explains as follows.

> If we consult Scripture we will find it clearly spelled out that the ... self-same Christ is simultaneously two things: the root of the life of creation as well as the root of the life of the new creation.

---

[100] Abraham Kuyper gives the first constructive theological analysis of the Reformed doctrine of common grace in his three volume work, *De Gemeene Gratie* ["Common Grace"]—published 1902, 1903, and 1904, respectively by Höveker & Wormser in Amsterdam. For a selection from these volumes, see "Common Grace," in *Abraham Kuyper: A Centennial Reader*, ed. James D. Bratt, 165–201 (Grand Rapids: Eerdmans, 1998). See also the recent translation of the appendices on science and art in Volume III of *De Gemeene Gratie*, namely, *Wisdom & Wonder, Common Grace in Science & Art*, Translated by Nelson D. Kloosterman, Edited by Jordan J. Ballor and Stephen J. Grabill (Grand Rapids, MI: Christian's Library Press, 2011). On the development of Kuyper's mature views regarding the relationship between common grace and Christ's redemption, see the magisterial study of S. U. Zuidema, "Common Grace and Christian Action in Abraham Kuyper," in *Communication and Confrontation: A Philosophical Appraisal and Critique of Modern Society and Contemporary Thought* (Toronto: Wedge, 1972), 52–104. For a contemporary discussion of the doctrine of common grace, see Richard J. Mouw, *He Shines in All That s Fair: Culture and Common Grace*, Stob Lectures (Grand Rapids: Eerdmans, 2001). For a general introduction to Kuyper's thought, see Peter S. Heslam, *Creating a Christian Worldview: Abraham Kuyper s Lectures on Calvinism* (Grand Rapids: Eerdmans, 1998).

[101] Kuyper, *Abraham Kuyper: A Centennial Reader*, 168 (*De Gemeene Gratie*, 1:222).

Introduction 49

First we read that Christ is "the first-born of all creation, for in him all things were created, in heaven and on earth," so that he is "before all things and in him all things hold together" [Col. 1:15–17]. It could hardly be stated more plainly and clearly that Christ is the root of the creation and therefore of common grace, for it is common grace that prevents things from sinking into nothingness. (Does not the text say that all things *hold together* in him?) But we immediately note in the second place that the same Christ is "the *Head of the Body* and the first-born from the dead" [Colossians 1:18], hence also the root of the life of the new creation or special grace. The two things are even stated in parallel terms: he is the root of common grace for he is *the first born of all creation* [v. 15], and simultaneously the root of special grace, for he the *first-born from the dead* [v. 18]. There is thus no doubt whatever that common grace and special grace come most intimately connected from their origin, and this connection lies in Christ.[102]

---

[102] Kuyper, *Abraham Kuyper: A Centennial Reader*, 186–87 (*De Gemeene Gratie*, 2:645; see also 183). I am reminded here of John Paul II who in his 1998 Encyclical Letter, *Fides et Ratio*, makes a similar point about the selfsame Christ. "The unity of truth is a fundamental premise of human reasoning, as the principle of non- contradiction makes clear. Revelation renders this unity certain, showing that the God of creation is also the God of salvation history. It is the one and the same God who establishes and guarantees the intelligibility and reasonableness of the natural order of things ... and who reveals himself as the Father of our Lord Jesus Christ. This unity of truth, natural and revealed, is embodied in a living and personal way in Christ, as the Apostle [Paul] reminds us: "Truth is in Jesus" (cf. Eph 4:21; Col 1:15–20). He is the *eternal Word* in whom all things were created, and he is the *incarnate Word* who in his entire person reveals the Father (cf. John 1:14, 18).... [W]hat is revealed in him is 'the full truth '(cf. John 1:14-16) of everything which was created in him and through him and which therefore in him finds its fulfillment (cf. Col 1:17)" (§34).

Yet, there is one more point I need to make about the relationship between common grace and particular grace in order to avoid the image that they run along parallel tracks, existing independently side-by-side, with completely independent purposes, having only an extrinsic relationship to each other. The purpose of common grace does not exist outside of particular grace, given that the latter "restores creation in its root." In other words, Kuyper rightly sees that nature and grace belong together. "You cannot see grace in all its riches if you do not perceive how its tiny roots and fibers everywhere penetrate into the joints and cracks of the life of nature. And you cannot validate that connectedness [between nature and grace] if, with respect to grace, you first look at the salvation of your soul and primarily on the *Christ of God*." Kuyper explains:

> For if grace exclusively concerned atonement for sin and salvation of souls, one could view grace as something located and operating outside of nature. One could picture it as oil poured on turbulent waters, floating on those waters while remaining *separate* from them, solely so that the drowning person can save his life by grabbing the life buoy thrown out to him. But if it is true that Christ our Savior has to do not only with our soul but also with our body, that all things in the world belong to Christ and are claimed by him, that one day he will triumph over every enemy in that world, and that in the end Christ will not gather a few separated souls around him, as is the case now, but will rule as king on a new earth under a new heaven—then, of course, everything is different.
>
> For that reason Scripture continually points out that the *Savior* of the world is also the *Creator* of the world, indeed that he could become its Savior only *because* he already was its

Creator. Of course, it was not the *Son of man*, not the *incarnate Word*, who created the world.... Still, Scripture repeatedly points out that he, the first-born of the dead, is also the first-born of creation, that the Word Incarnate nevertheless always was and remained the same eternal Word who was with God and was God, of whom it is written that without that Word nothing was made that is made [John 1:1–3]. Christ then is connected with *nature* because he is its Creator, and at the same time connected to *grâce* because, as Re-creator, he manifested the riches of grace in the midst of that nature.[103]

Turning now back to Dooyeweerd after this brief introduction to Kuyper's doctrine of common grace, we can understand the specific sense in which Christ limits evil. Says Dooyeweerd,

Common grace in the first place consists in the maintenance of the temporal world-order in all its structures against the disintegration by sin. In this sense common grace embraces "the evil and the good together" and is restricted to temporal life. Special grace, however, is concerned with the renewal of the religious root of the creation in Christ Jesus as the Head of the regenerated human race and [hence] must not [be] considered in an *individualistic* soteriological sense. From this it follows that particular grace is the real root and foundation of common grace. It is therefore absolutely contrary to the Biblical standpoint when a distinction is made between two independent realms or spheres of grace.[104]

---

[103] Kuyper, *Abraham Kuyper: A Centennial Reader*, 173 (*De Gemeene Gratie*, 1:228).

[104] Dooyeweerd, *A New Critique of Theoretical Thought*, 3:506–7.

He explains, following Kuyper, that Christ's redemption is the source of common grace, in other words, the source of a restraining or "preserving grace," which is "a counterforce against the destructive work of sin in the cosmos."

> Common grace is meaningless without Christ as the root and head of the regenerated human race.... It is grace shown to mankind as a whole, which is regenerate in its new root Jesus Christ, but has not yet been loosened from its old apostate root. This is the meaning of Jesus 'parable of the tares among the wheat. The wheat and the tares must grow together until the harvest.... It is all due to God's common grace in Christ that there are still means left in the temporal world to resist the destructive force of the elements that have got loose; that there are still means to combat disease, to check psychic maladies, to practice logical thinking, to save cultural development from going down into savage barbarism, to develop language, to preserve the possibility of social intercourse, to withstand injustice, and so on. All these things are the fruits of Christ's work.
>
> ... From the very beginning God has viewed His fallen creation in the light of the Redeemer.[105]

Thus, we are now in a position to understand why it is when we survey cultures from a Christian standpoint, we see *both* goodness *and* fallenness, grace *and* sin, *both* truth *and* falsity. It follows from this point that the Christian should accept truth and goodness wherever it appears

---

[105] Dooyeweerd, *A New Critique of Theoretical Thought*, 1:523, and 2:34–35.

among fallen human beings, even among unbelievers. Of course, the grasp of truth in that context may be incomplete, inadequate, even distorted, but because the Spirit of God is the sole foundation of all that is true, we honor him by accepting that truth. *All truth is God's truth.*[106]

This is by no means the whole picture. "The good news of Christ continually renews the life and culture of fallen man; it combats and removes the error and evil which flow from the ever-present attraction of sin. It never ceases to purify and elevate the morality of peoples. It takes the spiritual qualities and endowments of every age and nation, and with supernatural riches it causes [man's life and culture] to blossom, as it were, from within; it fortifies, completes and restores them in Christ" (*GS*, §58).

At this point, I move on to unpack the claim that Christ is the fulfiller of culture by attempting to give a definition of culture in order to get a better grasp of what exactly is being fulfilled. We may define a culture, following Charles Taylor, as a specific intellectual, moral, symbolic, and institutional formation. This cultural formation expresses an understanding of "personhood, social relations, states of mind/soul, goods and bads, virtues and vices." Alternatively put, it expresses "a constellation

---

[106] Both St. Thomas Aquinas (1225–1274) and, centuries later, the Protestant reformer John Calvin (1509–1564) held similar views on this score. Aquinas wrote, "Although some minds are enwrapped in darkness, that is, deprived of clear and meaningful knowledge, yet there is no human mind in such darkness as not to participate in some of the divine light ... because all that is true by whomsoever it is uttered, comes from the Holy Spirit." I found this passage by Aquinas in John Paul II, "Method and Doctrine of St. Thomas in Dialogue with Modern Culture," in *The Whole Truth about Man*, ed. with an intro. by James V. Schall, S.J. (Boston: Daughters of St. Paul, 1981), 268–69. Similarly, Calvin wrote: "If we regard the Spirit of God as the sole fountain of truth, we shall neither reject the truth itself, nor despise it wherever it shall appear, unless we wish to dishonor the Spirit of God" (*Institutes of the Christian Religion*, ed. John T. McNeill [Philadelphia: Westminster, 1960], 2.2.15.273–74).

of understandings of person, nature, society, and the good" as well as about the relationships of the human person to "God, the cosmos and other humans."[107] Further, man is a culture-bearing creature whose cultures are diverse, permeable, which includes an openness to influence from each other, and changeable because he is developing and therefore historical.[108]

In particular, says the former Joseph Cardinal Ratzinger, now Benedict XVI, "Each particular culture not only lives out its own experience of God, the world, and man, but on its path it necessarily encounters other cultural agencies and has to react to their quite different experiences." In that intercultural exchange, he adds, "that culture's own perceptions and values [may be] deepened and purified," leading to a "profound reshaping of that culture's previous form" (*TT*, 63). Yet, this is precisely where the objection is raised that this exchange is necessarily violent of that culture and alienating it from its own specific cultural formation. If so, then even inculturating the gospel and evangelizing in the faith-knowledge of the great and universal commission that Jesus Christ himself gave his disciples is unjustified (Matt. 28:19f.). Behind this objection is the assumption that there is no universal truth about God, man, or reality, which is in principle accessible to all men and belongs to all. We are left with the idea that we are only, in differing cultural formations, as Benedict puts it, "just touching on the mystery that never unveils itself to us" (*TT*, 57). "Thus the multiplicity of cultures serves to demonstrate the relativism of all cultures. *Culture is set against truth.*

---

[107] Charles Taylor, "Two Theories of Modernity," *Hastings Center Report*, 25, no. 2 (March-April 1995): 24–33, and for these quotes 24, 29. I discovered this reference to Taylor in Tracey Rowland, *Culture and the Thomist Tradition After Vatican II* (New York: Routledge, 2003), 12–13. Similar definitions of culture can be found in Niebuhr, *Christ and Culture*, 32–39.

[108] Nichols, "Re-relating Faith and Culture," 10–11.

This relativism, which is nowadays to be found, as a basic attitude of enlightened people, penetrating far into the realm of theology, is the most profound difficulty of our age" (*TT*, 72; italics added).

Benedict XVI faces this difficulty head on. "Only if it is true that all cultures are potentially universal and have an inner capacity to be open to others can interculturality lead to new and fruitful forms [of culture]" (*TT*, 64). He undercuts the assumption of relativism by arguing that inculturation "assumes the potential universality of every culture" (*TT*, 59). That is, the union of all cultures is in principle possible because the "same human nature is at work in all of them and there is a common truth of humanity alive within that human nature that aims towards union" (*TT*, 60). There is more: the very same Logos who has become man in Jesus Christ, the self-revelation of truth itself, is at work in all these various cultural formations leading them toward truth. If this is so, then no violence is necessarily being done to a specific cultural formation because each and every culture is *commonly oriented*, in light of our common human nature, *to the truth of our humanity*. "A meeting of cultures is possible because man, in all the variety of his history and of his social structures and customs, is *a single being, one and the same. This one being, man, is however touched and affected in the very depth of his existence by truth itself*" (*TT*, 64–65; italics added). This common truth of humanity is that man is *created by God and for God*, that God unceasingly draws man to himself, and that only in communion with God will he find the truth and wholeness for which he never stops searching (cf. *CCC*, §§27–30). Thus, inculturating the faith as well as evangelizing others "opens up" and further develops the direction of a specific cultural formation to the common truth of humanity. The truth to be found in a given formation coexists with falsehood. If I understand Benedict XVI correctly, then, a critical engagement with those cultures is required, not merely to discern falsehoods, but also to "open up" the fragments of truth found there in the direction of Christ, with the aim of assimilating that truth into a larger synthesis, "within which the truth about God and about reality as a whole is always involved" (*TT*, 66). "A process of this kind can in fact lead to a breaking open of the silent alienation of man from the truth and from himself that exists within that culture ... to let itself be purified and thus to become better adapted to the truth and to man" (*TT*, 63, 60). Because of the potential universality of every culture, breaking open their fragments of truth in the direction of Christ will lead to a full unfolding of the truth.[109]

Because no culture is unqualifiedly either good or evil, then "whatever elements in any culture exclude such opening up ... represent what is inadequate in that culture" (*TT*, 60). In some cases, however, intercultural exchange may lead to the recognition of the limits of some specific cultural outlook or formation and hence to *complementary* perspectives that are neither contradictory nor self-sufficient but rather "incomplete and approximate portrayals of an enormously complex reality."[110] Therefore, says Benedict, "only in the interrelating of all great works of culture can man approach the unity and wholeness of his true nature" (*TT*, 65). Next, intercultural exchange may also lead to the recognition that different cultural formations are *genetically* related as "successive stages in some process of development. Each later stage presupposes earlier stages, partly to include them, and partly to transform them."[111] Most importantly, however, the perspectives embedded in cultural formations

---

[109] John Paul II, *Fides et Ratio*, §71. See also, "Faith and Inculturation," 220: "One conviction dominates the preaching of Jesus: in Jesus—in his word and in his person—God perfects the gifts he has already made to Israel and to all nations, by transcending them. *Jesus is the sovereign light and true wisdom for all nations and all cultures*" (italics added).

[110] Bernard Lonergan, S.J., *Method in Theology* (New York: Herder and Herder, 1972), 219.

[111] Lonergan, *Method in Theology*, 236.

may also be "opposed *dialectically*." "What for one is true, for another is false. What for one is good, for another is evil."[112] Indeed, says Benedict, "the potential universality of cultures is often blocked by quite insurmountable obstacles that prevent it from turning into an actual universality." Thus: "Not only a [common] dynamic exists, but equally [common] divisions, barriers against others, contradictions that exclude, an impossibility of transition because the waters between are far too deep. This [is] a negative factor in human existence: an alienation that hinders our perceiving things and that, *at least partially*, cuts men off from the truth and thus also from each other" (*TT*, 65; italics added). Notwithstanding these negative dynamics, the openness to the truth endures within human nature and hence "every culture contains within itself and displays an indestructible urge for some sort of fulfillment." "We can therefore say," adds John Paul II, "that culture contains within itself the capacity for receiving divine revelation," which is "the immutable truth of God, which he himself has revealed in the history and culture of a people."[113]

> At this point, what is special about the self-understanding of Christian faith can be seen. It knows very well, if it is aware and uncorrupted, that there is a great deal of what is human in its particular cultural forms, *a great deal that needs purifying and opening up*. But it is also certain that it is at heart the self-revelation of truth itself [the Logos who has become man, Jesus Christ] and, therefore, redemption. For the real problem of mankind is the darkening of truth. This distorts our action and sets us against one another, because we bear our own evil within

---

[112] Lonergan, *Method in Theology*, 236.
[113] John Paul II, *Fides et Ratio*, §71.

ourselves, are alienated from ourselves, cut off from the ground of our being, from God. If truth is offered, this means a leading out of alienation and thus out of the state of division; it means the vision of a common standard that does no violence to any culture but that guides each one to its own heart, because each exists ultimately as an expectation of truth.... It is then clear that this truth is the sphere within which everyone can find and relate to one another and, in so doing, lose nothing of his own value or his own dignity. (*TT*, 65–67, 72)

Thus, on the one hand, the Christian faith is open to all that is true, good, and beautiful in world cultures. Significantly, it will also oppose "whatever in the culture bars the doors against the gospel." "Therefore," adds Benedict, "it has always been critical of culture also, and it must continue fearlessly and steadfastly to critique culture, especially today."[114] The assumption here is that whatever good is found sown in, say, Greek thought, in the minds and hearts of men such as Plato, Aristotle, Plotinus, and others, must be taken captive for the truth of Christ and for the glory of God (cf. 2 Cor. 10:5). In short, in Etienne Gilson's wonderfully apt phrase, Christian thinkers must "put these fragments of truth in the service of revelation."[115] This service is, as Hans Urs von Balthasar rightly urges, "no mechanical adoption of alien chains of thought

---

[114] Pope Benedict XVI, "Communication and Culture," in *On the Way to Jesus Christ*, trans. Michael J. Miller (San Francisco: Ignatius Press, 2005), 42–52, and for this quote, 49.

[115] Etienne Gilson, *The Philosopher and Theology*, trans. Ralph MacDonald, C.S.B., (London: Sheed & Ward, 1939). 188. Gilson's approach stands in the line of the "spoils from Egypt" trope. For an important discussion of this trope, see Fr. Thomas G. Guarino, *Foundations of Systematic Theology* (New York: T&T Clark, 2005), 269–310. He explains this trope as one "that characterized the

with which one can adorn and garland the Christian dimension externally."¹¹⁶ In other words, as Calvin Seerveld puts it, "The reforming Christian approach to unchristian culture is not one of highway robbery and synthetic adoption but is one of serious, anti-sympathetic vibration, if you can take a metaphor; in forming, in building a re-formational Christian culture we scrutinize unchristian genius (to know what is going on!) to see what they are mistakenly getting at in God's world and to use them for a good thing in fashioning our own wineskins."¹¹⁷ Thus, the task implied in Gilson's phrase could be distinguished, says Balthasar, into the "art of *breaking open* all finite, philosophical truth in the direction of Christ, and the art of *clarifying transposition*."¹¹⁸ Regarding the former, Christians are deeply committed to the "all-embracing authority

---

work of so many early Christian writers. Insofar as God had created the world, had communicated himself to humanity by a primordial act of grace and love inscribed in creation itself, wisdom and truth could be found in many places. All such wisdom, however, the traditional spoils metaphor insists, must ultimately be disciplined by, and incorporated into, the revelatory narrative. Athens, whatever its own insights into truth, must ultimately be chastened by Jerusalem" (269).

[116] Hans Urs von Balthasar, "On the Tasks of Catholic Philosophy in Our Time," *Communio: International Catholic Review* 20 (Spring 1993): 147-87, and for this quote, 155-56. That Balthasar's point is in agreement with Aquinas may be seen from the following statement of Aquinas: "So those who use the works of the philosophers in sacred doctrine, by bringing them into the service of faith, do not mix water with wine, but rather change water into wine" (Questions 1-4 of Aquinas '*Commentary on the* De Trinitate *of Boethius*, trans. with intro. and notes Armand Maurer [Toronto: Pontifical Institute of Medieval Studies, 1987], Q. 2, art. 3, reply 5.) Clearly, Aquinas also rejects, in Balthasar's words, a "mechanical adoption of alien chains of thought with which one can adorn and garland the Christian dimension externally."

[117] Seerveld, *A Christian Critique of Art and Literature* (Ontario: Association for Reformed Scientific Studies, 1964), 27.

[118] Balthasar, "On the Tasks of Catholic Philosophy in Our Time," 156.

of Christ" (cf. Matt. 28:18) over all forms of creaturely truth because in Christ are hid all the treasures of wisdom and knowledge (cf. Col. 2:2–3), and hence Christians "cannot rest until they have brought all these forms of truth into the service of the one truth. 'Everything is yours; but you belong to Christ, and Christ to God '(1 Cor. 3:23).'"[119] Regarding the art of clarifying transposition, Balthasar writes,

> The fragment or stone that they pick up may come from the bed of a Christian stream, or of a pagan or heretical stream, but they know how to cleanse it and to polish it until that radiance shines forth which shows that it is a fragment of the total glorification of God. Such a methodology may appear dangerous, because the clear and sharp outlines of the evangelical decision threaten to become blurred in it. This is the form of thought which necessarily *had* to be confused by unbelieving criticism with the syncretism of late Antiquity, the form of thought which permitted Christianity to amalgamate itself with the elements of Hellenism which were alien to its own being. But everything depends here on the disposition in which the synthesis is made: if the knowledge of the absoluteness of the truth of Christ stands at the abiding origin of such thought, and if the decision for him has been made with the entire purity of a loving soul, then it is legitimate and safe to adopt the intellectual mission to go out into all the world and to take captive all truth for Christ. "Test *everything* and retain what is good!" (1 Thess. 5:21). But "do not conform yourselves to the spirit of the world" (Rom. 12:2).[120]

---

[119] Balthasar, "On the Tasks of Catholic Philosophy in Our Time," 158.
[120] Balthasar, "On the Tasks of Catholic Philosophy in Our Time," 159.

Benedict illustrates this "path of cultural encounter and conflict" by using an image from the writings of the fourth-century Cappadocian, Basil of Caesarea (ca. 330–379), who took the same path with the Greek culture of his time. "I was one who slits the fruit of the sycamore" (Amos 7:14). Basil writes:

> The sycamore is a tree that bears very plentiful fruit. But it is tasteless unless one carefully slits it and allows its saps to run out, whereby it becomes flavorful. That is why, we believe, the sycamore is a symbol for the pagan world; it offers a surplus, yet at the same it is insipid. This comes from living according to pagan customs. When one manages to slit them by means of the Logos, it [the pagan world] is transformed, becomes tasty and useful.[121]

Benedict cites a recent German commentator of Basil's passage that is illuminating:

> In this symbol [of the sycamore] are found the plenteousness, the wealth, the luxuriance of the pagan world ..., but its deficiency is found therein as well. As it is, it is insipid, unusable. It needs a complete transformation, whereby the change does not destroy its substance; rather, it gives to it the qualities it lacks.... The fruit remains fruit; its abundance is not diminished; rather it is recognized as an advantage.... On the other hand, the necessary transformation can scarcely be more keenly evident in this image than through the fact that what formerly could not

---

[121] Benedict XVI, "Communication and Culture," 46.

be enjoyed now becomes edible. In the "running out" of the sap, furthermore, the process of purification is suggested.[122]

One final point, adds Benedict XVI, is that the source of the transformation alluded to above is not internal to the tree itself and its fruit. In keeping with the image of the shepherd and the dresser of the sycamore tree, an intervention from outside is necessary. Says Benedict, "Applied to the pagan world, to what is characteristic of human culture, this means: The Logos itself must slit our cultures and their fruit, so that what is unusable is purified and becomes not only usable but good...." Yes, ultimately only the Logos himself can guide our cultures to their true purity and maturity, but the Logos makes us his servants, the "dresser of sycamore trees.... An ongoing and patient encounter between the Logos and the culture is necessary, mediated by the service of the faithful."[123]

I do not think it is reaching too far to suggest that the "dresser of the sycamore trees" resonates with the words of Jesus to his disciples recorded in the gospel of Matthew, "The harvest is plentiful but the workers are few. Ask the Lord of the harvest, therefore, to send out workers into His harvest field" (9:37–38). Indeed, deeply mindful of the words of Saint Paul, "I am not ashamed of the Gospel: it is the power of God for salvation to every one who has faith" (Rom. 1:16), the Christian cannot help but proclaim the gospel in the conviction that Jesus Christ is the answer to the question that is every human life. Jesus Christ, the revelation of truth itself, is the Way, the Truth, and the Life (cf. John 14:6). "In reality it is only in the mystery of the Word made flesh that the mystery of man truly becomes clear" (*GS*, §22). Christ alone, not only reconciles us to the Father but also reveals the totality of the mystery of man. "He

---

[122] Benedict XVI, "Communication and Culture," 47.
[123] Benedict XVI, "Communication and Culture," 47.

is the truth in person and, thereby, the way to be human" (*TT*, 67). That is the "high claim" (*TT*, 67) to truth that the Christian faith brings, indeed *must* bring, to the cultures of the world.

Christ *and* Culture

Some versions of the fourth approach—typically called *dual-ism*—to the enduring question of how Christ relates to culture urge us to distinguish the progress *of* history from the progressive realization of the kingdom of God *within* history because the final consummation of all things is an eschatological event. The kingdom of God is both present and future, both now and not yet. In and by the singularly unique revelation of Jesus Christ, the kingdom of God is presently inaugurated but it will reach its final consummation only when the Lord Jesus returns to bring about the renewal of all things: "Behold, I make all things new" (Rev. 21:5). For the present, between the already and the not yet, all our works, including the works of culture, the structures of society, are fallen and distorted by sin. The reason then for insisting on distinguishing the progress *of* history from the progress of the kingdom of God *within* history is clear: "*Before the holiness of God* as disclosed in the grace of Jesus Christ … there is corruption and degradation in all man's work." There exists a tension between faith and culture that manifests a *dualism* between sin and grace, that is, "the situation of cultured, sinful man confronting the holiness of divine grace." Short of eschatological fulfillment, then, Christ's lordship and historical progress is not one and the same thing. John Paul II puts this point admirably well:

> Man, who was created for freedom, bears within himself the wound of original sin, which constantly draws him towards evil and puts him in need of redemption. Not only is *this doctrine an*

integral part of Christian revelation; it also has great hermeneutical value insofar as it helps one to understand human reality. Man tends towards good, but he [is] also capable of evil.... [Thus] when people think they possess the secret of a perfect social organization which makes evil impossible, they also think that they can use any means, including violence and deceit, in order to bring that organization into being. Politics then becomes a 'secular religion 'which operates under the illusion of creating paradise in this world. But no political society—which possesses its own autonomy and laws—can ever be confused with the Kingdom of God. The Gospel parable of the weeds among the wheat (cf. Matt. 13:24-30, 36-43) teaches that it is for God alone to separate the subjects of the Kingdom from the subjects of the Evil One, and that this judgment will take place at the end of time. By presuming to anticipate judgment here and now, man puts himself in the place of God and sets himself against the patience of God. (*CA*, §25)

This version of dualism is, therefore, a needed *corrective* to the optimism that is implied by views that identify the growth of the kingdom of God with human progress. In this respect, dualism, or at least some versions of it, shares with anticultural Christianity a profound sense of sin even in the whole world of human activity. Unlike the latter, however, "the dualist knows that he belongs to that culture and cannot get out of it, that God indeed sustains him in it and by it; for if God in His grace did not sustain the world in its sin it would not exist for a moment."[124] Notwithstanding this positive note, this view raises the important question of whether it leaves cultural life and its institutions with

---

[124] Niebuhr, *Christ and Culture*, 152-53, 156.

Introduction

a merely *negative* function in a fallen world—restraining sin from becoming as destructive as it might otherwise be—rather than with a certain *positive* value of its own.[125] It leaves unanswered the equally important question of whether living the Christian life here and now in the temporal world is necessary because intrinsically meaningful for the realization of God's redemptive work.[126]

Significantly, humanism in the last several centuries has reacted against this version of dualism by asserting "the autonomy and inherent worth of human life in this world."[127] Obviously, the orthodox Christian faith rejects the notion of autonomy and inherent worth when that is understood as a self-sufficiency entailing a denial, as it surely does for many, of the theology of creation—"every creature, man included, naturally depends upon God"[128]— and the theology of the Incarnation: "The Truth is that only in the mystery of the Incarnate Word does the mystery of man take on light" (*GS*, §22; cf. §36). Unfortunately, however, some Christians—both Protestant and Catholic—have framed their whole concept of the Christian life with the understanding that nature and grace are separated into two quasi- independent orders of reality, namely, one temporal, the other spiritual, one natural, and the other supernatural. This "parallelistic dualism of separated spiritual and temporal life," as Niebuhr describes this concept,[129] entails the idea of the autonomy of the temporal order, meaning thereby that this order falls outside the scope of the fall into sin as well as being unrelated to, or autonomous from, grace.

---

[125] Niebuhr, *Christ and Culture*, 171.

[126] Again, helpful here with the formulation of this question is Germain Grisez, *The Way of the Lord Jesus*, 1:16–17, 1:807–30.

[127] Grisez, *The Way of the Lord Jesus*, 1:811.

[128] John Paul II, *Fides et Ratio*, §80.

[129] Niebuhr, *Christ and Culture*, 179.

This concept leads Christians to *live double rather than integral lives*, putting their faith and their daily lives into separate compartments, which the Second Vatican Council called one of the most serious errors of our age (cf. *GS*, §43). Most importantly, this dualistic concept of nature and grace leaves nature untouched by grace. It has not been radically affected by sin and therefore is not in need of renewal and transformation in its own realm. This results in a cultural naturalism or secularism. Unlike anticultural Christians who take nature to be so corrupt that grace, no longer able to transform it, merely replaces it altogether by adding the spiritual realm over and above creation, this dualistic concept leaves nature untouched by grace and, in the process, effectively limits the scope of sin and redemption to the supernatural realm.[130] In other words, cultural life, indeed the whole of temporal life, does not need Christ!

Following Maritain, I argued earlier in the Introduction to this study that it is erroneous to ignore not only the distinction between nature and grace but also their union.[131] There remains to ask how best to understand the union of nature and grace. The brief answer to this question here must be that *grace restores nature*, meaning thereby the totality of created reality. In the words of Henri Cardinal De Lubac, "The supernatural does not merely *elevate* (this traditional term is correct, but it is

---

[130] Especially influential in my thinking on the relationship between nature and grace have been the reflections of Dutch neo-Calvinist philosopher Dooyeweerd (1894–977). For a brief introduction to his thinking, see *In the Twilight of Western Thought*. Extremely helpful also to me was De Lubac, *The Mystery of the Supernatural*. See also, David L. Schindler, "Introduction: Grace and the Form of Nature and Culture," 10–30, esp. 11, 20–21.

[131] Maritain, *Clairvoyance de Rome*, 222 (italics added), "*There is one error that consists in ignoring the distinction between nature and grace. There is another that consists in ignoring their union.*" I discovered this quote in De Lubac, "Apologetics and Theology," 91–104, and this citation at 103n28.

inadequate by itself) ... [Rather] it *transforms it* ... 'Behold, I make all things new! '(Rev. 21:5). Christianity is 'a doctrine of transformation ' because the Spirit of Christ comes to permeate the first creation and make of it a 'new creature. 'What is true of the final great transformation, on the occasion of the 'Parousia 'at which there will arise 'new heavens and a new earth '(Rev. 21), is already true now, according to Saint Paul, of each one of us."[132]

Christ *Saving Transformer* of Culture

Shortly before his death, the Holy Father, John Paul II, published his final book, thus leaving the Church, indeed the whole of humanity, the beautiful gift of his reflections entitled, *Memory and Identity*. Relevant to the question of the indivisible unity of nature and grace is the following passages from this work:

> The resurrection of Christ clearly illustrated that only the measure of good introduced by God into history through the mystery of Redemption is sufficient to correspond fully to the truth of the human being. The Paschal Mystery thus becomes the definitive measure of man's existence in the world created by God. In this mystery, not only is eschatological truth revealed to us, that is to say the fullness of the Gospel, or Good News. There also shines forth a light to enlighten the whole of human existence in its temporal dimension and this light is then reflected onto the created world. Christ, through his Resurrection, has so to speak "justified" the work of creation, and especially the creation of man. He has "justified" it in the sense that he revealed the 'just

---

[132] De Lubac, *A Brief Catechesis on Nature and Grace*, 81–82.

measure" of good intended by God at the beginning of human existence. This measure is not merely what was provided by him in creation and then compromised by man through sin; it is a superabundant measure, in which the original plan finds a higher realization (cf. Gen. 3:14–15). In Christ, man is called to a new life, as son in the Son, the perfect expression of God's glory.[133]

At the core of the Christian worldview is an interlocking set of life-orienting beliefs regarding the creation, fall into sin, and Redemption (i.e., incarnation, passion, resurrection, and ascension). First, God created the world good. Given the cultural mandate to subdue and have dominion over created reality, this "goodness" extends to the work of man's hands when accomplished in the light of "the truth about ourselves and about the world."[134] Indeed, the totality of creation, especially man who is its crown, actually manifests God's goodness, being created in the image and likeness of God. This manifestation of goodness is God's thesis, his affirmation, his *yes* to the creation (Gen. 1:31).

Second, all creation (i.e., nature, culture, history, society) is fallen through original sin. Human nature as a whole has lost its original harmony, and man is wounded at the very root of his being, estranged from God, from himself, and from his fellow man. His humanity exhibits the marks of being sinful, prone to sin, with sin being a violation of God's will and purpose. This sinfulness denies God's thesis and has its beginnings in Genesis 3. God's response to man's sin is *yes* but also *no*. *Yes*, because God, full of love, mercy, and grace does not abandon the fallen creation. Indeed, Genesis 3:15 contains the first proclamation of the Messiah, the *proto-evangelium*; also *no*, because God, judging man in the

---

[133] John Paul II, *Memory and Identity*, 25.
[134] John Paul II, *Memory and Identity*, 81.

Introduction

light of his perfect justice and holiness is the author of the antithesis, of the sign of contradiction between good and evil; between the seed of the woman and the seed of the serpent.

Third, the redemption accomplished through the mystery of the Incarnation and Christ's finished work—his life, passion, death, resurrection, and ascension—abrogates the antithesis between sin and creation. Put differently, the incarnation, passion, and resurrection in Jesus Christ means that his grace restores an original good creation. God's original thesis is reasserted and reestablished, but also, as John Paul II asserts in the above quote, enriched, fulfilled, and perfected. This redemption restores the very heart of human nature, causing the rebirth of the human self in Christ (Col. 2:13; 2 Cor. 5:17). "Christ alone, through his humanity, reveals the totality of the mystery of man.... The key to his self-understanding lies in contemplating the divine Prototype, the Word made flesh, the eternal Son of the Father." "Without the Gospel," John Paul adds, "man remains a dramatic question with no adequate answer. The correct response to the question about man is Christ, *Redemptor Hominis*."[135] This rebirth manifests itself in the integral redemption of the whole man in Christ through the fellowship of the Father, Son, and Holy Spirit, and with one another in them, which has been given to us in grace (Rom. 5:5). Indeed, this redemption in Christ becomes a vision of cosmic redemption for the whole creation, including the life of culture. Indeed, God's grace in Christ restores all life to its fullness, penetrating and perfecting and transforming the fallen creation from within its own order, bringing creation into conformity with his will and purpose.[136]

---

[135] John Paul II, *Memory and Identity*, 110, 114.

[136] Portions of these three paragraphs were originally published in my article, "Living Truth for a Post-Christian World: The Message of Francis Schaeffer and Karol Wojtyla," *Religion & Liberty* 12, no. 6 (November/December 2002).

The *New Evangelization* of Culture[137]

"God is preparing a *great springtime for Christianity*," John Paul II proclaimed throughout his pontificate of almost twenty-seven years.[138] To prepare for that rich harvest, the people of God, the whole Church—especially the lay faithful, the Holy Father stresses—must be committed to the *new evangelization*. "The new evangelization that can make the twenty-first century a springtime of the Gospel is a task for the entire People of God, but will depend in a decisive way on the lay faithful being fully aware of their baptismal vocation and their responsibility for bringing the good news of Jesus Christ to their culture and society" (*SE*, 89).

If the new evangelization is to meet the challenge of this hour, the first and most urgent imperative is that the Church must remain true to her *evangelical* identity. As Paul VI wrote, "*Evangelization is the grace and vocation proper to the Church, her deepest identity. She exists in order to evangelize*, that is to say, in order to preach and teach, to be the channel of the gift of grace, to reconcile sinners with God, and to perpetuate Christ's sacrifice in the Mass, which is the memorial of His death and glorious resurrection."[139] In other words, the Church will fulfill the task in which its deepest identity is based when it proclaims throughout the world "the full truth of the Gospel ... with renewed vigor '*Jesus Christ, the one Savior of the world, yesterday, today and for ever*'" (*SE*, 40, 42).

---

[137] Portions of the concluding section of this essay were published in *John Paul II and the New Evangelization*, ed. Ralph Martin and Peter Williamson (Cincinnati: Servant Books, 2006), 288–95, 312–13.

[138] John Paul II, *Springtime of Evangelization*, The Complete Texts of the Holy Father's 1998 ad Limina Addresses to the Bishops of the United States, ed. and intro. Fr. Thomas D. Williams, L.C. (San Francisco: Ignatius Press, 1999), 38. Subsequent references to *SE* will be made parenthetically in the text.

[139] Paul VI, *Evangelii Nuntiandi*, §14.

John Paul II called his Christ-centered approach to the transformation of culture, the *new evangelization*. Why does he call this evangelization *new*?

The reason that comes readily to mind in reference to Europe, but surely a similar point could be made about America, is because of: "*the loss of Europe's [and America's] Christian memory and heritage*, accompanied by a kind of practical agnosticism and religious indifference whereby many Europeans [and Americans] give the impression of living without spiritual roots and somewhat like heirs who have squandered a patrimony entrusted to them."[140] Significantly, there is also the "advance of secularism," which includes a relativistic attitude toward truth itself, in the flow of the culture and society, gradually changing cultural institutions such as marriage and family and broader societal structures such as mainstream media, political, legal, educational, and health care institutions. Furthermore, with the Christian faith under attack by this advancement, many Christians have *privatized* their faith, adopting a "citadel mentality," retreating behind the walls of the Church, and hoping that secularization will not reach them. Thus: "Many people are no longer able to integrate the Gospel message into their daily experience; living one's faith in Jesus becomes increasingly difficult in a social and cultural setting in which that faith is constantly challenged and threatened. In many social settings, it is easier to be identified as an agnostic than a believer. The impression is given that unbelief is self- explanatory, whereas belief needs a sort of social legitimization which is neither obvious nor taken for granted." Alternatively, "European culture gives the impression of 'silent apostasy 'on the part of people who have all that they need and who live as if God does not exist." In sum, John Paul adds,

---

[140] John Paul II, *Ecclesia in Europa*, 2003 Post-Synodal Apostolic Exhortation, §7.

"We are witnessing the emergence of a new culture ... whose content and character are often in conflict with the Gospel and the dignity of the human person."[141]

Western culture is failing because its Christian roots are eroding. This failing culture has reached its lowest point in the emerging *culture of death*, which is antithetical to what John Paul II also calls the *culture of life* in the 1995 encyclical *Evangelium Vitae*. There are four specific roots of the culture of death: individual autonomy; a debased notion of freedom detached from objective truth; the eclipse of the sense of God and, in consequence, of the human person; and the darkening of human conscience, indeed, moral blindness, resulting in a confusion between good and evil in the individual and in society.[142] In short, the Church is engaged in a battle for the soul of Western culture. What is the consequence of this conclusion for the Church? What ought *we* to do in engaging this failing culture?

In response, John Paul II has provided us with an all-embracive "plan of action" involving the whole Church in the whole spectrum of life and in the whole culture (*SE*, 59, 76).[143] We are called to be the people of God at the *service of life*. We need to bring the gospel of Jesus to the heart of every man and woman. There is a deep spiritual hunger in every human heart "for fullness of life and truth" (*SE*, 56). In no uncertain terms, Pope John Paul II boldly proclaims the truth of the gospel: "Jesus Christ is the answer to the question that is every human life" (cf. *SE*, 44, 58, 85). *"No demand ... is more urgent than the 'new evangelization' needed to satisfy the spiritual hunger of our times"* (*SE*, 148).

Most important for its overall approach to culture, however, the Church must include each one of the typical answers, but now only as

---

[141] John Paul II, *Ecclesia in Europa*, §§7, 9.

[142] John Paul II, *Evangelium Vitae*, §§19–24.

[143] John Paul II, *Evangelium Vitae*, §§78–101.

aspects of its total approach, to the enduring question of how Christ relates to culture. The *culture* that embodies the *gospel of life* is *opposed* to the *culture of death*— abortion, infanticide, physician-assisted suicide, euthanasia, cloning, along with issues regarding bioethics, sexual ethics, marriage, and family life (cf. *SE*, 148–49). Christians are not only called to be *against* these practices but also to be agents of Christ-centered cultural *renewal*. The Church must evangelize, indeed, transform not only individuals but also cultural institutions and broader societal structures that support and promote the *gospel of life*. God's people are called to be in service to life by *building a new culture of human life*.

At the core of the new evangelization is the good news that *human life is a good, a gift of God*: Man is made in the image of God (Gen. 1:26), who is the crown of creation given dominion over all of creation (Gen. 1:28), possessing human dignity, and incomparable value. Man's image was marred by sin but is "restored, renewed, and brought to perfection" in and through the redemptive incarnation of the eternal Son of God, Jesus Christ. John Paul says: "All who commit themselves to following Christ are given the fullness of life ... God's plan for human beings is this: that they should be 'conformed to the image of his Son '(Rom. 8:29)." Furthermore: "The dignity of [human] life is linked not only to its beginning, to the fact that it comes from God, but also to its final end, to its destiny of fellowship with God in knowledge and love of him." Thus, *"The Gospel of God's love for man, the Gospel of the dignity of the person and the Gospel of life are a single and indivisible Gospel."*[144]

In order to be fully equipped as God's people to be at the service of life this "single and indivisible Gospel" must be taught and lived from the outset in the life of the family. Indeed, the family has a decisive and irreplaceable role to play in building a culture of life. Children must be

---

[144] John Paul II, *Evangelium Vitae*, §2, but also, §§32–36, and 38.

raised by their parents with the understanding that *procreation* is about receiving, not possessing, the divine *gift of human life*. Human life is not only a *gift*, however, it is also a *task*. That is, they must learn that in receiving this gift they have a corresponding responsibility to affirm and protect human life as a good. They do this by making choices that show respect for others, not only by respecting their rights, but also, indeed chiefly, by the sincere *gift of self* shown in being hospitable, in engaging in dialogue, in generous service, in bearing each others 'burdens, and in expressing solidarity with others. At the root of this self-giving is the divine commandment *to love, respect, and promote life*, especially but not only where life is weak and defenseless but also where life is challenged by hardship, sickness or rejection, and suffering. "Human life is sacred and inviolable at every stage and in every situation; it is an indivisible good.[145]

The truths of this single and indivisible gospel of life must be taught thereafter "*in catechesis, in the various forms of preaching, in personal dialogue, and in all educational activity.*" Yet, there is more: the gospel of life should be culturally embodied. As John Paul II constantly urged, "A faith that does not become culture [that is, inculturated] is a faith not fully accepted, not entirely thought out, not faithfully lived."[146] To that end, we must support and express solidarity with agencies and centers of service to life such as hospitals, clinics, and convalescent homes by emphasizing the intrinsic and undeniable *moral dimension* of their responsibility. In particular, to be actively prolife for the common good of society requires Christian health-care professionals—doctors, nurses,

---

[145] John Paul II, *Evangelium Vitae*, §§92–93, 96, and 52, 4, and for this quote at no. 87.

[146] Pontifical Council for Culture. *Towards a Pastoral Approach to Culture*, §1.

pharmacists, administrators, and chaplains— to bear witness to the gospel of life *in* their respective areas of responsibility. The apostolate of the laity "is exercised ... when they endeavor to have the Gospel spirit permeate and improve the temporal order, going about it in a way that bears clear witness to Christ and helps forward the salvation of men. Characteristic of the lay state is a life led in the midst of the world and of secular affairs, and hence laymen are called by God to make of their apostolate, through the vigor of their Christian spirit, a leaven in the world."[147] This apostolate is particularly important today given the current temptation of health-care professionals "to become manipulators of life, or even agents of death." This temptation may be resisted by recovering the meaning of the *Hippocratic Oath*, "which requires every doctor to commit himself to absolute respect for human life and its sacredness."[148]

Furthermore, Christians involved in the political, social, and civic arenas of cultural life are also responsible for implementing the gospel of life by "shaping society and developing cultural, economic, political, and legislative projects that, with respect for all and in keeping with democratic principles will contribute to the building of a society in which the dignity of each person is recognized and protected and the lives of all are defended and enhanced."[149] Moreover, Christian scholars—philosophers, theologians, indeed all those intellectuals engaged in the study of man—at work in institutions of higher education, centers, institutes, and committees addressing bioethical questions are also obligated by virtue of their calling in Christ to contribute to building a new culture of life.

At the start of this study, I referred to the central role that natural law plays in Catholic social teaching. What is the place of the natural law

---

[147] Vatican II, *Apostolicam Actuositatem*, §2.
[148] John Paul II, *Evangelium Vitae*, §§88–89.
[149] John Paul II, *Evangelium Vitae*, §90.

in building a new culture of life? Gerhard Cardinal Müller states that Pius XI in his 1937 encyclical *Mit Brennender Sorge* held the natural moral law, in principle accessible to all men, to be the highest guarantor against moral relativism and subjectivism.[150]

> It is on faith in God, preserved pure and stainless, that man's morality is based. All efforts to remove from under morality and the moral order the granite foundation of faith and to substitute for it the shifting sands of human regulations, sooner or later lead these individuals or societies to moral degradation. The fool who has said in his heart "there is no God" goes straight to moral corruption (*Psalms* xiii. 1), and the number of these fools who today are out to sever morality from religion, is legion. They either do not see or refuse to see that the banishment of confessional Christianity, i.e., the clear and precise notion of Christianity, from teaching and education, from the organization of social and political life, spells spiritual spoliation and degradation. No coercive power of the State, no purely human ideal, however noble and lofty it be, will ever be able to make shift of the supreme and decisive impulses generated by faith in God and Christ. If the man, who is called to the hard sacrifice of his own ego to the common good, loses the support of the eternal and the divine, that comforting and consoling faith in a God who rewards all good and punishes all evil, then the result of the majority will be, not the acceptance, but the refusal of their duty. The conscientious observation of the ten commandments of God and the precepts of the Church (which are nothing but practical specifications of rules of the Gospels) is for everyone

---

[150] *The Pope, His Mission and His Task*, translated by Brian McNeil (Washington, DC: Catholic University of America Press, 2021), 22.

an unrivaled school of personal discipline, moral education and formation of character, a school that is exacting, but not to excess. A merciful God, who as Legislator, says - Thou must! - also gives by His grace the power to will and to do. To let forces of moral formation of such efficacy lie fallow, or to exclude them positively from public education, would spell religious underfeeding of a nation. To hand over the moral law to man's subjective opinion, which changes with the times, instead of anchoring it in the holy will of the eternal God and His commandments, is to open wide every door to the forces of destruction. The resulting dereliction of the eternal principles of an objective morality, which educates conscience and ennobles every department and organization of life, is a sin against the destiny of a nation, a sin whose bitter fruit will poison future generations.[151]

This moral law not only grounds human dignity in a source of truth and morality outside the state itself, but it also leads to the rejection of the absolute state, subordinating the latter's power to the rule of law. Furthermore, the natural law, given its moral objectivity, leads to the rejection of a democracy that is based on the absolutization of the majority principle. As Benedict XVI correctly argues, "The majority cannot be an ultimate principle, since there are values that no majority is entitled to annul. It can never be right to kill innocent persons, and no power can make this legitimate."[152] Elsewhere, Benedict writes, "But majorities, too, can be blind or unjust, as history teaches us very plainly.... The majority principle always leaves open the question of the ethical foundations of

---

[151] Pius XI, *Mit Brennender Sorge*, §29.

[152] Joseph Cardinal Ratzinger, "To Change or to Preserve? Political Visions and Political Praxis," in *Values in a Time of Upheaval*, trans. Brian McNeil, C.R.V. (New York: Crossroad, 2006), 11–29, and for this quote, 27.

law. This is the question of whether there is something that can never become law but always remains injustice [remains wrong]; or, to reverse this formulation, whether there is something that is of its very nature inalienably law, something that is antecedent to every majority decision and must be respected by all such decisions."[153] Who would disagree? The brief answer to this question here must be: those who lack confidence in the truth-attaining capacities of human reason. Such a lack signifies, according to Benedict XVI, *"a crisis of political reason, which is a crisis of politics as such."* We come thus to the nub of the issue before us. Both Benedict and John Paul II are persuaded that what is ultimately at stake in an authentic democracy is the "defense of reason." "Reason," adds Benedict, "that is, moral reason is above the majority." "But how is it possible to discern these ultimate values that are the basis of all 'rational' and morally correct politics and are therefore binding on every person, irrespective of how majorities may shift and change? What are these values?"[154]

In reply to the question in the concluding sentence of this passage, here is a summary statement of these core values:

> In the face of *fundamental and inalienable ethical demands*, Christian must recognize that what is at stake is the essence of

---

[153] Ratzinger, "What Keeps the World Together, The Pre-political Moral Foundations of a Free State," in *Values in a Time of Upheaval*, 31–44, and for this quote, 34. There is another translation of this same essay available in Joseph Cardinal Ratzinger (Pope Benedict XVI) and Jürgen Habermas, *Dialectics of Secularization: On Reason and Religion*, ed. with foreword Florian Schuller, trans. Brian McNeil, C.R.V. (San Francisco: Ignatius Press, 2006), 53–80, and for this quote, 60. It is the translation from this book that I am citing in the text. See also my article, "Lessons from the Habermas and Ratzinger Debate," *Fellowship of Catholic Scholars Quarterly*, Spring/Summer 2017, 42-54.

[154] Ratzinger, "To Change or to Preserve?" 27.

the moral law, which concerns the integral good of the human person. This is the case with laws concerning *abortion* and euthanasia.... Such laws must defend the basic right to life from conception to natural death. In the same way, it is necessary to recall the duty to respect and protect the rights of the *human embryo*. Analogously, the *family* needs to be safeguarded and promoted, based on monogamous marriage between a man and a woman, and protected in its unity and stability in the face of modern laws on divorce: in no way can other forms of cohabitation be placed on the same level as marriage, nor can they receive legal recognition as such. The same is true for the freedom of parents regarding the *education* of their children; it is an inalienable right recognized also by the Universal Declaration on Human Rights.... In addition, there is the right to *religious freedom* and the development of an *economy* that is at the service of the human person and of the common good, with respect for social justice, the principles of human solidarity and subsidiarity.[155]

I would add here that John Paul II and Benedict XVI are persuaded that, in the former's words, "authentic democracy is possible only in a State ruled by law, and on the basis of a correct concept of the human person" (*CA*, §46). Hence, they both argue against the thesis that "the

---

[155] Ratzinger, "Doctrinal Note on Some Questions Regarding the Participation of Catholics in Political Life," Congregation for the Doctrine of the Faith, November 24, 2002, §4, http://www.vatican.va/roman_curia/congregations/cfaith/documents/rc_con_cfaith_doc_20.

modern concept of democracy [is] indissolubly linked to that of relativism" (as Benedict puts it).[156] John Paul elaborates: "Nowadays there is a tendency to claim that agnosticism and skeptical relativism are the philosophy and the basic attitude which correspond to democratic forms of life. Those who are convinced that they know the truth and firmly adhere to it are considered unreliable from a democratic point of view, since they do not accept that truth is determined by the majority, or that it is subject to variation according to different political trends" (*CA*, §46). What started out as a mere recognition of the fact of moral and religious diversity, and hence disagreement, in contemporary society has turned into the stronger epistemological claim that excludes the recognition of moral and religious truth claims. If we cannot be sure of the truth, or if truth is culturally, socially, and individually relative, that is, nothing but a matter of interpretation and perspective, then everyone's freedom is best protected from manipulation, coercion, and deception—so the argument goes. In response to this argument, John Paul observes in this regard, "if there is no ultimate truth to guide and direct political activity, then ideas and convictions can easily be manipulated for reasons of power" (*CA*, §46). Indeed, agnosticism and skeptical relativism about truth do not protect human freedom and hence the dignity of the human person. The very opposite is true, according to both popes. In a world without truth in the objective sense, might makes right. Without transcendent truth, which provides a foundation for human rights and basic freedoms, we actually open the door to totalitarianism, and man is vulnerable to the violence of manipulation, coercion, and deception. In short, argues John Paul, the dignity of the human person cannot be inviolable unless it is objectively grounded in truth about human nature.

---

[156] Ratzinger, "*What Is Truth?* The Significance of Religious and Ethical Values in a Pluralistic Society," in *Values in a Time of Upheaval*, 53–72, and for this quote, 55.

Introduction

"If there is no transcendent truth, in obedience to which man achieves his full identity, then there is no sure principle for guaranteeing just relations between people.... Thus, the root of modern totalitarianism is to be found in the denial of the transcendent dignity of the human person who, as the visible image of the invisible God, is therefore by his very nature the subject of rights which no one may violate—no individual, group, class, nation or State" (*CA*, §44). What rights is the pope talking about?

> Among the most important of these rights, mention must be made of the right to life, an integral part of which is the right of the child to develop in the mother's womb from the moment of conception; the right to live in a united family and in a moral environment conducive to the growth of the child's personality; the right to develop one's intelligence and freedom in seeking and knowing the truth; the right to share in the work which makes wise use of the earth's material resources, and to derive from that work the means to support oneself and one's dependents; and the right freely to establish a family, to have and to rear children through the responsible exercise of one's sexuality. In a certain sense, the source and synthesis of these rights is religious freedom, understood as the right to live in the truth of one's faith and in conformity with one's transcendent dignity as a person (*CA*, §47).

In speaking of modern totalitarianism, we should understand that John Paul is thinking here not only of national socialism and the Marxist-Leninism of the twentieth century, but also, indeed chiefly, of the "thinly disguised totalitarianism" of a "democracy without [absolute] values" (*CA*, §46). Although the pope does not explicitly say so, we can safely surmise that he means here the thinly disguised totalitarianism of a secularist political liberalism that moves religion or a religiously based morality into the private sphere, appearing to take up a neutral position on religion, but holding that it should not be invoked in matters of public policy, indeed, should not even be given public recognition. Put differently, given the fact of diversity in our society on moral and religious matters, making and assessing truth claims regarding such matters is out of bounds in public life—or so we are regularly told. "Truth is controversial." "The concept of 'truth 'has in fact," adds Benedict, "moved into the zone of antidemocratic intolerance. It is not now a public good, but something private.... [I]t is not the truth of society as a whole."[157] Religion and public life are therefore compartmentalized in the name of liberal values such as tolerance and diversity. "The question must be asked," however, "whether all this is as fair as it appears." As Roger Trigg rightly observes,

> It may seem tolerant to take up a neutral position on religion, but excluding any agreement involving religion is far from neutral. Many religious believers will be excluded from public debate as their beliefs are ruled a private matter.... When, however, an issue like abortion is fought over, the exclusion of religious grounds will only leave religious believers disgruntled and feeling that their voice has not been heard. They have not even been overruled. They have not been listened to.... It is not clear why someone who believes on religious grounds that a human fetus

---

[157] Ratzinger, *"What Is Truth?* The Significance of Religious and Ethical Values in a Pluralistic Society," 55.

is a person should be excluded from the debate while a non- believer is under no such restraint and is free to argue that the fetus is not a person.[158]

We reach here the crux of John Paul's charge that the specter of a thinly disguised totalitarianism looms large in a democracy that is intolerant toward moral and religious truth claims. He is drawing our attention to a secularist totalitarianism whose perspective often goes undetected. This form of totalitarianism—secular political liberalism—is therefore far from neutral.[159]

Thus, the moral truth regarding the intrinsic goodness and inviolability of human life is a fundamental value for all human beings, indeed for the common good of the whole of human society, and hence is indispensable to democracy. Furthermore, moral know-ledge of this good can be had by the light of human reason.

> The *Gospel of life* is not for believers alone: *It is for everyone.* The issue of life and its defense and promotion is not a concern of Christians alone. Although faith provides special insight and strength, this question arises in every human conscience which seeks the truth and which cares about the future of humanity. Life certainly has a sacred and religious value, but in no way is that value a concern only of believers. *The value at stake is one*

---

[158] Roger Trigg, *Rationality and Religion* (Oxford: Blackwell, 1998), 16.

[159] On this point, see also Nicholas Wolterstorff, "The Role of Religion in Decision and Discussion of Political Issues," in *Religion in the Public Square: The Place of Religious Convictions in Political Debate*, ed. Robert Audi and Nicholas Wolterstorff (New York: Rowman & Littlefield, 1997), 67–120, esp. 105.

which every human being can grasp by the light of reason; thus it necessarily concerns everyone."[160]

Christians should therefore form alliances with all men of good will and sound judgment who share a commitment to the sanctity of human life, unconditionally respecting "the right to life of every innocent person—from conception to natural death—[as] one of the pillars on which every civil society stands."[161] What is more, they should communicate this commitment and other moral principles on the field of rational debate, in the public square, dispelling the misconception that prolife principles are a matter of *pure faith* rather than rationally grounded beliefs about human nature. In the words of Princeton professor and author Robert P. George, "These principles are available for rational affirmation by people of good will and sound judgment, even apart from their revelation by God in the Scriptures and in the life, death, and resurrection of Christ."[162]

Of course, presupposed here by Robert George and John Paul II is an understanding of the relationship between faith and reason and hence of the role of religion in public life that is not generally accepted, indeed, is controversial. Why should not religious and moral truth claims be publicly recognized? In particular, does the Christian faith have no public role to play? At issue here is not a political theocracy. "*Christian truth* is not of this kind." "In constantly reaffirming the transcendent dignity of the person," adds John Paul, "the Church's method is always that of respect for freedom" (*CA*, §46). That is, the freedom to choose reason over coercion, argument over force. Indeed, as Roger

---

[160] John Paul II, *Evangelium Vitae*, §101; italics added to the last sentence.
[161] John Paul II, *Evangelium Vitae*, §101.
[162] Robert P. George, *The Clash of Orthodoxies: Law, Religion, and Morality in Crisis* (Wilmington, Del.: ISI Books, 2001), 7.

Trigg rightly notes, "freedom may be seen as the precondition of rationality."[163] Significantly, says John Paul, "freedom attains its full development only by accepting the truth." Here again the pope emphasizes his critique of a so-called post-truth democracy (to borrow a phrase from Jürgen Habermas):[164]

> In a world without truth, freedom loses its foundation and man is exposed to the violence of passion and to manipulation, both open and hidden. The Christian upholds freedom and serves it, constantly offering to others the truth which he has known (cf. John 8:31–32), in accordance with the missionary nature of his vocation. While paying heed to every fragment of truth which he encounters in the life experience and in the culture of individuals and of nations, he will not fail to affirm in dialogue with others all that his faith and the correct use of reason have enabled him to understand. (*CA*, §46)

I should like then to summarize in three theses the principles informing the Christian's role in public life:

1. The Christian should reject the pernicious error of compartmentalizing his faith and life. Rather, given the integral role that the Christian faith should play in his entire life, the Christian should affirm and thus display "the unity of Christian life: coherence between faith and

---

[163] Roger Trigg, *Rationality and Religion*, 26.

[164] Jürgen Habermas, "Religion in the Public Sphere" (public lecture, University of San Diego, March 4, 2005), *European Journal of Philosophy* 14:1, 1-25, and for this phrase, 18. Online: http://www.sandiego.edu/pdf/pdf_library/habermaslecture031105_c939cceb2ab087bdfc6df291ec0fc3fa.pdf.

life, Gospel and culture, as recalled by the Second Vatican Council."[165] This is not only a Catholic principle but also a Reformed one. "It belongs to the *religious convictions* of a good many religious people in our society that *they ought to base* their decisions concerning issues of justice *on* their religious convictions. They do not view it as an option whether or not to do so. It is their conviction that they ought to strive for wholeness, integrity, integration, in their lives."[166]

2. The Christian should affirm the principle regarding the necessary correlation between reason and faith, reason and revelation, as sources of knowledge serving as checks on one another. "They need each other, and they must acknowledge one another's validity."[167] Faith needs reason, and vice-versa: reason needs faith.[168] Benedict XVI applies this principle to the context in which we live today where, he says, "there exist

---

[165] " Doctrinal Note on Some Questions Regarding the Participation of Catholics in Political Life," Congregation for the Doctrine of the Faith, 2002, §9. In *Gaudium et spes*, the Council Fathers spoke of "the dichotomy between the faith which many profess and the practice of their daily lives" as "pernicious" (§43).

[166] Wolterstorff, "The Role of Religion in Decision and Discussion of Political Issues," 105. Habermas agrees with Wolterstorff's "compelling objection." He writes, "If we accept this to my mind compelling objection, then the liberal state, which expressly protects such [religious] forms of life in terms of a basic right [First Amendment], cannot at the same time expect of *all* citizens that they also justify their political statements independently of their religious convictions or world views" ("Religion in the Public Sphere," 8).

[167] Ratzinger, "What Keeps the World Together, The Pre-political Moral Foundations of a Free State," 43.

[168] John Paul II, *Fides et Ratio*, "Faith and reason taken by themselves are fragile and weak. Reason, bereft of Revelation, runs into devious paths which deprive it of the ability of discovering its ultimate goal. Faith, bereft of reason, exalts the feeling and experience of the spirit, and so is in danger of being no

Introduction 87

pathologies of religion, as well as pathologies of reason."[169] He adds, "Religion must continually accept the purification and regulation that reason carries out.... [R]eason too must be admonished to keep to its own boundaries and to learn to listen to what the great religious traditions of mankind have to say. If reason becomes fully emancipated and lays aside this willingness to learn, this correlation [of reason] with religion, it takes on a destructive character."[170]

---

longer a universal gift" (§48). For a similar view, see Joseph Ratzinger, "Faith, Philosophy and Theology," in *The Nature and Mission of Theology*, Translated by Adrian Walker (San Francisco: Ignatius Press, 1995), 13-29.

[169] Ratzinger, "Searching for Peace, Tensions and Dangers," in *Values in a Time of Upheaval*, 101-16, and for this quote, 108-9.

[170] Ratzinger, "What Keeps the World Together, The Pre-political Moral Foundations of a Free State," 42-43. For some examples of these pathologies, see "Searching for Peace, Tensions and Dangers," in *Values in a Time of Upheaval*, 109- 10. On religion: "God or the divine can turn into the absolutization of one's own power and one's own interests.... This is made even worse by the fact that the intention to act on behalf of one's cause is charged with a fanaticism centered on the absolute, a religious fanaticism, and thus becomes completely brutal and blind. God has become an idol in which human beings adore their own will. We see this in the terrorists 'ideology of martyrdom.... Sects in the Western worlds also provide examples of an irrationality and a perversion of religion that show how dangerous religion becomes when it loses its orientation."

On reason: "But there also exists a pathology of reason that is completely detached from God, as we have seen in the totalitarian ideologies that parted company with God and wanted to construct the new man, the new world." Benedict gives as examples here Hitler, Marxism, and Pol Pot, but also refers to Western intellectual developments. "Was not the atomic bomb already a transgression of boundaries, where reason refused to be a constructive force but instead sought its strength in the ability to destroy? Now that reason is reaching for the very roots of life in its investigation of the genetic code, there is an increasing tendency to stop seeing man as a gift of the Creator (or of "nature") and to make him a product. Man is "made," and what one can "make" one can

3. This basic principle should guide the discussions in public life between the religious and secular citizens of a democratic community. Both citizens must be willing to reason about what is true, that is, to enter seriously and engage in a discussion on moral and religious truth claims. But I believe that this will happen only if both sides "have cognitive reasons to take seriously each other's contributions to controversial subjects in the public debate."[171] In keeping with the principle regarding the necessary correlation between reason and faith, on the one hand, the Christian citizen can take seriously the contributions of fellow citizens who are secular. On the other hand, the secular citizen who has a secularist consciousness lacks the correct epistemic attitude to his fellow citizens who are religious because he presumes that religion makes no cognitive claims. Consequently, I think that secular citizens should engage in a "self-critical assessment of the limits of secular reason," as Habermas puts it, "rejecting a narrow scientistic concept of reason and the exclusion of religious doctrines from the genealogy of reason."[172] This recommendation by agnostic Habermas is remarkably similar to Benedict's own analysis. He, too, rejects a "reason [that] reduces itself to those things that are open to experimental examination." The result of this reductionist notion of reason is, he says, to banish all morality and religion "to the sphere of the 'subjective, 'and this entire sphere has nothing to do with shared reason. Religion and morality do not fall within the province of reason; there are no longer any 'objective 'shared criteria of morality."[173]

---

also unmake. Human dignity dissolves. And where are we then to find an anchor for human rights? How is respect for man—even the one who is conquered, weak, suffering, or handicapped—to survive?"

[171] Jürgen Habermas, "Pre-political Foundations of the Democratic Constitutional State," in *Dialectics of Secularization*, 19–52, and for this quote, 47.

[172] Habermas, "Religion in the Public Sphere."

[173] Ratzinger, "Searching for Peace," 110.

By contrast, Benedict's proposal for restoring faith in reason's truth-attaining capacities goes further than Habermas. Ratzinger has consistently argued throughout his writings that modern conceptions of reason are caught in a "strange oscillation between irrationalism and irrationality."[174] At the root of this oscillation is the world view of naturalism: God doesn't exist, nature is all there is, and man is just a part of nature; man himself being the chance product of impersonal matter-in-motion. Given that, according to naturalism, man is the chance product of matter-in-motion, the fundamental question arises, says Ratzinger: "Does the irrational stand at the beginning of all things, is the irrational the real origin of the world, or does it come creative reason?"[175] Elsewhere Ratzinger writes, the question is, "whether reason, being a chance by-product of irrationality and floating in an ocean of irrationality, is ultimately just as meaningless [as man]; or whether the principle that represents the fundamental conviction of Christian faith and of its philosophy remains true: '*In principio erat Verbum*'—at the beginning of all things stands the creative power of reason."[176] The brief answer to this question here must be: The Christian holds that "faith in God who is Logos is at the same time faith in the creative power of reason." "God is Logos—meaning, reason, and word, and that is why man corresponds to God when his reason is open and he pleads the cause of a reason that is not allowed to be blind to the moral dimensions of existence." "But," Ratzinger adds, "a reason that completely detaches itself from God, and is willing to accept his existence only in the realm of the subjective, loses

---

[174] For the argument that follows in the text, see Joseph Ratzinger/Benedict XVI, *A Turning Point For Europe*, Second Edition, Translated by Brian McNeil, C.R.V. (San Francisco: Ignatius Press, 2010), 112. For a fuller statement of the argument, see Ratzinger, *Truth and Tolerance*, 179-183.

[175] Ratzinger/Benedict XVI, *A Turning Point for Europe*, 112.

[176] Ratzinger/Benedict XVI, *Truth and Tolerance*, 181.

its orientation, thereby opening the door to the powers of destruction." Indeed, such a concept of reason is sick. "Sick reason ultimately regards as fundamentalism all knowledge of definitively valid values and every insistence that reason is capable of discerning truth." Sick reason "paralyzes and destroys itself."[177]

Of course, the Christian citizen should urge the secular citizen to notice that the biblical revelation about faith in the God who is Logos not only grounds our understanding of the dignity of human reason,[178] but also, indeed chiefly, discloses the whole truth that human dignity is revealed in Jesus Christ, God truly become man. In other words, "When he presents the heart of his redemptive mission, Jesus says: 'I came that they may have life, and have it abundantly '(John 10:10). In truth, he is referring to that 'new 'and 'eternal 'life which consists in communion with the father, to which every person is freely called in the Son by the power of the Sanctifying Spirit. It is precisely in this 'life 'that all the aspects and stages of human life achieve their full significance."[179] In a nutshell, this is the *leitmotif* of John Paul II's call for the *new evangelization*, echoing Vatican II: "In reality it is only in the mystery of the Word made flesh that the mystery of man truly becomes clear" (*GS*, §22), which is to say that there is no true self- knowledge apart from Jesus Christ.

Pope John Paul II summed up the call:

---

[177] Ratzinger, "Searching for Peace," 111.

[178] John Paul II has written: In our culture where "there are signs of a widespread distrust of universal and absolute statements, especially among those who think that truth is born of consensus and not of a consonance between intellect and objective reality," the Christian faith is an "advocate of reason," that is, "of the human capacity to *know the truth*, to come to a knowledge that can reach objective truth," meaning thereby *adaequatio rei et intellectus* (*Fides et Ratio*, §§56, 82, respectively).

[179] John Paul II, *Evangelium Vitae*, §1.

Indeed, the Church's mission of spreading the Gospel not only demands that the Good News be preached ever more widely and to ever greater numbers of men and women, but [also] that the very power of the Gospel should permeate thought patterns, standards of judgment, and the norms of behavior; in a word, it is necessary that the whole of human culture be steeped in the Gospel. The cultural atmosphere in which a human being lives has a great influence upon his or her way of thinking and, thus, of acting. Therefore, a division between faith and culture is more than a small impediment to evangelization, while a culture penetrated with the Christian spirit is an instrument that favors the spreading of the Good News.[180]

This last point makes clear the intrinsic connection between the new evangelization and the cultural mandate, namely, a commitment to the new evangelization entails a commitment to the renewal of culture, indeed, the whole spectrum of life. This renewal is ongoing because it is caught in the eschatological tension between the present (the now) and future (not yet) dimensions of the kingdom of God until its culminating fullness at the end of time.

---

[180] John Paul II, "A Deep Commitment to Authentic Christian Living," *The Whole Truth about Man*, ed. with intro. James V. Schall, S.J. (Boston: St. Paul Editions, 1981), 84–91, and for this citation, 89.

Chapter 1

Hermeneutical Considerations on Meaning and Truth

The Idea of Doctrinal Development

> The Word of God is not addressed to any one people or to any one period of history. Similarly, dogmatic statements, while reflecting at times the culture of the period in which they were defined, formulate an unchanging and ultimate truth. This prompts the question of how one can reconcile the absoluteness and the universality of truth with the unavoidable historical and cultural conditioning of the formulas that express that truth. The claims of historicism, I noted earlier, are untenable; but the use of a hermeneutic open to the appeal of metaphysics can show how it is possible to move from the historical and contingent circumstances in which the texts developed to the truth that they express, a truth transcending those circumstances. Human language may be conditioned by history and constricted in other ways, but the human being can still express truths that surpass the phenomenon of language. Truth can never be confined to time and culture; in history it is known, but it also reaches beyond history.
>
> —John Paul II[1]

Certainly, there is a need to seek out and to discover *the most adequate formulation* for universal and permanent moral

---

[1] John Paul II, *Fides et Ratio*, §95.

norms in the light of different cultural contexts, a formulation most capable of ceaselessly expressing their historical relevance, of making them understood and of authentically interpreting their truth. This truth of the moral law — like that of the "deposit of faith" — unfolds down the centuries: the norms expressing that truth remain valid in their substance, but must be specified and determined *"eodem sensu eademque sententia"* in the light of historical circumstances by the Church's Magisterium, whose decision is preceded and accompanied by the work of interpretation and formulation characteristic of the reason of individual believers and of theological reflection.

—John Paul II[2]

By its nature, the task of religiously guarding and loyally expounding the deposit of divine Revelation (in all its integrity and purity), implies that the Magisterium can make a pronouncement "in a definitive way" on propositions which, even if not contained among the truths of faith, are nonetheless intimately connected with them, in such a way, that the definitive character of such affirmations derives in the final analysis from revelation itself, What concerns morality can also be the object of the authentic Magisterium because the Gospel, being the Word of Life, inspires and guides the whole sphere of human behavior.... By reason of the connection between the orders of creation and redemption and by reason of the necessity, in view of salvation, of knowing and observing the whole moral law, the competence of the Magisterium also extends to that which concerns the natural law. Revelation also contains moral teachings which *per se* could

---

[2] John Paul II, *Fides et Ratio*, §53.

be known by natural reason. Access to them, however, is made difficult by man's sinful condition. It is a doctrine of faith that these moral norms can be infallibly taught by the Magisterium.

—Joseph Cardinal Ratzinger[3]

[T]he Church grounds her teachings regarding marital morality and sexual ethics on the nature of marriage itself. And what marriage is flows from a metaphysical view of the human person, which is based on Holy Scripture, the Tradition of the Church, and the pronouncements of the Magisterium. This view of the human person and the resulting view of marital morality can also be discovered and explained philosophically, without appealing to Revelation.

—Willem Jacobus Cardinal Eijk[4]

In 2017, James K.A. Smith published a reflection[5] that I will argue raises the question that the Catholic tradition addresses in its teaching on the relationship between revelation and dogma/doctrine and the corresponding idea of doctrinal development. The issue raised by Smith is about the relationship between the fundamentals of orthodoxy, namely,

---

[3] *Donum Veritatis*, Congregation for the Doctrine of the Faith, May 24, 1990, §16.

[4] Willem Jacobus Kardinaal Eijk, *De Band van de Liefde: Huwelijksmoraal and Seksuele Ethiek* (Utrecht: KokBoekencentrum UItgevers, 2022), 47.

[5] James K.A. Smith, "On 'Orthodox Christianity': some observations and a couple of questions," *Fors Claviga*, Friday, August 4, 2017. Online: Fors Clavigera: On "orthodox Christianity": some observations, and a couple of questions.

the ecumenical councils and creeds of the Church[6] that are grounded in the nature of God (Triune), the Incarnation, the means of our salvation, the church, and the life to come, on the one hand, and non-fundamentals, as he suggest, on the other, that reflect a "particular view of sexuality and marriage." The issue here is, according to Smith, not whether one can be indifferent to the latter view since they are not a matter of creedal definition, but whether a standard of sexuality and marriage pertain essentially to orthodoxy, namely, "right beliefs" or "correct beliefs," beliefs that are true rather than false."[7]

Smith does not say what particular view of sexuality and marriage he has in mind, a view that he refers to as traditional, as the "historic teaching of the Church." I surmise that he means the idea that sexual difference between a man and woman is constitutive of our humanity (Gen 1:27), and hence of sexual morality such that only a sexual union of male and female persons makes bodies in any real sense "one flesh" (Gen 2:24), with the latter organic bodily union being a necessary condition for the existence of authentic conjugal love; thus, in this light, marriage is the two-in-one-flesh union of a man and a woman.

The *Catechism of the Catholic Church* explains, "Sexuality, in which man's belonging to the bodily and biological world is expressed, becomes personal and truly human when it is integrated into the relationship of one person to another, in the complete and lifelong mutual gift of a man and a woman." The virtue of chastity involves not only the in-

---

[6] There are seven ecumenical councils in the first eight centuries of the Church's history: The First Council of Nicaea, 325; the First Council of Constantinople, 381; The First Council of Ephesus, 431; The Council of Chalcedon, 451; the Second Council of Constantinople, 553; the Third Council of Constantinople, 680-681; and the Second Council of Nicaea, 787.

[7] Eleonore Stump, "Orthodoxy and Heresy, *Faith and Philosophy*, Volume 16, Issue 2, April 1999, 147-163.

tegrity of the person but also the integrality of the gift of self that presupposes sexual differentiation between a man and a woman, which according to Christian anthropology, means "the successful integration of sexuality within the person and thus the inner unity of man in his bodily and spiritual being."[8] That is, "Everyone, man and woman, should acknowledge and accept his sexual *identity*. Physical, moral, and spiritual *difference* and *complementarity* [between man and woman] are oriented toward the goods of marriage and the flourishing of human life.[9]" The virtue of chastity, therefore, presupposes the sexual differentiation of male and female, such that only a sexual union of male and female persons makes bodies in any real sense "one flesh" (Gen 2:24), with the latter organic bodily union being a necessary condition for the existence of authentic conjugal love.

Cardinal Eijk writes, "Homosexual acts are sexual acts performed between persons of the same sex."[10] The moral criteria used to judge homosexual behavior is whether or not it corresponds "with norms that arise from human nature, or the moral natural law, and are therefore presented by Holy Scripture, Tradition, and the Magisterium."[11] Therefore, as Gerhard Cardinal Müller correctly states, "we cannot modify the *Catechism* on the question of homosexuality because it directly concerns revealed doctrine. St. Paul and the four evangelists spoke about it, transmitting one sole version—that marriage is between a man and a woman,

---

[8] *CCC* §2337.
[9] *CCC* §2333.
[10] Eijk, *De Band van de Liefde*, 281.
[11] Eijk, *De Band van de Liefde*, 282.

exactly as Jesus intended (Matt 19:4-6)."[12] Jesus refers us back to the creation texts of Gen 1:27 and 2:24.[13] These texts are absolutely normative for marriage, indeed, for the Christian anthropology that ungirds sexual ethics, according to the *Catechism of the Catholic Church*. (§§2331-2345) The truth of this judgment is grounded in objective reality, according to the order of creation or natural law– the way things really are, and this creation order or natural law is contained in the deposit of faith.[14] This raises the epistemological question regarding the authority of the Church's Magisterium "to decide—not in the sense of choosing but in the sense of judging—what belongs to revelation,"[15] and that includes the natural moral law. The natural moral law objectively exists, it is of divine origin (Rom 2:14-5], we did not have a hand in making it but discovered it by reflection on experience. Francis Sullivan adds a crucial point: "the existence of such a law, our obligation to live according to it, and some of its basic norms, are not only naturally knowable but also revealed."[16]

---

[12] Cardinal Gerhard Müller, with Franca Giansoldati, *Vatican Confidential: A Candid Conversation with Cardinal Gerhard Müller*, translated by Nicholas Reitzug (Manchester, New Hampshire: Sophia Institute Press, 2023), 70.

[13] Cardinal Eijk, *De Band van de Liefde*, 48.

[14] Denzinger §3074. See also, Eijk, *De Band van de Liefde*, 43.

[15] Germain Grisez, *The Way of the Lord Jesus*, 1, *Christian Moral Principles* (Chicago: Franciscan Herald Press, 1983), 840.

[16] Francis A. Sullivan, SJ, *Magisterium: Teaching Authority in the Catholic Church* (Eugene, OR: Wipf and Stock Publishers, 2002 [1983]), 136. See also, Pius XII, Allocution "Magnificate Dominum" (1954), "The power of the Church is not bound by the limits of "matters strictly religious," as they say, but the whole matter of the natural law, its foundation, its interpretation, its application, so far as their moral aspects extend, are within the Church's power. For the keeping of the Natural Law, by God's appointment, has reference to the road by which man has to approach his supernatural end. But, on this road, the Church is man's guide and guardian in what concerns his supreme

For example, Jesus grounds sexual ethics and the corresponding ethic of marriage in the order of creation. Müller explains, "Sexuality can be contextualized only if a conjugal design exists."[17] This, too, is the view of Cardinal Eijk. He explains: "God's intention at the beginning, His plan of creation (which coincides with what the scholastics call the '*lex aeterna*'), is normative and has ethical significance for human life, including for marriage and sexuality, in all times and under all circumstances." He adds, "If we want to find answers to the many ethical issues surrounding marriage and family, then we must therefore orient ourselves to the beginning, as that is expressed in the creation narrative. The foundation of the moral natural law lies in God's order of creation."[18] In this connection, we must note all the offenses against chastity: lust, masturbation, fornication, pornography, prostitution, rape, and homosexuality.[19]

Smith acknowledges the support these views on marriage and sexuality have received. "The weight of Scripture, tradition, and perhaps even 'natural law' have sustained these views [of marriage and sexuality] and beliefs for millennia." Again, this, too, is the view of Cardinal Eijk that is found in the fourth epigraph to this Introduction.[20] But Smith presup-

---

end." Online: Pope Pius XII, Allocution "Magnificate Dominum" (1954) – Novus Ordo Watch.

[17] Müller, *Vatican Confidential*, 67.

[18] Eijk, *De Band van de Liefde*, 48.

[19] CCC §2351-59. See also, Eijk, *De Band van de Liefde*, 291-330.

[20] Eijk, *De Band van de Liefde*, 47; see also 388. This is no longer the view of the Archbishop of Canterbury: "Where we've come to is to say that all sexual activity should be within a committed relationship and whether it's straight or gay." See Gavin Ashenden, "The Archbishop of Canterbury's new position on sex and marriage: a 'journey' or a departure?" in *Christian Today*, 26 October 2024.

poses the distinction between those articles of faith which are *fundamental* and those which are not fundamental. The former are creedal and hence are to be accepted by all such that doubt or denial falls under the censure of heresy. The latter may be left to the free assent of the faithful because there is, according to Smith, not a standard of sexuality and marriage essential to orthodoxy. Smith explains:

> But it is surely also worth pointing out that conciliar standards of orthodoxy do not articulate such [sexual and marital] standards. If the adjective "orthodox" is untethered from such ecumenical standards, it quickly becomes a cheap epithet we idiosyncratically attach to views and positions in order to write off those we disagree with as "heretics" and unbelievers. If "orthodox" becomes an adjective that is unhooked from these conciliar canons, then it becomes a word we use to make sacrosanct the things that matter to "us" in order to exclude "them."

Smith's article was written shortly after the Christian Reformed Church (CRC) began a process in 2016 to form a study committee to produce a report on the "biblical theology" of human sexuality. This report was released in 2020 for Synod 2021. It was a 175-page report, *Committee to Articulate a Foundation-Laying Biblical Theology of Human Sexuality*.[21] Because of the pandemic, the annual synod did not vote in person to accept this report until 2022. The synod decided to "codify its opposition to homosexual sex by elevating it to the status of confession,

---

[21] Human_sexuality_report_2021.pdf (crcna.org) My reflection on this report is found in Eduardo Echeverria, "Male and Female He Created Them: Ecumenical Reflections," *Homiletic & Pastoral Review*, December 23, 2020.

Ch. 1: Hermeneutical Considerations on Meaning and Truth

or declaration of faith."[22] This means that "unchastity" in *Heidelberg Catechism* Q&A 108 "encompasses adultery, premarital sex, extra-marital sex, polyamory, pornography, and homosexual sex," which violate the Seventh Commandment, and "this interpretation has confessional status."[23]

Does Smith's position presuppose that the nature of marriage and moral norms regarding sexual ethics are not part of the proper content of revelation, and hence for that reason are not matters of creedal definition? He does not say. The question that arises is whether Smith is denying, in the words of John Paul II, "that there exists, in Divine Revelation, a specific and determined moral content, universally valid and permanent."[24] Aren't there moral norms found in Scripture having not only the status of fundamental revealed moral truth but also are in themselves relevant for salvation (1 Cor 6:9–11)? Aren't the biblical commandments against incest, bestiality Exod 22:19), homosexuality (Lev 18:22; Rom 1:26–27; 1 Cor 6:9), adultery (Exod 20:14), child sacrifice, prostitution (Lev 19:29; Deut 23:17–18), and rape (Deut 22:25–29), contained in the deposit of faith and, indeed, absolute and universally valid? Is it morally acceptable to oppress the poor? Commit idolatry (Exod 20:4; Deut 13:6–11)? Bribery (Exod 23:8; 2 Chr 19:7)? Bearing false witness against one's neighbor (Exod 23:1–2)? Surely not. Of course, I am not suggesting that Smith thinks that any of these practices are morally acceptable. But it does seem that his apparent denial of fundamental *revealed* moral truth, which is universally valid, holding for all times and

---

[22] Yonat Shimron, "Christian Reformed Church Brings LGBT Stance into Faith Statement," *Christianity Today*, June 15, 2022.

[23] Rev. Aaron Vriesman, "The Difficult Synod of 2023 and What it Says about the CRC," *The Banner*, July 28, 2023. See Robert Gagnon, "Why a New Translation of the Heidelberg Catechism is not Needed: And why Homosexualist Forces in the PCUSA Seek it," June 19, 2008.

[24] John Paul II, *Veritatis Splendor*, §37.

places throughout the centuries, makes it difficult for him to justify his acceptance of these moral precepts as constitutive of orthodoxy.

Moreover, the Catholic tradition rejects the sharp distinction made by Smith between creedal Christianity and the Church's historic teaching on sexuality and marriage. His position, then, raises the basic question alluded to in the second epigraph regarding the relation of moral and theological propositions and the truths of faith. The then Cardinal Ratzinger explains the three-fold relationship of such propositions and the truths of faith, and the role of the magisterium with regard to the natural moral law.

> [1] When the Magisterium of the Church makes an infallible pronouncement and solemnly declares that a teaching is found in Revelation, the assent called for is that of theological faith. This kind of adherence is to be given even to the teaching of the ordinary and universal Magisterium when it proposes for belief a teaching of faith as divinely revealed. [2] When the Magisterium proposes "in a definitive way" truths concerning faith and morals, which, even if not [explicitly] divinely revealed, are nevertheless strictly and intimately connected with Revelation, these must be firmly accepted and held. [3] When the Magisterium, not intending to act "definitively," teaches a doctrine to aid a better understanding of Revelation and make explicit its contents, or to recall how some teaching is in conformity with the truths of faith, or finally to guard against ideas that are incompatible with these truths, the response called for is that of the religious submission of will and intellect. This kind of re-

sponse cannot be simply exterior or disciplinary but must be understood within the logic of faith and under the impulse of obedience to the faith.²⁵

Before going on to discuss the points made in this passage by Ratzinger, it is important to describe briefly the theological notes—"what doctrines are binding, on what grounds, and in what measure"²⁶—by explaining them briefly and the corresponding authority of doctrinal statements. Given the purpose of this chapter, I can best begin here by citing Karl Rahner's statement regarding the Second Vatican Council's assumptions about levels of authoritative teaching. These assumptions, I contend, are necessary for a clear and fruitful discussion of doctrinal development. The Council assumes:

> [1] the distinctions to be made between the wielders of the teaching authority in the Church (individual bishops, the collective episcopate, the pope, a general council); [2] the distinctions to be made between the doctrine taught (revealed truths, truths not revealed but necessarily linked with revelation as its presupposition or its consequence etc.); [3] the distinctions to be made between the types of authority claimed by the teacher and his intention of binding his hearers; [4] the distinctions to be made between the "theological qualifications" of the truths proposed (dogma, common teaching, irreformable truths, reformable truths which still demand a conditional assent, etc.);

---

²⁵ *Donum Veritatis*, On the Ecclesial Vocation of the Theologian, Congregation for the Doctrine of the Faith, May 24, 1990, §23. See also, *Lumen Gentium*, §25.

²⁶ Avery Dulles, S. J., *Magisterium, Teacher and Guardian of the Faith* (Naples, FL: Sapientia Press, 2007), 84.

[5] the distinctions to be made in the assent of the hearer (from the absolute assent of faith to a genuine but not necessarily irreformable inner assent and on to mere "obedient silence").[27]

For my purpose here, I will pare down and summarize the different levels of magisterial authority to be attributed to dogmas and doctrines as follows:

(1) *De fide*: dogmas of the faith. These are divinely revealed truths contained in the Word of God, written or handed down, either (a) formally defined by a pope or Council; or (b) taught by the ordinary and universal magisterium. They constitute basic truths of faith that must be believed by Catholics, since they concern matters of faith, and they are called the primary objects of infallibility. The natural moral law that marriage is the two-in-one-flesh union of a man and a woman is an example of a primary object of infallibility. Thus, as Sullivan rightly adds, "the magisterium could infallibly define propositions of this law if they are clearly confirmed by revelation."[28] These dogmas require the assent of theological faith by all members of the faithful. Thus, whoever obstinately places them in doubt or denies them falls under the censure of heresy.

---

[27] Karl Rahner, "Dogmatic Constitution on the Church: Chapter III, Articles 18–27," in *Commentary on the Documents of Vatican II*, 5 volumes, 1: ed. Herbert Vorgrimler, trans. Lalit Adophus, et al. (London: Burn & Oates; New York: Herder & Herder, 1967–69), 208–16, at 209.

[28] Sullivan, *Magisterium: Teaching Authority in the Catholic Church*, 137.

(2) *Fides ecclesiastica*: doctrines that are infallibly taught as inseparably connected with revelation, concerning matters required to support the faith, and called secondary objects of infallibility. Examples of these would be the offenses against chastity listed earlier. These truths are necessarily connected with revelation by virtue of either an historical relationship, or a logical connection, expressing a stage in the development of the understanding of revelation, and "are required for the defense and explanation of the deposit of revelation."[29] These truths are (a) formally defined by a pope or Council; or (b) taught infallibly by the ordinary and universal magisterium of the Church as a *sententia definitive tenenda*. This is why these are called the "faith of the Church." Both primary and secondary objects of infallibility are such that they are at one and the same time not only fundamentally irreversible, or irreformable, and hence can never be contradicted, but also may need to be clarified over time. Whoever denies these truths would be in a position of rejecting a truth of Catholic doctrine and would therefore no longer be in full communion with the Catholic Church.

(3) *Sententia fidei proxima*: doctrine authoritatively but non-infallibly taught by the magisterium. This is for a doctrine that is not formally promulgated, but is regarded as teaching a truth of revelation. It is proximate to the faith. Examples of

---

[29] Bishop Gasser, the spokesman for the *Deputatio de Fide* of Vatican I cited by Sullivan, Sullivan, *Magisterium: Teaching Authority in the Catholic Church*, 226n21.

these would be the Church's moral teaching on reproductive technologies and contraceptive sex.[30]

(4) *Sententia ad fidem pertinens*, or *theologice certa*: theological conclusions logically deduced from a proposition of faith and taught by the magisterium, which have a high degree of certainty.

(5) *Sententia probabilis*: denotes probable opinion, although in theological discussion there are many other levels operating: well founded, pious, and tolerated opinions (with the least authority).[31]

After the 2022, CRC Synod decided to "codify its opposition to homosexual sex by elevating it to the status of confession, or declaration of faith, in Catholic terms either a primary or secondary object of infallibility, Smith now seems to be moving in the direction of theological note 5 to which judgments about marriage and sexual ethics belong. He sug-

---

[30] Congregation for the Doctrine of the Faith, *Donum Vitae*, Instruction on Respect for Human Life in is Origin and on the Dignity of Procreation; replies to certain questions of the Day, February 27, 1987. Online: Instruction on respect for human life (vatican.va). Pope Paul VI, *Humanae Vitae*, July 25, 1968. Humanae Vitae (July 25, 1968) | Paul VI (vatican.va).

[31] Gavin D'Costa, *Vatican II: Catholic Doctrines on Jews & Muslims* (Oxford: Oxford University Press), 2014, with some adaptation. Helpful here is Joseph Cardinal Ratzinger, the 1988 CDF document, "Doctrinal Commentary on the Concluding Formula of the Professio fidei." Similarly, Ludwig Ott, *Fundamentals of Dogma*, trans. Patrick Lynch, ed. James Canon Bastible; 2018 edition fully revised and updated by Robert Fastiggi (London: Baronius Press, 2018 [1952]), Introduction, The Theological Grades of Certainty §8, 10. Dulles, *Magisterium, Teacher and Guardian of the Faith*, 83–84. Harold E. Ernst, "The Theological Notes and the Interpretation of Doctrine," *Theological Studies* 63 (2002): 813–25.

Ch. 1: Hermeneutical Considerations on Meaning and Truth

gests this position, "I worry that Calvin University, like some of our congregations, are going to have to face the possibility that you can either be CRC [Christian Reformed Church] or you can be reformed." Smith adds, "To be reformed is to be always reforming [32]... It means a spirit of intellectual and deep theological inquiry and wrestling with the ongoing work of the Spirit to discern what it means to be faithful now."[33] In the contrast here between the CRC and the dynamic of always reforming, Smith is suggesting that the CRC is committed to *confessionalism*. The Dutch master of dogmatic theology, G.C. Berkouwer, defines confessional-ism in his 1949 study, *Conflict met Rome*, "Confessionalism in effect takes the position that the Scriptures have been given their final form in the confession. The Bible lies behind; ahead of us is the 'extract'. The Scriptures have no longer any actuality."[34] Berkouwer frames the issue before us especially with respect to Catholicism.

> The tensions in Catholicism may remind us that no "position" or "mind" ever is free from danger of perversion. One side runs the greatest danger of static irrelevance to the times, of traditional*ism* and confessional*ism*, and of seeking to put the church under the control of a school of theology, notwithstanding the assumption that the "school" identifies itself with the gospel. For the Church to be guardian of the truth could be twisted so badly that the church would lose perspective for the future, lose power

---

[32] For an historical account of this Reformation slogan, see Jeff Fisher "Reformed and Always Reforming," *Banner*, September 30, 2024.

[33] Calvin University board charged with examining faculty dissent (religionnews.com).

[34] *Conflict met Rome* (Kampen: Kok, 1949, 43; translated by David Freeman as *The Conflict with Rome* (Grand Rapids, MI: Baker Book House, 1958), 31.

to test the gospel in new situations of life, and lose the willingness to attempt new answers to new questions. The other side runs the danger of being so open and fearless in the face of the problems of the time that it does not sufficiently honor the critical, testing power of the gospel. It faces the temptation to engage the issues of the day so openly that it neglects to bring the power and hence the blessings of the unchangeable gospel to bear on the situation.[35]

The above passages suggest something about doctrinal development, namely, as Aidan Nichols rightly states, "What we should look for is a theory which allows for genuine development in doctrine yet respects the substantial homogeneity of revealed truth."[36]

Smith appeals to the slogan, "*ecclesia semper reformanda est*," the church reformed, always reforming is a critique of confessional*ism* or traditional*ism*. What does this critique entail? Does this slogan "always reforming" presuppose an unqualified fallibilism? What is fallibilism? "Fallibilism does not challenge the claim that we can know the truth, but rather the belief that we can know that we have attained the final truth with absolute certainty."[37] There is an inconsistency generated by an unqualified fallibilism by virtue of implying the reversibility, in principle,

---

[35] G.C. Berkouwer, *Vatikaans Concilie en de Nieuwe Theologie*, (Kampen: J.H. Kok, 1964), 323; ET: *The Second Vatican Council and the New Catholicism*, translated by Lewis Smedes (Grand Rapids, MI: Eerdmans, 1965), 255-56.

[36] Aidan Nichols, OP, *From Newman to Congar: The Idea of Doctrinal Development from the Victorians to the Second Vatican Council* (Edinburgh: T&T Clark, 1990), 169.

[37] This definition of fallibilism is by Richard Bernstein, "Philosophers respond to [John Paul II's] *Fides et Ratio*," *Books and Culture* 5 (July/august 1999): 30–32.

Ch. 1: Hermeneutical Considerations on Meaning and Truth 109

at some later point, of all Christian doctrinal and dogmatic truths that are putatively irreversible, irreformable, or final.

Consider leading Evangelical Protestant theologian Kevin Vanhoozer who approvingly cites the claims of Robert McAfee Brown who insists that Catholic ecclesiology and its corresponding notion of the Church's teaching authority is such that its position is "'incompatible with the notion that the church is *semper reformanda*, always to be reformed'."[38] Adds Vanhoozer, this position, "along with the teaching about the indefectibility of the church, effectively forecloses the possibility of reforming the church's teaching."[39] In short, again approvingly citing Brown, Vanhoozer concludes, "'Roman Catholicism has become master of the gospel rather than servant'."[40]

Nevertheless, Vanhoozer himself acknowledges permanent truth: "There is a sense in which … different insights, all generated by particular occasions [e.g., the errors of Arianism and the judgments of Nicaea], represent *permanent* [emphasis added] gains in the church's grasp of the gospel and its implications. What originated in specific contexts is now part of the catholic tradition."[41] If permanently true, then, it is equally

---

[38] Robert McAfee Brown, *Spirit of Protestantism* (Oxford: Oxford University Press, 1965), 167, cited in Kevin Vanhoozer, *Biblical Authority After Babel* (Grand Rapids, MI: Brazos Press, 2016), 222.

[39] Vanhoozer, *Biblical Authority After Babel*, 228.

[40] Brown, *Spirit of Protestantism*, 167, cited in Vanhoozer, *Biblical Authority After Babel*, 228. Vanhoozer, *Biblical Authority After Babel*, 228. Vanhoozer's claims open up onto a field of questions to which I respond throughout my book, *Revelation, History, and Truth: A Hermeneutics of Dogma* (New York: Peter Lang Publishing, 2018). I refute his claims in Chapters 1 and 2 of this book when addressing the issue of the hermeneutics of Vatican II, particularly the essentialist vs. historicist dispute regarding the truth-status of dogmatic formulations, as well as the question of Scripture, tradition, and the Church.

[41] Vanhoozer, *Biblical Authority After Babel*, 222–23.

true for others living at any time, and in any place. Vanhoozer, thus, rejects historicism, which denies the "enduring validity of truth," as the philosopher-pope John Paul II describes historicism.[42] According to Vanhoozer, permanent truths are dogmas that he calls "first-level doctrines," that is, "formulations of revealed biblical truth that the whole church considers authoritative."[43] Furthermore, with respect to what Vanhoozer is calling "first-level doctrines," does not Christianity require propositional infallibility in respect of them, that is, true affirmations or judgments that possess the highest degree of certainty? In this connection, consider the late Lutheran theologian George Lindbeck's argument supporting an affirmative answer to this question:

> The New Testament writers early designated "Jesus is Lord" as a statement essential to Christian identity, and they meant it, not only as a profoundly meaningful symbol, but in the emphatically propositional sense of referring to a specific man in a definite time and place. It is systematically impossible to include the statement "Jesus is not Lord," within an identifiably Christian context. There are also many other propositional affirmations which, while they do not by themselves, in the absence of existentially or symbolically significant appropriation, make men Christian, still cannot be denied without destroying or gravely damaging the identity or integrity of Christian language systems and correlated forms of life. These propositions, then, are intra-

---

[42] John Paul II, *Fides et Ratio*, §87.
[43] Vanhoozer, *Biblical Authority After Babel*, 205.

systematically infallible. Within a Christian context, they cannot be denied, they cannot be false.⁴⁴

Thus, Lindbeck correctly adds, "From this point of view, the original Reformation tradition, like historic Christianity in general, is just as deeply committed to infallible dogmatic propositions as is the Catholic."⁴⁵ "Infallibility," then, he concludes, "may be regarded as the objective property of unquestionability derived from the logically indispensable role which an affirmation plays within a given religion."⁴⁶ Surely, this, too, is Vanhoozer's position. There are, he says, "Doctrines that are essential to the logic of the gospel story." Although he does not use the terms "infallible dogmatic propositions," something like the meaning of those terms is in play in his understanding of dogmas. They are an absolutely authoritative element in the creedal tradition because they are necessary to the intelligibility of the gospel. He explains:

---

⁴⁴ George A. Lindbeck, *Infallibility*, The 1972 Pere Marquette Theology Lecture (Milwaukee, WI: Marquette University Press, 1972), 49. By "intra-systematic," which he distinguishes elsewhere from categorical and ontological truth, Lindbeck means epistemically justified. "What the text [*The Nature of Doctrine*] calls 'intrasystematic' (that is, coherence with the relevant context of beliefs and behavior) is better thought of as a necessary (though not sufficient) condition for justified belief. When to this is added 'categorical truth' (that is, adequate words and grammar or, more technically expressed, adequate concepts and appropriate patterns for deploying them), one has two necessary (but not sufficient) conditions for successful truth claims (that is, for assertions that are not only justified but also 'ontologically' true" (Afterword to the 25th anniversary edition [2009] of *The Nature of Doctrine*). See also, idem., "Response to Bruce Marshall," *The Thomist* 53 (1989): 403–06.

⁴⁵ Lindbeck, *Infallibility*, 50.

⁴⁶ George A. Lindbeck, "The Infallibility Debate," in *The Infallibility Debate*, ed. John J. Kirvan (New York: Paulist Press, 1971), 118.

Dogmatic statements reflect the mind of the church as to the mind of the Scriptures. It is no accident that the doctrine of the Trinity was the first dogma on which the communion of saints formed a consensus, at the Council of Nicaea (325). ... That there is one God in three persons is a level-one teaching because it identifies the main persons of the gospel story. To differ at this first level is to disagree about the gospel itself. Level-one doctrines concern what the apostle Paul says is of "first importance" (1 Cor 15:3), namely, doctrines such as the bodily resurrection of Jesus (1 Cor 15:4), without which the gospel story loses its integrity. As to what and how many these level-one doctrines are, catholicity is a helpful criterion. Simply put: level-one doctrines are catholic doctrines—what every follower of Jesus, anywhere and at all times, must believe to preserve both the intelligibility of the gospel and the fellowship of saints.[47]

Surely, then there are infallible dogmas, expressive of true affirmations or judgments, implying a certain infallibility in teaching.[48] As Avery Cardinal Dulles explains, "The irreformability of dogma implies that it cannot be reversed or cancelled out by future developments. . . . What is infallibly taught is therefore irreformable in the sense of irreversible." Nevertheless, Dulles clarifies,

The question of reformability should not be confused with that of *reformulation*. Reformability has to do with the content or meaning of statements; reformulation, with the mode of expression. The two are of course intimately related, since changes of language generally involved at least minor changes in meaning.

---

[47] Vanhoozer, *Biblical Authority After Babel*, 205.
[48] Lindbeck, *Infallibility*, 16.

Sometimes, however, reformulation is called for precisely *in order to* retain the meaning of an old formula in a situation in which the terms have changed their meaning. Infallibility therefore does not preclude reformulation; in fact, it may positively call for this.[49]

Some critics, such as Berkouwer, of "confessional*ism*" or "uncritical traditional*ism*,"[50] or even Vanhoozer who claims that Catholicism is incompatible with the notion that the Church is *semper reformanda* ignore that church teaching has different levels of authority and certainty; while some are fundamental, definitive, indeed, infallible, and hence irreformable, others are not and so may be subject to reform, the possibility of reversals (e.g., the church's previous teachings on religious freedom, church/state relations, ecumenism have been reformed). So not all church teaching carries the same weight or authority because the church has never held that every magisterial teaching is, ipso facto, infallible.

Notwithstanding this fundamental point about irreformable statements, which are statements protected by infallibility, even teaching that is fundamental, definitive, and hence irreformable is such that it may "require further thought and elucidation." Earlier we defined an unqualified fallibilism. We now need to distinguish it from a *qualified* fallibilism. A qualified fallibilism presupposes the distinction between the propositional truths of faith and their linguistic expressions, between

---

[49] Avery Dulles, SJ, "Infallibility: The Terminology," in *Teaching Authority & Infallibility in the Church, Lutherans and Catholicis in Dialogue VI*, edited by Paul C. Empie, T. Austin Murphy, and Joseph A. Burgess (Minneapolis: Augsburg Publishing House, 1978), 69-80, and at 75.

[50] Berkouwer, *De Heilige Schrift*, I-II (Kampen: J.H. Kok, 1966-67), and here Vol. II, 272; translated and edited by Jack B. Rogers as one volume, *Holy Scripture* (Grand Rapids, MI: Eerdmans, 1975), 278.

truth-content and context, such that those truths are "open to reconceptualization and reformulation, and that [is because] no statement comprehensively exhausts truth, much less divine truth."[51] As Dulles also puts it, "Irreformable statements may, however, require completion, refinement, reinterpretation, and restatement in accordance with new conditions, which raise new questions and provide new information, new conceptual categories, new methods, and new vocabulary."[52] For, adds Dulles, "The 'irreformability' of a definition [definitive teaching about matters of faith and morals], though it rules out subsequent reversals, *leaves room for considerable 'reformulations'*."[53] The distinction between irreformable statements and reformulations is dependent upon the distinction between a proposition and a sentence. As Francis Sullivan rightly notes:

> A sentence is a particular verbal expression, in a particular language; the proposition is the *meaning* which the sentence intends to express. The same proposition is capable of various linguistic expressions: otherwise it would be impossible to translate it from one language into another.... So when we speak of 'true propositions', we do not identify the propositions, as such, with the sentences in which they have been expressed. A proposition is true if its *meaning* is true: strictly speaking, the proposition *is* the meaning.[54]

---

[51] Thomas G. Guarino, *Foundations of Systematic Theology* (New York/London: t&t clark, 2005), 139, n. 59.

[52] Dulles, *Magisterium, Teacher and Guardian of the Faith*, 60.

[53] Dulles, Magisterium, *Teacher and Guardian of the Faith*, 60, italics added.

[54] Sullivan, *Magisterium: Teaching Authority in the Catholic Church*, 15.

Ch. 1: Hermeneutical Considerations on Meaning and Truth 115

Bernard Lonergan makes clear the ontological realism that is presupposes by this claim about meaning, namely, a proposition is true if and only if what it says corresponds to the way objective reality is; otherwise, it is false. In other words, regarding the status of meaning, the way things are is what makes "meanings" true or false. Lonergan clearly explains the relationship between meaning and truth:

> Meaning of its nature is related to a meant, and what is meant may or may not correspond to what in fact is so. If it corresponds, the meaning is true. If it does not correspond, the meaning is false. . . . To deny correspondence is to deny a relation between meaning and meant. To deny the correspondence view of truth is to deny that, when the meaning is true, the meant is what is so. Either denial is destructive of the dogmas. . . . If one denies that, when the meaning is true, then the meant is what is so, one rejects propositional truth. If the rejection is universal, then it is the self-destructive proposition that there are no true propositions. If the rejection is limited to the dogmas, then it is just a roundabout way of saying that all the dogmas are false.[55]

Moreover, there is even an eschatological qualification to knowledge of church teaching that is fundamental, definitive, and irreformable. Ratzinger explains, "all knowledge in the time of the church remains knowledge seen in a mirror—and hence fragmentary. The direct relation to reality, to the face of God himself, is still kept for the *eschaton* (cf. 1

---

[55] Bernard Lonergan, SJ, "The Dehellenization of Dogma," in a *Second Collection*, Papers by Bernard J.F. Lonergan, SJ, edited by William F.J. Ryan, SJ, and Bernard J. Tyrrell, SJ. (Toronto: University of Toronto Press, 1974), 14, 16. 11-32.

cor 13:12)."⁵⁶ Berkouwer reminds us that no dogmatic definition is adequate given the fullness of divine truth. Still, inadequacy of expression does not mean inexpressibility of divine truth. We can say something determinate and true about divine truth, even if the fullness of divine truth remains inexhaustibly beyond us. Francis Sullivan reminds us: "If we grant that a proposition can have all these limitations, and still be true, I think there is no reason to deny the very possibility that the Church could express its normative faith in propositions that are really true."⁵⁷

This latter point was clearly taught by Vatican councils I (1869-70) and II (1962-1965). So teaches Vatican I citing the 5th century monk, Vincent of Lérins:

> May understanding, knowledge and wisdom increase [of the meaning of sacred dogmas] as ages and centuries roll along, and greatly and vigorously flourish, in each and all, in the individual and the whole church: but this only in its own proper kind, that is to say, in the same doctrine, in the same meaning, and in the same judgment [in eodem scilicet dogmate, eodem sensu eademque sententia].⁵⁸

Michael Bauwens explains admirably well a Lérinian hermeneutics:

---

⁵⁶ Ratzinger's commentary on *Dei Verbum*, the dogmatic constitution on divine revelation, 183.

⁵⁷ Sullivan, *Magisterium: Teaching Authority in the Catholic Church*, 15.

⁵⁸ Denzinger §3020. See my "Vincent of Lérins: The Development of Christian Doctrine," in *The Faith Once For All Delivered: Doctrinal Authority in Catholic Theology*, ed. Kevin L. Flannery, S.J. (Steubenville, OH: Emmaus Academic, 2023), 171–98.

Hence identity over time ("the same doctrine, in the same sense, and in the same meaning") is maintained, while allowing for genuine growth and hence progress—not merely in the subjective understanding of the objectively present Truth, but in the very historical and contingent mode in which the Truth becomes manifest.[59]

The Latin clause *eodem sensu eademque sententia* has been either omitted in translations, such as the English and Spanish, or translated in the Dutch and German versions of the opening speech. It is also missing in *Gaudium et Spes*, §62. When that subordinate clause has been translated into English, it has almost always been inadequately translated as "provided their sense and meaning are retained," "with their meaning preserved intact," or "retaining the same meaning and message" or as Walter Abbott's translation renders it: "For the deposit of faith or revealed truths is one thing; the manner in which they are formulated without violence to their meaning and significance is another." In my view, because of the connection between meaning and truth such that what is meant is judged to be true to reality, the most fitting translation is "keeping the same meaning and the same judgment."[60]

---

[59] Michael Bauwens, "Synchronic Progress in the Understanding of Doctrine: A Marian Perspective," in *Progress in Theology: Does the Queen of the Sciences Advance?*, edited by Gijsbert van den Brink, Rick Peels and Bethany Sollereder (London/New York: Routledge, 2025), 64-83, and at 76.

[60] I follow Fr. Joseph Komonchak's translation of the official Latin text (available at https://jakomonchak.files.wordpress.com/2012/10/john-xxiii-opening-speech. pdf.), which also happens to be the translation in Heinrich Denzinger, *Compendium of Creeds, Definitions, and Declarations on Matters of Faith and Morals*, Latin-English, ed. Peter Hünermann, 43rd ed., English edition ed. Robert Fastiggi and Anne Englund Nash (San Francisco: Ignatius Press, 2012), §3020.

So teaches Vatican II's *Unitatis Redintegratio*, "Christ summons the Church... to that continual reformation of which she always has need, insofar as she is an institution of men here on earth. Therefore, if the influence of events or of the times, has led to deficiencies in conduct, in church discipline, or even in the formulations of doctrine (which must be carefully distinguished from the deposit of faith itself), these should be rectified at the proper moment." (§6) Again, Vatican II, but this time, *Dei Verbum*: "For there is a growth in the understanding of the realities and the words which have been handed down. this happens through the contemplation and study made by believers, who treasure these things in their hearts (see Luke, 2:19, 51) through a penetrating understanding of the spiritual realities which they experience, and through the preaching of those who have received through episcopal succession the sure gift of truth. For as the centuries succeed one another, the Church constantly moves forward toward the fullness of divine truth until the words of God reach their complete fulfillment in her." (§8)

Returning to the critics of confessionalism, they seem to ignore those defenders of confessions and creeds that they are aware of hermeneutical and historical considerations.[61] Let us briefly consider the claim that integral to the truth of the Christian faith are certain historical events, as well as statements about these events, such as we find in the Nicene creed: "For us men and for our salvation, Jesus Christ came down from heaven: by the power of the holy Spirit he was born of the Virgin Mary, and became man. For our sake he was crucified under Pontius Pilate; he suffered, died, and was buried. On the third day he rose again in fulfillment of the Scriptures." Yes, Berkouwer is correct to say that to understand confessions of faith, such as the Nicene Creed, "a hermeneutical problem arises that creates an honest need for consideration of the

---

[61] Adapted from my book, *Berkouwer and Catholicism: Disputed Questions* (Boston/Leiden: Brill, 2013), 60-2, 82-3

background and the orientation of a given confession. to insist that there is a direct, verbal clarity in the statements of the past, apart from historical context and the need for hermeneutical principles of interpretation is to betray an ignorance of church history."[62] Consider also the first part of the Nicene Creed: "we believe in one Lord, Jesus Christ, the only Son of God, eternally begotten of the Father, God from God, Light from Light, true God from true God, begotten, not made, one in Being with the Father." Berkouwer is right, "the real intentions of the church's language have had to be clarified within the total message of the church. The use of the word co-substantial [one in Being] in the Church's condemnation of Arianism in 325 is very illustrative."[63] Thus, we need to understand the historical context and background of these creedal statements in order to get at "the intention of the church as it witnesses to the truth of God in each historical era."[64] Again: we should ask "what the real intention of the church was in its use of these philosophical concepts."[65] The question of intention is particularly important to Berkouwer because it is bound up with the question regarding the "criterion for distinguishing between form and content, representation and affirmation."[66] Berkouwer explains:

> If the word "intention" is sometimes used here, it is not meant to designate a psychological problem, as though one's concern were not actually with the text but with the intention of its framers. Rather, one's concern is with an intentionality in the confessions themselves, which often comes clearly to light. But this

---

[62] Berkouwer, *Vatikaans Concilie en de Nieuwe Theologie*, 90 [ET: 78].
[63] Berkouwer, *Vatikaans Concilie en de Nieuwe Theologie*, 85 [ET: 75].
[64] Berkouwer, *Vatikaans Concilie en de Nieuwe Theologie*, 90 [ET: 79].
[65] Berkouwer, *Vatikaans Concilie en de Nieuwe Theologie*, 88 [ET: 77].
[66] Berkouwer, *Vatikaans Concilie en de Nieuwe Theologie*, 73 [ET: 65].

directedness is concretized in a definite time, which is connected to the understanding of Scripture then. Often, too, it is connected to limited ideas and thoughts, which were characteristic of that time but can now be reflected on critically—unless one believes that all formulations of dogma has taken place under the special, providential leading and sanction of the holy Spirit.... When we look back at that confession in later times and trace its intentionality, tensions can arise concerning continuity. However, they [tensions] cannot be abolished by starting from an abstract idea of 'unchangeability' and minimizing the differences [between then and now] and seeking the confessional continuity in those differences.[67]

Berkouwer alludes in this passage to the distinction between irreformable propositions and their reformulations, suggesting that the latter cannot be absolutized. In this connection, he says there can be tensions concerning the issue of material continuity. In his first Vatican II book, *Vatikaans Concilie en de Nieuwe Theologie*, Berkouwer addresses the question regarding the relationship between unchangeable truth and the human expression of that truth in the variety of historically conditioned forms of thoughts, inclusive of different philosophical concepts that have played a role in explicating the content of revelation. Berkouwer himself is persuaded that "Modernism has definitely seen a very real problem—despite its untenable solutions—that has not been seen by anti-modernistic reaction in upholding the '*semper eadem*,' namely the absolutizing of continuity in a way that had no appreciation

---

[67] *De Kerk*, Vol.I, *Eenheid en Katholiciteit* (Kampen: J.H. Kok, 1970); Vol. II, *Apostoliciteit en Heiligheid* (Kampen: J.H. Kok, 1972), 111. Both volumes were translated into one English edition by James E. Davison as *The Church* (Grand Rapids, MI: Eerdmans, 1976), 294-95.

for the historical nature of human expression. In more recent times, this compelling problem naturally resurfaced and the distinction between form and content returned."[68] Succinctly put, the real question is, according to Thomas Guarino, how to explain "the material identity of christian truth over the course of time." Thus, the distinction between abiding truth and its historically conditioned formulation resurfaced with the *nouvels théologiens* and with that came the problem regarding the relation between history and truth. Of course, Berkouwer is right that the distinction itself cannot "be used as a magician's wand to clear up every burning question."[69] The problem is that the presupposition of the hermeneutic of continuity no longer seemed self-evident, given that truth's expressions are historically conditioned, and that these expressions are never absolute, wholly adequate, and irreplaceable. Berkouwer elaborates:

> that harmony had always been presumed, virtually self-evidently, to be an implication of the mystery of the truth "*eodem sensu eademque sententia.*" Now, however, attention is captivated primarily by the historical-factual process that does not transcend the times but is entangled with them in all sorts of ways. It cannot be denied that one encounters the undeniable fact of the situated setting of the various pronouncements made by the church in any given era.[70]

How, then, exactly is a single and unitary revelation homogeneously expressed, keeping the same meaning and the same judgment, given the

---

[68] G.C. Berkouwer, *Nabetrachting op het Concilie* (Kampen: J.H. Kok, 1968), 72.

[69] Berkouwer, *Vatikaans Concilie en de Nieuwe Theologie*, 99 [ET: 84]

[70] Berkouwer, *Nabetrachting op het Concilie*, 52.

undeniable fact "of time-conditioning, one can even say: of historicity."[71] Says Berkouwer, "all the problems of more recent interpretation of dogma are connected very closely to this search for continuity.... Thus, the question of the nature of continuity has to be faced."[72] Furthermore, how did the ecclesiastical magisterium respond to the *nouvels théologiens* and the issue of truth and theological epistemology raised by them? I have addressed this question elsewhere and so I will not return to it here.[73]

We need, however, to say more about ontology of meaning in order to provide the material identity of truth, its substantial homogeneity, with a metaphysical buttress. Guarino is right that "the issue of stability within change, unity within multiplicity, perdurance within temporality, inevitably raise questions concern-ing the metaphysical and ontological dimensions of reality."[74]

Briefly, pared down for my purpose here, I shall draw on Hans-Georg Gadamer's ontology of the meaning of the text that he inherited from F. L. Gottlob Frege (1848-1925) via Edmund Husserl (1859-1938).[75] Nicholas Wolterstorff has given the clearest account of this ontology and its bearing on the hermeneutic tradition, especially Gadamer. He explains:

> Suppose we assume that the right way to analyze belief and judgment is into a content, on the one hand, and the stance of belief or the action of judgment, on the other hand. The context of the

---

[71] Berkouwer, *Nabetrachting op het Concilie*, 52-3.

[72] Berkouwer, *De Kerk*, I, 236, 237 [190–91].

[73] See my book, *Berkouwer and Catholicism*, 58-101.

[74] Guarino's review of Anthony C. Thiselton, *The Hermeneutics of Doctrine*, 347.

[75] Adapted from my book, *Berkouwer and Catholicism*, 88-90.

belief that 2+3=5, is that 2+3=5, and the content of the judgment that today is warm and sunny, is that today is warm and sunny. Let us further suppose that the content of beliefs and judgments are entities of some sort, so that believing something consists of taking up the stance of belief toward that entity which one believes, and judging something consists of performing the action of judging on that entity which one judges to be true. Frege called such entities *Gedanken*, that is, *thoughts . . . Gedanken* are not states of mind. He argues that whereas you and I can believe and assert the same *Gedanke*, we cannot share the same state of mind. Obviously *Gedanken* are also not physical entities. and neither, so Frege argued, are they to be identified with sentences, for the reason that two distinct sentences may express one and the same *Gedanke*. *Gedanken* have to be abstract entities—or as the hermeneutic tradition preferred to call them, *ideal* entities. What distinguishes them from such other abstract entities as properties is that they can be believed and asserted, and that they are all either true or false.[76]

Indeed, Gadamer calls the ontological status of the meaning of the text an "ideal" entity. On this point, we find him saying, "What is stated in the text must be detached from all contingent factors and grasped in

---

[76] Nicholas Wolterstorff, "The Promise of Speech-act Theory for Biblical Interpretation," in *After Pentecost: Language and Biblical Interpretation*, edited by Craig Bartholomew, Colin Greene, Karl Moeller (Grand rapids, MI: Zondervan, 2001), 73–90, and for this quote, 77–78. See also, Wolterstorff, "Resuscitating the Author," in *Hermeneutics at the Crossroads*, edited by Kevin J. Vanhoozer, et al. (Bloomington and Indianapolis: Indiana university press, 2006), 35–49, especially, 39.

its full ideality, in which alone it has validity."⁷⁷ Gadamer explains himself more fully in the following often overlooked passage that Wolterstorff brings to our attention.

> [The] capacity for being written down is based on the fact that speech itself shares in the pure ideality of the meaning that communicates itself in it. In writing, the meaning of what is spoken exists purely for itself, completely detached from all emotional elements of expression and communication. A text is not to be understood as an expression of life but with respect to what it says. Writing is the abstract ideality of language. Hence the meaning of something written is fundamentally identifiable and repeatable. What is identical in the repetition is only what was actually deposited in the written record. This indicates that "repetition" cannot be meant here in its strict sense. It does not mean referring back to the original source where some thing is said or written. The understanding of something written is not a repetition of something past but the sharing of a present meaning.⁷⁸

The Fregean-Husserlian ontology of textual meaning then affirms the objectivity of meaning in general and is thus anti-historicist. I join Wolterstorff in siding "with Frege and Husserl that the right analysis of judgment is that, in judgment, there is something that one judges to be

---

⁷⁷ Hans-Georg Gadamer, *Wahrheit und Methode*, 3., erweiterte auflage (Tubingen: J.C.B. Mohr, 1972), 372. English translation: *Truth and Method*, Second revised edition, translation revised by Joel Weinsheimer and Donald G. Marshall (New York: Continuum, 1994), 394.

⁷⁸ Gadamer, *Wahrheit und Methode*, 370; *Truth and Method*, 392.

true that's to be distinguished from both that particular act and the sentence one uses to make the judgment."[79] What is more, thoughts, meanings, and propositions—what Wolterstorff elsewhere calls noematic content[80]— are true if and only if what they assert is in fact the case, being the way things are; otherwise, they are false. In short, regarding the status of meaning, the way things are, objective reality, is what makes "meanings" true or false.

Furthermore, adds Wolterstorff, "readers of texts can often find out the noematic content of the discourse of which the text is the medium—so that, in that sense, noematic content is 'transferable' from one mind to another."[81] One could add here: propositions are transferable as well to different contexts and conceptualities in which we seek to understand and communicate truth, including divine truth. This conclusion brings us back John XXIII's famous statement in his opening address to Vatican II, *Gaudet Mater Ecclesia*: "the deposit or the truths of faith [2 Tim 1:14], contained in our sacred teaching, are one thing, while the mode in which they are enunciated, keeping the same meaning and the same judgment [*eodem sensu eademque sententia*], is another."[82] Yves Congar, for one, has argued that this distinction summarizes the meaning of the entire council.[83] Although the propositional truths of the faith may be expressed differently, we must always determine whether those new re-

---

[79] Wolterstorff, "The promise of Speech-act theory for Biblical Interpretation," 80.

[80] Wolterstorff, *Divine Discourse, Philosophical Reflections on the Claim that God Speaks* (Cambridge: Cambridge University Press, 1995), 138, 155, 157–158.

[81] Wolterstorff, *Divine Discourse*, 155.

[82] Ioannes XXIII, "Allocutio habita d. 11 oct. 1962, in initio Concilii," 54. *Acta Apostolicae Sedis* [1962], 796, and for this quote, 792.

[83] Yves Congar, OP, *A History of Theology*, Translated by Hunter Guthrie (Garden City, N. Y.: Doubleday, 1968), 18–19.

formulations are preserving the same meaning and judgment (*eodem sensu eademque sententia*), and hence the material continuity, identity, and universality of those truths.

In this volume, the project of redeeming sex involves the battle for the body, one that is fought on many fronts in this book: the need for a philosophical and theological anthropology on the nature of the human person, particularly the body that has a proper subjectivity encompassing the whole man; the foundation of sexual ethics in a normative creation order/natural law and its relation to the flourishing of persons and communities, and the cultural and religious dynamics that contributed to the sexual revolution and the rise of homosexualism, same-sex marriage, and gender ideology.

In a wide-ranging discussion of a theology of revelation, doctrinal development, and a perspective on philosophical ethics and moral theology, the sources of Christian ethics are considered, as well as the nature of human experience and judgment, and how a theory of experience grounds a sound epistemology but also a sound metaphysics for Christian ethics. We address the question of what is a sound epistemology and a corresponding sound metaphysics.

In the spirit of genuine ecumenism, I engage the thought of leading Dutch Reformed (liberal) theologian, Ad. L. Th. De Bruijne (1959-), the Dutch Reformed master of dogmatics and ecumenical theology, G. C. Berkouwer (1903-1996), and Dutch philosopher Herman Dooyeweerd (1894-1977). They are all brought into conversation with the philosopher Karol Wojtyla/St. John Paul II (1920-2005), and the latter is brought into conversation with the revisionist (liberal) moral theology of Margaret A. Farley, RSM (1935-). Finally, the moral and theological underpinnings of the nature and purpose of pastoral care of individuals in morally and spiritually problematic relationships is considered in critical dialogue with, inter alia, influential Jesuit theologian, James Martin, SJ.

Chapter 2

Christian Anthropology, the Unity of Human Nature, and the Bodily Subjectivity of the Human Person

> The person, including the body, is completely entrusted to himself, and it is in the unity of body and soul that the person is the subject of his own moral acts. ... A doctrine which dissociates the moral act from the bodily dimensions of its exercise is contrary to the teaching of Scripture and Tradition. ... In fact, body and soul are inseparable: in the person, in the willing agent and in the deliberate act they stand or fall together.
>
> —John Paul II[1]

> The human body is man himself in the structural whole of his temporal appearance. ... [T]he human spirit cannot carry out any real acts outside its temporal corporal individuality-structure. For that reason, we said: it is the individual human being in the integral unity of "body" and "soul" who accomplishes the acts. The full person as a totality is the subject of the act.
>
> —Herman Dooyeweerd[2]

---

[1] John Paul II, *Veritatis Splendor*, §§48–9.

[2] Herman Dooyeweerd, *A New Critique of Theoretical Thought*, III, 89. Dooyeweerd, *Reformation and Scholasticism in Philosophy*, III, *Philosophy of Nature and Philosophical Anthropology*, Part II, chapters 1–3, 162–3.

This is one of the pressing questions of our day. The answer, of course, is "the whole counsel of God." That is true but also somewhat glib. Do peculiar times not call for specific emphases in our teaching? ... What does it mean to be human? More specifically, what does it mean to be an embodied human? For we now find ourselves in a battle for the body. The status of the body as it relates to us as human persons seems to be the issue that lies, often unseen, behind many of the other more prominent debates of our age. Take the most controversial question of recent years: What is a woman? This is remarkably simple to answer if bodies have importance, but it is now staggeringly difficult to answer because our culture denies the authority of the body in this matter.

—Carl Trueman[3]

I devote my very rare free moments to a work that is close to my heart and devoted to the metaphysical sense and mystery of the PERSON. It seems to me that the debate today is being played on that level. The evil of our times consists in the first place in a kind of degradation, indeed in a pulverization, of the fundamental uniqueness of each human person. This evil is even much more of the metaphysical order than of the moral order. To this disintegration, planned at times by atheistic ideologies,

---

[3] The subtitle of my book is borrowed from Carl Trueman, "The Battle for the Body," *First Things* (September 21, 2023), https://www.firstthings.com/web-exclusives/2023/09/the-battle-for-the-body. See also, Nancy R. Pearcey, *Love the Body* (Grand Rapids. MI: Baker Books, 2018), Chapter 1, "I Hate Me. The Rise and Decline of the Human Body," 17-46.

we must oppose, rather than sterile polemics, a kind of "recapitulation" of the inviolable mystery of the person.

—Archbishop of Kraków, Karol Wojtyla[4]

According to the Church's teaching, the human being is a substantial unity of soul and body. Her marital morality and sexual ethics are based on this. . . . The concept of the human being as a substantial unity of soul and body leads to a clear answer to the question of what constitutes the mutual, total self-giving of man and woman to each other in marriage: this self-giving cannot, in essence, be a total gift of the person if it does not also encompass the physical level, including sexuality.

—Willem Jacobus Cardinal Eijk[5]

In the epigraphs to this chapter, it is evident that both Herman Dooyeweerd, John Paul II, and Cardinal Eijk share a common emphasis regarding the unity of the human person and his integral relation to the body.[6] So, too, does Trueman who alerts us to the "battle for the body"

---

[4] Karol Wojtyla expressed this concern in a well-known letter to Henri de Lubac, SJ, found in Henri de Lubac, *At the Service of the Church: Henri de Lubac Reflects on the Circumstances That Occasioned His Writings*, trans. Anne Englund (San Francisco, CA: Ignatius Press, 1993), 171–2. The work he is referring to here is *Person and Act and Related Essays*. Translated by Grzegorz Ignatik. (Washington, DC: Catholic University of American Press, 2021).

[5] Willem Jacobus Cardinal Eijk *De Band van de Liefde: Huwelijksmoraal and Seksuele Ethiek* (Utrecht: KokBoekencentrum Ultgevers, 2022), 83, 90.

[6] This chapter is an adapted and shortened version of chapter 3 of my book, *Roman Catholicism and Neo-Calvinism: Ecumenical and Polemical Engagements* (New York: Peter Lang, 2024).

in contemporary culture.[7] The body refers to the whole of man's temporal existence. In this introduction, we turn to Dooyeweerd's philosophical anthropology and his critique of the substance ontology of classical Catholic anthropology in the scholastic tradition, particularly Thomistic, as a form of dualism between soul and body.[8] He argues that substance ontology does not do justice to the unity of human nature. In addition, I consider the relation of Dooyeweerd's critique to Karol Wojtyla's approach to anthropology in his philosophical magnum opus, *The Person and Act*. We begin, however, with Berkouwer's discussion of Catholic anthropology and the *nouvelle théologie*[9] in the context of the charge of substantial dualism against that anthropology and its alleged failure to maintain the unity of human nature.[10]

---

[7] "Protestants need to recover both natural law and a high view of the physical body,"Carl R. Trueman, *The Rise and Triumph of the Modern Self: Cultural Amnesia, Expressive Individualism, and the Road to the Sexual Revolution* (Wheaton, Illinois: Crossway, 2020), 405,

[8] Herman Dooyeweerd, *Reformation and Scholasticism in Philosophy*, II, Chapter VII, "The Idea of the Individuality-Structure and the Thomist Substance-Concept, as Applied to Anthropology," 246–432.

[9] *Nouvelle théologie* refers to a historical and theological analysis by Catholic theologians involved in the *ressourcement* movement for renewal in twentieth-century Catholic theology in the period 1930 to 1960, contributing to the reforms in the Second Vatican Council. On the *nouvelle théologie* and its influence on Vatican II, see G.C. Berkouwer, *Vatikaans Concilie en de Nieuwe Theologie* (Kampen: Kok, 1964); ET: *The Second Vatican Council and the New Catholicism*, trans. Lewis Smedes (Grand Rapids, MI: Eerdmans, 1965), 250. The phrase "nieuwe theologie" (literally "new theology") in the Dutch title of the book is a clear reference to the *nouvelle théologie* of Henri de Lubac, et al. That reference is lost in the English translation, which speaks of "New Catholicism."

[10] G.C. Berkouwer, *De Mens Het Beeld Gods*, (Kampen: J. H. Kok, 1957), 211–58. English Translation: *Man: The Image of God*, trans. Dirk W. Jellema (Grand Rapids: Eerdmans, 1962), 194–233.

Dualism, Duality, and Unity

What is man? On the one hand, man exists in a threefold set of relations, according to Bavinck, "to God, to other human beings, and to nature."[11] Relationality is constitutive of man's being. On the other hand, man exists in his own right as a self-transcending subject, a fully constituted, self-subsisting individual, who is a unique, unrepeatable, and incommunicable human person. The unity of this self-subsisting individual "lies in his or her *I*." Bavinck explains, "That is the root, the center, the kernel, the core of every person. Everything else lies around it and is near to it and attaches to it: I *have* intellect, feelings, a will, a body, hand, foot, etc., but I *am* ... *I*. Holy Scripture calls this the heart, out of which are the issues of life (Prov 4:23)." "The heart is the central midpoint of human being and living, and also the seat of self-consciousness."[12]

Furthermore, Bavinck's anthropology is such that the "body belongs integrally to the image of God." He explains that he is neither a materialist nor a dualist. "Scripture reconciles the two." He is not the former because "the soul is essentially different from the body. It is not a property or quality of matter, but something on its own, yet related to the body."[13] He is not a dualist either because he does not see the self as something merely having a body. Rather, he sees man as a living, bodily entity, a unified totality.

Man has a "spirit" (*pneuma*), but that "spirit" is psychically organized and must, by virtue of its nature, inhabit a body. It is of

---

[11] Herman Bavinck, *Reformed Ethics*, Vol. I: *Created, Fallen, and Converted Humanity*, ed. by John Bolt with Jessica Joustra, Nelson D. Kloosterman, Antoine Theron, and Dirk Van Keulen (Grand Rapids: Baker Academic, 2019) I, 50; see also 49–62.

[12] Bavinck, *Reformed Ethics*, I, 191.

[13] Bavinck, *Reformed Ethics*, I, 44.

the essence of humanity to be corporeal and sentient. ... The body is not a prison, but a marvelous piece of art from the hand of God Almighty, and just as constitutive for the essence of humanity as the soul. ... The nature of the union of the soul with the body though incomprehensible, is much closer than the theories of "occasionalism" or "preestablished harmony" (*harmonia praestabilitia*) or "a system of influence" (*systema influxus*). ... The nature of the union of the soul with the body ... is so intimate that one nature, one person, one self is the subject of both and of all their activities. ... It is always the same soul that peers through the eyes, thinks through the brain, grasps with the hands, and walks with the feet.[14]

Indeed, Bavinck holds to a position he calls "Harmonism"—meaning thereby, as I understand him, that the body of man is irreducible to mere matter: it is a *spiritualized body*; just as man's spirit is so closely united to the body that he can be described as *an embodied spirit*.[15] Moreover, Bavinck elaborates, "We are persons because we can say 'I'. This *I* is what forms our humanity in us, what is actually human. This *I* always and under all circumstances remains the same and identical with itself. The *I* is a wonder, inexplicable, and simply to be accepted."[16] He continues: "That *I* has a real existence, it is ... a being, or rather *the* being in us (all the others are but revelations of the *I*." In other words, all the manifestations of man's whole existence are revelations of the one same, undivided, individual, and entire I revealing itself.

[I]t is always the one, *whole I* that reveals itself. ... It is the same

---

[14] Bavinck, *Gereformeerde Dogmatiek*, II 521[559].

[15] Bavinck, *Reformed Ethics*, 46.

[16] Bavinck, *Reformed Ethics*, 46.

single and entire *I* which thinks, wills, and feels. It is not one part of the *I* which thinks and another part which wills, but it is the same *I* which, when it works, reveals three sides of itself [thinks, wills, and feels]. All three abilities presume the *I*, the self-consciousness, the foundation on which the [anthropological] edifice stands.[17]

This, too, is Kuyper's anthropology, "there is no way that the body is a matter of secondary importance." He adds, "Christ is King not only of our soul but is just as decidedly King of our body. ... The body is a creation of God just as much as the soul is. ... Christ's kingship over our body, no less than his kingship over our soul, is the very pillar and foundation of the Christian family."[18]

We find another argument in Cardinal Eijk's defense of the body as an intrinsic dimension of the human person.[19]

However, this is not about the body in its outward appearance as a physiological entity, but rather about the ensouled body, which is the visible expression of the human person. Moreover, three considerations must be taken into account:

1. God is the creator of the body;
2. God's Son became human and in that connection took on a human body;

---

[17] Bavinck, *Reformed Ethics*, I, 46–8.

[18] Abraham Kuyper, *Pro Rege: Living Under Christ the King*, Vol. 2, *The Kingship of Christ in its Operation*, Collected Works in Public Theology, ed. John Kok with Nelson D. Kloosterman, trans. Albert Gootjes, Introduction by Govert Buijs (Bellingham, WA: Lexham Press), 436, 438.

[19] Eijk, *De Band van de Liefde*, 85.

3. and the body will rise again at the end of time.

In this sense, knowledge of God sheds light also on the meaning of the body, including masculinity or femininity.[20]

Thus, the upshot of all these arguments is that the body is intrinsic to personhood. This view is shared by Kuyper, Dooyeweerd, Eijk, and also by John Paul II. In particular, as I will show in Chapter 3, this anthropology undergirds the nature of marriage from the order of creation in that it requires sexual difference, the bodily-sexual act, as a foundational prerequisite, indeed, as *intrinsic* to a one-flesh conjugal union.

In the light of this anthropological vision, Kuyper reiterates Jesus' "back-to-creation" model. "Jesus points to creation as the starting point that determines everything." In creation, the difference between man and woman was indicated from the very beginning."[21] Kuyper presciently saw that modernism ended in "transgenderism," which "denies and abolishes every difference, [and] cannot rest until it has made woman man and man woman, and putting every distinction on a common level."[22] Furthermore, Bavinck holds that marriage is the basis of the family in the order of creation. What, then, is marriage? Bavinck affirms the conjugal view of marriage in which marriage is a comprehensive two-in-one-flesh-union—mind, will, and bodily union—of man and woman, ordered to family life, to having and rearing children, and requiring a permanent and exclusive commitment to each other. Significantly, he regards sexual differentiation—and its corollary the "twoness" of male and female bodily union—as not only a created reality that

---

[20] Eijk, *De Band van de Liefde*, 66.

[21] Kuyper, *Pro Rege: Living Under Christ the King*, Vol. 2, 305.

[22] Abraham Kuyper, *Lectures on Calvinism*, 1898 Princeton University Stone Lectures (Grand Rapids, MI: Eerdmans, 1931), 27.

is good but also a fundamental prerequisite for marriage.[23] On the goodness of sexual differentiation, Bavinck writes:

> God is the Creator of the human being, and simultaneously also the Inaugurator of sex and of sexual difference. This difference did not result from sin; it existed from the very beginning, it has its basis in creation, it is a revelation of God's will and sovereignty, and is therefore wise and holy and good. ... Together in mutual fellowship [man and woman] bear the divine image. God himself is the Creator of duality-in-unity. Within that unity, they are and remain two.[24]

As to sexual differentiation being a fundamental prerequisite for marriage, Bavinck elaborates on the concluding claim of the last quote. He says,

> In order to make such unity, fellowship, and cooperation in soul and body both possible and real, God created the woman *from* the man and *for* the man (1 Cor. 11:8–9), but also simultaneously unto the man, even as he created the man unto the woman. God made two out of one, so that he could then make the two into one, one soul and one flesh. This kind of fellowship is possible only between two. From the very beginning, marriage was and is by virtue of its essential nature monogamous, an essential

---

[23] Herman Bavinck, *Het Christelijke Huisgezin*, 2nd rev. ed. (Kampen: Kok, 1912; first edition 1908). Translated by Nelson D. Kloosterman as *The Christian Family*, introduction by James Eglinton (Grand Rapids, MI: Christian's Library Press, 2012), 70. See my article review, "Bavinck on the Family and Integral Human Development," *Journal of Markets and Morality* 16.1 (Spring 2013): 219–37.

[24] Bavinck, *The Christian Family*, 5.

bond between one man and one woman, and therefore also a lifelong covenant.[25]

Thus, man and woman were made for each other, these two sexually differentiated people being united comprehensively in the full and complete communion of husband and wife—again, mind, will, and bodily union—in one body, "one flesh" (Gen. 2:24). This is the essence of marriage.[26]

Contemporary Catholic philosophical theologian, Cardinal Eijk, following Vatican II (*Gaudium et Spes* §48), also refers back to the creation texts to which Jesus refers in Matt 19:4-5 and Mark 10:6-8. "The intimate partnership of married life and love has been established by the Creator and qualified by His laws, and is rooted in the conjugal covenant of irrevocable personal consent." Explains Cardinal Eijk:

> In its definition of marriage, the Second Vatican Council clearly indicates that marriage was instituted by God at creation. The Council states here that a concrete marriage comes into being through the mutual consent of man and woman to each other, but that this is an "institution rooted in God's law" and "established by the Creator" (Ibid.). The Creator designed the nature of the human person, and thereby also the nature of one of the most fundamental communities known to humanity—marriage. . . . Humanity does not determine the meaning of marriage but, through natural law that is established in Holy Scripture—by, among other things, the Ten Commandments—*discovers* the essence of marriage, along with the values and norms

---

[25] Bavinck, *The Christian Family*, 7.
[26] Bavinck, *The Christian Family*, 85.

for marriage that flow from that essence.[27]

Is marriage, then, a two-in-one-flesh union between a man and a woman because the Church says so, positing or postulating its existence and nature according to its own judgment, that is, Church law? If so, then, one accepts ecclesial "positivism," the view that these are basically mere conventions. This positivism is similar to one thinking that human beings have rights because the state or society says so. Alternatively, does the Church judge that marriage is a two-in-one-flesh union between a man and woman because that judgment is true to an objective reality, according to the order of creation? The *Catechism of the Catholic Church* adds, "The vocation to marriage is written in the very nature of man and woman as they came from the hand of the Creator" (§§ 1603; 1614-1615). If so, then one is a Christian realist: marriage is grounded in the order of creation, of an independently existing reality, and therefore has an objective structure judged by the Church to be the case or the way things really are. On this view, the fact that the Church teaches that marriage is a two-in-one-flesh union between a man and a woman adds nothing to the truth-status of this dogma. This realism about the truth-status of dogmatic propositions is similar to one holding that human beings have rights by virtue of their nature as human beings, and the state simply secures, rather than confers, those rights by writing them down in a constitution. I contend that the Church holds to Christian realism, and Cardinal Eijk expresses that view in the above passage.

Berkouwer stands in the line of Bavinck and Kuyper in his Christian anthropology. He rightly notes in his reflections on man as the image of God, that man here refers to the "whole man" in the totality of his existence, including his bodily existence, rather than mere functions of the

---

[27] Eijk, *De Band van de Liefde*, 62.

soul like the powers of intellect, will, and others. These functions are an abstraction from the whole man, says Berkouwer, "especially in relation to the human body."[28] Explains Berkouwer,

> Though Scripture gives us no exposition of all the relationships in man, the whole Scriptural witness deals with the whole man in the actuality of his existence. ... But we can never see man from the biblical viewpoint as long as we *abstract* the "real man" from his bodily existence. ... Scripture does not at all view man's bodiliness as something secondary; rather, the moment one devalues the body, one has "deactualized" man's whole reality as a creature of God.[29]

Berkouwer, thus, rejects the idea that the body is, in some sense, spiritually inferior, or even ontologically inferior, such that the image of God is functionally localized in man's soul, his intellect and will, in distinction to his body. This idea holds that there is a hierarchical relationship between the soul and the body.

Once again, here, too, we find Cardinal Eijk: "The body is thereby an intrinsic dimension of the human person. . . . This understanding is fundamental to Catholic sexual morality and medical ethics."[30] In this connection, Eijk cites *Gaudium et Spes* (§14):

> Though made of body and soul, man is one. Through his bodily composition he gathers to himself the elements of the material world; thus they reach their crown through him, and through him raise their voice in free praise of the Creator. For this reason

---

[28] Berkouwer, *De Mens Het Beeld Gods*, 210 [194].
[29] Berkouwer, *De Mens Het Beeld Gods*, 255 [230–1].
[30] Eijk, *De Band van de Liefde*, 85.

man is not allowed to despise his bodily life, rather he is obliged to regard his body as good and honorable since God has created it and will raise it up on the last day. Nevertheless, wounded by sin, man experiences rebellious stirrings in his body. But the very dignity of man postulates that man glorify God in his body and forbid it to serve the evil inclinations of his heart.

Hence, Cardinal Eijk hits hard against the anthropological vision of transgenderism.[31] This is the idea "that the body, and along with it biological sexuality, are not intrinsic dimensions of the human person, also underlies gender theory. According to this theory, the social role of man or woman, the so-called gender, is entirely separate from physical sexuality, allowing individuals to freely choose their gender identity."[32]

The anthropological vision of Vatican II, as Cardinal Eijk rightly sees it, is not always captured by Catholic theologians. Consider, for example, the claim of Peter Kwasniewski, who holds to a hierarchical relationship between the soul and the body. "[T]here is a proper hierarchy to all that we are and do; God first, the soul second, the neighbor third, the body last."[33] Although he adopts the idea that "man [is] a body-soul hylomorphic composite," there is a lop-sided emphasis on the intellect such that the *bodily* nature of the human person is not distinctive in its own right, that is, not due to bodiliness as such, says Kwasniewski, but

---

[31] See the recent "Joint Declaration on 'Diversity of Gender and Sexuality,'" A Norwegian Christian Ecumenical Project 2024. https://www.felleskristen.no/the-declaration-in-english.

[32] Eijk, *De Band van de Liefde*, 81.

[33] Peter Kwasniewski, *Treasuring the Goods of Marriage in a Throwaway Society* (Manchester, NH: Sophia Press, 2023), 58.

because of "its animation by a rational soul."[34] Yes, the intellectual substance that is the soul is united to the body as its form; in other words, the human person's "rational soul is *per se et essentialiter* the form of his body."[35] But I have my doubts whether Kwasniewski is able to account for the *"Church's teachings on the unity of the human person,"* which is the person himself in the unity of soul and body, as John Paul II and Cardinal Eijk put it, and hence is unable to grasp the specifically human meaning of the body. "Only in reference to the human person in his 'unified totality', that is, as 'a soul which expresses itself in a body and a body informed by an immortal spirit,' [*Familiaris Consortio*, §11], can the specifically human meaning of the body be grasped."[36] That is, adds John Paul, "The spiritual and immortal soul is the principle of unity of the human being, whereby it exists as a whole—*corpore et anima unus*—as a person."[37] Cardinal Eijk elaborates the problem here:

> That the human being is a substantial unity of body and soul aligns with our direct, everyday experience. Each of us perceives ourselves as the center of various activities of a highly diverse nature. Some of our actions are of a highly spiritual level, such as praying and studying. . . . We engage in physical, psychological, and spiritual actions. Yet, at the same time, we experience ourselves as a unity. All these different activities stem from one and the same subject. How is it possible that a human can perform such diverse activities and still be a unified being?[38]

---

[34] Kwasniewski, *Treasuring the Goods of Marriage in a Throwaway Society*, 59.

[35] John Paul II, *Veritatis Splendor*, §48.

[36] John Paul II, *Veritatis Splendor*, §50.

[37] John Paul II, *Veritatis Splendor*, §48.

[38] Eijk, *De Band van de Liefde*, 83.

Ch. 2: Christian Anthropology, the Unity of Human Nature... 143

We will return to this question below. For now, I shall focus on John Paul II's elaboration of the bodily nature of the human person, "The person, by the light of reason and the support of virtue, discovers in the body the anticipatory signs, the expression and the promise of the gift of self, in conformity with the wise plan of the Creator."[39] Indeed, Kwasniewski seems unable to account for the specifically human meaning of the body and its integral place in the unified totality that is the human person. This is evident, I argue, when Kwasniewski states, rather than bodily unity being the foundation of the moral community that is conjugal marriage, "the "union of souls is the higher and proper end of matrimony as regards the persons of the spouses."[40] Hence, "In its very bodiliness, the nuptial act ... cannot be the summit of spousal union, for bodiliness is not what is highest in man; the body is not the purest expression of a person's spiritual uniqueness or capacity for giving and receiving."[41] Now, the hierarchical relationship, higher and lower parts, that Kwasniewski sees between the soul and the body, makes it difficult for him to honor the integral place of man's body, as Berkouwer puts it, in "his full and genuine creatureliness and humanness,"[42] and hence sexual differentiation, as such, in regard to spousal union, conjugal marriage.[43]

---

[39] John Paul II, *Veritatis Splendor*, §48.

[40] Kwasniewski, *Treasuring the Goods of Marriage in a Throwaway Society*, 63.

[41] Kwasniewski, *Treasuring the Goods of Marriage in a Throwaway Society*, 64.

[42] Berkouwer, *De Mens Het Beeld Gods*, 222 [203].

[43] In my view, Kwasniewski fails to understand the fundamental significance of sexual differentiation in John Paul II's anthropology as it bears upon the nature of marriage, and hence of its sacramental validity. See Kwasniewski, *Treasuring the Goods of Marriage in a Throwaway Society*, 57–8.

By contrast, in his theological magnum opus, *Man and Woman He Created Them: A Theology of the Body*,[44] John Paul II understands sexual differentiation, maleness and femaleness, as foundational to the human body, and hence to marriage, having then "*the meaning of a gift of the person to the person.*"[45] Indeed, he explains, "[T]he *original* [i.e., creational] and fundamental *meaning of being a body*, as also of being, as a body, male and female ... *is united to the fact that man is created as a person and is called to a life 'in communione personarum'.*"[46] And as to the structure of the sacramental sign of marriage and what it signifies, John Paul argues, "The sacramental sign is constituted in the intentional order inasmuch as it is simultaneously constituted in the real order."[47] By the intentional order, John Paul means that the sign of the sacrament of marriage is constituted by the words intentionally spoken "on the level of intellect and will, of consciousness and the heart," by both the man and the woman, words that must then correspond to the reality, that is, the real order, of the full and real visible sign of the sacrament itself, of the human subjectivity of the man and woman. "Thus, from the words with which the man and the woman express their readiness to become 'one flesh' according to the eternal truth established in the mystery of creation [Gen 1:27; 2:24], we pass *to the reality* that corresponds to these words. Both the one and the other element are important *with regard to the structure of the sacramental sign.*"[48] Otherwise, the words spoken by the man and the woman would not correspond to the sexual

---

[44] Pope John Paul II, *Man and Woman He Created Them: A Theology of the Body* (Boston, MA: Pauline Books & Media, 2006). Carl Trueman regards this work of John Paul II as "the best work on the body from a Christian perspective," *The Rise and Triumph of the Modern Self*, 406n17.

[45] John Paul II, *Man and Woman He Created Them*, 61.1.

[46] John Paul II, *Man and Woman He Created Them*, 69.4.

[47] John Paul II, *Man and Woman He Created Them*, 103.3.

[48] John Paul II, *Man and Woman He Created Them*, 103.4.

differentiation that is a fundamental prerequisite for the two to become one flesh.

Again, in contrast to a hierarchical relationship between soul and body, higher and lower parts, John Paul II states, "Man is a subject not only by his self-consciousness and by self-determination, but also based on his own body. *The structure of this body is such that it permits him to be the author of genuinely human activity.*"[49] Yet, the body is not the totality of the human person. Ridderbos correctly states, "it is in this being a body that there is the possibility of the distinction between man and himself, between the 'I' and its realization in thoughts and acts."[50] In a biblical sense, the human body is the temple of the Holy Spirit (1 Cor 6:19), but it isn't the center and the root of human existence. This, too, is Dooyeweerd's view regarding what he calls "man's integral spiritual individuality." He explains, "[A] person's individuality is rooted in the spiritual center of his existence, of which the selfhood is the expression, and that precisely because human nature possesses such an integral religious unity in its root, it expresses that it is created after God's image."[51] As we shall show below, Dooyeweerd rejects the alleged dualism in the substance ontology of Thomist anthropology, because it destroyed the unity of human nature, but this doesn't mean that he abandons a duality between "heart" and "body."[52] Says Dooyeweerd:

---

[49] John Paul II, *Man and Woman He Created Them*, 7.2. See also, John Paul II, *Veritatis Splendor*, no. 48: "The person, including the body, is completely entrusted to himself, and it is in the unity of body and soul that the person is the subject of his own moral acts."

[50] Herman Ridderbos, *Paulus: Ontwerp Van Zijn Theologie* (Kampen: Kok, 1973), 122–4. English translation: *Paul: An Outline of His Theology*, trans. John Richard De Witt (Grand Rapids, MI: Eerdmans, 1975), 115-17.

[51] Dooyeweerd, *Reformation and Scholasticism in Philosophy*, II, 352.

[52] Berkouwer, *De Mens Het Beeld Gods*, 233 [212].

Man's very soul or spirit—in the signal, religious meaning of divine revelation—is the radical unity of his "body" which encompasses his entire temporal existence in one integral "enkaptic structural whole," including man's temporal act-life with its three basic directions of knowing, imagining, and willing. But here the "body" is something entirely different from the abstract "material body" of Aristotelian scholasticism, just as the soul in its succinctly religious, Scriptural sense is something entirely different from the abstract "*anima rationalis*."[53]

Accordingly, the duality between "heart" and "body" is alternatively addressed in Scripture with its distinction between "the outward man" and "the inward man" (Rom 7:22; 2 Cor 4:16; Eph 3:16), as Ridderbos puts it, "describing the outward, visible, physical, and the inward, invisible spiritual side of human existence." The "inward man" is further defined as "'understanding' (*nous*), 'heart' (*kardia*), 'will' (*thelēma*), 'soul' (*psychē*), 'spirit' (*pneuma*), 'conscience' (*syneidēsis*)." In this connection, "heart" is taken to denote the center of a person's self. In particular, adds Ridderbos, "the heart is still more inclusive than the *nous*," Ridderbos explains, "in that the *nous* speaks of the human ego from the viewpoint of thinking … whereas the affections, aspirations, passions, desires dwell in the heart and spring forth from it."[54] Helpfully, the *Catechism of the Catholic Church* describes the *person* as someone and not just something. "He is capable of self-knowledge, of self-possession and of freely giving himself and entering into communion with other persons" (§357). In addition, it refers to the person by the term of "heart," meaning thereby "the whole man as he functions in all his aspects in the midst

---

[53] Dooyeweerd, *Reformation and Scholasticism in Philosophy*, II, 353.

[54] Ridderbos, *Paulus*, 126 [119]. This, too, is Dooyeweerd's view in *Reformation and Scholasticism in Philosophy*, III, 141.

of his created actuality."[55] In particular, says Berkouwer, "The term 'heart' deals with the total orientation, direction, concentration of man, his depth dimension, from which his full human existence is directed and formed. He who gives his heart to the Lord gives his full life (cf. Prov 23:26)."[56] Recently, Pope Francis has expressed a similar point about the "heart":

> The word "heart" proves its value for philosophy and theology in their efforts to reach an integral synthesis. Nor can its meaning be exhausted by biology, psychology, Anthropology or any other science. It is one of those primordial words that [wrote Karl Rahner] "describe realities belonging to man precisely in so far as he is one whole (as a corporeo-spiritual person)." It follows that biologists are not being more "realistic" when they discuss the heart, since they see only one aspect of it; the whole is not less real, but even more real. Nor can abstract language ever acquire the same concrete and integrative meaning. The word "heart" evokes the inmost core of our person, and thus it enables us to understand ourselves in our integrity and not merely under one isolated aspect.[57]

In this light, we can easily understand the *Catechism*:

---

[55] Berkouwer, *De Mens Het Beeld Gods*, 236 [214].

[56] Berkouwer, *De Mens Het Beeld Gods*, 221 [203].

[57] Pope Francis, *Dilexit Nos*, October 24, 2024, Encyclical Letter, "On the Human and Divine Love of the Heart of Jesus Christ," §15. Similarly, see also, §21: "This profound core, present in every man and woman, is not that of the soul, but of the entire person in his or her unique psychosomatic identity. Everything finds its unity in the heart, which can be the dwelling-place of love in all its spiritual, psychic and even physical dimensions."

The heart is the dwelling-place where I am, where I live; according to the Semitic or Biblical expression, the heart is the place "to which I withdraw." The heart is our hidden center, beyond the grasp of our reason and of others; only the Spirit of God can fathom the human heart and know it fully. The heart is the place of decision, deeper than our psychic drives. It is the place of truth, where we choose life or death. It is the place of encounter, because as image of God we live in relation: it is the place of covenant. (§2563)

Furthermore, the term "soul" refers to the entire human person. Hence, the whole man is composed of both body and soul. The reference to "soul and body" raises the question "whether we must accept as Biblical teaching that man is composed of two substances, soul and body,"[58] or rather the duality-in-unity, a substantial unity, of "two inseparable elements of one and the same substance."[59] Berkouwer asks, "With this question we face an issue which has aroused deep and complex theological and philosophical discussion: the issue of whether dichotomy [duality] is necessarily dualistic and thus necessarily involves a dialectic of mediation [between soul and body] which must destroy the unity of man."[60] The brief answer here to this question must be that duality and dualism are not identical. There is a duality within created reality be-

---

[58] Berkouwer, *De Mens Het Beeld Gods*, 227 [207].

[59] Etienne Gilson, *The Spirit of Medieval Philosophy*, Gifford Lectures 1931-1932, trans. A. H. C. Downes (New York: Scribners, 1940), 76, and also, 198: "Neither the soul nor the body is the man, but the composite of both." Also helpful is John D. Finley, "Metaphysics: A Note on Soul, Body, and Sexuality," in *Sexual Identity, The Harmony of Philosophy, Science, and Revelation*, ed. John D. Finley (Steubenville, Ohio: Emmaus Road, 2022), 237–50.

[60] Berkouwer, *De Mens Het Beeld Gods*, 232 [211].

tween man and fellow man, man and world, without a substantial dualism between the two terms. Dualism destroys the unity of human nature, but duality does not preclude the unity of human nature. Says Berkouwer, "The attempt is made to show the unity of man despite—or, rather, in this duality, by calling attention to some relation which, in whatever way it is more closely described and defined, unites soul and body."[61] How, then, could man's unity be maintained when man was created a duality-in-unity, soul and body, according to Catholic Anthropology?

The Council of Vienne (1312), the Fifth Lateran Council (c. 1513–17), chaired by Pope Leo X, and the rejection of the errors of Anton Günther (1857), affirmed the Aristotelian-Thomist doctrine of the rational and intellectual soul of itself and essentially the form of the human body, "the *soul is 'per se et essentialiter'* the form of the body."[62] Indeed, in 1878, Tomasso Cardinal Zigliara stated, in his *De Mente concilii Viennensis*, that the "Council's aim [was] to defend the truth of man's *substantial unity* and to refute the error of *dualism* in relation to man himself."[63] Berkouwer judges that these statements on the soul as the form of the body are "undoubtedly intended to emphasize the unity of man." He explains:

> This is clear from the ideas which Vienne condemned, those of Olivi. Olivi, too, affirmed a relation between soul and body, but held that the soul was the form of the body only through a lower

---

[61] Berkouwer, *De Mens Het Beeld Gods*, 232 [212].

[62] For Vienne, see DH 902; the Fifth Lateran Council, DH 1440, and the rejection of Günther's ideas, DH 2828.

[63] As cited in Réginald Garrigou-Lagrange, *Thomistic Common Sense: The Philosophy of Being and the Development of Doctrine*, trans. Matthew K. Minerd (Steubenville, OH: Emmaus Academic, 2021), 241, n. 29.

form of the soul, an idea arising from his Platonic dualism, which implied that an intermediate form was necessary between the *anima intellectiva* and the body; and it was in opposition to this mediating lower form of the soul that Vienne formulated its statement that the soul is "*per se et essentialiter*" the form of the body. Though the lower aspects of the soul are not denied, they are no mediating form between soul and body, for they are led and controlled by the rational soul. Vienne felt that only through this *per se*, through this rejection of a mediating form, was a truly substantial unity of man possible, and only could the *unio personalis* in Christ be maintained. Thus, we must conclude that Vienne in its statement on the soul as the form of the body clearly did not mean to affirm dualism, but rather to reject it.[64]

It is not a hylomorphic view of human nature as such that has dualistic tendencies because on this view the soul is the form of the body. The Catholic Church used a hylomorphic concept to affirm what the Church actually meant to assert, namely, the unity of human nature. This point was made by the *nouvelle théologie*. Still, Berkouwer correctly adds that the problem with Catholic anthropology cannot simply be "reduced to an attempt to maintain this unity."[65] Critics, such as Dooyeweerd, take the substance-concept in Thomist anthropology to be the problem.

No matter how far one was willing to go along with the Aristotelian conception concerning the "soul" as the substantial form of the material body, one shrank back from abandoning the "independence" of the body vis-à-vis the soul and of the soul vis-à-

---

[64] Berkouwer, *De Mens Het Beeld Gods*, 241–2 [219–20].
[65] Berkouwer, *De Mens Het Beeld Gods*, 244 [221].

vis the body. Church dogma confessed to the continued existence of the soul after the shedding of the body, and the resurrection of the latter. When thought through within the metaphysical framework of the substance-concept, this dogma therefore had to lead in pre-Thomist scholasticism to the doctrine of the two "independent" entities. With this, however, scholastic philosophy landed in a veritable maze of contradictions.[66]

Dooyeweerd argues, as I shall show below, that there is a contradiction between holding that the soul is an intellectual substance and, at one and the same time, the form of a body. The dualistic tendency, then, arises from considering the soul as both a substance and a form, that is, in itself, a substance, and with respect to the body a form. Thus, Catholic anthropology, such as Aquinas's view, maintains that "the human soul, besides being the form of the body, is a substance in its own right."[67] That is, Gilson rightly describes the soul being a substance as "a self-subsisting immaterial reality endowed with its own essence and its own act of being [*esse*]."[68] As the Council of Vienne states about the confessional status of this truth about substance (Denzinger, §902):

> We reject as erroneous and contrary to the truth of the Catholic faith any doctrine or opinion that rashly asserts that *the substance of the rational and intellectual soul is not truly and of itself the form of the human body or that calls this into doubt* (emphasis added).

---

[66] Dooyeweerd, *Reformation and Scholasticism in Philosophy*, II, 392.

[67] Etienne Gilson, *Elements of Christian Philosophy*, Part IV, (Garden City, NY: Doubleday & Company, 1960), "Man," Chapter 9, "The Human Soul," 203–19, and at 206.

[68] Gilson, *Elements of Christian Philosophy*, 207.

Also, the Fifth Lateran Council repeats the same claim (Denzinger, §1440):

> The intellectual soul is not only truly, of itself and essentially, the form of the human body, as it is stated in the canon of Clement V, Our predecessor of blessed memory, issued by the Council of Vienne [§902], but it is also immortal and according to the great number of bodies into which it is individually infused, it can be, and is multiplied.

The dilemma here is: affirming the substance of the soul in its own right, jeopardizes the unity of man; and affirming the soul as the form of the body, risks losing the substantiality of the soul and hence its personal immortality.[69] Dooyeweerd critically comments: "This 'problem' did not exist for Thomas' Greek teacher. For Aristotle, the *anima rationalis* is merely the 'form of the material body', not a substance (*ousia*). It can therefore not exist apart from the body; it perishes with it."[70] This dilemma is insoluble, according to Dooyeweerd, obstructing the way to a philosophical anthropology affirming the concrete unity of human nature.

Hence, we cannot extricate the emphasis on unity from the substance-concept, meaning thereby not merely that the soul is the form of the body but also that the soul is a substance in its own right. This extrication would be, says Berkouwer, "a striking simplification [e.g., by the

---

[69] Gilson, *The Spirit of Medieval Philosophy*, 176, and *Elements of Christian Philosophy*, 204. See also, Anton C. Pegis, *St. Thomas and the Problem of the Soul in the Thirteenth Century* (Toronto, Ontario: Pontifical Institute of Mediaeval Studies, 1978 [1934]).

[70] Dooyeweerd, *Reformation and Scholasticism in Philosophy*, II, 343.

nouvelle théologie] that it becomes meaningful to ask whether then the whole history of the doctrinal authority of the Catholic Church, and the official use of various philosophical ideas, should not be completely rewritten."[71] No, that history need not be rewritten once we understand that the issue before us is how can we safeguard "the substantial character of the soul and its radical independence of the body"[72] without endangering the unity of man.[73] Cardinal Eijk asks:

> If the human being consists of spirit and body, the question arises as to how we can explain this unity without falling into a dualism. How can these two principles constitute a single being, a unity?[74]

He explains:

> We can find an answer to this only by viewing the spiritual dimension and the material dimension as two principles that together constitute the human being. This is the classical metaphysical view of the human person, as developed by Aristotle and Thomas Aquinas, [[75]] by means of the thesis that the human being is constituted by the human soul as substantial form and that matter that by the soul, as substantial form, has shaped into a human body.[76]

---

[71] Berkouwer, *De Mens Het Beeld Gods*, 244 [221].
[72] Pegis, *St. Thomas and the Problem of the Soul in the Thirteenth Century*, 121.
[73] Gilson, *Elements of Christian Philosophy*, 209.
[74] Eijk, *De Band van de Liefde*, 84.
[75] On the soul as "forma subsistens," see Aquinas, *Summa Theologiae* I, 75, 2.
[76] *De Band van de Liefde*, 84.

In other words, Eijk elaborates:

> Its connection with the body is not a degradation [humiliation] for the soul, for this is thereby the *forma subsistens* of nature directed toward matter. That the body is shaped by a spiritual principle does, however, signify an elevation of the body. . . . It is important to realize that if the soul forms matter into the human body, it also forms matter into human sexual organs. . . . The human sexual organs, shaped by the soul, are therefore not comparable to those of the animals. This comparison would be possible only within a purely biological-materialistic view of humanity. Because the human sexual organs, like the body as a whole, are shaped by the soul, they possess a specifically human and therefore also a moral value. Like the body as a whole, the sexual organs share in the intrinsic dignity of the human person. They are an intrinsic dimension of the human person and therefore are always more than merely instrumental in value.[77]

Cardinal Eijk gives an illuminating account of the unity of man as body and soul. But how does he safeguard, as we asked above, "the substantial character of the soul and its radical independence of the body"[78] We return to this question below.

We turn now to Dooyeweerd's own anthropology, and his critique of Catholic anthropology, particularly the substance-concept in Thomist

---

[77] *De Band van de Liefde*, 84-6.
[78] Pegis, *St. Thomas and the Problem of the Soul in the Thirteenth Century*, 121.

anthropology.[79] Following that, we turn to a discussion of Christian personalism in Wojtyla's Christian anthropology.

Individuality Structure That is Man

Berkouwer, wrote clearly and emphatically on the matter of the place of the human body in Christian anthropology.

> The New Testament community is to strive towards the full reality of man: "glorify God therefore in your body" (1 Cor 6:20). Though Scripture gives us no exposition of the nature of all the relationships of man, the whole Scriptural witness deals with the whole man in the actuality of his existence. … But we can never see man from the Biblical viewpoint as long as we abstract the

---

[79] In *Reformation and Scholasticism in Philosophy*, II, Dooyeweerd also criticizes the predominant role of the substance-concept in Reformed Scholasticism. "This is true despite the fact that our theologians try to accommodate it [substance-concept] to the reformational line of thought" (271). He adds, "Given that Reformed Scholasticism rejected this Roman Catholicism dogma [i.e., transubstantiation], it is the more astonishing that it blithely took over the Thomist substance-concept 'for theological usage'. Without question, here too it was utilized in order to find a 'metaphysical basis' for certain doctrines of the Christian faith, such as the resurrection of the body and the continuous existence of the soul after it has shed the body" (310). "[G.H.H.W.J.] Geesink and [Herman] Bavinck, too, adopted the Thomist conceptions from first to last. What strikes us especially is their rejection of the Augustinian-Franciscan concept of the 'plurality' of the substantial forms' and their acceptance of the Aristotelian-Thomist view of the unity of the substantial form of human nature in the '*anima rationalis*', which they also adopted *in toto* in their elaboration of the psycho-creationist standpoint" (431). For an account of the disputes at the Free University regarding Dooyeweerd's critique of the substance ontology in Reformed Scholasticism, see Marcel E. Verburg, *Herman Dooyeweerd: The Life and Work of a Christian Philosopher*, Translated and edited by Herbert Donald Morton and Harry Van Dyke (Jordan Station, Ontario: Paideia Press, 2015), 229–59.

"real man" from his bodily existence. ... [Thus] we may never justify an anthropology which would assert a special relation of sin to bodiliness, and which would separate salvation and resurrection from bodiliness. ... Scripture does not at all view man's bodiliness as something secondary; rather the moment one devalues the body, one has "deactualized" man's whole reality as a creature of God.[80]

Lastly, then, in this biblical light, we consider the structures of individuality, the typical structure of an individual whole, even with respect to a human being, who is only one, a whole one, functioning as a subject in all the modal law-spheres. Dooyeweerd states, "The thing-structure is the meaning-individual structure of cosmic reality."[81] Thus: "Does man also possess a thing-structure, and, if so, what then distinguishes man from other things?"[82] The individual bodily existence, says Dooyeweerd, this whole, "which we call the human body, can likewise not be classified among the thing structures, as it is indissolubly connected to the human soul or spirit (in the sense of religious root of life)."[83] In this connection, Dooyeweerd argues that plants and animals, too, are not "things," meaning thereby "inanimate objects and matters." In sum, "plants, animals and men are referred to as 'beings' or 'creatures'." He adds, "But both

---

[80] Berkouwer, *De Mens Het Beeld Gods*, 255–6. ET: 230–1. This, too, is the view of Berkouwer's fellow countryman and great Reformed New Testament theologian and biblical scholar in his own right, Herman Ridderbos (1909–2007) in his book, *Paulus*, 133: "[T]he body represents not merely a certain constituent part of man [in distinction from the soul], but rather man himself in his concrete corporeal mode of existence." ET: 125.

[81] Herman Dooyeweerd, *The Crisis in the Humanistic Political Theory*, Collected Works, Series B, Vol. 7, ed. D.F.M. Strauss (Grand Rapids, MI: Paideia Press, 2010 [1931]), 92.

[82] Dooyeweerd, *Reformation and Scholasticism in Philosophy*, III, 221.

[83] Dooyeweerd, *Reformation and Scholasticism in Philosophy*, VI, 263.

things and *living beings* are sharply distinguished from all other temporal individualities according to their reality status. Exactly what accounts for this ontic difference?"[84] Dooyeweerd explains this ontic difference:

> In the case of the animal, however, we cannot speak of a real act-structure because it is not a subject in the normative aspects of reality, and above all because it has no *spiritual act-center*. ... The animal has no concept of language, logic, or culture, nor any other normative subject-function. Certainly we cannot deny some *sensory* "intelligence" to the more highly developed animals. ... However, "sensory intelligence" remains a sensitive function in an undisclosed sense. It moves within the narrow boundaries of an only more highly differentiated psychical corporal individuality-structure. It is based on sensitive fantasy, which pre-senses the causal-purposeful relationship between two things in its sensory imagination. It even lacks the sensorily bound conceptual representation of the causal relationship such as we [man] form in our pre-scientific thinking. In animals, distinction and knowledge remain limited to their biotic and sensitive environment. They serve the instinctive biotic urges, also insofar as they cannot be explained by knowledge. ... Identification of properties, which is the essence of logical analysis, is altogether lacking both in animal intelligence and in instinctual distinction.[85]

Dooyeweerd implicitly alludes here to a point made by the Hungarian/British polymath, Michael Polanyi (1891–1976), when contrasting

---

[84] Dooyeweerd, *Reformation and Scholasticism in Philosophy*, VI, 263.
[85] Dooyeweerd, *Reformation and Scholasticism in Philosophy*, III, 159, 160, 161.

the mental development of a child and a chimpanzee at the age of 15 to 18 months. In that period, states Polanyi,

> the mental development of the chimpanzee is nearing completion; that of the child is only about to start. By responding to people who talk to it, the child soon begins to understand speech and to speak itself. By this one single trick in which it surpasses the animal, the child acquires the capacity for sustained thought and enters on the whole cultural heritage of its ancestors.[86]

Regarding the individual human being, then, Dooyeweerd assigns subject-functions in the logical and post-logical aspects of the temporal reality to the entire human body. "[T]he human spirit cannot carry out any real acts outside its temporal corporal individuality-structure. For that reason, we said: it is *the individual human being* in the integral unity of "body" and "soul" who accomplishes the acts. The full person is the subject of the act."[87] In particular, says Dooyeweerd, "The human body, therefore, is not to be conceived as an abstract material body, but as the whole of man's temporal existence, which receives its deeper unity only

---

[86] Michael Polanyi, *Personal Knowledge: Towards a Post-Critical Philosophy*, Gifford Lectures 1951–52 (New York: Harper & Row, 1964 [1958]), 69. Polanyi made important theoretical contributions to physical chemistry, economics, human sciences, and philosophy. See also, Herman Dooyeweerd, "Creation and Evolution," in *Philosophia Reformata* 24 (1959): 113–59, "Man cannot be understood starting from the animal, but, conversely, the animal can only be understood starting from man, because it is only within the act-structure of the human body that the latter's animal sub-structure can disclose its relation to our inner acts and can therefore be known to us."

[87] Dooyeweerd, *Reformation and Scholasticism in Philosophy*, III, 162.

by virtue of its concentration in the 'soul'."[88] The whole man functions as a subject in the full array of modal spheres. In sum:

> The numerical sphere of discrete quantity serves as the foundation of the spatial sphere of continuous, dimensional extension. The latter founds the kinematic sphere that lies at the foundation of the biotic sphere. This sphere forms the foundation of the sensory function of consciousness, which provides the foundation for the analytical sphere of logical thinking. The analytical sphere lies at the foundation of the historical sphere of cultural development, which in turn founds the lingual sphere of symbolical signification. That sphere is the basis for the social sphere of sociability and interaction, which itself is the basis for the economic sphere of the frugal balancing of values. The economic sphere in turn founds the aesthetic sphere of beautiful harmony, which founds the jural sphere of retribution. The jural sphere lies at the basis of the moral sphere of the disposition of love, which lies at the basis of the temporal sphere of faith.[89]

Human acts, then, function in all aspects of reality.

> In the acts, the "soul" is actually operative in the entire enkaptic structure of the body, and only in the body does the soul have the capacity to do so, insofar as the acts are included in the temporal order of the body. In other words, we can take the "acts" neither to be purely "corporeal" nor purely "spiritual." They are

---

[88] Herman Dooyeweerd, *The Theory of Man: 32 Propositions on Anthropology*, Proposition IX. https://jgfriesen.files.wordpress.com/2016/12/32 propositions.pdf.

[89] Dooyeweerd, *The Crisis in the Humanistic Political Theory*, 80.

both inseparably connected and properly for that reason they bear a *typically human* character.⁹⁰

What gives these bodily acts their typically human character? Dooyeweerd replies, "Only the act-structure *in its fundamental dependence upon the spirit* stamps the body as human. Viewed from the *temporal* order, the human body is the bearer of the acts: viewed from the *spiritual, religious* order, it is the human soul or spirit."⁹¹ Dooyeweerd makes clear that he does not use these terms as a contrast to the material body. He explains, "The logical and post-logical functions [for example, juridical, ethical, cultural, lingual] of our temporal existence are not 'spiritual'; they function in the temporal body structure of human existence. But they are, along with all other modal functions, *concentrated* in the *spirit* or *soul*. This spirit or soul involves the spiritual root, and the modal functions are its temporal ramifications."⁹² In other words, this multi-dimensional functionings of man are all manifestations of the one same, individual subject. "It is the entire person, and not merely [his] 'soul', which thinks, wills, imagines or judges."⁹³

What, then, is the enkaptic structure of the human body? Dooyeweerd refers to the individuality-structures of the human body: a typical physico-chemical qualification, a typically biotic qualification, a typically psychic qualification, and a fourth individuality-structure, which Dooyeweerd calls "the *individuality-structure of the human acts* or *act-individuality structure of the body*."⁹⁴ How, then, does Dooyeweerd construe the enkaptic structural whole of the human body

---

⁹⁰ Dooyeweerd, *Reformation and Scholasticism in Philosophy*, III, 163.
⁹¹ Dooyeweerd, *Reformation and Scholasticism in Philosophy*, III, 163.
⁹² Dooyeweerd, *Reformation and Scholasticism in Philosophy*, III, 140.
⁹³ Dooyeweerd, *Reformation and Scholasticism in Philosophy*, III, 152.
⁹⁴ Dooyeweerd, *Reformation and Scholasticism in Philosophy*, III, 148.

and the person? He replies:

> If this body is indeed an enkaptic rather than a simple structural whole, then the lower individuality-structures can only participate in the intrinsic unity of the human body through their being bound within the highest individuality-structure.[95]

Dooyeweerd distinguishes the relationship between these individuality-structures from a part-whole relation. "Enkapsis expresses much rather an interwovenness of individuality-structures that cannot be qualified as the relation of a whole and its parts."[96] In other words, explains Dooyeweerd,

> The lower individuality-structures do not become *parts* of the highest individuality-structure in this way, for they are only parts of the enkaptic whole. But the structural whole builds itself up only in the binding of all lower individuality-structures within the highest one. According to their internal sphere sovereignty, i.e., viewed apart from the enkapsis, the lower individuality-structures are not really parts of, but merely the necessary *substrates* for, *the highest corporal individuality structure.*[97]

Bernard Lonergan, SJ, defines sublation helping us to construe the enkaptic structural whole of the human body. "What sublates goes beyond what is sublated, introduces something new and distinct, yet so far from interfering with the sublated or destroying it, on the contrary needs it, includes it, preserves all its proper features and properties, and carries

---

[95] Dooyeweerd, *Reformation and Scholasticism in Philosophy*, III, 147.
[96] Dooyeweerd, *Reformation and Scholasticism in Philosophy*, III, 112.
[97] Dooyeweerd, *Reformation and Scholasticism in Philosophy*, III, 146.

them forward to a fuller realization within a richer context."[98] The highest corporal individuality structure refers to the "the individuality-structure of the human acts or act-individuality structure of the body." He explains: "By the word 'acts'—differentiated in their basic dimensions of knowing, imagining and willing—I understand those activities which issue from the human selfhood but function within the enkaptic body individuality-structure."[99] The lowest individuality-structure of the human body is the physico-chemical qualification. Dooyeweerd explains:

> It consists of atomic compounds, which as such, i.e., outside the actual enkapsis, cannot yet be called a corporal individuality-structure. We can only call them so in their enkaptic binding within the next individuality-structures within the physical body. This individuality-structure, which forms the substratum for all the succeeding ones, liberates itself out of the enkaptic morphological binding during the corruption process of corporal death. This is, however, at the same time its end as a corporal individuality-structure.[100]

Furthermore, adds Dooyeweerd, the second individuality of the enkaptic body individuality-structure is of a *typically biotic qualification*. Dooyeweerd explains:

> In its internal sphere-sovereignty it governs the vegetative body processes insofar as these do not fall under the typical guidance of the sensitive function and of the latter (normative) functions. It is only in individuality-structure that the living cells and other

---

[98] Lonergan, *Method in Theology*, 241.
[99] Dooyeweerd, *Reformation and Scholasticism in Philosophy*, III, 148.
[100] Dooyeweerd, *Reformation and Scholasticism in Philosophy*, III, 147.

biotically qualified structures make their appearance. It provides the vegetative substratum for both of the subsequent individuality-structures. It governs the so-called autonomous nervous system with the muscular and glandular tissues insofar as they are innervated by this system; the so-called smooth muscles of the eye, the hair, the bronchi, the intestines and the striated muscles of the heart.[101]

This is not yet to be seen as a human corporal individuality-structure. The new enkaptic binding within a third individuality-structure is a typically qualified sensitive function. Dooyeweerd explains:

In its internal sphere-sovereignty this third individuality-structure dominates those functions of the sensory and motor nervous system—particularly those of the brain (the sensory brain), the spinal cord, and the gland system (including the endocrine glands) which in their being typically directed by the subjective sensitive function fall outside the domination by a person's acts of will, at least up to a certain point.[102]

The fourth individuality-structure, sublating the previous individuality-structures, Dooyeweerd calls the highest individual-ity-structure of the person, namely, "the *individuality-structure of the human acts* or *act-individuality-structure of the human body*."[103] The previous three individuality-structures must be seen in connection with this structure so

---

[101] Dooyeweerd, *Reformation and Scholasticism in Philosophy*, III, 147–8.
[102] Dooyeweerd, *Reformation and Scholasticism in Philosophy*, III, 148.
[103] Dooyeweerd, *Reformation and Scholasticism in Philosophy*, III, 148.

that it might be considered as "essential parts of the enkaptically structured whole called the 'human body'."[104] Thus, given the sublated individuality-structures, Dooyeweerd's anthropology of man and woman includes not only a biological dimension, but also the anatomic, reproductive, genetic, and molecular dimensions. Dooyeweerd explains the meaning of the act-individuality structure of the human body.

> By the word "acts"—differentiated in their basic dimensions of knowing, imagining, and willing—I understand those activities which issue from the human selfhood but function within the enkaptic body individuality-structure. Through them, one orients oneself *intentionally* (i.e., with a purpose) towards states of affairs in temporal reality—or in the world of one's imagination—under the guidance of normative points of view. One internalizes these intentional (or intended) states of affairs by relating them to one's *I-ness*. Their "innerness" is involved in the intentional character of the "acts." Only the action realizes the intention of the act. In this realization, the acts of knowing, imagining and willing are intertwined with the motivated process of decision-making, and then the decision is converted into the action. ... The action has an external causality.[105]

---

[104] Dooyeweerd, *The Theory of Man*, Proposition XI.

[105] Dooyeweerd, *Reformation and Scholasticism in Philosophy*, III, 148–9. Dooyeweerd, *Reformation and Scholasticism in Philosophy*, II, 417, "Not a single human act of thinking can exist in which the human body as a temporal whole is not active in all its aspects. Not a single 'act' is given to us in human experience otherwise than in this concrete coherence of reality. If this be the case, then we must be able to point at an individuality structure also in the human body that makes the theoretical act of thinking possible and within which alone it can operate. ... [T]his individuality structure is called the act-structure of the human body."

According to Dooyeweerd, then, cognitive acts, for example, function within the enkaptic body individuality-structure, meaning thereby in all aspects of temporal reality, for the entire body is internally active in those acts.[106] Regarding the exceptional act-structure of the human body, Dooyeweerd argues that the ultimate structure, the act-structure, of the human body is an undifferentiated one.

> The human body has no differentiated qualifying function in a modal aspect of temporal reality, since in its act-structure it must retain a field of free self-expression for the soul or spirit, which transcends all temporal structures of reality as the religious root of human existence.[107]

In his early writings, for example in 1937, Dooyeweerd held that the act-structure of the human body was "a *pistically* (i.e., by the function of faith) *qualified body*."[108] But by 1942, Dooyeweerd reverses his view, now arguing that the "act-structure that is decisive for the human body ... is not qualified, not even by a normative function."[109] If I understand Dooyeweerd correctly, there are two reasons why he came to find this view untenable. If faith qualified all human acts, then all acts, historical, social, juridical, ethical, would "necessarily bear the character of *typical faith* acts." But then we would be unable to account for the differentiated character of human acts. For example, says Dooyeweerd, "A theoretical

---

[106] Dooyeweerd, *Reformation and Scholasticism in Philosophy*, III, 171.

[107] Dooyeweerd, *Reformation and Scholasticism in Philosophy*, VI, 341n1.

[108] Dooyeweerd, "The Significance of the Philosophy of the Law Idea for the Theory of Human Society," 119.

[109] Dooyeweerd, "The Significance of the Philosophy of the Law Idea for the Theory of Human Society," 119n7.

thought-act ... is of a typically *scientific* qualification through its theoretical-logical function. This does not mean ... that it is exhausted in this function, but rather that it functions in *all* aspects of reality without exception."[110] There is an even more significant reason why the act-structure of the human body is undifferentiated one. Dooyeweerd holds that acts of the human body are ordered to the heart of man, which is "the spiritual-religious center of a person's entire temporal existence, which participates in the religious root-community of the human race."[111] In particular, according to Dooyeweerd,[112] religion is the "*ex-sistent* condition [of the heart], ... the mode of being of the ego itself ... and it is nothing *in itself*. Veritable religion is absolute *self-surrender*." In a passage I quoted earlier, Dooyeweerd elaborates:

> [T]rue self-*knowledge* discovers the ex-sistent character of the selfhood also in the fact that the ego is centrally bound with other egos in a religious community. The central and radical unity of our existence is at the same time individual and supra-individual; that is to say, in the individual I-ness it *points beyond* the individual ego toward that which makes the whole of mankind spiritually *one in root* in its creation, fall and redemption. According to our Christian faith, all humanity is spiritually included in Adam. In him the whole human race has fallen and in mankind also the entire temporal cosmos, which was concentrated in it. In Jesus Christ, the entire *new* humanity is one in root, as the members of one body. Our I-ness is, in other words, rooted in the spiritual community of mankind. It is no self-sufficient "substance," no "windowless monad," but it lives in the

---

[110] Dooyeweerd, *Reformation and Scholasticism in Philosophy*, III, 176.
[111] Dooyeweerd, *Reformation and Scholasticism in Philosophy*, III, 166.
[112] Dooyeweerd, *A New Critique of Theoretical Thought*, I, 58.

Ch. 2: Christian Anthropology, the Unity of Human Nature... 167

spiritual community of the *we*, which is directed to a Divine *Thou*, according to the original meaning of creation.[113]

In short, adds Dooyeweerd, regarding the transcendent condition of our knowledge he returns to the religious root-community of the human race, "In a transcendent sense the horizon enclosing all human experience is formed by the communal structure of the religious root of human existence."[114]

Furthermore, Dooyeweerd avoids "materialism" and "idealism" regarding his philosophy of man. In regard to idealism, Dooyeweerd is decidedly anti-Cartesian and hence anti-modernist in his epistemology since he does not isolate the individual human being from the rest of the world. In other words, he does not take the individual to be an enclosed consciousness in which the ideas in the mind of the isolated thinking subject are the starting point from which we infer what the state of affairs, the real world, must be like.[115]

All acts issue from the indivisible center of human existence, from the spirit or the soul in its religious unity, in which the human I-ness is seated. All acts are oriented upon the I. ... The acts themselves, however, do function within the temporal order of reality. They possess modalities in the various aspects, they have various modal subject-functions in them, and within this temporal differentiation they can be enacted in a person's corporal existence. It is the entire person, and not merely [his] "soul," which thinks, wills, imagines or judges.[116]

---

[113] Dooyeweerd, *A New Critique of Theoretical Thought*, I, 60.
[114] Dooyeweerd, A New Critique of Theoretical Thought, I, 552.
[115] Dooyeweerd, *Reformation and Scholasticism in Philosophy*, III, 164.
[116] Dooyeweerd, *Reformation and Scholasticism in Philosophy*, III, 152.

Indeed, Dooyeweerd makes clear that the human body as such is "not identical with an abstract 'physico-psychical soma'; it is the structural whole of temporal human existence in the intermodal coherence of all its modal aspects."[117] (*NC* II, 147).

Moreover, Dooyeweerd makes clear that his anthropology steers clear of a materialist view of the person's cognitive states of mind—such as knowing—or a purely "immaterial" characterization of such states. On the one hand, it is not merely his "soul" that thinks or judges; on the other hand, "we cannot say that the human 'body' thinks, wants, imagines."[118] Regarding the latter materialist view, it leads to the denial of "all logical and post-logical subjectivity to the body. ... But this view, if consistently worked out, must also deny the biotic and psychical subjectivity of the body. For these functions do not fit in the abstract view of the pure 'material body' either."[119] He subjectively functions in various aspects, including various modal subject functions, and that characterizes the entire person. That is, human knowing, which includes thinking and sensing, is always full-fledged bodily human action. On the one hand, Dooyeweerd purports to steer clear of both in the following argument. He explains:

> The "acts" such as knowing, willing, desiring, imagining, remembering, etc., which appear to operate even within the sphere of the unconscious or subconscious, do not, as modern phenomenology teaches, differ from the outwardly, projected actions in that they are merely "intentionally" oriented towards

---

[117] Dooyeweerd, *A New Critique of Theoretical Thought*, II, 147.
[118] Dooyeweerd, *Reformation and Scholasticism in Philosophy*, III, 162.
[119] Dooyeweerd, *Reformation and Scholasticism in Philosophy*, III, 162, and 163.

corporal reality *without possessing a corporal character themselves.* For the acts are, according to their entire structure of expression, *within* temporal reality, and our entire body is *internally active* in them, also in its physico-chemically qualified substrate. No act of knowing, willing, desiring, imagining or any other is possible without energy consumption. The "acts" function in *all* aspects of temporal reality, and not just in the sensitive and subsequent aspects.[120]

Dooyeweerd concludes, "It is therefore necessary to assign *subject-functions* in the logical and post-logical aspects [ethical, jural, cultural, lingual, confessional] of temporal reality to the entire body in the act-structure."[121] In sum, according to Dooyeweerd, and John Paul II as well, "The full person as a totality is the subject of the act."[122] The latter writes: "Man is a subject not only by his self-consciousness and by self-determination, but also based on his own body. *The structure of the body is such that it permits him to be the author of genuinely human activity.* In this activity, the body expresses the person."[123] I will turn to the philosophical anthropology of Karol Wojtyla/John Paul II in Chapter 4.

Dooyeweerd's Critique of the Substance-Concept in Thomist Anthropology

We get a fuller picture of Dooyeweerd's critique of Thomist anthropology when we consider his claim that "Thomist scholasticism took

---

[120] Dooyeweerd, *Reformation and Scholasticism in Philosophy*, III, 171–2.
[121] Dooyeweerd, *Reformation and Scholasticism in Philosophy*, III, 162.
[122] Dooyeweerd, *Reformation and Scholasticism in Philosophy*, III, 152.
[123] John Paul II, *Man and Woman He Created Them*, 7.2. See also, John Paul II, *Veritatis Splendor*, §§48–50.

over the Aristotelian view regarding the principle of individuation," namely, matter is the principle of individuation of the soul, of individual human differences, indeed, being numerically distinct. Here is, according to Dooyeweerd, the root of the "antinomy between [Thomism's] view of individuality and the church dogma concerning the individual survival of the human soul. ... This antinomy caused scholastic theology—insofar as it followed Thomas' conception—no small embarrassment." Now, according to Dooyeweerd, Aristotle held matter to be the *principium individuationis*, and hence the form of the body, which is the soul, cannot be individual by itself, a substance in its own right. In other words, on the one hand, "If the *principium individuationis* for the 'rational nature' of man stems from 'matter'—in this case, from the 'material body'—how could one maintain the continued existence of an individual 'anima rationalis' as a substance after its separation from the material body?"[124] On the other hand, if the soul is merely the form of the body, then its existence would not be independent of matter and it would cease to exist once the body did.[125] Although this may be the Aristotelian view of the soul, it is inconsistent with the Church's teaching regarding personal immortality, that is, the individual immortality of the soul.

Thomas Aquinas's attempt to resolve this difficulty was, claims Dooyeweerd, "more ingenious that convincing."[126] He adapts the doc-

---

[124] Dooyeweerd, *Reformation and Scholasticism in Philosophy*, II, 342–3.

[125] A.G. Sertillanges, O.P., *The Foundations of Thomistic Philosophy*, translated from the French by Godfrey Anstruther, O.P. (Providence, RI: CLUNY, 2020), 184.

[126] Dooyeweerd, *Reformation and Scholasticism in Philosophy*, II, 344.

Ch. 2: Christian Anthropology, the Unity of Human Nature… 171

trine of creation to a "psycho-creationist theory" in which the soul is immediately created by God.[127] Dooyeweerd elaborates, "Psycho-creationism has the *anima rationalis* emerge through a separate creative act of God in a previously formed *corpus organicum*. This required that the material body must be viewed as an 'independent entity' vis-à-vis the 'rational soul'."[128] On this view, the rational soul is independent of the material body, "can exist by itself as a 'spiritual', albeit 'incomplete', substance."[129] Although the soul is a substance, existing in its own right, its separation from its body means that it is not a complete substance.[130] This position distinguishes Thomas from the Platonic tradition. As Pegis describes the "two conditions which every substance must fulfill":

> In order to be a substance, a being must be both subsistent and complete. The soul fulfills only one of these requirements. It is subsistent, being capable of acting within itself, and to this extent can be called a *hoc aliquid*. But the soul is not the complete nature of man, and therefore man cannot be called a soul. Furthermore, since the soul, though subsistent, is nevertheless an incomplete nature, it is not composed of matter and form. To consider the soul as the complete nature of man or to hold that it is composed of matter and form is really to leave unexplained the union of soul and body.[131]

---

[127] Dooyeweerd, *Reformation and Scholasticism in Philosophy*, II, 344–5, 346, 348. For a critical discussion from a biblical theological standpoint of "psycho-creationism," see Berkouwer, *De Mens Het Beeld Gods*, 311–45 [278–309].

[128] Dooyeweerd, *Reformation and Scholasticism in Philosophy*, II, 396.

[129] Dooyeweerd, *Reformation and Scholasticism in Philosophy*, II, 344.

[130] Pegis, *St. Thomas and the Problem of the Soul in the Thirteenth Century*, 183.

[131] Pegis, *St. Thomas and the Problem of the Soul in the Thirteenth Century*, 184–5.

Dooyeweerd, then, turns to the real issue for Thomas, namely, the soul is necessarily the substantial form of the body and the manner and form of the union of soul and body. He responds, "Consequently God must have created it [the soul] separately, and it must still be created separately in the body. As well, since the rational soul by its very nature is the substantial form of the material body, God must have created it within a body suited to it."[132] In other words, says Dooyeweerd, "the soul is created as the form of the body with a view to an individual body."[133] This soul is a numerically distinct individual, individuated by virtue of its relation to the material body, having been called into being "in and for the body," says Dooyewe-erd, "according to the measure of the body."[134] Hence, human souls not only numerically differ from one another, but also have a material cause. Significantly, Dooyeweerd grasps the difference between individuality and individuation. The former is not caused by the quantitative matter of bodies, dimensional extension, place and time, "but is merely produced by God Himself in accordance with the numerical specifics of the bodies."[135] Thus, the soul "possesses," says Dooyeweerd, "'absolute being' (i.e., a 'being' independent of the body) in which it has acquired its individuality, this 'being' always remains individual."[136] Indeed, "after the body perishes, the soul nevertheless retains this measure and adaptation to this body. In a certain sense it remains individualized through 'matter', even though it is no longer

---

[132] Dooyeweerd, *Reformation and Scholasticism in Philosophy*, II, 344.
[133] Dooyeweerd, *Reformation and Scholasticism in Philosophy*, II, 344.
[134] Dooyeweerd, *Reformation and Scholasticism in Philosophy*, II, 347.
[135] Dooyeweerd, *Reformation and Scholasticism in Philosophy*, II, 344–5.
[136] Dooyeweerd, *Reformation and Scholasticism in Philosophy*, II, 345.

Ch. 2: Christian Anthropology, the Unity of Human Nature... 173

connected with the 'material body'."[137] Yet, although as a matter of principle the soul is independent of the body, that is not its purpose, meaning thereby the goal of being united with the body.

Dooyeweerd finds this argument unpersuasive. He argues that, on this view, the soul's relation to the material body would be a *natural relation*, a substantial and not just an accidental union with the body, and this means a retreat to the original Aristotelian conception that has "no room for an '*anima separata*'."[138] He elaborates, "If the human soul is an *anima rationalis* which by nature is 'individualized' in accordance with the material body, then it cannot be a 'substance', but merely a 'substantial form or *actus* of the body."[139] Gilson provides a critical response to Dooyeweerd's assessment of Thomas's anthropology.

As Gilson correctly states regarding the fact that the soul, while subsistent, is not the complete nature of man, "in order to be 'human', it [the soul] needs to be united with the body of a man. ... And, indeed, how could there be a soul where there is no body for it to animate? There is no human soul where there is no man. ... The real substance, fully construed in its own species, is neither the human body nor the human soul; it is *man*."[140] Furthermore, although Dooyeweerd rightly understands that the human soul is the form of a body, according to Thomas, he is mistaken that Thomas has to choose between the soul being a substance and it being the form of man's body. Rather, it is not in spite of being a substance that the soul is the form of its body. Rightly argues Pegis, "the human soul is the form of a body *because* it is the precise kind

---

[137] Dooyeweerd, *Reformation and Scholasticism in Philosophy*, II, 347.
[138] Dooyeweerd, *Reformation and Scholasticism in Philosophy*, II, 351.
[139] Dooyeweerd, *Reformation and Scholasticism in Philosophy*, II, 351.
[140] Gilson, *Elements of Christian Philosophy*, 223.

of substance it is."[141] In other words, "the soul of man is not the form of its body in spite of being a substance; on the contrary, it is *qua* substance that it is form."[142] This is Gilson's rebuttal of Dooyeweerd's objection. This means that "the substantiality of the soul is the very foundation of the substantiality of man."[143] Why? Because it is the substantiality of the soul that is communicated to the matter by the form. The source of the substantiality of the whole man is the form, not the matter.

> In Thomas' own terms, it is the act of being proper to the form that is, by the same token, the act of being of the whole compounded substance, namely, man. The soul, Thomas says, has the being of a substance, and nevertheless it shares its being with the body; more precisely, it receives the body in the communion of its own act of being.[144]

Otherwise, man's whole being would not be one, and the unity of man's nature would be lacking a substantial unity. On the contrary, the soul is the one single act of being for man, namely, "the whole individual human substance, including the form, the matter, and all the individuating accidents."[145] In sum, "while there is no concrete substance without matter, the substantiality of the human composite is not due to the matter, but is that substantiality which is communicated to the matter by the form."[146] With Thomas's emphasis on the concrete substance that is man in the unity of his whole existence, we may now turn to personalism.

---

[141] Pegis, *St. Thomas and the Problem of the Soul in the Thirteenth Century*, 185.

[142] Gilson, *Elements of Christian Philosophy*, 208.

[143] Gilson, *Elements of Christian Philosophy*, 209.

[144] Gilson, *Elements of Christian Philosophy*, 209.

[145] Gilson, *Elements of Christian Philosophy*, 209.

[146] Gilson, *The Spirit of Medieval Philosophy*, 199.

What Is Christian Personalism?

> [I]n contemporary Protestant and Catholic theology today in general, the category of the "person" is strongly stressed. ... to emphasize the central moment of man, the center, from which the whole man unfolds himself. ... This centering of man in his "person" is generally referred to as "personalism," and it is of importance to us, in our reflection on the whole man, to consider exactly what the term means.[147]

Now, we see this personalism at work in Wojtyla's pre-papal philosophical writings, "Thomistic Personalism," "On the Dignity of the Human Person," "The Human Person and Natural Law," and "The Person: Subject and Community," to name just a few of his most significant essays.[148]

Wojtyla states that "Personalism is not primarily a theory of the person or a theoretical science of the person. Its meaning is largely practical and ethical: it is concerned with the person as a subject and object of activity, as a subject of rights, etc."[149] He traces the roots of this personalism to the philosophical theologians of the Patristic period, and especially to Aquinas's doctrine of the person, who in seeking to clarify the mysteries of the Trinity and the Incarnation of the Second Divine Person thoroughly examined the concept of person. In Aquinas's philosophical theology, the concept *persona* plays a crucial role in his treatises on the Trinity and the Incarnation, as well as in his treatise on man. The idea

---

[147] Berkouwer, *De Mens Het Beeld Gods*, 245–6 [223].

[148] All these essays are in Karol Wojtyla, *Person and Community: Selected Essays*, trans. Theresa Sandok, O.S.M. (New York: Peter Lang, 1993), 165–86, 219–62.

[149] Wojtyla, "Thomistic Personalism," in *Person and Community*, 165.

of the person is at the center of Thomistic anthropology. The mystery of the Incarnate Word involves a hypostatic union of two natures, divine and human, distinguishing "a concept of person and an understanding of the relation that occurs between person and nature."[150] In this light, Wojtyla argues that Christian thought distinguished "theological personalism" from "humanistic personalism," with priority being given to the former with, one might say, God being the primary analogate and the human person being the secondary analogate. Wojtyla explains Aquinas's view thusly:

> [W]hatever is a true perfection in the created world must be found in the highest degree in God, and so the person, too, which signifies the highest perfection in the world of creatures, must be realized in an incomparably more perfect degree in God. ... St. Thomas takes precisely this occasion to assert that in the created world the person is the highest perfection: the person is *perfectissimum ens*. And this forms the basis for St. Thomas's conception of a personal God.[151]

Gilson explains admirably well the very point that Wojtyla is making in the above paragraph about the starting-point and basic principle of Christian personalism.

> [H]ow could personality be anything but the mark of being at the very summit of its perfection, in a philosophy like the Christian philosophy where everything is suspended from the creative act of a personal God? For all the things were made by the

---

[150] Wojtyla, "Thomistic Personalism," in *Person and Community*, 166.
[151] Wojtyla, "Thomistic Personalism," in *Person and Community*, 166–7. See Thomas Aquinas's *Summa Theologiae* I, questions 75–6.

Ch. 2: Christian Anthropology, the Unity of Human Nature...

Word, and the Word is with God, and the Word is God; that is to say precisely this being Who presents Himself as personal in virtue of the sole fact that He presents Himself as Being: *Ecce personalis distinctio; Exodi tertio, ego sum qui sum.* Christian personalism also, like the rest, has its roots in the metaphysics of Exodus; we are persons because we are the work of a Person; we participate in His personality even as, being good, we participate in His perfection; being causes, in His creative power; being prudent, in His providence; and, in a word, as beings in His being. To be a person is to participate in one of the highest excellences of the divine being. But then it seems, when that is said, all is said. ... Of all admirable things in nature, says the Greek poet, I know none so admirable as man. But from the opening of the Christian era it is no more of man that we speak of but of the human person: *persona significat id quod est perfectissimum in tota natura* [Aquinas, *Sum. Theol.*, I, 29, 3, Resp.].[152]

Aquinas's philosophical reflections on the concept of the person appear elsewhere in his treatise on man. He draws on Boethius's definition: *persona est rationalis naturae individua substantia*—"the human being is an individual (*individua substantia*) of a rational nature." This means that being a person is different from being an individual member of the

---

[152] Gilson, *The Spirit of Medieval Philosophy*, Chapter IX, "Christian Anthropology," 168–88, and 176; Chapter X, "Christian Personalism," 189–208, and at 204–5, 206. See also, Gilson, *The Spirit of Medieval Philosophy*, 433n9: "Of course we do not maintain that the text of Exodus [3:14] is a revealed metaphysical definition of God; but if there is no metaphysics *in* Exodus there is nevertheless a metaphysics *of* Exodus; and we shall see it developed in due course by the Fathers of the Church, whose indications on this point the mediaeval philosophers merely follow up and exploit." Gilson, *Elements of Christian Philosophy*, Part IV, "Man," Chapter 9, "The Human Soul," 203–19.

human species.[153] As John M. Rist describes this difference, although "persons have a nature," we are "unique subjects," that is, "each of us is a human being in a significantly different way from all others."[154] As Italian philosopher Antonio Malo explains with respect to human sexuality,

> Thus, a study of human sexuality needs to look at both the particular individual of the species *homo sapiens* (the human male or female), and his or her individualization (the personalization of this particular male or female). For although the person can be viewed as an individual member of the human species, his or her individuality is not the same as an animal's. ... [T]his is because the person transcends the individuality of the species through his or her own ontological difference, that is, his or her personal being; for every man and every woman is a unique person.[155]

Garrigou-Lagrange agrees. He, too, distinguishes "person" and "things." "The person is a rational and free being, the master of his acts, independent, *sui iuris*, as opposed to the animal, the plant, and the mineral." Furthermore, the selfhood of the human person is a substance, but a unique sort of substance. Garrigou-Lagrange adds, "for prior to phenomena and to becoming, there is the *being* that appears and changes

---

[153] See Robert Sokolowski, *Eucharistic Presence, A Study in the Theology of Disclosure* (Washington, D.C.: Catholic University of America Press, 1994), 119.

[154] John M. Rist, *What Is a Person? Realities, Constructs, Illusions* (Cambridge: Cambridge University Press, 2020), 64.

[155] Antonio Malo, *Transcending Gender Ideology: A Philosophy of Sexual Difference*, trans. Alice Pavey, Foreword by John M. Rist (Washington, DC: Catholic University Press, 2020), 25.

appearance."[156] Moreover, we distinguish between "person and nature." He elaborates:

> Everyone says, "my arm, my body, my soul, my intellect, my will, my resolution," meaning thereby: "the arm that is *mine*, the soul and body that are *mine*." Everyone says again, "*I* run, *I* think." In this way, we contrast to a *self*, to one and the same self, everything else that we attribute to it: our spiritual and bodily nature, our existence, our faculties, our acts. The self is already, for common sense, the first subject of attribution that cannot itself be attributed. ... Therefore, the person is a whole composed of essential and permanent elements, as well as passing elements, and it is to this whole and not to its parts that we attribute existence and action. ... The person is a whole existing or subsisting separately, *that which* exists, *that which* acts, whereas the nature is *that by which* this whole is essentially constituted, the intellect *that by which* it emits acts of knowledge, and so.[157]

The "person" is strongly stressed here, according to Garrigou-Lagrange, as the central moment of man, the unity of human nature, the center from which the various aspects of the whole man unfold. This, too, is personalism.

Significantly for our reflections here in Aquinas's personalism, Aquinas draws on his theological reflections on the Trinity and the Incarnation, concluding that "a rational nature does not possess its own subsistence as a nature, but subsists in a person." What is a person, according to Aquinas?

---

[156] Garrigou-Lagrange, *Thomistic Common Sense*, 262.
[157] Garrigou-Lagrange, *Thomistic Common Sense*, 262–3.

In a more special and perfect way, the particular and the individual are found in the rational substance which have dominion over their own actions; and which are not only made to act like others, but which can act of themselves; for actions belong to singulars. Therefore, also the individuals of the rational nature have a special name even among other substances; and this name is "person."[158]

In other words, Wojtyla elaborates:

The person is a subsistent subject of existence and action—which can in no way be said of a rational nature. That is why God must be a personal being. In the visible world, every human being is such a created being. St. Thomas says that this being is objectively the most perfect being. Its perfection is undeniably the result of its rational, and thus spiritual, nature, which finds its natural complement in freedom. ... The person, therefore, is always a rational and free concrete being, capable of all those activities that reason and freedom alone make possible.[159]

Furthermore, in Aquinas's treatise on man he adopts a hylomorphic view, regarding man as a composition of matter and form. Says Aquinas, "[M]an is not a mere soul, nor a mere body; but both soul and body."[160] This means that man is not two substances of body and soul, but rather a substantial unity of "two inseparable elements of one and the same

---

[158] Aquinas, *Summa Theologiae* I, q. 29, a. 1, as cited in Rist, *What Is a Person?*, 64.

[159] Wojtyla, "Thomistic Personalism," in *Person and Community*, 167.

[160] Aquinas, *Summa Theologiae*, I, q. 75, a. 4.

substance."¹⁶¹ That is, "Man, consequently, is a concrete substance."¹⁶² He is an indivisible unity such that he is a concrete substance and complete in himself. This means that when I say *I know* it is this "concrete being 'I', taken in its unity, [that] performs an act of knowing. The same thing holds when I say that *I live*, or simply that *I am*."¹⁶³

Wojtyla, too, adopts a hylomorphism, stating in *Person and Act*, "it is fitting to fully approve the vision of human reality bestowed on us by traditional philosophy (Aristotle and Thomas Aquinas), which, besides the element of 'matter-*hýle*', discovers in man just as in other beings of the visible world yet another element, namely, 'form-*morphē*'."¹⁶⁴ In other words, adds Wojtyla, "In the metaphysical sense, the soul is a 'form', and its relation to the body, according to Aristotle or Thomas Aquinas, is the same as the relation of 'form' to 'matter'."¹⁶⁵ The human soul in this *compositum* is the substantial form of the body, actualizing and structuring matter in a distinctive manner.¹⁶⁶ Still, the question is raised as to whether the rational soul that is *per se et essentialiter* the form of the body, is something more? Aquinas replies, "[T]he nature of the human intellect is not only incorporeal, but it is also a substance, that is something subsistent." That is, "For it is clear that by means of the intellect man can have knowledge of all corporeal things. Now whatever knows certain things cannot have any of them in its own nature; because that which is in it naturally would impede the knowledge of anything

---

¹⁶¹ Gilson, *The Spirit of Medieval Philosophy*, 176, and also, 198: "Neither the soul nor the body is the man, but the composite of both." Also helpful is Finley, "Metaphysics: A Note on Soul, Body, and Sexuality."

¹⁶² Gilson, *The Spirit of Medieval Philosophy*, 463n19.

¹⁶³ Gilson, *The Spirit of Medieval Philosophy*, 181.

¹⁶⁴ Wojtyla, *Person and Act*, 311.

¹⁶⁵ Wojtyla, *Person and Act*, 371.

¹⁶⁶ Finley, "Metaphysics: A Note on Soul, Body, and Sexuality," 241. Aquinas's *Summa Theologiae*, I, q. 75, a. 5.

else."[167] Thus, as a principle of operation, the intellect exercises its activity independently of the body, namely, as the substantiality of the soul. But then, as Gilson asks, "what, then, becomes of the substantial unity of the human being? How can that which is the form of the individual body, at the same time be separate from this individual body?"[168] In the next section, this question will be the focus of my analysis of Dooyeweerd's critique of the substance-concept in Thomist anthropology.[169] For now, the brief answer to this question here must be that the concrete substance that is "'man' is not a combination of two substances but a complex substance which owes its substantiality to only one of its two constitutive principles."[170] Thus, although man is a concrete substance, an indivisible unity and complete in himself, "he nevertheless owes all his substantiality to that of the soul."[171] In sum:

> [T]he man, therefore, is neither his body, since the body subsists only by the soul, nor his soul, since this would remain destitute without the body: he is the unity of a soul which substantializes his body and of the body in which this soul subsists.[172]

According to Wojtyla, then, the human soul is a spiritual substance, and hence the principle and source of the whole spirituality of man, of his reason and free will, and hence "that by virtue of which the human being may properly be ascribed the character of a person."[173] As John Paul II put it years later, "The spiritual and immortal soul is the principle

---

[167] Aquinas, *Summa Theologiae*, I, q. 75, a. 2.
[168] Gilson, *The Spirit of Medieval Philosophy*, 177.
[169] Dooyeweerd, *Reformation and Scholasticism in Philosophy*, II, 342–432.
[170] Gilson, *The Spirit of Medieval Philosophy*, 187–8.
[171] Gilson, *The Spirit of Medieval Philosophy*, 187.
[172] Gilson, *The Spirit of Medieval Philosophy*, 188.
[173] Wojtyla, "Thomistic Personalism," in *Person and Community*, 168.

of unity of the human being, whereby it exists as a whole—*corpore et anima unus*—as a person."[174] Additionally, the soul has faculties that are intrinsically dependent on matter, namely, sensory faculties that are cognitive and appetitive. Says Wojtyla, "These faculties, as belonging to the concrete human being, are likewise found in the person and contribute in their own way to the shaping of the psychological and moral personality."[175] Moreover, adds Wojtyla, Aquinas reflects on the spirituality of the human being such that it is "eminently suited to unite into a substantial whole with the corporeal, and thus also with the sensory,"[176] a substantial whole that I referred to above as a concrete substance. Man is a unity, substantial unity of "two inseparable elements of one and the same substance,"[177] and this union plays a "special role in shaping the human personality."[178] This follows from the presupposition that "man is not a soul only, but something composed of soul and body."[179]

Wojtyla urges us to understand that this anthropology differs from the anthropology of Plato but also of Descartes. In this latter anthropology, soul and body are two distinct beings as such and hence are a mere conjunction of these two things, an accident rather than any kind of metaphysical necessity.[180] Regarding Descartes's anthropology he divides man into an extended substance (the body) and a thinking substance (the soul). Wojtyla argues that, according to Descartes, soul and body

---

[174] John Paul II, *Veritatis Splendor*, §48.

[175] Wojtyla, "Thomistic Personalism," in *Person and Community*, 168–9.

[176] Wojtyla, "Thomistic Personalism," in *Person and Community*, 169.

[177] Gilson, *The Spirit of Medieval Philosophy*, 176, and also, 198: "Neither the soul nor the body is the man, but the composite of both." Also helpful is Finley, "Metaphysics: A Note on Soul, Body, and Sexuality."

[178] Wojtyla, "Thomistic Personalism," in *Person and Community*, 169.

[179] Aquinas, *Summa Theologiae*, I, q. 75, art. 4. On this, see Gilson, *Elements of Christian Philosophy*, 223.

[180] Gilson, *The Spirit of Medieval Philosophy*, 181.

"are related to one another in a parallel way and do not form an undivided whole, one substantial *compositum humanum*."[181] It is only by chance that these two things, soul and body, exist together. Finley explains the implication of soul and body being a mere conjunction of these two things rather than a unified whole:

> There would be no reason why souls and bodies always appear *together*, or why the *same kinds* of soul and body appear together. For example, if souls and bodies are really separate things in their own right, then we ought to find *some* falcon bodies with falcon souls, but others without them. And we ought to find different kinds of souls coming to different kinds of bodies; falcon souls in crow bodies, fish bodies, or even flower bodies.[182]

One might add here that another implication of seeing the soul and body as two separate things being a mere conjunction of these two is found in so-called "trans-genderism," namely, that a man's soul could be in a female body, or vice-versa. Of course, that's where we find ourselves in contemporary culture with those who insist that a so-called "trans-man"—in reality, a biological woman—could be pregnant. Finley correctly states in response:

> But of course we encounter none of these situations. We always find that the same kind of soul (life-principle) accompanies the same kind of body. More fundamentally, we don't even get a falcon body in the first place unless the falcon life-principle is present. This, after all, *is* conception: the beginning of life, yes, but as the beginning of a new living body of a certain kind. Which

---

[181] Wojtyla, "Thomistic Personalism," in *Person and Community*, 169.
[182] Finley, "Metaphysics: A Note on Soul, Body, and Sexuality," 240.

is to say that we don't get a falcon *soul* unless and until the new embryonic body has come to be.[183]

In sum, a man's soul could only be in a man's body, and in fact we don't get a human soul until the new embryonic male body has come to be. On this view, a living being is truly one substance, a unified whole, consisting of two principles, soul and matter, not just a mere conjunction of these two principles, with the union of soul and body being an accident.

Thus Cartesianism, according to Wojtyla, puts the unity of man in jeopardy.[184] It "[1] lacks a sufficient basis for including the body, the organism, within the structural whole of the person's life and activity; [2] it lacks the notion of a spiritual soul as the substantial form of that body and as the principle of the whole life and activity of the human being."[185] As I shall argue below, *contra* both the substantial dualism of Platonism and Cartesianism and its inability to include the body in a structural anthropological whole, according to Wojtyla, "*we cannot examine the human body in separation* from the totality that is man, that is, *without understanding that he is a person.*"[186] On the one hand, explains Wojtyla, in view of the unity of the subjectivity of the human person, "the human body is not a separate subject in relation to the subject that is the man-person. Its unity with man's ontic subjectivity, with the human *suppositum*, is beyond any doubt." On the other hand, adds Wojtyla, "within the integral subjectivity of the person—the consciousness-related sub-

---

[183] Finley, "Metaphysics: A Note on Soul, Body, and Sexuality," 240.
[184] This is true for any radical dualism of soul and body, such as Platonism. See Gilson, *The Spirit of Medieval Philosophy*, 176.
[185] Wojtyla, "Thomistic Personalism," in *Person and Community*, 169.
[186] Wojtyla, *Person and Act*, 311.

jectivity—the body possesses a somewhat separate 'subjectivity'—without, of course, violating the ontic unity of man."[187] The same holds for Wojtyla's claim that *"through his body the man-person is an authentic part of nature."*[188] Wojtyla's personalism does not alienate the person from nature. I return below to a discussion of the body's proper subjectivity.

Thus, Wojtyla aims to honor man's body as integral to his full humanity. Furthermore, the substantial dualism of Platonism and Cartesianism cannot account for the unity of the human person. But this doesn't preclude a duality-in-unity of two substances, soul and body, what Wojtyla calls the complexity of man, integral to the unity of the man-person. "[T]he problem of man's complexity as a bodily-spiritual being, [is] where the 'body' is understood as 'matter' not in a merely physical but above all in a metaphysical sense."[189] Regarding the soul, however, Wojtyla refers to the "spiritual element of the human being." On this crucial point, the *Catechism of the Catholic Church* states the teaching of the Catholic tradition: the human soul is the form of the body and is spiritual. In other words,

> The unity of soul and body is so profound that one has to consider the soul to be the "form" of the body: i.e., it is because of its spiritual soul that the body made of matter becomes a living, human body; spirit and matter, in man, are not two natures united, but rather their union [of two elements of soul and body] forms a single nature.[190]

---

[187] Wojtyla, *Person and Act*, 320–1.
[188] Wojtyla, *Person and Act*, 317.
[189] Wojtyla, *Person and Act*, 286.
[190] *Catechism of the Catholic Church*, §§362–5, and here 365.

Ch. 2: Christian Anthropology, the Unity of Human Nature… 187

Wojtyla explains "that this [spiritual] element determines the unity of man," and "this notion of spirituality is the key to understanding the complexity of man."[191] This is because the concrete substance that is man "owes all his substantiality to that of the soul."[192] Wojtyla then describes the powers of man's spiritual nature, namely, man's cognitive function's dynamic relation to truth, and freedom's dynamic dependence on truth in the function of self-determination.[193] Wojtyla elaborates:

> For man appears to us as a person, and in this way he appears to us above all in action, in the act. *He then stands* in the scope of our integral experience *as "somebody" material, being a body, while at the same time the spirit, spirituality, the spiritual life, determines the personal unity of this material "somebody."* Precisely the fact that spirituality determines the personal—and also ontic—unity of man who is a "body" allows and commands us to see in this man the ontic composite of soul and body, of the spiritual and material elements.[194]

Spirituality then determines the personal unity of man who is a "body." It deals with the total orientation of man, his depth dimension from which the unity of his full human existence is directed and formed. Let's turn now to develop Wojtyla's personalism.

Cosmological and Personalist

Wojtyla's personalism is chiefly at work in *Person and Act*. He shifts

---

[191] Wojtyla, *Person and Act*, 288.
[192] Gilson, *The Spirit of Medieval Philosophy*, 187.
[193] Wojtyla, *Person and Act*, 287.
[194] Wojtyla, *Person and Act*, 288.

philosophical visions from the vision he calls "cosmological" to the vision he calls "personalistic."[195] In his essay, "Subjectivity and the Irreducible in Man,"[196] Wojtyla distinguishes the more personalist focus of his phenomenology from the cosmological focus of the Aristotelian-Thomistic metaphysics of human nature—which studies man in terms of cosmological categories like substance, potentiality, rationality, freedom—which he unequivocally accepts but which has its own limits, such as failing to do justice to that which makes man irreducibly a person and hence threatening to reduce man to a cosmological type (i.e., an individual member of the human species).

Of course, man does hold a place in the cosmic order of things, and hence Wojtyla/John Paul II does make use of the "Aristotelian tradition in logic and in anthropology" to analyze man's nature in terms of a "proximate genus" and "specific differentia."[197] *Homo est animal rationale*: "This definition does not only correspond to the Aristotelian demands of denoting the species (man) through the proximate genus (a living being) and the factor differentiating the given species in this genus (endowed with reason)."[198] Elsewhere, he writes, "The usefulness of the Aristotelian definition [man is a rational animal or an individual substance of a rational nature] is unquestionable." Still, Wojtyla acknowledges the limits of this definition for a philosophy of man. He explains:

> *This definition* is also built in a way that excludes—at least when

---

[195] Wojtyla, *Person and Act*, 420, 429.

[196] It is found in the critical edition of *Person and Act*, "Subjectivity and 'the Irreducible' in Man," 536–45. Originally in *Analecta Husserliana* VII, "Subjectivity and 'the Irreducible' in Man," 107–14. This essay has been retranslated by Theresa Sandok, O.S.M., with a slightly altered title, "Subjectivity and the Irreducible in the Human Being," in *Person and Community*, 209–17.

[197] John Paul II, *Man and Woman He Created Them*, 5.5, and n10.

[198] Wojtyla, *Person and Act*, 537–8.

we take it directly and immediately—the possibility of manifesting what is *"irréductible dans l'homme."* It contains—at least in the foreground—*a conviction of the reducibility of man to the world*. The reason for this reducibility was and is the need to understand man. We can call this *type of understanding cosmological*.[199]

There is also a philosophy of man where the "person" stands at the foundation of understanding the subjectivity of the selfhood, meaning thereby self-presence and inwardness. Wojtyla explains: "Today it stands at the foundation of a growing manifestation of the person as a subject and of many efforts aiming at personal interpretation of the subjectivity of man." Wojtyla doesn't pit these two visions, however, against each other. There is the metaphysical sense of the subjectivity of man, which guarantees the identity of this man in being and acting; and the subjectivity that is proper to the person, which is the selfhood of the human person.[200]

In the philosophical and scientific tradition originating from the definition *homo—animal rationale, man was* first and foremost an object, *one of the objects of the world*, visibly and physically belonging to it. *Objectivity*, thus understood, *was linked* with the general presupposition of *man's reducibility*. Subjectivity, on the other hand, is, so to speak, a term bringing forth the fact that in his proper essence man cannot be reduced and completely explained by the most proximate genus and the specific difference.

---

[199] Wojtyla, "Subjectivity and 'the Irreducible' in Man," in *Person and Act*, 537–8.

[200] Wojtyla, "The Person: Subject and Community," in *Person and Act*, 472, 475.

Thus, in a sense, *subjectivity is a synonym of the entire* l'irréductible dans l'homme. If we make an opposition in this context, this opposition is not between objectivism and subjectivism but only between two ways of a philosophical (but also common and practical) treatment of man: as an object and a subject. For we cannot forget that the subjectivity of the man-person is also sometimes objective.[201]

We'll return below to the question of how the selfhood of the human person is also something objective. For now, I will consider Wojtyla's reflections on the irreducibility of personal subjectivity. First, Wojtyla regards man to be a unique and unrepeatable person, that is, that each human creature is "the one and ontically unique person" (as Wojtyla phrases it[202]), and given this irreducibility, Wojtyla says that the category of lived experience takes on greater significance and hence so, too, does a method he refers to as *"pausing at the irreducible."* He explains:

L'irréductible denotes what by its essence cannot be subjected to reduction, what cannot be "reduced" but can only be manifested, revealed. *By its essence, lived-experience opposes reduction*; this, however, does not mean that it breaks away from our cognition. It only demands to be *known in another way*, namely, by such a method, *by way of such an analysis that only reveals and manifests its essence*. ... By dwelling on the lived-experience of *l'irréductible* we attempt to cognitively penetrate its entire essence. In this way, we grasp not only the structure of lived-experience, subjective in its essence, but also its structural bond

---

[201] Wojtyla, "Subjectivity and 'the Irreducible' in Man," in *Person and Act*, 538–9.

[202] Wojtyla, *Person and Act*, 186.

with the subjectivity of man. ... So, this manifestation—one that is as profound as possible—seems to be an indispensable way to know man on account of his personal subjectivity. This subjectivity is also a distinct reality, a reality we attempt to understand in the objective totality whose name is "man." ... After all, *lived-experience too—and above all—is reality*. ... The thinker seeking the ultimate truth—in the philosophical sense—about man already moves not in a "purely philosophical terrain," but finds an abundance of elements attesting to both the bodiliness and spirituality of man, and better manifesting the one and the other. These are the elements of further philosophical development.[203]

Adds Wojtyla,

a belief in the primordial uniqueness of the human being, and thus in the basic irreducibility of the human being to the natural world, seems just as old as the need for reduction expressed in Aristotle's definition. This belief stands at the basis of understanding the human being as a person, which has an equally long tenure in the history of philosophy; it also accounts today for the growing emphasis on the person as a subject and for the numerous efforts aimed at interpreting the personal subjectivity of the human being.[204]

Still, without severing the person from his objective nature, the objective totality, as Wojtyla calls it above, namely, the objectivity of the *suppositum humanum*, Wojtyla hastens to remind us, however, "that we cannot forget that the subjectivity of the man-person is also something

---

[203] Wojtyla, *Person and Act*, 544–5.
[204] Wojtyla, *Person and Act*, 539.

objective."²⁰⁵ Wojtyla queries:

> However, the question always remains: Do the "cosmological" type of understanding man and the "personalistic" type ultimately exclude each other? In which place, if it all, do reduction [to substance, potentiality, rationality] and the manifestation of *l'irréductible* in man meet? In what sense is the philosophy of the subject to manifest the objectivity of man in his personal subjectivity itself?²⁰⁶

How does philosophical reflection on the subject disclose the *objectivity* of the human being in the personal *subjectivity* of this being? The brief answer to this question here must be: Wojtyla assures us that *"we protect the authentic subjectivity of man, that is, his personal subjectivity, in the realistic interpretation of his being."* Wojtyla explains, "The ontic subject is the substantial existence of the human subject, which is "metaphysical subjectivity … [and] the guarantor of the identity of this man in being and acting."²⁰⁷ In other words, man is an objective reality, "an individual substance of a rational nature" (as it is phrased by the Boethian definition), a *"suppositum humanum,"* which is "subjectivity in the metaphysical and fundamental sense," says Wojtyla, and representing human nature itself in the "metaphysical terrain" of being.²⁰⁸ This metaphysical realism of the person expresses "the individuality of the human being as a substantial being with a rational (spiritual) nature," marks out the "'metaphysical terrain'—the dimension of being—in which personal

---

[205] Wojtyla, *Person and Act*, 539.
[206] Wojtyla, "Subjectivity and 'the Irreducible' in Man," in *Person and Act*, 545.
[207] Wojtyla, "The Person: Subject and Community," in *Person and Act*, 472.
[208] Wojtyla, "The Person: Subject and Community," in *Person and Act*, 539.

Ch. 2: Christian Anthropology, the Unity of Human Nature... 193

human subjectivity is realized, creating, in a sense, a condition for 'building upon' this terrain on the basis of experience."[209] In short, "this personal human subjectivity is a determinate *reality*: it is a reality when we strive to understand it within the *objective totality* that goes by the name *human being*."[210] Otherwise, without this metaphysical terrain, the focus on personal human subjectivity, degenerates into a subjectivism. Thus, personal human subjectivity is understood in a metaphysical realist sense when it is connected with the person's being as its subject. Subjectivity divorced from the being of the person and treated as an autonomous subject of activity is understood as a version of subjectivism.

Second, Wojtyla gives us his perspective, in the Preface to *Person and Act*, on the significance of rejecting a departure of philosophical thought from a Cartesian starting point. Rather than start with the *cogito*, "pure consciousness" or the "pure subject," Wojtyla begins his study of man "by approaching him through action." Otherwise, "we do not interpret the real subjectivity of man any longer."[211] He explains:

> Since Descartes, the knowledge of man and his world has been identified with the cognitive function. As if only in cognition, and especially through knowledge of himself, would man manifest his nature and his prerogative. And yet, in reality, does man reveal himself in thinking or in the actual enacting of his existence?—in observing, interpreting, speculating or reasoning are changeable, flexible already in their acts, and mostly futile when confronted with the facts of reality, or in this confrontation itself when he has to take an active stand upon issues of vital decisions and with vital consequences and repercussions. In fact, it is in

---

[209] Wojtyla, "The Person: Subject and Community," in *Person and Act*, 539.
[210] Wojtyla, "The Person: Subject and Community," in *Person and Act*, 216.
[211] Wojtyla, *Person and Act*, 471.

reversing the classic attitude toward man that we undertake our study: by approaching him through action.[212]

In other words, Wojtyla's study of the *Person and Act* is concerned with the "*act that reveals the person; it will be a study of the person through the act.*"[213] Cardinal Eijk explains, "Agere sequitur esse, that is to say: acting follows being."[214] Wojtyla adds, "For such is the nature of the correlation inhering in experience, in the fact 'man acts': the act constitutes a particular moment of *revealing* the person. The act allows us to have the most proper insight into his essence and to understand it most fully. We experience that man is a person, and we are convinced of this because he performs acts."[215] The person is both a subject and agent of the act, and performing the act is of the authentic *actus personae*. Wojtyla explains:

> *The phrase "to perform an act" conceals in itself, in a sense, the entire subject matter of this study* [*Person and Act*]. For, in fact, we concern ourselves here with person and act not as two realities separate from each other but ... as one deeply coherent reality. This coherence takes place in reality; thus it must also take place in understanding, that is, in interpretation.[216]

Significantly for Wojtyla's philosophical anthropology, "*The human*

---

[212] Wojtyla, *Person and Act*, 587.

[213] Wojtyla, *Person and Act*, 103.

[214] Eijk, *De Band van de Liefde*, 84. See also, Aquinas, *Summa Theologiae* II, 69: "*agere sequitur ad esse.*"

[215] Wojtyla, *Person and Act*, 103–4.

[216] Wojtyla, *Person and Act*, 252.

body participates in the act."²¹⁷ Later, John Paul II argues, "Man is a subject not only by his self-consciousness and self-determination, but also based on his own body. The structure of this body is such that it permits him to be the author of genuinely human activity."²¹⁸ The subjectivity of the human person includes the body's proper subjectivity. Wojtyla distinguishes a static view of the relation between the body and the human person such that the body enters the definition of man from the dynamic view in which "*the human body* in its visible dynamic *is the terrain and, in a sense, even the means of expression for the person.*"²¹⁹ In other words, "The strictly personal structure of self-governance and self-possession runs, in a sense through the body and is expressed in it. As is known, this structure is manifested in the act and realized through the act."²²⁰

Elsewhere in his theological magnum opus, *Man and Woman He Created Them*, we find a sample of statements expressing the same point: "The body reveals man," "the body is an expression of man's personhood," and "the body *manifests* man and, in manifesting him, acts as an intermediary that allows man and woman, from the beginning, to 'communicate' with each other according to the that *communio personarum* willed for them in particular by the Creator."²²¹ In addition, John Paul makes a significant point in a long passage pertaining to his anthropology that repays reflection.

> Bodiliness and sexuality are not simply identical. Although in its normal constitution, the human body carries within itself the signs of sex and is by its nature male or female, *the fact that man*

---

²¹⁷ Wojtyla, *Person and Act*, 25.
²¹⁸ John Paul II, *Man and Woman He Created Them*, 7.2.
²¹⁹ Wojtyla, *Person and Act*, 312.
²²⁰ Wojtyla, *Person and Act*, 312, and also 313.
²²¹ John Paul II, *Man and Woman He Created Them*, 9.4; also n18, and 12.5.

is a "body" belongs more deeply to the structure of the personal subject than the fact that in his somatic constitution he is also male or female. ... This unity through the body ("and the two will become one flesh") possesses a multiform dimension: an ethical dimension, as is confirmed by Christ's response to the Pharisees in Matthew 19 (see also Mk 10), and also a sacramental dimension, strictly theological, as confirmed by the words of Paul to the Ephesians [Eph 5:29–32], that likewise refer to the tradition of the prophets (Hosea, Isaiah, Ezekiel). And this is so because the unity that realized through the body indicates from the beginning [from the creation] not only the "body," but also the "incarnate" communion of persons—*communio personarum*—and requires this communion right from the beginning [from the creation]. Masculinity and femininity express *the twofold aspect of man's somatic constitution* ("this time she is flesh from my flesh and bone from my bone") and *indicate*, in addition, through the same words of Genesis 2:23, *the new consciousness of the meaning of one's body*. This meaning, one can say, consists in *reciprocal enrichment*. Precisely this consciousness, through which humanity forms itself anew as a communion of persons, seems to constitute the layer in the account of creation of man (and in the revelation of the body contained in it) that is deeper than the somatic structure as male and female. In any case, this structure is presented from the beginning with a deep consciousness of human bodiliness and sexuality, and this established an inalienable norm for the understanding of man on the [philosophical and] theological plane.[222]

---

[222] John Paul II, *Man and Woman He Created Them*, 8.1, 9.5.

Several points may be made regarding this passage. First, John Paul II distinguishes between "bodiliness" and "sexuality." What does he mean by making this distinction? The body has a proper subjectivity that encompasses the whole man such that "reason and free will are linked with all the bodily and sense faculties." Explains Wojtyla, "The human person is not just a consciousness prolific in experiences of various content, but is basically a highly organized being, an individual of a spiritual nature composed into a single whole with the body (hence, a *suppositum humanum* [that is a person]."[223] Indeed, "The human body shares in the dignity of the image of God."[224] John Paul II's theology of the body is central to understanding the basic issues in, say, sexual ethics, in my judgment, because that theology emphasizes the bodily nature of the human person, meaning thereby that the body is intrinsic to human beings as bodily persons. Given that my body is intrinsic to myself, there is a unitary activity such that, as the pope says, "The person, including the body, is completely entrusted to himself, and it is in the unity of the body and soul that the person is the subject of his own moral acts."[225] In short, since the human person is bodily, then sexual moral choices are exercised in and through an act in which my bodily "activity is as much the constitutive subject of what one does as one's act of choice is."[226] This emphasis on the body being intrinsic to one's own self is rooted in the Church's teaching on the unity of the human person. As John Paul II says, "In fact, *body and soul are inseparable*: in the willing agent and in

---

[223] Wojtyla, "The Problem of Catholic Sexual Ethics," in *Person and Community*, 287.

[224] *Catechism of the Catholic Church*, §364.

[225] John Paul II, *Veritatis Splendor*, §48.

[226] John Finnis, "Personal Integrity, Sexual Morality and Responsible Parenthood," in *Why Humanae Vitae Was Right: A Reader*, ed. Janet E. Smith (San Francisco: Ignatius Press, 1993), 171–92, particularly 177.

the deliberate act *they stand or fall together*."[227]

Second, the body's proper subjectivity encompasses the foundation of sexual difference between male and female, that is, the somatic constitution of the personal subject. It is here that sexual differentiation is the basis for reciprocal enrichment in the two-in-one-flesh-unity between a man and a woman. Cardinal Eijk explains the Thomistic roots of this vision of man.

> The distinction between being male and being female is not a specific or formal difference but an accidental and material one, for otherwise man and woman would be two essentially different beings. From the perspective of the Thomistic understanding of the human person, this accidental material difference is owed to the differences in the disposition of matter to be formed by the substantial form, the soul. This difference is not a simple distinction that places masculinity on one side and femininity on the other, but actually holds a mutual complementarity. . . . The difference between man and woman encompasses two different and mutual forms of participating in the same perfection of human nature.[228]

Furthermore, in light of considering the human person as a unity of body and soul, we can understand why the *body is personal*. Rather than bodily existence being a mere instrument or extrinsic tool of man's personal self-realization, the body is the indispensable medium, argues Wojtyla, in and through which I reveal myself. In other words, Wojtyla's basic point is that the body and bodily action is in some sense communicative activity that reveals the person as a whole. As John Paul II says

---

[227] John Paul II, *Veritatis Splendor*, §49.
[228] Eijk, *De Band van de Liefde*, 112-3.

Ch. 2: Christian Anthropology, the Unity of Human Nature... 199

in *Person and Act*, "For us action *reveals* the person, and we look at the person through his action."[229] Later he says, "man manifests himself ... through his body. ... It is generally recognized that the human body is in its visible dynamism the territory where, or in a way even the medium whereby, the person expresses himself."[230] And in the theology of the body, we find a sample of statements expressing the same point: "the body reveals man," "the body is an expression of man's personhood," and "the body *manifests* man and, in manifesting him, acts as an intermediary that allows man and woman from the beginning, to 'communicate' with each other according to that *communio personarum* willed for them in particular by the Creator."[231] In sum, "In this sense, the body is the territory and in a way the means for the performance of action and consequently for the fulfillment of the person."[232] Herman Dooyeweerd nicely puts this point, "The human body is man himself in the structural whole of his temporal appearance."[233]

---

[229] Wojtyla, *Person and Act*, 11.

[230] Wojtyla, *Person and Act*, 203–4.

[231] John Paul II, *Man and Woman He Created Them*, 1.9.4, n18, and 1.12.5.

[232] Wojtyla, *Person and Act*, 205.

[233] Herman Dooyeweerd, *A New Critique of Theoretical Thought*, III, 89. This, too, is the view of Herman Dooyeweerd's philosophical anthropology, *Reformation and Scholasticism in Philosophy*, III, Part II, chapters 1–3, "[T]he human spirit cannot carry out any real acts outside its temporal corporal individuality-structure. For that reason, we said: it is the *individual human being* in the integral unity of 'body' and 'soul' who accomplishes the acts. The full person as a totality is the subject of the act. ... In the acts, the 'soul' is actually operative in the entire enkaptic structure of the body, and only in the body does the soul have the capacity to do so, insofar as the acts are included in the temporal order of the body. In other words, we can take the 'acts' neither to be purely 'corporal' nor purely 'spiritual'. They are *both* inseparably connected and precisely for that reason they bear a *typically human* character. Only the act-structure in *its fundamental dependence upon the spirit* stamps the body as human" (162–3).

We have here a communion of persons that is deeper than the somatic structure of male and female but presupposes that structure without which there could not be unity. What, then, does Wojtyla mean by "body"? The body in this sense is given in integral experience, meaning thereby the body as soma (*sōma*),[234] which does not constitute an object of observation, of scientific study, but rather the body in the sense of being such that it is an "organism," possessing "not only its external shape, but also its proper inwardness."[235] Later he says, "man manifests himself ... through his body ... . It is generally recognized that the human body is in its visible dynamism the territory where, or in a way even the medium whereby, the person expresses himself."[236] Hence, the body has a comprehensive significance being "man himself in his concrete corporeal mode of existence."[237]

Any concrete act of man, Wojtyla argues, is a bodily expression of the person given the unity of the person as body and soul. Thus, the body grounds human subjectivity, so that all knowledge and thought has bodily roots. It is impossible to pause here to give an account of the sense in which all knowledge and thought has bodily roots.[238] Still, in this light,

---

[234] John Paul II, *Man and Woman He Created Them*, 55.3. See Ridderbos, *Paulus*, 122–4 [115–17], and Berkouwer, *De Mens Het Beeld Gods*, 223–6 [204–7].

[235] Wojtyla, *Person and Act*, 311.

[236] Wojtyla, *Person and Act*, 313.

[237] Ridderbos, *Paulus*, 131 [125].

[238] For such an account see, Michael Polanyi's writings: *The Study of Man* (Chicago: University of Chicago Press, 1959). *Personal Knowledge: Towards a Post-Critical Philosophy* (New York: Harper & Row, 1964 [1958]). *The Tacit Dimension* (Chicago: University of Chicago Press, 1966). "The Logic of Tacit Inference," in *Knowing and Being, Essays by Michael Polanyi*, ed. Marjorie Grene (London: Routledge & Kegan Paul, 1969), 138–58. "Knowing and Being," in *Knowing and Being, Essays by Michael Polanyi*, ed. Marjorie Grene (London:

we can see the import of the point made by Wojtyla, "This relation [of the body and the human person] is expressed in the philosophical adage: *operari sequitur esse*."[239] *Operari* means thereby the total dynamism of man, particularly the subjectivity of the human person. This subjectivity is not just the subject in the metaphysical sense, namely, the dynamism of man includes what "happens" to man on "both the somatic and the psychical (the somatic-reactive and psycho-reactive) dimensions," as well as "what he 'does by acts'."[240] Regarding the latter, explains Wojtyla, "The act is a separate form of the human *operari*, and above all man reveals himself as a person in and through it."[241] He does not begin here with the discovery of the person because he identifies the human being with his actions, without any remainder that might admit a person distinct from his actions. On the contrary, Wojtyla distinguishes two complementary principles of the dynamic person-action reality: the "'integration of the person in the action', which is complementary to the notion of the 'transcendence of the person in the action'."[242] Thus, on the one hand, Wojtyla emphasizes the inalienable unity of the person in his bodily existence. Yet, on the other hand, this inalienable unity of the person does not mean that "the person is … to be identified solely with the body alone."[243] That is, "The belonging of the body to the subjective 'I'

Routledge & Kegan Paul, 1969), 124–37. "Sense-Giving and Sense-Reading," in *Knowing and Being, Essays by Michael Polanyi*, ed. Marjorie Grene (London: Routledge & Kegan Paul, 1969), 181–207.

[239] Wojtyla, "The Person: Subject and Community," in *Person and Community*, 223.

[240] Wojtyla, *Person and Act*, 473.

[241] Wojtyla, *Person and Act*, 473.

[242] Wojtyla, *Person and Act*, 296.

[243] Wojtyla, *Person and Act*, 313. This, too, is Dooyeweerd's view, "Van Peursen's Critische Vragen Bij 'A New Critique of Theoretical Thought'," *Philosophia Reformata* 25 (1960): 97–150, at 133, "The human 'I' is not to be identified with its subjective bodiliness."

does not consist in an identification with it. *Man 'is' not his body but 'possesses' his body.*"²⁴⁴

What does this distinction mean as far as the ability man has to take up distance vis-à-vis his own body? What is he suggesting with the distinction between "being" and "having" a body? "I *am* my *Leib*, which I also *possess* as *Körper.*"²⁴⁵ Wojtyla clarifies this difference.

> To "have" his own body leads to its objectification in actions and at the same time it is in this objectification that it expresses itself. Man has his body in a special way and also in a special way he is aware of his "possession," when in his acting he employs *his* body as a compliant tool to express his self-determination.²⁴⁶

Wojtyla, in an effort to explain the "special way" in which man has his body, cites Dutch phenomenologist Wilhelmus Antonius Luijpen.²⁴⁷ He says that Luijpen "protests against treating the body as an object of possession (of course, he means possession literally)." Says Luijpen, "*My Body is not the Object of 'Having'.* ... I 'have' a car, a pen, a book. In this 'having' the object of the 'having' reveals itself as an exteriority. There is a distance between me and what I 'have'. What I 'have' is to a certain extent independent of me." Thus, if my body is not the object of having, then I may not conceive of either sperm or eggs, either penis or vagina, in impersonal terms. For thinking of my body in impersonal terms is to think of it as a mere instrument or extrinsic tool of man's personal reality. Therefore, Luijpen continues, "My body is not something external to me like my car. I cannot dispose of my body or give it away as I dispose

---

²⁴⁴ Wojtyla, *Person and Act*, 314.
²⁴⁵ Schockenhoff, *Natural Law & Human Dignity*, 209.
²⁴⁶ Schockenhoff, *Natural Law & Human Dignity*, 206.
²⁴⁷ Wojtyla, *Person and Act*, 314n4.

Ch. 2: Christian Anthropology, the Unity of Human Nature...   203

of money. ... All this stems from the fact, that my body is not 'a' body, but *my* body ... in such a way that my body *embodies* me."[248] In short, the lived body is myself ("I") in my many activities; my subjectivity. It's not that I *am* a soul but *have* a body.[249] Rather, any concrete act of man, the pope seems to be arguing, is a bodily expression of the person given the unity of the person as body and soul.

Put differently, rather than beginning with human nature and its existence, Wojtyla begins with human action, in order to understand the relation between existence and activity. Yes, action is a way of knowing existence but action is also the most proper way to know *esse*, namely, the selfhood of the human person. "In this way we draw from the human *operari* the cognition not only of the fact that *man is its 'subject'*, but also *who man is as the subject of his action*."[250] This principle of *operari sequitur esse* is methodologically fundamental in Wojtyla's *Person and Act*. He explains, "In its basic conception, the whole of *Person and Act* is grounded on the premise that *operari sequitur esse*: the act of personal existence has its direct consequences in the activity of the person (i.e., in action). And so action, in turn, is the basis for disclosing and understanding the person."[251] In other words, it means that we can come to know more about *esse* by way of *operari*. He explains: "the form of human *operari* that has the most basic and essential significance for grasping the subjectivity of the human being is *action*: conscious human activity, in which the freedom proper to the human person is simultaneously expressed and concretized." "Thus," adds Wojtyla, "remaining always within the context of the *suppositum* (the *suppositum humanum*,

---

[248] Luijpen, *Existential Phenomenology*, 187–8.

[249] See Paul Helm, "Created Body and Soul," *The Gospel Coalition*, https://www.thegospelcoalition.org/essay/created-body-soul/.

[250] Wojtyla, *Person and Act*, 473.

[251] Wojtyla, *Person and Act*, 473n5.

of course), or subjectivity in the metaphysical and fundamental sense, we can arrive at a knowledge and explanation of subjectivity in the sense proper to the human being, namely, subjectivity in the personal sense."[252]

---

[252] Wojtyla, *Person and Act*, 474.

Chapter 3

Culture Wars, The Sexual Revolution, Ethics, and Hermeneutics[1]

The Pathos of Liberal Theology

When we undertake the analysis of the "beginning" according to the dimension of the theology of the body, we do so by basing ourselves on the words of Christ with which he himself appealed to that "beginning." When he said, "Have you not read that from the beginning the Creator created them male and female?" (Mt 19: 4), he ordered us and always orders us to return to the depth of the mystery of creation. And we do so in the full awareness of the gift of original innocence, which belonged to man before original sin. Although an insurmountable barrier divides us from what man was then as male and female, through the gift of grace united to the mystery of creation, and from what both were for each other as a reciprocal gift, we are nevertheless *trying to understand that state of original innocence in its link with man's "historical" state after original sin, "the state of fallen and at the same time redeemed nature* [status naturae lapsae simul et

---

[1] This chapter is a revised and expanded version of my published article, "Is the Sexual Revolution a Renewal Movement within the Traditional Sexual Morality of Orthodox Christianity," *Mid-America Journal of Theology*, Vol. 31 (2020): 103–132. It was also published in Dutch: "Is de seksuele revolutie een vernieuwingsbeweging binnen de traditionele seksuele moraal van het orthodoxe christendom?" in *Communio, Internationaal Katholiek Tijdschrift* 2020/3: 176-212.

redemptae]

—John Paul II[2]

It remains crucial to keep "creation" connected with "beginning." We cannot hear often enough—as anthropocentrically living and thinking people—that the beginning began with us. [T]he basics of human beings are guaranteed in creation ... and they also include an original difference (male-female) that not only gives depth to the power of attraction between men and women but also makes covenanting between human beings a first priority. This all is included in the connection between "creation" and "in the beginning." We did not think this up, we are not the ones who—with our "creative" beginnings or restarts—have to give significance to "creation." ... When, today, special attention is requested for what is original about the "sexual difference," a reformational philosophy that includes "creation" in its ground motive need not react nervously.

—Johan van der Hoeven[3]

---

[2] John Paul II, *Man and Woman He Created Them*, 18.3 (original emphasis).

[3] Johan van der Hoeven, "Na 50 Jaar: Philosophia Reformata—Philosophia Reformanda," *Philosophia Reformata* 51.1–2 (1986): 5–28, and at 19–20. The late Reformational philosopher, a disciple of Herman Dooyeweerd, Johan van der Hoeven (1932–2015), underscores the importance of creation regarding the matter of sexual differentiation in the second epigraph. Unfortunately, Gerrit Glas, who holds the Dooyeweerd Chair in Christian Philosophy at the Vrije Universiteit, Amsterdam, has abandoned the creational significance of sexual difference in affirming homosexuality, and hence has abandoned Dooyeweerd's

It is because homosexual activity lacks the full complementarity of the man-woman relationship, and also procreative openness to life, that the Catholic Church cannot recognize it as a legitimate expression of the human sexual inclination. As the 1986 letter [*Homosexualitatis problema*] to the bishops of the Catholic Church by the Roman Congregation for the Doctrine of the Faith observes, while the Church must be open to enlightenment from the human sciences, she must also remain confident that her own more "global vision," transcending that of the particular sciences, "does greater justice to the rich reality of the human person.

—Aidan Nichols, OP[4]

In the currently dominant secularized and highly individualistic culture in the Western world, great emphasis is placed on individual autonomy. Marriage, sexuality, the unity of marriage, and procreation are seen as neutral values in themselves, given meaning only by the individual within his autonomy. Sexual acts are primarily intended as experiences of pleasure. It is a personal choice whether or not one wishes to connect sexual acts with a (marital) relationship or with procreation. This also applies to the type of relationship or the manner of procreation. There is no objective truth, and as a result, there are no objective

---

social ontology of marriage. See his essay, "Homoseksualiteit en homo-ervaring," in *Open en kwetsbaar: Christelijk debat over homoseksualiteit*, ed. Ad de Bruijne (Barneveld: De Vuurbaak, 2012), 19–30.

[4] Nichols, *Epiphany*, 422.

principles for ethics. The ethics of contemporary secularized society, therefore, has a permissive character.

—Cardinal Eijk[5]

In his essay, "Seksualiteit en cultuurstrijd: Een theologische voorstel tot dialog,"[6] Dutch Reformed theologian, Ad L. Th. de Bruijne, a professor of ethics and spirituality at the Kampen Theological University, argues that the culture war between orthodox Christians and proponents of the sexual revolution, so-called, emancipatory liberals, and their sexual liberationist ideology, should be left behind. In general, De Bruijne stands in the line of the neo-Calvinism of Abraham Kuyper and Herman Bavinck by continuing to develop a hermeneutic of culture for the sake of renewal. In a recent collection of essays, *Gereformeerde hermeneutiek vandag: Theologische perspectieven*,[7] De Bruijne describes the increasing attention to hermeneutics among Kampen theologians. He explains:

---

[5] Eijk, *De Band van de Liefde*, 31.

[6] Ad de Bruijne, "Seksualiteit en cultuurstrijd: Een theologische voorstel tot dialog" ["Sexuality and Cultural Conflict: A Theological Proposal for Dialogue"] in *Religie en Samenleving* 11, nr. 2, September 2016, *God, seks en politiek*, 271–287. See also, for a fully revised version of the previous 2016 essay, Ad de Bruijne, "Culture Wars About Sexuality: A Theological Proposal for Dialogue," *Public Discourses About Homosexuality and Religion in Europe and Beyond*, editors. Marko Derks, Mariecke Van den Berg (Cham: Palgrave MacMillan 2020): 105-124. More recently, Ad de Bruijne, *Verbonden voor het Leven: Een theologisch-ethisch voorstel rond homoseksualiteit en seksuele diversiteit* (Utrecht: KokBoekencentrum, 2022).

[7] Ad de Bruijne en Hans Burg, eds. *Gereformeerde hermeneutiek vandag: Theologische perspectieven* [*Reformed Hermeneutics Today: Theological Perspectives*] Barneveld: De Vuurbaak, 2017.

Since the 1990s, more attention has been paid in Kampen to hermeneutics. . . . In that connection, we are convinced that attention to hermeneutics is necessary in order to remain faithful to God and His word within a secularized culture. . . . Within the neo-Calvinism of Kuyper, Bavinck, and others, there was an awareness from the outset that modern questions about the authority, interpretation, and application of the Bible could not be fully answered from the Reformed confessions and theology that existed at the time. That is why neo-Calvinist theologians time and again developed ideas that were hermeneutical in character, even though the term was often omitted. . . . Reformed reflection on the Bible in the Kampen tradition is mainly marked by the neo-Calvinist renewal movement of Abraham Kuyper, Herman Bavinck, and their students.[8]

Now, as an example of this neo-Calvinist hermeneutics with the aim of renewal, De Bruijne proposes a move from confrontation to dialogue between the traditional sexual morality of orthodox Christians and sexual liberationism. He claims the latter may be seen as a renewal movement within the understanding of traditional sexual morality. Indeed, he regards the sexual liberationist ideology as a *corrective* moment within the orthodox Christian understanding of the meaning, purpose, and morality of human sexuality.

His argument resembles a "theology of compromise,"[9] that is, a revisionist theology committed, as David Tracy rightly states, to "the dramatic confrontation, the mutual illuminations and corrections, the possible basic reconciliation between the principal values, cognitive claims,

---

[8] Ad de Bruijne, "De kunst van het verstaan: Hermeneutiek in Kampen," 13-34, and at 16, 26.

[9] Eijk, *De Band van de Liefde*, 34.

and existential faiths of both a reinterpreted post-modern consciousness and a reinterpreted Christianity."[10] In short, this critical correlation between the "Christian tradition and contemporary understandings of human existence"[11] in revisionist theology is best described as the pathos of liberal theology. As the late American liberal theologian, Van A. Harvey (1923-2021) succinctly describes that pathos. "The pathos of the liberal is that, by adopting modernity and accommodating Christianity to it, he is confronted by a solution of his own making in which Christianity has lost its 'transcendence' over common experience and is simply a representation of its own self-understanding. On the other hand, if the theologian identifies himself with a faith that transcends and judges modernity, he must appear to that modernity and to himself, perhaps, as out of joint with the times."[12]

This revisionist theology is not a form of retrieval theology, namely, the project of *ressourcement*. In other words, the theological project of retrieval theology is a "mode or style of theological discernment that looks back [to authoritative sources of faith] in order to move forward."[13] As Kevin Vanhoozer correctly states, "*Ressourcement* describes a return to authoritative sources for the sake of revitalizing the present."[14] Indeed, adds Vanhoozer, on the one hand, "we ought not to confuse retrieval with either retrenchment or repristination." Rather, "the main purpose of retrieval is the revitalization of biblical interpretation,

---

[10] David Tracy, *The Blessed Rage for Order: The New Pluralism in Theology* (New York: The Seabury Press, 1975), 32.

[11] Tracy, *The Blessed Rage for Order*, 23.

[12] Van A. Harvey, "The Pathos of Liberal Theology." *Journal of Religion* 56, no. 4, October 1976, 382-391, and at 391. This is Harvey's article review of David Tracy's book, *The Blessed Rage for Order: The New Pluralism in Theology*.

[13] Buschart, W. David and Eilers, Kent D, *Theology as Retrieval: Receiving the Past, Renewing the Church* (Downers Grove, IL: IVP Academic, 2015), 12

[14] Vanhoozer, *Biblical Authority After Babel*, 23.

theology, and the church today. *To retrieve is to look back creatively in order to move forward faithfully.*"[15] On the other hand, moving faithfully forward involves "*aggiornamento*," the meaning of which is best captured in Vatican II's *Gaudium et Spes*, §4:

> To carry out such a task, the Church has always had the duty of scrutinizing the signs of the times and of interpreting them in the light of the Gospel. Thus, in language intelligible to each generation, she can respond to the perennial questions which men ask about this present life and the life to come, and about the relationship of the one to the other. We must therefore recognize and understand the world in which we live, its explanations, its longings, and its often dramatic characteristics.

Significantly, as Oscar Cullman rightly stressed, "*aggiornamento* should be a consequence, not a starting point,"[16] of renewal, of *ressourcement*. Indeed, he adds, aggiornamento should not be understood as an "*isolated motive for renewal.*"[17] Therefore, in the interplay between *ressourcement* and *aggiornamento*, the former has normative priority.

In this chapter, first, I critically examine de Bruijne's argument that he gives supporting his claims. In this context, I consider the relationship between creation, fall, redemption, and eschatology. Both G.C. Berkouwer (1903-1996) and Karol Wojtyla/John Paul II (1920-2005) views on this relationship are examined. I also explore the foundation of ethics as it pertains to human sexuality. Second, I present the critique of

---

[15] Vanhoozer, *Biblical Authority After Babel*, 24; italics are Vanhoozer's.

[16] Oscar Cullman, "Have Expectations Been Fufilled?" In: *Vatican II, The New Direction*. Essays Selected and Arranged by James D. Hester. New York: Harper & Row, 1968, 54–63, and at 57.

[17] Cullman, "Have Expectations Been Fufilled?", 58.

Wojtyla/John Paul II) of the sexual liberationist ideology but also his response to each of de Bruijne's claims. Furthermore, I present Wojtyla's arguments for a Christian sexual ethics, along with the supporting arguments of Cardinal Eijk throughout the chapter.[18] There is also a critical discussion on the Christian Reformed Church (CRC) Synod 2022 document *A Foundation-Laying Biblical Theology of Human Sexuality*.

Erotic Wars[19]

How does De Bruijne describe "orthodox Christians," on the one hand, and emancipatory liberals, proponents of sexual liberation on the other? Regarding the former, he says, "By 'orthodox Christians' I am re-

---

[18] The arguments for sexual ethics in Eijk, *De Band van de Liefde* dovetails with that of Wojtyla's.

[19] For an informative study on the sexual revolution and the dynamics of erotic wars, see Lillian Rubin, *Erotic Wars: What Happened to the Sexual Revolution* (New York: HarperPerennial, 1990). For a devastating account of the effects of the sexual revolution, see Gabriele Kuby, *The Global Sexual Revolution, Destruction of Freedom in the Name of Freedom*, Foreword by Robert Spaemann, trans. James Patrick Kirchner (Kettering, OH: Angelico Press, 2012). See also, Jennifer Roback Morse, *The Sexual State* (Charlotte, NC: Tan Books, 2018). Robert R. Reilly, *Making Gay Okay, How Rationalizing Homosexual Behavior Is Changing Everything* (San Francisco, CA: Ignatius Press, 2014). J. Budziszewski, *On the Meaning of Sex* (Wilmington, DE: ISI Books, 2012). Louise Perry, *The Case Against the Sexual Revolution* (Cambridge: Polity, 2022). David R. Carlin, *Three Sexual Revolutions: Catholic-Protestant-Atheist, A sociological & Historical Perspective* (Hobe Sound, Florida: Lectio Publishing, 2022). Nancy R. Pearcey, *Love Thy Body: Answering Hard Questions about Life and Sexuality* (Grand Rapids, MI: Baker Books, 2018). Voddie T. Baucham, Jr., *It's Not like Being Black: How Sexual Activists Hijacked the Civil Rights Movement* (Delaware: Regnery Faith, 2024). Mary Eberstadt, *Adam and Eve after the Pill, Revisited*, Foreword by Cardinal George Pell (San Francisco: Ignatius Press, 2023 [2012]).

Ch. 3: Culture Wars, The Sexual Revolution, Ethics, Hermeneutics 213

ferring to those within divergent confessional traditions (Roman Catholic, Protestant, Anglican, Eastern Orthodox) who with intention seek to remain faithful to traditional views of sexuality, based, for example, on the authority of the Bible or the teaching authority of the church."[20] This claim raises the question not only of which orthodox Christians does De Bruijne have in mind—he refers to none—but also whether they have defended their understanding of sexual ethics on the ground of authority alone. Surely Augustine, Thomas Aquinas, Karl Barth, Helmut Thielicke, Herman Dooyeweerd, Karl Wojtyla/John Paul II, Germain Grisez, John Finnis, Cardinal Eijk, et al., have defended their views of sexual morality on the grounds not only of biblical revelation and the Church's teaching authority, but also of reason and the natural law (order of creation). By enlightened proponents of sexual emancipation, emancipatory liberals, he means those who embrace the "modern ideal of individual freedom and autonomy" that leads them to "breaking radically with traditional views about sexuality."[21] This resembles a theology of compromise. De Bruijne's major thesis is that these groups will be less confrontational and more dialogical if they come to recognize that "at the deepest level they share the same story."[22] He adds, "Orthodox Christians and enlightened advocates of sexual liberation display more affinity with each other on some points than both groups realize. Both groups fit within the same story."[23] Where, then, is there common ground?

De Bruijne claims that orthodox Christians have accommodated

---

[20] De Bruijne "Seksualiteit en cultuurstrijd: Een theologische voorstel tot dialog," 273.

[21] De Bruijne "Seksualiteit en cultuurstrijd: Een theologische voorstel tot dialog," 274.

[22] De Bruijne "Seksualiteit en cultuurstrijd: Een theologische voorstel tot dialog," 272, 283.

[23] De Bruijne "Seksualiteit en cultuurstrijd: Een theologische voorstel tot dialog," 283.

and hence changed some of their traditional understanding of sex to the views of the sexual revolution.[24] They have changed their understanding of the meaning and purpose of human sexuality by accepting, for example, contraception. Human sexuality is consequently no longer about procreation and the ordering of one's sexual desires to the goods of human sexuality; rather engaging in sexual acts is a matter of physical needs, indeed a private matter that renders such acts an instrument of pleasure, or about individual self-realization. Given this change in their view of sexuality, some orthodox Christians have come to accept pre-marital sex, cohabitation, and even extra-marital sex. Divorce and re-marriage have also become more acceptable. Significantly, there has been an accommodation to homosexuality insofar as a distinction is drawn between homosexual acts and homosexual orientation; the former is rejected and the latter is accepted. Finally, some orthodox Christians have even come to tolerate homosexuality and even increasingly openly accepted it.[25]

De Bruijne is surely correct that this accommodation has in fact taken place, not just in the wider culture but also among diverse ecclesial

---

[24] In an earlier article, De Bruijne resists compromising particularly on the question of homosexuality. See Ad de Bruijne, "Homosexuality: Improving the Traditional Theory?" in *Familie: Verwandtschaft, die den Unterschied macht, Family: Kinship that matters*, (Hrsg.) Gerard den Hartog/Jan Roskovec (Leipzig: Evangelische Verlagsanstalt, 2012), 103–112, especially 109–110. De Bruijne has a more extensive discussion of the sexual revolution in his more recent book, *Verbonden voor het Leven*, 55-62. But it doesn't add to the points made in the sources I am discussing here.

[25] De Bruijne, "Seksualiteit en cultuurstrijd: Een theologische voorstel tot dialog," 274.

Ch. 3: Culture Wars, The Sexual Revolution, Ethics, Hermeneutics 215

communities.²⁶ For instance, the United Church of Canada in her 37ᵗʰ General Meeting of 2000 confirmed sexual diversity—homosexual, lesbian, bisexual, heterosexual—as a gift of God reflecting the wonderful diversity of creation.²⁷

However, he does not give us an example of orthodox Christian thinkers who have made this accommodation but also never asks whether they are biblically, theologically, and philosophically justified in doing so in light of Scripture, tradition, human reason, and the natural law (creation order). What de Bruijne tries to do in justifying this accommodation is to claim that the sexual revolution is in some respects not only a break with Christian tradition but also "in some respects also the positive legacy of that tradition."²⁸ In other words, De Bruijne claims, in some respects the sexual revolution is a legacy of Christianity. "At least [four] aspects of late modern sexual morality can be understood on the basis of the preceding Christian story." Indeed, he claims, "Between the struggle for sexual liberation and the classical Christian tradition there exists, however, not only a psychological relationship, but also a *conceptual* relationship," indeed, De Bruijne adds, "manifold conceptual connections between sexual emancipation and the Christian tradition."²⁹ In what follows, I summarize the four aspects manifesting a common conceptual understanding that de Bruijne describes.

---

²⁶ On this, see Ad de Bruijne, "Homosexuality and Moral Authority: A Theological Interpretation of Changing Views in Evangelical Circles," in *Evangelicals and Sources of Authority*, ed. Miranda Klaver, Stefan Paas, and Eveline van Sataalduine-Sulman (Amsterdam: VU Press, 2016), 143–162.

²⁷ Eijk, *De Band van de Liefde*, 281.

²⁸ De Bruijne, "Seksualiteit en cultuurstrijd: Een theologische voorstel tot dialog," 275.

²⁹ De Bruijne, "Seksualiteit en cultuurstrijd: Een theologische voorstel tot dialog," 276, emphasis added. De Bruijne actually describes four aspects rather

First, individual freedom is central to contemporary sexual morality. This freedom is self-constituting, an expressive individual-ism, insofar as human beings are free to give meaning and structure/form to their sexuality and sexual practice. We are the architects of the structure and nature of human sexuality. Thus:

> Purported meanings that the past supplies us are not binding in that context. A person may look forward and develop their own life. Individual preferences are more important than traditional frameworks. People may break with those frameworks if necessary. That applies as well to boundaries that traditionally were characterized as being natural.[30]

This freedom is absolute so that its exercise has consequently led to considering gender and sex apart from the body's natural determinations, a sexually differentiated body, a gendered body, even to the extent of dissolving the meaning of the masculine/feminine difference. These natural determinations of a gendered body are alleged to impede self-determination. Admittedly, says de Bruijne, this ideal of absolute freedom is the dynamic behind the emancipatory drive to break free from traditional Christian sexual morality, according to the sexual emancipator. Louise Perry, a staunch critic of this idea of freedom writes:

> I am critical of any ideology that fails to balance freedom against

---

than just three that are alleged legacies of orthodox Christianity in the sexual revolution. On this, see "Culture Wars About Sexuality: A Theological Proposal for Dialogue," 110.

[30] De Bruijne, "Seksualiteit en cultuurstrijd: Een theologische voorstel tot dialog," 276.

other values, and I'm also critical of the failure of liberal feminism to interrogate where our desire for a certain type of freedom comes from, too often referring to a circular logic by which a woman's choices are good because she chooses them, just like *Sex and the City's* Charlotte York yelping "I choose my choice, I choose my choice!"[31]

On this view of freedom, one is free to make whatever one chooses right. It also opposes freedom and nature, material and biological nature, and, as John Paul II puts it, "progressively asserts itself" over nature.[32] He explains, "This ultimately means making freedom self-defining and a phenomenon creative of itself and its values. Indeed, when all is said and done man would not even have a nature; he would be his own personal life-project. Man would be nothing more than his own freedom."[33] Contra this view of freedom, The philosopher-pope argues:

> It must certainly be admitted that man always exists in a particular culture, but it must also be admitted that man is not exhaustively defined by that same culture. Moreover, the very progress of cultures demonstrates that there is something in man which transcends those cultures. This "something" is precisely human nature: this nature is itself the measure of culture and the condition ensuring that man does not become the prisoner of any of his cultures, but asserts his personal dignity by living in accordance with the profound truth of his being.

---

[31] Louise Perry, *The Case Against the Sexual Revolution* (Cambridge: Polity, 2022), 10.
[32] John Paul II, *Veritatis Splendor*, §46.
[33] John Paul II, *Veritatis Splendor*, §46.

Most significant, John Paul adds,

> To call into question the permanent structural elements of man which are connected with his own bodily dimension would not only conflict with common experience, but would render meaningless Jesus' reference to the "beginning" [creation order], precisely where the social and cultural context of the time had distorted the primordial [creational] meaning and the role of certain moral norms (cf. Mt 19:1-9).[34]

Nevertheless, de Bruijne claims, astoundingly, there is an underlying continuity with the Christian tradition in the latter's understanding of not only freedom where man is "nothing more than his own freedom,"[35] but also "the uniquely exalted place that people receive within created reality as image of God and in relationship to Jesus Christ. . . . They are called and emerge subsequently as co-designers of history."[36]

Second, human sexuality is an intrinsic good that ought to be sought after for its own sake and not for the sake of something else, such as procreation. "Sexuality no longer needs to serve higher purposes beyond itself, as it did in earlier cultural stages and in most other cultures. Sex is what it is." De Bruijne refers to those who take sex to be an intrinsic good to mean that "sex is . . . nothing more and nothing less than a physical primary need and means of pleasure."[37] Although he acknowledges that it might seem farfetched to see this understanding of sex as a Christian legacy, he nevertheless finds traces of this view in the Christian doctrine

---

[34] John Paul II, *Veritatis Splendor*, §53.

[35] John Paul II, *Veritatis Splendor*, §46.

[36] De Bruijne, "Seksualiteit en cultuurstrijd: Een theologische voorstel tot dialog," 276.

[37] De Bruijne, "Seksualiteit en cultuurstrijd: Een theologische voorstel tot dialog," 276.

of the creation of all things after their proper nature because it affirms sex's intrinsic goodness rather than merely an instrumental good for the sake of procreation. "The doctrine of creation implied that reality was allowed to be itself under the sovereignty of the creator. Each sphere of life could manifest itself according to its own nature."[38]

Third, human sexuality is at the core of one's identity as well as of individual self-realization or self-expression. De Bruijne appeals here again to the "biblical emphasis on the value of the individual person and their specific gifts. The . . . emphasis on the freedom of personal conscience functions in this as well. The notion of an internally anchored unique personal identity does not exist apart from the Christian emphasis on the heart."[39] However, achieving self-realization requires an interpersonal relationship because man by nature is a social being. This view, too, has its roots in the Christian tradition. Furthermore, self-realization and relationality go hand in hand because the latter is at the heart of the Christian doctrine of the Trinity, and this doctrine, too, has influenced Christian anthropology.[40]

Fourth, on the one hand, De Bruijne emphasizes that the meaning, nature, and structure of human sexuality is open-ended, future oriented rather than oriented to the normative order of creation and the nature of things with its embedded principles and the inherent meanings of the human sexual design. On the other hand, he attends to the order of creation, the reality of general revelation in creation, creation texts, in particular, Genesis 1:27 and 2:24, referred to by Jesus (see Mark 10: 6-8),

---

[38] De Bruijne, "Seksualiteit en cultuurstrijd: Een theologische voorstel tot dialog," 277.

[39] De Bruijne, "Seksualiteit en cultuurstrijd: Een theologische voorstel tot dialog," 277.

[40] De Bruijne, "Seksualiteit en cultuurstrijd: Een theologische voorstel tot dialog," 277–278.

which underscore the nexus between permanence, the twoness of male and female, and sexual differentiation as a fundamental prerequisite for the two to become one flesh. The biblical passages, such as, Leviticus 18 and 20, says De Bruijne, are best understood against the backdrop of the creation texts: ""the creation of man and woman and the sexual union intended between them."[41] He adds,

> In the New Testament, no change on that point can be found in Christ. He [Christ] also goes back to the creation of man and woman, and reserves sexual union for the intercourse of husband and wife within marriage.[42]

De Bruijne says that this is the sore point ("pijnpunt") for the interpretation of homosexuality as a creational variance because it refers to a normative state of affairs that is an enduring basis to judge the morality of homosexuality. This back to creation perspective, and in the light of the fall, "approaches homosexuality as part of the brokenness inherent in a creation fallen in sin, comparable to an illness or disability."[43] De Bruijne acknowledges the extremely plausible nature of this interpretation regarding the brokenness of homosexuality. But he is not satisfied with this interpretation because it does not allow for sexual variety, creational variance, such that homosexuality is seen, not as a disorder, but "as a full and equal variant of human life as created by God."[44]

Back, then, to the eschatological perspective. De Bruijne claims that this future orientation is derived from the Christian eschatological per-

---

[41] De Bruijne, *Verbonden voor het Leven*, 272.

[42] De Bruijne, *Verbonden voor het Leven*, 272.

[43] De Bruijne, *Verbonden voor het Leven*, 232, and also 243-244.

[44] De Bruijne, *Verbonden voor het Leven*, 232-233.

spective of the new creation "in which existing structures would be fulfilled and transformed. Then, for example, procreation would cease, whereas marriage and sexuality would be fulfilled in the communal love relationship of Christians with Christ."[45] In his recent book, he underscores this eschatological perspective. "In eschatological light, homosexuality is to be seen as further diversification of being male and female. As in every form of being human, the dimensions of creation, fall, and redemption are present therein. Homosexuality too is—no less and no more—a form of being human in route to the transformation of corporeality and eros-love that already exists in Christ (1 Pet. 1:3ff)."[46] I'll return below to a discussion of these two perspectives: creational and eschatological.

For now, I underscore that De Bruijne claims to hear echoes of this eschatological perspective—now secularized—in "a project of people themselves who pursue their own variation of this." Examples of this project that may receive new positive meaning in light of the future, according to de Bruijne, includes "polyamory, . . . transsexuality, intersexuality, and homosexuality."[47] Admittedly, says de Bruijne, polyamory—

---

[45] De Bruijne, *Verbonden voor het Leven*, 278. In an earlier article, de Bruijne raises this transformation as a possible objection to a creation-based ethics. De Bruijne, "Homosexuality: Improving the Traditional Theory?" 106, "When the kingdom approaches, marriage and family will be transformed into new forms of community, and perhaps also sexuality will undergo such a transformation." What he left there an open question, in this article, under examination, he tries to develop a case for giving an affirmative response to that question. In his new book, *Verbonden voor het Leven*, he attempts to provide a justification for homosexuality as a variant within the order of human sexuality. I discuss De Bruijne's attempted justification later in this chapter.

[46] De Bruijne, *Verbonden voor het Leven*, 254, and 250-251.

[47] De Bruijne, "Seksualiteit en cultuurstrijd: Een theologische voorstel tot dialog,", 280, 281. On December 7, 2015 the Theological University of Kampen

which is the practice of sexual relationships with more than one partner, and thus rejects monogamy—"as such does not fit with the dominant biblical ideal for marriage."⁴⁸ Still, de Bruijne claims the emancipatory liberals can help orthodox Christians recover the future orientation of sexuality and hence of sexual diversity that deviates from the natural order of creation, or at least a "static natural law model of creation ordinances," as he puts it.⁴⁹ De Bruijn makes a plea for an approach that is more dynamic "than classical variants of nature- or creation-oriented ethics. After all, these latter usually look back to an unchanging initial order and explain it normatively."⁵⁰ Christians have typically and exclusively oriented sexual ethics to the "creation and the natural context of marriage and family."⁵¹ However, De Bruijne tries to make a case for ontic innovation, ontic structural novelty, radical innovation, as it were, for "human relationality,"⁵² such that "[transsexuality, intersexuality, and homosexuality] would be able perhaps to receive a new meaning in light of the future."⁵³ So, the creation order must be such that, according to De Bruijne, that we can see "the actions of the biblical God as *surprisingly new again and again.*"⁵⁴ De Bruijne claims that this plea for "ontic

---

celebrated the 161st anniversary of her existence. Prof. Ad. de Bruijne gave an address entitled, "Seksualiteit in de laatste dagen." https://www.youtube.com/watch?v=QY66hisTfDI.

⁴⁸ De Bruijne, "Seksualiteit en cultuurstrijd: Een theologische voorstel tot dialog," 278.

⁴⁹ De Bruijne, "Homosexuality: Improving the Traditional Theory?," 106.

⁵⁰ De Bruijne, *Verbonden voor het Leven*, 42.

⁵¹ De Bruijne, "Seksualiteit en cultuurstrijd: Een theologische voorstel tot dialog," 280.

⁵² De Bruijne, *Verbonden voor het Leven*, 245.

⁵³ De Bruijne, "Seksualiteit en cultuurstrijd: Een theologische voorstel tot dialog," 280.

⁵⁴ De Bruijne, *Verbonden voor het Leven*, 42.

novelty" does not mean that God can deny or contradict the law of creation. "He constantly and transformatively transcends the given. At the same time, that given turns out nevertheless to be connected to and included in that newness in an unexpected way."⁵⁵

Can this quest for "ontic novelty" be shown to be the historical unfolding of inner laws given with the original order of creation, particularly since De Bruijne eschatologically situates this radical innovation? No, according to De Bruijne, "Because the Bible does not know our contemporary concept of homosexual orientation or identity, and does not shed direct light on it anywhere, therefore any conclusion on this point is somewhat speculative."⁵⁶ Still, De Bruijne acknowledges as most plausible the creation perspective in which sexual differentiation is a fundamental prerequisite for the two to become one-flesh, and hence the postfall interpretation of homosexuality as a reflection of a broken world.⁵⁷ Nevertheless, De Bruijn insists that "In addition to a creation perspective, as I used that in the foregoing, a kingdom- or eschatological-perspective also fits."⁵⁸

Here, too, de Bruijne claims to find continuity, or an affinity, between the sexual revolution and the Christian tradition in order to justify the eschatological possibility of the moral legitimacy of "transsexuality, intersexuality, and homosexuality." He says:

> Rather than retreating to their traditional morality, orthodox Christians should acknowledge the consequences of their own story and still should develop explicitly Christian versions of

---

⁵⁵ De Bruijne, *Verbonden voor het Leven*, 42.
⁵⁶ De Bruijne, *Verbonden voor het Leven*, 235.
⁵⁷ De Bruijne, *Verbonden voor het Leven*, 242-243, 247.
⁵⁸ De Bruijne, *Verbonden voor het Leven*, 249.

what their environment has earlier harvested in a secular manner. Suited to this is a renewed and future oriented interaction with sexuality and forming relationships. Even where the conviction remains that the biblical arrangement disallows a vision in which sexual union would henceforth also be suitable outside the context of a lifelong covenant between a man and a woman, various new sexual-ethical accents remain conceivable.[59]

De Bruijne attempts to justify his claim that a Christian sexual ethic that accepts the corrections of sexual liberationist ideology is an alternative version of the same liberationist dynamic by showing that there is a *conceptual* relation[60] between the affirmations of the Christian tradition and the alternative expressions of the proponents of sexual liberation regarding these four aspects distinguished above. Put differently, if I understand de Bruijne correctly, the sexual revolution is at its core a Christian renewal movement! In sum, de Bruijne concludes:

> Therefore, it is unsatisfactory when orthodox Christians simply oppose this sexual revolution. They [orthodox Christians] must acknowledge the *correction* that this revolution is bringing also to their tradition, a correction whose benefits, as we saw, they need not hesitate to share. Often the suitable response, on the basis of Christian traditions, is not confrontational rejection but their own alternative version of the same movement.[61]

---

[59] De Bruijne, "Seksualiteit en cultuurstrijd: Een theologische voorstel tot dialog," 281.

[60] De Bruijne, "Seksualiteit en cultuurstrijd: Een theologische voorstel tot dialog," 276.

[61] De Bruijne, "Seksualiteit en cultuurstrijd: Een theologische voorstel tot dialog," 276.

However, is that the case? What would have to be the case for there to be a conceptual relation between the affirmations of the Christian tradition and these alternative expressions of the emancipators? De Bruijne does not say.

Hermeneutics of Continuity

De Bruijne's colleague, Theo Boer, in Christian Healthcare Ethics at the Kampen Theological University, gives a brief account of the importance of preserving the continuity of "fixed anchor points" of the Christian moral tradition. They provide a justification for our moral judgments and choices when addressing contemporary moral challenges and issues.[62] The consequence of losing these fixed points of reference is that over time it entails "the end of the entire tradition." "Stated differently, a tradition must remain recognizable." He adds, "What is appealing in Roman Catholic thinking is the resolve to test every change by the question: How much change can a tradition endure before it ceases to be tradition?"[63]

This last sentence describes the pathos of liberal theology, as I described earlier contrasting with it the project of *ressourcement*. I find evidence of this pathos in De Bruijne's work. Boer does not properly frame the question that informs Roman Catholic thinking on the propositional truths of faith and morals and their alternative expressions in reflecting on the sense in which a doctrine, already confirmed and defined, is more fully known and deeply understood. Although he correctly focuses here on the question of continuity, he does not tell us that these fixed points

---

[62] Theo Boer, "Waarom ik Katholieke Ethiek nodig heb," in *Flirten met Rome, Protestanten naderen Katholieke*,ed., Almatine Leene (Amsterdam: Buijten & Schipperheijn, 2017), 37–47, especially 46.

[63] Boer, "Waarom ik Katholieke Ethiek nodig heb," 46.

of reference ground the tradition in affirmations of faith and morals that possess a *determinate* content of truth. Briefly, John XXIII drew this distinction in his opening address at the Second Vatican Council:

> For the deposit of faith, the truths contained in our venerable doctrine, are one thing; the fashion in which they are expressed, but with the same meaning and the same judgment [*eodem sensu eademque sententia*], is another thing.[64]

The subordinate clause, which I have cited in its Latin original, is part of a larger passage from the First Vatican Council's Dogmatic Constitution on Faith and Reason, *Dei Filius* (1869–1870). The phrase is earlier invoked by Pope Pius IX in the bull of 1854, *Ineffabilis Deus*, and also cited by Pope Leo XIII in his 1899 encyclical letter, *Testem benevolentiae Nostrae*. And this formula in *Dei Filius* is itself taken from the *Commonitorium* of St. Vincent of Lérins (445 AD), a Gallic monk, and the chief theologian of the Abbey of Lérins:[65] "Therefore, let there be growth and abundant progress in understanding, knowledge, and wisdom, in each and all, in individuals and in the whole Church, at all times and in the progress of ages, but only within the proper limits, i.e., *within the same dogma, the same meaning, the same judgment*" [*in eodem scilicet dogmate, eodem sensu eademque sententia*]."[66] In short, it is about "evolution within the same truth," or as Karl Rahner also put it, "it is change

---

[64] *Gaudet Mater Ecclesia*, §14.

[65] See Echeverria, "Vincent of Lérins: The Development of Christian Doctrine," 171-198. Eduardo Echeverria, *Revelation, History, and Truth: A Hermeneutics of Dogma* (New York: Peter Lang Publishing, 2018).

[66] Denzinger, §3020.

in, not of identity."⁶⁷ Aidan Nichols explains Rahner's Lérinian point about "development as change within identity—not change of identity. The decisive feature, in other words, is not [change], nor does the Church become cleverer as time proceeds. In this context, [progress] takes place within a self-identical reality and truth."⁶⁸ This italicized phrase of Vincent above means to say that the truth of a proposition is inextricably connected with its meaning. As to meaning, the way things are is what makes "meaning" true or false. Therefore, a proposition is true if what it says corresponds to the way objective reality is; otherwise, it is false. In other words, an account of the truth of dogma requires an ontological framework in which such truths correspond to what is basically an objective reality. So, this ontology is about "a relationship between language and reality in respect of truth."⁶⁹ Gavin D'Costa suggests that "any dogmatic expression must bear some determinative relationship to truth" and that is because "language," and one presumes D'Costa means, assertions, have a "proper referencing function to reality."⁷⁰ Furthermore, in the words of Bernard Lonergan, "Meaning of its nature is related to a 'meant,' and what is meant may or may not correspond to

---

⁶⁷ Karl Rahner, "The Development of Dogma," in *Theological Investigations*, vol. 1, trans. Cornelius Ernst, O. P. (Baltimore, MD: Helicon Press, 1961), 39–77, and at 45. Rahner is consistent with Vatican I, *Dei Filius*: "For the doctrine of faith that God has revealed has not been proposed like a philosophical system to be perfected by human ingenuity; rather, it has been committed to the spouse of Christ as a divine trust to be faithfully kept and infallibly declared," Denzinger §2020.

⁶⁸ Nichols, *From Newman to Congar*, 220.

⁶⁹ Paul Helm, *Faith, Form, and Fashion: Classical Reformed Theology and its Postmodern Critics* (Eugene, OR: Cascade Books, 2014), 157

⁷⁰ D'Costa, *Vatican II: Catholic Doctrines on Jews & Muslims*, 35.

what is so. If it corresponds, the meaning is true. If it does not correspond, the meaning is false."[71] Thus, a dogma's meaning is unchangeable because that meaning is true. The truths of faith are, if true, always and everywhere true; the different way of expressing these truths may vary in our attempts to communicate revealed truths more clearly and accurately, but these various linguistic expressions do not affect the truth of the propositions. This is a historically qualified foundationalism, a modest foundationalism, if you will.[72]

False Dilemma: Permanence and Change

In reply to De Bruijne's opposition between permanence and change, let me begin by making the point that natural-law morality, rightly understood, does not need to choose between permanence and change, between unchangeable principles and ongoing development of insight into their application.[73] De Bruijne seems to put the Catholic teaching in a false dilemma. Indeed, he is criticizing a straw man. John Paul II briefly addresses the very same concern voiced by De Bruijne regarding actual human existence and natural-law morality in his 1993 Encyclical Letter *Veritatis Splendor*: "The great concern of our contemporaries for historicity and for culture has led some to call into question

---

[71] Lonergan, "The Dehellenization of Dogma," 11–32, at 14 (scare quotes added).

[72] For an extensive discussion of this hermeneutics, see Echeverria, *Revelation, History, and Truth: A Hermeneutics of Dogma*, 1-45. See Echeverria, "Vincent of Lérins: The Development of Christian Doctrine," 171–98. Echeverria, "The Development of Christian Doctrine: Vincent of Lérins, G.C. Berkouwer, and Réginald Garrigou-Lagrange, OP," in *Roman Catholicism and Neo-Calvinism: Ecumenical and Polemical Engagements*, 249-339.

[73] This section is adapted from Echeverria, *"In the Beginning..." A Theology of the Body* (Eugene, Oregon: Pickwick Publications, 2011), 297-305.

the immutability of the natural law itself, and thus the existence of 'objective norms of morality' valid for all people of the present and the future, as for those of the past. Is it ever possible, they ask, to consider as universally valid and always binding certain rational determinations established in the past, when no one knew the progress humanity would make in it future?"[74] John Paul II's answer to this question avoids the horns of the dilemma between permanence and change. He argues that man, although as he actually and historically exists, exists in a particular culture, "is not exhaustively defined by that culture." In this connection, consider the mandate of Amnesty International.

> To seek the release of prisoners of conscience, people imprisoned solely for their beliefs, color, ethnic origin, sex, language, or religion, provided that they have neither used nor advocated the use of violence; to oppose the death penalty, torture, or other cruel, inhuman, or degrading punishment of all prisoners; to end extrajudicial executions or disappearances; to oppose abuses by opposition groups' hostage taking, the torture and killings of prisoners, and other arbitrary killings.[75]

This mandate raises the question of the foundation of human rights and the substantive nature of the human person in which these rights inhere. Some anti-foundational human rights skeptics have asked, "How on this earth, with all we know now about human variety and the elusive

---

[74] John Paul II, *Veritatis Splendor*, §53.

[75] John G. Healey, Executive Director, Amnesty Leadership Group mailing, December 5, 1991, quoted in Wayne Booth, "Individualism and the Mystery of the Social Self, or, Does Amnesty Have a Leg to Stand on?," in *Freedom and Interpretation: The Oxford Amnesty Lectures, 1992*, ed. Barbara Johnson (New York: Basic Books, 1993), 70-71.

nature of the self, how in the name of truth can Amnesty reasonably claim that certain actions committed by legitimate states are just plain wrong, regardless of circumstances?"[76] I hear an echo of this very point in De Bruijne's objection grounding moral norms in the creation order. And the answer to this question is to argue that certain acts like slavery and torture are fundamentally, universally wrong, not just in the USA and the Netherlands, but in all places and at all times. Indeed, 75 years ago the United Nations adopted a Universal Declaration of Human Rights. This document confirmed, as Pope John Paul II puts it in his 5 October 1995 speech to the U.N. General Assembly, that "there are indeed universal rights rooted in the nature of the person, rights that express the objective and inviolable demands of the universal moral law."[77]

This question regarding the permanence and universality of natural law grounded human right, was specifically addressed in the 1992 Oxford Amnesty Lectures. The lecture by Wayne Booth in this series stands out in my mind because he asks whether the idea of basic and inalienable human rights makes sense if human beings are centerless networks of beliefs and desires determined by historical circumstances. He says,

> Can we not expect that the world's ubiquitous torturers will welcome the rumor that advanced thinkers in the most advanced nations find no solid reality in that victim who cringes and weeps before their dry eyes? That precise fear was recently expressed to me by a young Chinese woman who had fled China

---

[76] This is the question that Wayne Booth raises and proposes to answer in his essay, "Individualism and the Mystery of the Social Self."

[77] John Paul II, *Make Room for the Mystery of God* (New York: Pauline Books and Media. 1995), 20.

after Tiananmen Square and then found, she said, that postmodernist Western thought seemed to deny her very existence as an individual protester.[78]

In this Chinese woman's plea, we see the tragic consequences of denying the idea of human rights—rights inherent in every person and prior to any Constitution and state legislation--and its ground in the transcendent dignity of the human person, of human nature itself.

Now, John Paul sees the permanent structural elements of man's human nature, the dynamic schemes of natural inclinations and their corresponding goods, to be integrally connected with man's own bodily dimensions. This particular spiritual and bodily structure is grounded in God's original plan of creation, the order of creation. Hence the import of "*Jesus' reference to the 'beginning'*," adds John Paul, "precisely where the social and cultural context of the time had distorted the primordial meaning and the role of certain moral norms (cf. Mt 19: 1-9)."[79] The truth of the natural law involves universality precisely because moral propositions grounded in that law are true. In this light, we can understand the following claim he makes:

> Inasmuch as [natural law] is inscribed in the rational nature of the person, it makes itself felt to all beings endowed with reason and living in history. . . . [And] inasmuch as the natural law expresses the dignity of the human person and lays the foundation for his fundamental rights and duties, it is universal in its precepts and its authority extends to all mankind. *This universality does not ignore the individuality of human beings*, nor is it op-

---

[78] Booth, "Individualism and the Mystery of the Social Self,"11.
[79] John Paul II, *Veritatis Splendor*, §53.

posed to the absolute uniqueness of each person. On the contrary, it embraces at its root each of the person's free acts, which are meant to bear witness to the universality of the true good.[80]

In this passage, John Paul assumes that the moral order flows from human nature itself. That is, he understands a human being as one who possesses a permanent nature or, as Jacques Maritain puts it, "an ontological structure which is a locus of intelligible necessities," meaning thereby, "man possesses ends which necessarily correspond to his essential constitution and which are the same for all."[81] In addition, according to Maritain, "But since man is endowed with intelligence and determines his own ends, it is up to him to put himself in tune with the ends necessarily demanded by his nature. This means that there is, by the very virtue of human nature, an order or a disposition which human reason can discover and according to which the human will must act in order to attune itself to the essential and necessary ends of the human being. The unwritten law, or natural law, is nothing more than that."[82] The ends to which human actions are ordered Maritain, following Aquinas, and John Paul agrees, considers as "goods" to be pursed, realized, and done, and these goods fulfill or perfect human beings because they are constitutive of their flourishing or well-being. Thus, the first principle of practical reason is as follows: "The good is to be done and sought; evil is to be avoided." This principle is fleshed out in the order of ends that is grounded in human nature and that is called by Maritain, a dynamic scheme of inclination and their corresponding goods. These inclinations that serve as principles of practical reason are summed up by William

---

[80] John Paul II, *Veritatis Splendor*, §51.

[81] Jacques Maritain, *Man and the State* (Chicago: Phoenix Books, The University of Chicago Press, 1951), 86.

[82] Jacques Maritain, *Man and the State*, 86.

May. Those permanent structural elements of man consist of that triple-tiered set of human goods described by Aquinas in *Summa Theologiae* I-II, Q. 94, art. 2.

> St. Thomas Aquinas identified a triple-tiered set of such human goods which, when grasped by our reason as ordered to action ("practical reason"), serve as first principles or starting points for practical deliberation—"what am I to do?" Aquinas' first set includes being itself, a good that human persons share with other entities, and since the being of living things is life itself, the basic human good at this level is that of life itself, including bodily life, health, and bodily integrity. His second set includes the sexual union of man and woman and the handing on and educating of human life, a set of goods human persons share with other sexually reproducing species but, of course, in a distinctive human way. His third set includes goods unique to human persons such as knowledge of the truth, especially truth about God, fellowship and friendship with other persons in a human community (friendship and justice, peace), and the good of being reasonable in making choices or what can be called the good of practical reasonableness.[83]

On the very question before us, then, Grisez argues, "human nature and natural-law morality are both stable and changing." In what sense is that the case? Human nature and natural-law morality are "stable, in that the givenness and fundamental unalterability of natural inclinations [to the basic human goods] account for the unalterability of the principles

---

[83] Ronald Lawler, O.F.M. Cap., Joseph Boyle, Jr., and William E. May, *Catholic Sexual Ethics, A Summary, Explanation and Defense*. Second Edition (Huntington, IN: Our Sunday Visitor, 1998), 9-10.

of natural law; but also changing, in that the dynamism of the inclinations [to the basic human goods], their openness to continuing and expanding fulfillment, accounts for the openness of natural law to authentic development."[84] Like Maritain, Grisez argues that those permanent structural elements of man's nature are the fundamental dynamic schemes of inclinations to human goods such as "the basic possibilities of human individuals as bodily creatures, endowed with intelligence, able to engage in fruitful work and creative play, psychically complex, capable of more or less completely reasonable action, in need of companionship, capable of love, and open to friendship with God in whose image they are made."[85] These structural elements of man's nature are creational givens, and hence do not change.

On the matter of human nature's unalterability, Finnis notes that "human nature in its basic possibilities of fulfillment, possibilities which are adequately known only by adverting to the basic forms of human flourishing which are understood in our grasp of fundamental reasons for action," does not change. He explains:

> Is there, then, anyone for whom it was not or is not or will not be the case that life and health, knowledge of truth and beauty, excellence in work and play, the harmony in friendship with others, the procreative friendship of marriage with another, personal harmony in interior integrity and peace and outer authenticity, and harmony with the source of all meaning and value, are the basic reasons for actions, the basic forms of the human fulfillment in which he. . . would wish to share and outside which no benefit or goal could seem really worthwhile? No. No such human person could be identified, and the talk of human

---

[84] Grisez, *The Way of the Lord Jesus*, I, 182.
[85] Grisez, *The Way of the Lord Jesus*, I, 183.

nature's changeability—equivocating between nature as actualized and nature as basic possibilities of fulfillment—fails to impinge on the foundations of morality.[86]

Hence, the moral precept forbidding murder is grounded on man's nature, namely, the basic good of human life, and that precept in its positive sense is meant to protect that good. What this means is that the murder of a human person is incompatible with "the general ends and innermost dynamic structure of [his] rational essence."[87] Maritain adds, "Hence the prohibition of murder is grounded on or required by the essence of man. The precept: thou shalt do no murder, is a precept of natural law."[88] In sum, there is a correlative relationship between the fundamental dynamic schemes of natural inclinations to the basic goods of human nature, on the one hand, and basic precepts of the natural law, corresponding to each natural inclination on the other.

In sum, the Catholic tradition does not remain caught in De Bruijne's false dilemma. On the one hand, then, human nature in its basic givenness does not change. On the other hand, says John Paul II, as I noted above, "Certainly there is a need to seek out and to discover *the most adequate formulation* for universal and permanent moral norms in the light of different cultural context, a formulation most capable of ceaselessly expressing their historical relevance, of making them understood and of authentically interpreting their truth."[89] Another Catholic theologian, David Tracy, takes a Lérinian position on the question of material continuity and discontinuity in respect of doctrine that

---

[86] John Finnis, *"Historical Consciousness" and Theological Foundations* (Toronto: Pontifical Institute of Medieval Studies, 1992), 25.
[87] Maritain, *Man and the State*, 88.
[88] Maritain, *Man and the State*, 88.
[89] John Paul II, *Veritatis Splendor*, §53.

is close to the one for which I am arguing in this chapter. His view is faithful to John XXIII's Lérinian conception. Tracy says, "Fidelity to orthodox judgment intrinsic to the particular meaning expressed in propositions is what counts, not the language itself." Again, "The judgments endure but always need new cultural and therefore linguistic formulations." And again, "A purely classicist understanding of language believes that a static unchanging, unchangeable, normative language is alone capable of expressing (*semper idem*) the community's *ortho-dox* beliefs."[90]

The first principle of the natural law is: we should do and seek good, and shun evil. For example, human life is a good to be sought, and sickness is to be shunned. Thus: "The natural inclination toward health and what protects and promotes it is constant and unchanging. Modern medicine, however, has given 'health' a much richer content for us than people of any previous era. Thus, even with regard to the basic good of life, the possibilities of human fulfillment are only gradually specified as humankind realizes and experiences them, then presses on to expand them further."[91] So the allegation that all natural-law morality of the sort that Church affirms cannot do justice to man's historical actuality is simply not the case. For the constancy of human nature and its corresponding unalterable principles of the natural law does not imply that all the possible applications of the natural law are already inscribed in the natural law. Rather, as the *Catechism of the Catholic Church* correctly notes, natural law thinking "can demand reflection that takes account of various conditions of life according to places, times, and circumstances."[92] In other words, the applications of universal and permanent

---

[90] David Tracy, "A Hermeneutics of Orthodoxy," in *Christian Orthodoxy*, eds. Felix Wilfred and Daniel F. Pilario, *Concilium* (2014/2), 71–81, 74–75.

[91] Grisez, *The Way of the Lord Jesus*, I, 182.

[92] *Catechism of the Catholic Church*, §1957.

moral norms, their most adequate formulation to existential situations of man, situations unheard of in human history, such as reproductive technologies, stem cell research, cloning, and the like, are not inscribed in the essential structure of human nature, and are known to man. The understanding of the truth of the moral law has unfolded in the interpretation and application of that law down the centuries. Drawing on the distinction between truth and its formulations, between moral propositions and their linguistic expressions, John Paul explains that the moral norms expressive of moral truths, although taking account of various conditions of life according to places, times, and circumstance, "remain valid in their substance" and hence "must be specified and determined '*eodem sensu eademque sententia*' [keeping the same meaning and the same judgment]" about that moral truth. So, there is growth in the understanding of moral truth, seeking our and discovering "the *most adequate formulation for universal and permanent moral norms*" without changing the substantive truth of morality. Maritain elaborates:

> Men know [natural law] with greater or less difficulty, and in different degrees, running the risk of error here as elsewhere. . . . That every sort of error and deviation is possible in the determination of these things merely proves that our sight is weak, our nature coarse, and that innumerable accidents can corrupt our judgment. . . . Man's knowledge of [natural law] has increased little by little as man's moral conscience has developed. . . . The knowledge which our own moral conscience has of this law is doubtless still imperfect, and very likely it will continue to develop and to become more refined as long as humanity exists. Only when the Gospel has penetrated to the very depth of hu-

man substance will natural law appear in its flower and its perfection.[93]

The concluding sentence of this passage from Maritain makes clear that not only the effects of sin upon human nature, but also the deepening of our knowledge regarding the fullest meaning of the natural law must be considered from the perspective of Christ's redemptive work. In short, , grace restores or renews nature, meaning thereby that God's grace in Christ restores all life to its fullness, penetrating and perfecting and transforming the fallen creation from within its own order, bringing creation into conformity with His will and purpose. Given this understanding of the relation between nature, sin and grace, we can understand why "'the Church affirms that underlying so many changes there are some things which do not change and are *ultimately founded upon Christ*, who is the same yesterday and today and forever'. Christ is the 'Beginning' who, having taken on human nature, definitively illumines it in its constitutive elements and in its dynamism of charity towards God and neighbor."[94]

Moral Authority?

In this connection, we cannot fail to note that De Bruijne leaves us confused about how to come to grips with the moral authority of the Bible. He works with a false dichotomy of narrative versus an approach to Scripture in which divine revelation consists (in part) of moral propositions, a divinely given revelation with cognitive content, in short, a propositional notion of revelation. Regarding the biblical narrative, De

---

[93] Maritain, *Man and the State*, 89-90.
[94] John Paul II, *Veritatis Splendor*, §53. The quote within the quote is from *Gaudium et Spes*, §10.

Bruijne states: "The Bible contains the story of the historical ways the Triune God in Christ chose to go with his people. Therefore, also ethics should not in the first place operate with biblical data [e.g., propositional truths] but be founded upon this salvation history."[95] De Bruijne adds, "Accordingly, ethics consists of making God's eschatological goal at the end of history into our own and of following him on his ways toward this goal."[96] As I shall argue below, De Bruijne, then, has a teleological approach to ethics. Although he doesn't say so, unlike De Bruijne, John Paul II clearly defines such an approach: "Consequently the moral life has an essential *'teleological character'*, since it consists in the deliberate ordering of human acts to God, the supreme good and ultimate end *(telos)* of man."[97] De Bruijne does give us a definition of ethics.

> We can describe ethics briefly as 'the reflection on the good life before God's face and, in that context, on good and evil.' Ethical hermeneutics therefore first of all requires an understanding of the good life and of good and evil. It is precisely ethics that involves us, our neighbor, and the world from the very outset.[98]

Most recently, he elaborates: "Christian ethics is not a puzzle of laying down biblical normative indications, but it is believing reflection

---

[95] De Bruijne, "Christian Ethics and God's Use of the Bible," in *Correctly Handling the Word of Truth, Reformed Hermeneutics Today*, edited by Mees te Velde & Gerhard H. Visscher (Eugene, OR: Wipf & Stock, 2014), 171-186, and at 175.

[96] De Bruijne, "Christian Ethics and God's Use of the Bible," 175.

[97] John Paul II, *Veritatis Splendor*, §73.

[98] De Bruijne, "Ethiek en hermeneutiek," in *Gereformeetde hermeneutiek vandaag, Theologische perspectieven*, eds. Ad de Bruijne en Hans Burger (Barneveld: De Vuurbaak, 2017),181.

about God, about his works and therefore about man, the world and everything that goes with that. In light of this, insight arises into what does and does not fit or accord with God."[99] Moral decisions are oriented to the true goal of human life.

According to De Bruijne's teleological approach to ethics, God is man's ultimate end, and hence human acts must be ordered to that end. But since De Bruijne rightly distinguishes good and evil, that means not all acts are as such, in their own essential character, capable of being ordered to God. How, then, does he morally assess whether a human act is capable of being ordered to God? Is it good intentions, circumstances, particularly the consequences, or is it the act itself, the moral object of his act?[100] As I shall show below, De Bruijne's approach to making moral decisions is such that since all human acts are historically bound they cannot be defined in the timeless abstract as absolutes.

However, the Catholic tradition disagrees because it has a significant place for concrete acts that are intrinsically immoral, meaning thereby as put by the late Dominican theologian, Benedict Ashley (1915-1913): "By their very nature [concrete acts] are contradictory to the true goal of human life, and can never serve as a means to it."[101] He elaborates:

> Moral wisdom requires us *first* to determine whether the act we are about to intend to perform is itself—objectively in its own essential character—capable of leading us toward God, or one which will frustrate this movement towards God. If then the latter [the act] is *intrinsically immoral*, not simply because it is contrary to God's command—although in fact God forbids that

---

[99] De Bruijne, *Verbonden voor het Leven*, 26.
[100] John Paul II, *Veritatis Splendor*, §73.
[101] Benedict Ashley, OP, *Living the Truth in Love: A Biblical Introduction to Moral Theology* (New York: Alba House, 1996), 132.

kind of actions—but because it obstructs the relation to God which the Christian and God mutually seek to strengthen, then no circumstances or good intentions can make such an action morally good.[102]

It is, then, the act itself that is intrinsically evil—*per se* and in itself incapable of being ordered to God and the good of the person.[103] In other words, since De Bruijne's ethics has no place for exceptionless moral norms, that is, moral absolutes, does he hold to the prominent alternative, namely, the system of "proportionate reason," in short, proportionalism, which denies that some acts are intrinsically immoral.[104] Ashley explains,

The fundamental thesis of the system of proportionate reason is that at least in the case of concrete moral norms it is never possible to judge that any human act is intrinsically immoral, without at the same time considering all the circumstances (including circumstantial intentions). Consequently, the basic principle of moral judgment is that to determine whether a concrete act is moral it is necessary to weigh the positive and negative values involved in this act, including its circumstances, and then to judge it good if there is a proportionate reason to perform the act, i.e., if the positive values outweighs the negative.[105]

Consider some examples of proportionate moral reasoning given by

---

[102] Ashley, *Living the Truth in Love*, 136.
[103] John Paul II, *Veritatis Splendor*, §81.
[104] Eijk, *De Band van de Liefde*, 35-6. See also, John Paul II, *Veritatis Splendor*, §75.
[105] Ashley, *Living the Truth in Love*, 134.

Cardinal Eijk. For one,

> However, there would be no absolute standards when it comes to concrete actions. This ethical theory was primarily developed to justify contraception. In itself, this would merely be an "ontic" evil, that is to say: a physical evil, but not yet a moral evil. Contraception, if used with selfish motives, is morally evil. If contraception is used for the realization of a value that is relatively more important than the physical evil of contraception (for example, preventing overpopulation), then contraception is morally good.[106]

For another example, consider homosexual conduct where the distinction between ontic and moral evil is applied. Homosexual conduct is considered contrary to nature and then something that possesses a certain ontic or physical evil, but not a moral evil. Eijk explains why on this view homosexual conduct is morally wrong when it is promiscuous.

> It [homosexual conduct] would be morally wrong only when it involves frequent changes in sexual partners, reflecting a selfish attitude that does not justify homosexual acts.[107]

However, homosexual conduct would be morally justified by a proportionate reason despite the conduct being contrary to nature and hence ontically evil when the goal is the search for an enduring interpersonal relationship of love between two men or two women.[108] Eijk criticizes this moral reasoning:

---

[106] Eijk, *De Band van de Liefde*, 35.
[107] Eijk, *De Band van de Liefde*, 35.
[108] Eijk, *De Band van de Liefde*, 35.

This attempt to legitimize homosexual acts is hardly convincing. Aristotle says that true friendship seeks the good of the other. How can a true loving relationship or friendship be built through an act that, upon closer inspection, is unnatural and therefore a moral evil? It is one of two things: either one considers sexual acts outside of marriage and separated from procreation to be compatible with human nature and thus permissible, or one holds the opposite view and considers them morally unacceptable.[109]

Eijk summarizes his objection to the system of proportionate reason, namely, that it is a "responsible relational" ethical position. There is no distinctive sexual ethics, considering the essence of sexual conduct; rather the morally decisive factor in a sexual relationship are none other than conformity to general moral norms governing relationships as such. Norms that prohibit lying, deception, and exploitation are sufficient to render sexual acts morally good. This is how Margaret Farley describes the norms for what she calls sexual justice: refusal to do unjust harm, free consent, mutuality, equality, commitment, fruitfulness, and social justice.[110] Furthermore, Eijk states:

---

[109] Eijk, *De Band van de Liefde*, 36.

[110] Margaret Farley, *Just Love: A Framework for Christian Sexual Ethics* (New York: Continuum, 2006), 231: "Sex should not be used in ways that exploit, objectify, or dominate; rape, violence, and harmful uses of power in sexual relationships are ruled out; freedom, wholeness, intimacy, pleasure are values to be affirmed in relationships marked by mutuality, equality, and some form of commitment; sexual relations like other profound interpersonal relations can and ought to be fruitful both within and beyond the relationship; the affections of desire and love that bring about and sustain sexual relationships are all in all

Acts, including sexual acts, are seen purely as a means to achieve an end. The nature of the act by which the end is realized is not decisive. Whatever the sexual act may be in itself—what matters is that it serves a loving relationship. *The fundamental problem here is that there is no clear definition of what love or sexuality is.*[111]

Ashley summarizes the chief objection to the system of proportionate reason.

Proportionalism is self-contradictory because it demands that one weigh the values and disvalues of an act *before* judging it to be moral or immoral. The values relevant to moral decision, however, must be weighed as they are appropriate or inappropriate means to the true final end of life; a value is positive if it is an effective means, negative if it is an ineffective or harmful means. But as soon as one considers an act as a means *in relation* to the end of life, one is judging it morally. Proportionalists therefore contradict themselves by claiming first to weigh pre-moral [ontic or physical] values to determine their proportionate weight when in fact they are either already weighing them as moral values, or they are weighing them with respect to characteristics which are morally irrelevant.[112]

We will return below to De Bruijne's teleological approach to the

---

genuinely to affirm both lover and beloved." Chapter 4 has an extensive analysis of Farley's moral theology.

[111] Eijk, *De Band van de Liefde*, 38. Emphasis added.
[112] Ashley, *Living the Truth in Love*, 136.

moral life.

Teleological Approach to the Moral Life

Turning now to De Bruijne's teleological approach, the Christian moral life, and the responsibility to make choices that are worthy of the calling that we have received in Christ, is located within the context of the overarching biblical narrative of creation, fall into sin, redemption, and eschaton. Of course, this authoritative biblical narrative is central for understanding the meaning and purpose of the moral life in Christ.[113] De Bruijne claims that the neo-Calvinism of Kuyper and Bavinck focused on revelation and salvation history, rather than moral propositions. He explains, "Separate truths gave way to the great trajectory of the work of the Triune God. That work progresses from creation to re-creation, centered on Christ's redemption. That new approach made the teaching less dependent on (the exegesis of) a few specific texts. Moreover, the historical context of those texts could now rise to the surface more clearly."[114]

In other words, De Bruijne suggests here that someone who operates in his appeal to Scripture with the presupposition of *biblicism*. Dutch theologian, the late Jochem Douma, and professor at Kampen Theological University, gives a helpful definition of biblicism: "By *biblicism* we understand that appeal to Scripture which uses Bible texts in an atomistic (isolated) way by lifting them out of their immediate contexts or out of the whole context of Scripture." Let's call this atomistic appeal to Scripture the bad sense of using proof-texts. But De Bruijne doesn't distinguish this bad sense from a good sense of using biblical proof-texts,

---

[113] De Bruijne, "Ethiek en hermeneutiek," 183.
[114] On this, see De Bruijne, "Ethiek en hermeneutiek," 184.

exegetically and scripturally. Otherwise, "It would be a hopeless situation," Douma correctly adds, "if by definition every appeal to Scripture were biblicistic. For then a pure appeal to Scripture in ethics [or theology] would be simply impossible."[115]

Furthermore, De Bruijne stresses narrative, namely, "the great story of God's works in Christ (Phil. 1:27)," as the foundation of Christian ethics rather than "God's work of creation or on 'nature' with its innate laws."[116] Still, since the historic Christian faith teaches the Scriptures to be divinely authoritative for morals, then, we must still come to terms with the moral authority of specific moral directives, commandments, and rules, in short, propositional truth. This classical view is well stated by John Paul II, and De Bruijne seems to deny it, namely, "that there exist, in Divine Revelation, a specific and determined moral content, universally valid and permanent."[117]

The use of Scripture as morally authoritative does not ascribe authority to everything that Scripture, from Genesis to Revelation, commands and forbids.[118] But the key to determining which moral teachings are binding lies in Scripture itself since we can identify what ceremonial

---

[115] Jochem Douma, "Appendix: The Use of Scripture in Ethics," in *The Ten Commandments: Manual for the Christian Life*, trans. Nelson D. Kloosterman (Phillipsburg,m NJ: P&R Publishing, 1996),363-364. Similarly, Berkouwer, *Heilige Schrift*, II, 443 [363]: "It is possible to read Scripture in a frame of reference whereby a method—though unscientific—or a prejudice deprives human understanding of the mystery of Scripture. It is possible to read and use Scripture out of context and coherence, to isolate and atomize it, and to abandon it to arbitrariness and literalistic exegesis."

[116] Douma, "Appendix: The Use of Scripture in Ethics," 363-364.

[117] John Paul II, *Veritatis Splendor*, §37. See also. Robert A.J. Gagnon, "Are There Universally Valid Sex Precepts?" in *Horizons in Biblical Theology* 24 (2002): 72-125.

[118] This section is adapted from Echeverria, *"In the Beginning..." A Theology of the Body* (Eugene, Oregon: Pickwick Publications, 2011), 97-100.

laws and civil laws, including the penal code, are no longer binding.[119] To understand the reason why not everything accurately recorded in Scripture has normative authority for our faith and conduct, but only has historical authority, that is, it has authority for the people of the time, we need to think through the implication of the principle that the economy of revelation was given in the form of a history, passing through a succession of periods, culminating in Jesus Christ, who is both the mediator and fullness of revelation.[120] In other words, as Bavinck succinctly put it, "The revelation contained in Scripture is a historical and organic whole." He explains:

> Much of what was commanded and instituted by God, or prescribed and enjoined by prophets and apostles, no longer applies to us directly and pertained to persons living in an earlier age. The command to Abraham to offer up his son, the command to Israel to kill all the Canaanites, the ceremonial and civil laws in force in the days of the OT, the decrees of the synod of Jerusalem, and many more things, while indeed useful for instruction and correction as history, cannot and may not any longer be obeyed by us. Furthermore, the record of revelation not only includes the good works of the saints but also the evil deeds of the

---

[119] In De Bruijne, "Ethiek en hermeneutiek," 187, he refers to this threefold distinction in passing but does not find it helpful for addressing the question of moral authority. Obviously, I disagree.

[120] Millard Erickson offers a set of criteria to distinguish what is "historically authoritative" and "normatively authoritative": (1) constancy across cultures, (2) universal setting, (3) a recognized permanent factor as a base, (4) indissoluble link with an experience regarded as essential, and (5) final position within progressive revelation," *Christian Theology*, (Grand Rapids: Baker Academic, 2013), 130-134.

ungodly. Frequently words and actions are recorded in Scripture, therefore, that, while they are represented as historically true, are not presented as normative. . . . Also the sins of the saints, of Abraham, Moses, Job, Jeremiah, Peter, etc., are given as a warning, not as models for our conduct.[121]

Perhaps it would be helpful for understanding Bavinck's point about the difference between historical and normative authority to distinguish two senses of "reveal."[122] First, there is the sense of "reveal" that means the "*recording* or *reporting* sense." "Revelation in this sense is simply the accurate recording of the often mistaken and wicked beliefs and opinions of men. It is revelation to us in that without these opinions and views being recorded it is highly probable that we would be ignorant of them. This is probably the case also with the recording of certain historical events."[123] There is a second of "reveal" that means the "*disclosing* or *endorsing* sense." "If God reveals in this sense, then his disclosure of whatever the matter is, is a necessary and sufficient condition for that matter being true or right." In other words, in the disclosing or endorsing sense of "reveal" what is revealed does correspond to what God himself regards as being true. Now, the difference between these two senses of "reveal" has the following implications. First, there are false beliefs, opinions and the like that are accurately recorded or reported in the Bible, but that does not count against identifying the Bible with God's special revelation because what is revealed, in the recording or reporting sense of "reveal," does not correspond to what God himself regards as

---

[121] Bavinck, *Gereformeerde Dogmatiek*, I, 428-429 [459].

[122] I am following Paul Helm's illuminating distinction between the two senses of "reveal" in his book, *The Divine Revelation; The Basic Issues* (Vancouver: Regent College Publishing, 2004), 68-70.

[123] Helm, *The Divine Revelation*, 68-70.

true, and is therefore false. Thus, "if the Bible in its entirety is God's revelation it does not follow that every sentence of the Bible is God's revelation [in the second sense of 'reveal'], any more than it follows that because a poem rhymes every word in the poem rhymes." There is a second important implication that follows from this distinction. That is, Paul Helm concludes, "this distinction imposes a considerable hermeneutical burden on any would-be interpreter of the special revelation. For he has to determine the exact limits of each kind of revelation, otherwise it may happen that the mistaken beliefs of men would be equated with the special revelation of God's will."[124] There remains to ask whether there is a way to ease the hermeneutical burden on the would-be interpreter of special revelation. I want to suggest the following criteria that Robert A.J. Gagnon stipulates for anyone who takes Scripture to be the primary authority for faith and practice. Gagnon writes:

> If that primacy counts for anything, it must count for core values. Core values are values that are held 1. pervasively throughout Scripture (at least implicitly), 2. absolutely (without exceptions), and ... 3. strongly (as a matter of significance). This applies all the more to instances in which: 4. such values emerged in opposition to contrary cultural trends and ... 5. have prevailed in the church for two millennia. *Such a [core] value is the biblical limitation of sex to intercourse between male and female, with its attendant opposition to same-sex intercourse.* If the authority of Scripture means anything, those who seek to overturn its core values must meet an extraordinary burden of proof. The evidence must be so strong and unambiguous that it not only

---

[124] Helm, *The Divine Revelation*, 68-70.

makes the witness of Scripture pale by comparison but also directly refutes the reasons for the Bible's position.[125]

One point of clarification here may be needed. Scripture is an integrated whole, a single, unified, authoritative Word of God, which means that the whole of Scripture, in light of its God-breathed character, has canonical authority. In that sense all of Scripture is normative. Hence, we cannot *abstractly separate* in Scripture the authority of history and normative authority. So, I reject the dualistic construal of the distinction between historical and normative authority that leads to the process of sifting and separating the Word of God and the word of men. The point I am making then—in line with Bavinck and Berkouwer—should not be interpreted as dualism.[126] Rather, the question has to do with distinct kinds of scriptural authority, namely, that not all Scriptural authority is the authority of a law enacted by a legislature. For God's Word has historical contours. Against that background, we can easily understand why Bavinck judges that the sins of the saints in Scripture, although given as a warning, still have authority for us. He elaborates: "Even in the deceptive words of Satan and the evil deeds of the ungodly, God still has something to say to us. Scripture is not only useful for teaching but also for warning and reproof. It teaches and corrects us, both by deterrence and by exhortation, both by shaming and by consoling us." Still, adds Bavinck, the distinction between historical and normative authority "does make clear that Scripture cannot and may not be understood as a fully articulated code of law. Appeal to a text apart from its context is not sufficient for a dogma. The revelation recorded in Scripture is a historical and organic whole. That is how it has to be read and interpreted. A

---

[125] Dan O. Via and Robert A.J. Gagnon, *Homosexuality and the Bible, Two Views* (Minneapolis: Fortress Press, 2003), 42; italics added.

[126] Berkouwer, *De Heilige Schrift*, II, 110-111 [190-192].

dogma that comes to us with authority and intends to be a rule for our life and conduct must be rooted in and inferred from the entire organism of Scripture. The authority of Scripture is different from the authority of an act of parliament or congress."[127]

Returning now to my charge that De Bruijne is confused on Scripture's moral authority. This confusion stems from his rejection of moral foundationalism, even a historically conscious foundationalism as I sketched above. He claims, "This combination of the traditional appeal to the Bible with modern foundationalism has rendered Christian ethics vulnerable to postmodernism."[128] Why? De Bruijne says that a foundationalist approach to biblical ethics renders it susceptible to skepticism because it "fails to establish one single interpretation and application that everyone accepts." But does epistemic moral diversity entail the denial of moral objectivity. De Bruijne seems to thinks so. For that reason, he rejects moral foundationalism on the following ground: "There are no privileged epistemic positions, and no certain foundations for beliefs. All claims are judged by conventions or language games, which have no deeper grounding. There are no neutral, transcultural standards for settling disagreements."[129] De Bruijne concurs with postmodernism, particularly with respect to ethical judgments. "Ethical conclusions are *by definition not objective*. Postmodernism exposed the underlying interests or motives that act as guiding principles behind finely constructed rational arguments and final conclusions."[130] Put differently, De Bruijne thinks not only that there are no universally valid moral precepts

---

[127] Bavinck, *Gereformeerde Dogmatiek*, I, 429 [460].

[128] De Bruijne, "Christian Ethics and God's Use of the Bible, 173.

[129] Alvin Goldman, *Knowledge in a Social World* (Oxford: Clarendon Press, 1999), 10.

[130] Ad de Bruijne, "De kunst van het verstaan: Hermeneutiek in Kampen," 191, emphasis added.

grounded in an objective moral order, but also that these precepts cannot be objectively known to be the case. His denial, then of objective judgments should be seen against the background of the distinction between ontological and epistemic objectivity.[131] Paul Helm helpfully distinguishes between the "conditions under which something is true" and the "conditions under which something is known to be true."[132] Corresponding to ontological objectivity, then, and hence to the conditions under which something is true, is a realist notion of truth: a proposition is true if and only if what that proposition asserts is in fact the case about objective reality; otherwise, the proposition is false. Corresponding to epistemic objectivity, and hence to the conditions under which something is known to be true, is the "question of how our beliefs about and knowledge of the world are to be properly arrived at, the question of the proper manner of human enquiry. Is it possible to gain knowledge and belief that is objective, that is not 'made up'? And if so, in what sense is

---

[131] Helm, *Divine Revelation*, 40. See also, Helm, "Why be Objective?," in *Objective Knowledge: A Christian Perspective*, editor, Paul Helm (Leicester, England: Inter-Varsity Press, 1987), 29–40. It is precisely the distinction between ontological and epistemic objectivity, and hence the "conditions under which something is true" and the "conditions under which something is known to be true," that is overlooked by the authors of the 1979 synodical report of the former Gereformeerde Kerk in the Netherlands, *God Met Ons, Over de Aard van het Schriftgezag*, [God with us: The Nature of Biblical Authority], especially Chapter I, "Veranderingen in het Waarheidsbegrip,"[Changes in the Concept of Truth] confuses ontological and epistemological questions: what there is and how we can know it are two different questions. The report calls for a "relational" as opposed to the traditional "objective" notion of truth, meaning thereby a "correspondence" understanding of truth, wrongly claiming that a "realist" notion of truth—a proposition is true if and only if what that proposition asserts is in fact the case about objective reality; otherwise, it is false—has no place for the conditions under which the truth-seeker knows something to be true.

[132] Helm, *Divine Revelation*, 39.

this objective?"¹³³ De Bruijne seems to think objective moral knowledge is not available.

Ethics and Hermeneutics

There is another reason why De Bruijne rejects moral foundationalism. The latter turns biblical moral instruction into a self-contained rigid whole of logical principles, leaving no room for historical development. "The Bible then functions as a collection of truths (propositions, theses). In addition to truths that focus on what one must believe (called *credenda*), there are also those that deal with what one must do (*agenda*)."¹³⁴ Is this a fair characterization of moral foundationalism, in particular, of a historically qualified foundationalism, as I sketched above. No, I don't think so. Briefly, let's consider ethics and hermeneutics in the light of several models of revelation.¹³⁵

> [1] Moral guidelines (norms) can and must be *deduced* from the Bible as the revealed Word of God:
>
> Variant (a): they can be deduced directly because Revelation=Word=Scripture=text;
> Variant (b): they can be deduced directly but not without taking account of the *historical distance* between the biblical writers and our time. This is done by factoring the difference in situation into the formation of a judgment;

---

¹³³ Helm, "Why be Objective?" 33.
¹³⁴ De Bruijne, "Ethiek en hermeneutiek," 182.
¹³⁵ This section is adapted from Echeverria, *"In the Beginning..." A Theology of the Body*, 109-114.

Variant (c): they can be deduced *indirectly* by way of an appeal to central biblical motifs (covenant, view of man, view of the body, the love-command), etc.).

[2] One can indeed deduce guidelines for action from the Bible, not primarily because their moral validity is rooted in the fact that they are laid down in Scripture, but because, from an ethical viewpoint, they are good for people. Consequently, we find them also in the Bible. To "deduce" means one can also trace them to Scripture. In the Bible, though morality often turns out to be crucial in the end, it is not the central issue. God's design is to continue to teach us even through a fallen nature, culture, and history.

[3] Central to our agenda must be the doing of God's will. That does not consist in following rules but is discovered in seeing what God is concretely doing in history. The church has found that God's action is liberating. The Bible is the story of liberation from oppression. For that reason we must not automatically do the same today as what God's people did in earlier times. The church must understand the Bible in light of its concrete experience with liberation and oppression.[136]

As I see it, model [1], in all its variants, has been consistently used by Christians throughout the centuries in appealing to the authority of Scripture—but only as long as the unity of Scripture and its reliability as the Word of God was accepted as a first principle of the moral life as well

---

[136] On these models, see Pim Pronk, *Against Nature? Types of Moral Argumentation regarding Homosexuality* (Grand Rapids, MI: Eerdmans, 1994), 283-284.

as in doctrinal matters, indispensable and decisive. The moral foundationalism that De Bruijne rejects is best understood as variant (a).

Variant (b) of Model (1), takes account of the *historical distance* between the biblical writers and our time without a wholesale abandonment of Scriptural norms. According to Jochem Douma, Scriptural revelation functions in a variety of ways as a moral authority—it functions as *guide, guard, compass,* and *example*.[137] Helpful here in distinguishing these various functions is Lewis Smedes' distinction between "primary commandments" and "concrete commandments." The former cover specific areas of life, such as human existence, property, communication, marriage, family. The latter demand or prohibit a specific act in the context of applying a primary command.

First, Scripture functions as a *guide* telling us specifically and concretely what is good and evil. There are primary commands against murdering my neighbor, against stealing or lying, or against committing adultery, and disrespecting parental authority in the family. These commands are meant to safeguard respect for persons. They are universal—they are always and everywhere valid, because it is true of all men that they should not kill, steal, lie, dishonor their parents, or commit adultery. Of course, not all men heed these commandments, but all men should. Yet, while these commands stand above cultural relativities—children should obey their parents is universally valid—some specific applications of these commands, so-called concrete commands—executing a son who swears at his father—are not accepted now as binding. Such commands are now understood to be a cultural rather than an absolute norm expressed in a primary commandment.

---

[137] Douma, "Appendix: The Use of Scripture in Ethics," 367-376. The remainder of this section is adapted from Echeverria, *"In the Beginning . . ." A Theology of the Body,* 114-119.

Biblical revelation also functions as a *guard*. This is especially the case when a direct appeal to Scripture is not possible because of the difference in situation between the biblical time and now. We're all aware of, and have been influenced by, cultural developments that have led to changes in, for example, the relationships between husbands and wives, parents and children, government and citizens. For instance, we cannot directly appeal to Scripture to justify the rise of human rights, democracy, freedom of religion, and better forms of government. In other words, Scripture cannot function as a direct guide (in the above stated sense of telling us specifically and concretely what is good and evil) on these and other related matters. This is not to say that the biblical revelation is irrelevant, say, for the notion of human rights.

Nonetheless, and here we can see the import of variant (c) of Model [1], the Biblical revelation has played a crucial and authoritative role as guard for various cultural changes and developments in human rights issues like the abolition of slavery, child labor, and colonialism. That man is created in the "image and likeness of God" (Gen. 1:26-27) is an inherent indication of human worth and, with it, personal dignity. Furthermore, the Biblical insistence that justice be done for the powerless, especially the poor, widows, orphans, and strangers, suggests that respect is due to them on the basis of their inviolable dignity. Moreover, the saving revelation of the Father's love in Jesus' death on the cross reveals to man, as John Paul II says, "not only the boundless love of God who 'so loved the world that He gave His only Son' (Jn. 3:16), but also the *incomparable value of every human person*."[138] In connection with the pope's point, we can easily understand what Douma rightly says about the function of Scripture as guard: "Scripture is . . . a guard that

---

[138] John Paul II, *Evangelium Vitae*, §2.

warns against corrupt developments. Old Testament prophets left behind no blueprint for political and social relationships, but they certainly denounced abuses where God was not being honored and people were not being respected. Scripture does not choose for or against democracy and other matters that we today value highly. But the Bible does sharpen our vision for seeing where people are abused and oppressed, regardless of political or economic system."

Biblical revelation also functions as a *compass* indicating the general direction we should go for finding an answer to the question of what is good or evil in a universally valid sense. For example, we could appeal to the universally valid Scriptural prohibitions or primary commands against homosexual relations (see Rom 1:21-27; 1 Cor 6:9-10), but we can also use Scripture as a compass for dealing with the question of the biblical validity of such relations. Consider the biblical account of God's original creation of sexual differentiation from the beginning ("male and female He created them" states Gen. 1:27), of His ordaining sexual relations to be in the form of male-female union, because man and woman were created for one another in full complementarity (Gen. 2:18-23), of man and woman—Adam and Eve—becoming "one flesh," one reality (Gen. 2:24), and last but not least, the procreative openness to new life that is divinely enjoined, "be fruitful and multiply" (Gen. 1:28) .

The creation account in God's Word presents the constant principles for sexual activity that remain valid in every age—sex belongs within the context of marriage, marriage is exclusively heterosexual in nature, whose rationale is the full complementarity of the man-woman relationship as well as procreative openness to new life. This creation account is reaffirmed in the New Testament by Jesus Christ (Matt 19:4-6), as well as St. Paul (Eph 5:31), as the original design of the Creator. Thus, in light of creation, there is no biblical defense for homosexuality, because it belongs to the realm of man's fall into sin and not to the divine order of creation. The Bible gives us, then, constant principles that help us to discover what we should think and do, and in this sense, it can be used as a compass.

We should now add, as Robert Gagnon correctly states, that every single scriptural text (whether narrative, law, proverb, poetry, and moral exhortation) treating the issue of homosexual practice treats it as an offense of great abhorrence to God. In short, all these texts presuppose a male-female prerequisite. In other words, as Gagnon puts it, "the male-female prerequisite is the foundational prerequisite for defining most other sexual norms." How so?

Well, the scriptural norm of marital monogamy and indissolubility are based on the foundational principle of the male-female prerequisite. The two-in-oneness of the sexes ordained by God at creation is the foundation limiting the number of persons in a conjugal bond. We must pause here to consider the objection, especially with respect to Jesus, that he "had no interest in maintaining a male-female requirement for sexual relations." In reply to this objection, Robert Gagnon persuasively writes: "What the evidence *really* shows: Jesus believed that a male-female requirement for sexual relations was foundational, a core value of Scripture's sexual ethics on which other sexual standards should be based, including the 'twoness of a sexual union'." [139] He elaborates:

> The male-female prerequisite is the foundation or prior analogue for defining other critical sexual norms. Jesus himself clearly predicated his view of marital monogamy and indissolubility on the foundation of Gen 1:27 and 2:24, texts that have only one thing in common: the fact that an acceptable sexual

---

[139] Gagnon, "What the Evidence *Really* Says about Scripture and Homosexual Practice: Five Issues," March 14, 2009, http://robgagnon.net/articles/homosexScripReallySays.doc.pdf.

bond before God entails as its first prerequisite (after the assumption of an intra-human bond) a man and a woman (Mark 10:6-9; Matt 19:4-6). Jesus argued that the "twoness" of the sexes ordained by God at creation was the foundation for limiting the number of persons in a sexual bond to two, whether concurrently (as in polygamy) or serially (as in repetitive divorce and remarriage). The foundation can hardly be less significant than the regulation predicated on it; indeed, it must be the reverse. . . . The principle by which same-sex intercourse is rejected is also the principle by which incest, even of an adult and consensual sort, is rejected. Incest is wrong because, as Lev 18:6 states, it involves sexual intercourse with "the flesh of one's own flesh." In other words, it involves the attempted merger with someone who is already too much of a formal or structural same on a familial level. The degree of formal or structural sameness is felt even more keenly in the case of homosexual practice, only now on the level of sex or gender, because sex or gender is a more integral component of sexual relations, and more foundationally defines it, than is and does the degree of blood relatedness. So the prohibition of incest can be, and probably was, analogically derived from the more foundational prohibition of same-sex intercourse.[140]

Now, following Douma, I have been arguing that Scriptural revelation functions in a variety of ways as a moral authority—it functions as *guide, guard, compass,* and *example.* I have already briefly shown how it functions in the first three senses. I now want say something about how

---

[140] Robert A. J. Gagnon, "What Should Faithful Lutherans in the ELCA Do?"September 30, 2009, http://robgagnon.net/articles/homosex-ELCAonWhatToDo.pdf.

it functions as an *example*: the Bible also provides the example that Christ and others have given. As a *model*, we have the lives of the saints in the Old and New Testament (Luke 4:25-27; 1 Cor 10:1-5; Phil 3:17; 2 Thess 3:9; Heb 6:12; Heb11-12:1; James 5:17-20). No doubt, following Christ, who is our great example, is even more essential to the Christian moral life (Matt 16:24; 19:21; John 13:15; 1 Cor 11:1; 1 Peter 2:21). Following Christ involves holding fast to His very person, indeed it is abiding in a living relationship with Him. Thus, following Christ is not an outward imitation, but the existential reality of being in love with God, because Christ dwells by faith in the heart of the believer (see Eph 3:17). In short, following Christ means being conformed to Him, which is the effect of grace, of the active presence of the Holy Spirit in the believer's life.[141]

Thus, being in love with Christ moves us to live differently than unbelievers. In the words of Douma, "The Christian must walk differently from the pagan, not (only) because the Ten Commandments require this of him, but because he has learned to know Christ (Eph 4:20). He must have an attitude of forgiveness, even as God in Christ has forgiven him (Eph 4:32). He must find out what is pleasing to Christ (Eph 5:10). In their marriage, husband and wife must reflect the relationship between Christ and His church (5:22). Christians must flee fornication because their bodies are members of Christ (1 Cor 6:3ff.)."[142]

Model (2), which is compatible with [1], should be understood in terms of natural law, which purports to defend the universal claims for biblical morality. On this Model [2], Scriptural moral norms are the Creator's norms, and they are expressions of his design for human life. Here, too, we need to distinguish unchangeable propositional truths of faith

---

[141] John Paul II, *Veritatis Splendor*, §§19-20.
[142] Douma, "Appendix: The Use of Scripture in Ethics," 374.

and morals, on the one hand, and their alternative expressions in reflecting on the sense in which a doctrine, on the other, already confirmed and defined, is more fully known and deeply understood. Unlike De Bruijne, John Paul II draws that distinction, following Vincent of Lérins:

> Certainly, there is a need to seek out and to discover *the most adequate formulation* for universal and permanent moral norms in the light of different cultural contexts, a formulation most capable of ceaselessly expressing their historical relevance, of making them understood and of authentically interpreting their truth. This truth of the moral law — like that of the "deposit of faith" — unfolds down the centuries: the norms expressing that truth remain valid in their substance, but must be specified and determined *"eodem sensu eademque sententia"* in the light of historical circumstances by the Church's Magisterium, whose decision is preceded and accompanied by the work of interpretation and formulation characteristic of the reason of individual believers and of theological reflection.[143]

In order, then, to work out the relation between Models [1] and [2] we need to discuss the larger question of how Christ relates creation and the will of God. "Is Christ in continuity with creation? Or is Christ in disjunction with creation?" In other words, what is the relation between redemption and creation? This theological question is fundamental to understanding John Paul II's in *Man and Woman He Created Them: The Theology of the Body*. The pope states that Genesis 2 and 3 theologically gives us an "account that is a description of events" that makes clear "the essential difference *between the state of man's sinfulness and that of his*

---

[143] John Paul II, *Veritatis Splendor*, §53. See also §29.

original innocence." That is, there are "two different states of human nature, '*status naturae integrae*' (state of integral nature) and '*status naturae lapse*' (state of fallen nature)."[144] Yet, John Paul argues that the order of creation is the essential continuity between creation, fall into sin, and grace in Christ. He writes, "*Christ's words* [in Mt 19: 3-8], which appeal to the 'beginning', *allow us to find an essential continuity in man and a link* between these two different states or dimensions of the human being ['*status naturae integrae*' and '*status naturae lapsae*', that is, the state of integral nature and the state of fallen nature]."[145] Redemption, then, is about the restoration of the fallen creation.

De Bruijn recognizes this perspective: ""There are traditions that conceive of the destiny of man and creation primarily as the restoration of the perfection of the beginning."[146] Adds De Bruijn, "But the Bible provides reason to expect an end that will surpass that beginning and will in many ways have been unimagined."[147] In other words, De Bruijne claims, we can justify in an eschatological light "further [sexual] variation within the framework of being a man and being a woman in accordance with our future."[148] This is the *crux* of De Bruijne's interpretation of creation and the eschaton, namely, his plea for "ontic novelty," he assures us, does not mean that God can deny or contradict the law of creation. It is hard to see how the search for "ontic novelty" does not deny or contradict the law of creation if that law justifies what "specifies sexual love as such from parental or filial or fraternal or friendly love. . . . by virtue of the differentiation of the human race into two complementary

---

[144] Pope John Paul II, *Man and Woman He Created Them*, 3.3.
[145] Pope John Paul II, *Man and Woman He Created Them*, 4.1.
[146] De Bruijne, *Verbonden voor het Leven*, 249.
[147] De Bruijne, *Verbonden voor het Leven*, 249.
[148] De Bruijne, *Verbonden voor het Leven*, 245.

sexes"[149] Ashley adds, "Thus what specifies sexual love is that humanity was created male and female with a drive to sexual union precisely in view of the *family* community through which only the expansion, continuity, and education of the human species can be attained."[150]

Furthermore, in the creation perspective before us, grace restores or renews nature, meaning thereby that God's grace in Christ restores all life to its fullness, penetrating and perfecting and transforming the fallen creation from within its own order, bringing creation into conformity with His will and purpose.

As the *Catechism of the Catholic Church* puts it: "Jesus came to restore creation to the purity of its origins."[151] Elsewhere in the *Catechism* we read: "In his preaching Jesus unequivocally taught the original meaning of the union of man and woman as the Creator willed it from the beginning.... *By coming to restore the original order of creation disturbed by sin*, [Jesus] himself gives the strength and grace to live marriage in the new dimension of the Reign of God."[152] This question is raised against the background of a fallen creation. Given the fallen creation, does new life in Christ oppose creation? Put differently: does grace replace fallen nature? "Nature" here has the chief meaning of ontological rather than physical or biological. So, when we ask about the relation between nature, sin and grace, we are asking in what manner and to what extent sin and grace affect the essence or structure of reality. On the one hand, are the structures of creation so corrupted that grace, no longer able to transform them, merely replaces them altogether by adding the spiritual realm over and above creation, a *donum superadditum*? On the other

---

[149] Ashley, *Living the Truth in Love*, 429.
[150] Ashley, *Living the Truth in Love*, 429.
[151] *Catechism of the Catholic Church*, §2336.
[152] *Catechism of the Catholic Church*, §2336; §1614-15; italics added.

hand, does grace leave nature untouched, merely completing or supplementing it, with nature taken to be unaffected by the Fall or, in turn, by Redemption internally, which effectively limits the scope of sin and redemption to the supernatural realm and results in naturalism on the level of nature.[153]

In the early twentieth century, the great French Catholic thinker, Jacques Maritain, wisely noted that it is erroneous to ignore that there is a distinction between nature and grace as well as a union.[154] How then should we understand the union-in-distinctness of nature and grace? In particular, how do we understand the Thomistic dictum that grace does not abolish nature but presupposes it? The brief answer to this question must be that *grace restores or renews nature*, meaning thereby that God's grace in Christ *restores all life to its fullness, penetrating and perfecting and transforming the fallen creation from within its own order*, bringing creation into conformity with His will and purpose.[155] In the words of Henri de Lubac, "The supernatural does not merely *elevate* (this traditional term is correct, but it is inadequate by itself) . . . [Rather] it *transforms it* . . . 'Behold, I make all things new!' (Rev 21:5). Christianity is 'a doctrine of transformation' because the Spirit of Christ comes to permeate the first creation and make of it a 'new creature'. What is true of the final great transformation, on the occasion of the 'Parousia' at which there will arise 'new heavens and a new earth' (Revelation 21), is already

---

[153] On this point, see De Lubac, *Catholicism: Christ and the Common Destiny of Man*, 313-314.

[154] "*There is one error that consists in ignoring the distinction between nature and grace. There is another that consists in ignoring their union,*" Jacques Maritain, *Clairvoyance de Rome*, 222 (italics added) as cited in De Lubac, "Apologetics and Theology," *Theological Fragments*, 91-104, and this citation at 103n28.

[155] This theological understanding of the relation between nature, sin and grace is fundamental to John Paul II's *Theology of the Body*.

true now, according to St. Paul, of each one of us."[156] Thus, the key idea here is that *grace restores nature*. "Faith in redemption cannot be separated from faith in the Creator." Redemption, adds the late Benedict XVI, "is an act of new creation, the restoration of creation to its true identity."[157]

What is the import of this latter understanding of nature and grace for understanding Model [2] as well as for the claim that Scriptural moral norms are the Creator's norms, that is, expressions of his design for human life? We can briefly respond to this question in the words of Lewis Smedes:

> Christ is continuous with creation, the restorer of creation's original intent. It comes to a universal claim for the morality taught by Jesus: it is the way all persons should live. The morality of the Bible is not an esoteric way of life for a relatively few disciples; it is the human way of life. But is it a way of life which ordinary people can be persuaded to accept? The continuity between Christ's law and God's original purpose with his creatures does not entail an ability of sinful people either to tune into it or live by it. Jesus' moral teachings assume that a conversion is necessary in the hearts of those who hear them, a personal conversion that includes both a new vision of God and new power to will to do his will. So, even though the special morality of the Gospel is—in the deepest sense—valid for all people, it is—in terms of its feasibility—applicable only to those who are prepared by the Spirit to accept it. Still, it is important that when one does accept Jesus' moral law, he is accepting, not an odd,

---

[156] De Lubac, *A Brief Catechesis on Nature & Grace*, 81-82.
[157] Joseph Ratzinger/Benedict XVI, *The Spirit of the Liturgy*, 24, 34.

esoteric, enclave morality, but the morality of the truly human existence.[158]

The *Catechism of the Catholic Church* illustrates Model [2] in its understanding of marriage. God himself is the author of marriage and hence the latter is grounded in the order of creation. Marriage is under the fall into sin and hence marital "union has always been threatened by discord, a spirit of domination, infidelity, jealousy, and conflicts that can escalate into hatred and separation." This brokenness "does not stem from the *nature* of man and woman, nor from the nature of their relations, but from *sin*. . . . Nevertheless, the order of creation persists, though seriously disturbed." The redemptive work of Christ is, however, continuous with the order of creation, with God's original intent for marriage, because he came "to restore the original order of creation disturbed by sin." Furthermore, Christ himself "gives the strength and grace to live marriage in the new dimension of the Reign of God. It is by following Christ, renouncing themselves, and taking up their crosses that spouses will be able to 'receive' the original meaning of marriage and live it with the help of Christ. This grace of Christian marriage is a fruit of Christ's cross, the source of all Christian life."[159] In short, redemption restores the creation to its true identity.

As to Model [3], its popularity arose with the surrender of the unity and reliability of Scripture under the influence of historical critical investigation, but also with the denial that there exists in Holy Scripture, as a special revelational act of God, fundamental revealed moral truth.

---

[158] Lewis Smedes, "The Bible and Ethics." Portions of this paper have been published in the first and last chapter of Smedes' *Mere Morality: What God Expects from Ordinary People* (Grand Rapids: Eerdmans, 1989).

[159] The quotations in this paragraph are from the *Catechism of the Catholic Church*, §§1603, 1606, and 1615.

With this denial came the acceptance of the claim that "the revelation of the will of God is not given in the form of immutable and universally valid ethical norms."[160] What encouraged this acceptance was the rejection of revealed truth, that is, propositional revelation. "It is for this reason that there is among scholars, across the Christian traditions, a movement away from what we might call a 'biblical rules' approach to theology. 'Realizing the impossibility of transposing rules from biblical times to our own, interpreters look for larger themes, values, or ideals which can inform moral reflection without determining specific practices in advance'"[161] So on this Model (3) biblical authority can be ascribed to themes like love, justice, freedom even though their concrete applications bring one into open conflict with biblical commandments. This is not the view of the Catholic Church, or for that matter of any orthodox Christian rooted in the historic moral teaching of Christianity. But it is the view of De Bruijne. Briefly, De Bruijne thinks the view that "In God's creation ordinance lies the basis for the moral natural law,"[162] as Cardinal Eijk puts it, but this is, according to De Bruijne, "too static an understanding of creation."[163]

Now, despite his denial of moral objectivity, De Bruijne does identify criteria under which we strive "to find out what is pleasing to God and what attitude and practice best suits God's purposes and coming kingdom in the given situation."[164] De Bruijne refers us to epistemic criteria such as, "the narrative we inhabit, the tradition that has formed us,

---

[160] Typical of this acceptance is a statement adopted by the Reformed Ecumenical Council, Athens 1992, *Hermeneutics and Ethics*.

[161] Michael G. Lawler, *What is and what ought to be: The Dialectic of Experience, Theology, and Church* (New York: Continuum, 2005), 84. The quote within the quote is from Lisa Sowle Cahill, "Is Catholic Ethics Biblical?"5-6.

[162] Eijk, *De Band van de Liefde*, 48.

[163] De Bruijne, *Verbonden voor het Leven*, 42.

[164] De Bruijne, "Christian Ethics and God's Use of the Bible," 178.

the authorities that we acknowledge, and the experiences we undergo."[165] "Likewise," he adds, "we should honestly consider possible results of scientific research. At the same time, the Bible keeps the final word."[166] But the Bible must be interpreted within the hermeneutical context where factors, such as, "experience, reason, community, and context remain within the framework of the comprehensive story of Scripture."[167]

Again, Hermeneutics of Continuity

Returning to Boer's stress on preserving fixed points of reference, we need to argue, *pace* De Bruijne, that there are privileged epistemic positions. A foundationalist theory of knowledge is needed in order to justify the claim that faith's knowledge of God, concepts and dogmatic formulations of the propositional truths of faiths, are objectively true in the sense of corresponding to reality. Non-foundationalist epistemologies presuppose an unqualified fallibilism such that all beliefs are open to revision. Unqualified foundationalism is the Achilles' heel of non-foundationalist epistemology for Christian belief. That is so because such an epistemology is unable to sustain the irrevocability, continuity, universality, material identity, and objective truth of Christian belief. In contrast, the contemporary Catholic philosophical theologian, Thomas Guarino, affirms a qualified fallibilism, otherwise referred to as a historically conscious foundationalism in which the propositional truths of faith may require further thought and elucidation, that is, propositional

---

[165] De Bruijne, "Christian Ethics and God's Use of the Bible," 174. See also, Ad de Bruijne, "Ethiek en hermeneutiek," 188-189.
[166] De Bruijne "Ethiek en hermeneutiek," 180.
[167] De Bruijne, "Ethiek en hermeneutiek," 190.

truth may be reconceptualized and reformulated in a conceptually different framework. Indeed, no single conceptualization or formulation can exhaust the propositional truths of faith, but not every alternative reformulation is true, meaningful, or in accordance with these truths. Therefore, suitable restatements of the propositional truths of faith must keep the same meaning and the same judgment, to quote St. Vincent of Lérins: *eodem sensu eademque sententia*.

This point brings us to the issues of meaning and truth in the hermeneutics of reinterpreting the affirmations of faith and morals. In brief, in order to maintain the continuity of the tradition in alternative formulations and expressions of the affirmations of faith and morals, those conceptual formulations and linguistic expressions must keep the same meaning and the same judgment (*eodem sensu eademque sententia*). This hermeneutics grounds continuity in a view of language that has a proper function of referring to reality by virtue of assertions that express propositions, which, if true, correspond to reality. Thus, beliefs about the reality of freedom, human sexuality, the individual's self-realization, and so forth, presuppose an understanding of the truth content of these beliefs.

Does De Bruijne actually accept the postmodernist claim that there are no privileged epistemic positions? Yes, he does. But aren't their moral norms formulated in Scripture not only having the status of fundamental revealed moral truth but also are in themselves relevant for salvation? Yes, there are. I argued for this affirmative response in Chapter 1.[168] Furthermore, the New Testament's moral teaching affirms not only the continuing validity of the Decalogue but also its perfection and superabundant fulfillment. As Germain Grisez correctly emphasizes, "In the Sermon on the Mount, Jesus broadens and deepens several of the

---

[168] Robert A.J. Gagnon, "Are there universally valid sex precepts?" 76-77.

commandments and demands their interiorization (see Mt 5:21-37). All the synoptics, moreover, present Jesus as affirming the commandments as a necessary condition for entering eternal life (see Mt 19:16-20; Mk 10:17-19; Lk 18:18-21)."[169] St. Paul, too, adds Grisez "assumes the truth of the Decalogue and its permanent ethical relevance."[170]

Of course, we can acknowledge that the application of these universally valid moral propositions contain a contingent element.[171] That is, there are concrete biblical commands, such as, "Anyone who curses his father or mother must be put to death" (Exod 21:17). Yes, they are culturally conditioned, and here is the contingent element. But this concrete command is an *application* of a primary commandment that is absolute and universal: "Honor your father and your mother" (Exod 20:12).[172] Christian's appeal to God's prohibition against same-sex relations in Lev 18:22 ("You shall not have intercourse with a man as you would with a woman. It is an abomination."), but ignore, as culturally conditioned, the punishment of death for same-sex relations in Lev 20:13. They find scriptural warrant in the sixth commandment for rejecting adultery as wrong (Exod 20:14), but ignore, as culturally conditioned, the scriptural warrant that the punishment for committing adultery is death (see Lev 20:10). The fourth commandment tells us that we should honor our parents (Exod 20:12), but Exod 21:17 says that we should execute a son who swears at his father. Christians readily cite scriptural warrant for parental authority but none accept execution as a punishment for disrespecting parents. Another instance of a concrete command ("Whoever sacrifices to any god other than the Lord must be

---

[169] Grisez, *The Way of the Lord Jesus*, 1, 838.

[170] Grisez, *The Way of the Lord Jesus*, 1, 838.

[171] De Bruijne, "Ethiek en hermeneutiek," 192; De Bruijne, "Christian Ethics and God's Use of the Bible," 176.

[172] On these distinctions, see Lewis Smedes' *Mere Morality*, especially chapter 1. Smedes develops these distinctions more fully in, "The Bible and Ethics."

destroyed" [Exod 22:20]) which is an application of a primary commandment from the Decalogue (Exod 20:1-6) prohibits the practice of idolatry (Exod 20:4; Deut 13:6-11). The concrete command is contextually conditioned but not the primary command on which it is based.

Helpful here in distinguishing between commandments that are still enduringly valid from those that are not, is Lewis Smedes' distinction between "primary commandments" and "concrete commandments." The former cover specific areas of life, such as human existence, property, communication, marriage, family. The latter demand or prohibit a specific act. At the root of each and every command is the "foundational commandment" that covers all of life, namely, the central commandment of Love: We are called to love God completely and to love our neighbor as we love ourselves.[173]

Of course, I'm not suggesting that De Bruijne thinks that any of these practices are morally acceptable. But it does seem to me that we cannot allow his rejection of a historically qualified moral foundationalism to pass without being challenged. By locating biblical authority primarily (exclusively?) in the Scripture's narratives rather than in its commandments he leaves us confused about how to come to terms with the Bible's authority for the moral life.

De Bruijne might respond to my criticism by distinguishing normative biblical instructions from their applications, which contain an element of contingency.[174] "Our main task is not to repeat the instantiations but to connect the narrative of God's work in Christ to situations and questions we face today."[175] He qualifies: "With this I certainly do not

---

[173] Helpful in understanding the central commandment of love is David E. Holwerda, "Jesus and the Law: A Question of Fulfillment," in Jesus and Israel: One Covenant or Two (Grand Rapids, MI: Eerdmans, 1995), 122-145.

[174] De Bruijne, "Christian Ethics and God's Use of the Bible," 176.

[175] De Bruijne, "Christian Ethics and God's Use of the Bible," 176.

want to imply that we can ignore the apostolic instantiations."[176] Since De Bruijne disavows the possibility of a knowledge which is objectively true, which includes even moral judgments, De Bruine's anti-foundationalist approach to the relation between ethics and hermeneutics, propounds a perpetual hermeneutics of biblical morality (e.g., the Beatitudes), which involves recontextualizing and reapplying that biblical instruction with the aim of answering the "central ethical hermeneutical question." Once again, De Bruijne states:

> We can describe ethics briefly as 'the reflection on the good life before God's face and, in that context, on good and evil.' Ethical hermeneutics therefore first of all requires an understanding of the good life and of good and evil. It is precisely ethics that involves us, our neighbor, and the world from the very outset.[177]

There may be a "fusion of horizons" à la Gadamer if the normative biblical instructions is sufficiently similar despite the hermeneutical distance between the Bible and us. De Bruijne explains:

1. We form a picture of the situation of the original readers and decide whether it corresponds sufficiently with our own context.
2. Additionally, we develop a conception of the underlying logic that leads the apostles to their instructions, and of how this logic should work out in our circumstances.[178]

What bridges the hermeneutical distance between the two contexts is not the universality and immutability of the natural law, the creation

---

[176] De Bruijne, "Christian Ethics and God's Use of the Bible," 176.
[177] De Bruijne, "Ethiek en hermeneutiek," 181.
[178] De Bruijne, "Ethiek en hermeneutiek," 192.

order, and the perception of the universality of the moral law on the part of reason.[179] For De Bruijne there is no objective moral knowledge, no moral foundational propositions, no moral propositions grounded in reality. Of course, he does not deny that many biblical instructions remain applicable today. "Nevertheless, such a direct application also implies that we—at least implicitly—recognize sufficient similarities between then and today."[180] However, this is not the case for homosexuality, according to De Bruijne. Indeed, late modern homosexuality is a "new phenomena that the Bible says nothing about."[181] It would take us too far afield to challenge De Bruijne's claim.[182] I will return below, briefly, and in latter chapters, to the matter of homosexuality.

What, then, is the central ethical hermeneutical question, according to De Bruijne? Looking back to what I called De Bruijne's teleological approach to ethics, here's the question: "what is the good life that fits or accords with God's works in Christ en route to the coming kingdom and *what is the optimal step forward in that direction within the margins of*

---

[179] John Paul II, *Veritatis Splendor*, §51.

[180] De Bruijne, "Ethiek en hermeneutiek," 193.

[181] De Bruijne, *Verbonden voor het Leven*, 257, and 270.

[182] This claim has become typical but many scholars challenge it, such as, Robert A.J. Gagnon, *The Bible and Homosexual Practice: Texts and Hermeneutics* (Nashville: Abingdon Press, 2001). For another, *Preston Sprinkle, People to Be Loved: Why Homosexuality is not just an Issue* (Grand Rapids: Zondervan, 2015). Still another is N.T. Wright's argument about same-sex relationships. "There is nothing in contemporary understanding and experience of homosexual condition and behavior that was unknown in the first century. The idea that in the first century, it was all about masters having odd relationships with slaves, or older men with younger men—yeah, sure, that happened, but read Plato's *Symposium*. They have permanent, faithful, stable male-male partnerships—lifelong stuff—Achilles and Patroclus in Homer, all sorts of things." Wright, N.T., live event at Serra Retreat Center in Malibu, California, February 2009. "N.T. Wright on Debate about Homosexuality 4."

the given situation."[183] Notice that the question here is not about doing the right thing in the boundaries of the given situation, objectively speaking, but rather of doing what optimally moves you in the direction of the Kingdom of God. That is, it is about doing the "responsible" thing, the "better" thing, when dealing "with genuine choice options in real human lives in *real-life* contexts."[184] Hence, De Bruijne rejects the binary distinction between absolute good and absolute evil entailed by a moral absolute, which is an exceptionless moral norm.[185] He explains, "given the sometimes narrow margins of such a moment that best accords with that destiny in God's kingdom]. It can refer to a less than ideal step in the right direction, but also to a less than at first sight inevitable step in the wrong direction."[186] De Bruijne's argument here calls to mind the distinction drawn by John Paul II between the "law of gradualism" and the "gradualism of the law."[187] The latter attempts to provide a justification of situation ethics, leading, I would argue, to a relativization of morality. The following diagram may help us to understand the difference between the "law of gradualism" and the "gradualness of the law."[188]

---

[183] De Bruijne, "Christian Ethics and God's Use of the Bible," 175. A developed version of the 2016 essay is found in Ad De Bruijne, "Ethiek en hermeneutiek," in *Gereformeetde hermeneutiek vandaag, Theologische perspectieven* (red.) Ad de Bruijne en Hans Burger (Barneveld: De Vuurbaak, 2017), 181-198, and at 184-185.

[184] De Bruijne, *Verbonden voor het Leven*, 45.

[185] De Bruijne, *Verbonden voor het Leven*, 44-45.

[186] De Bruijne, *Verbonden voor het Leven*, 45.

[187] Eduardo Echeverria, "Mercy and Truth: Pastoral Care of Individuals in Spiritually and Morally Problematic Relationships," in *Clerical Sexual Misconduct: An Interdisciplinary Analysis*, eds. Jane F. Adolphe and Ronald J. Rychlak (Providence, Long Island: CLUNY Media, 2020), 365-381, and for the following section, 368-372.

[188] I owe this diagram to Branislav Kuljovsky, "The Law of Gradualism or the Gradualism of Law? A Critical Analysis of *Amoris Laetitia.*"

The Law of Gradualism and the Gradualism of the Law

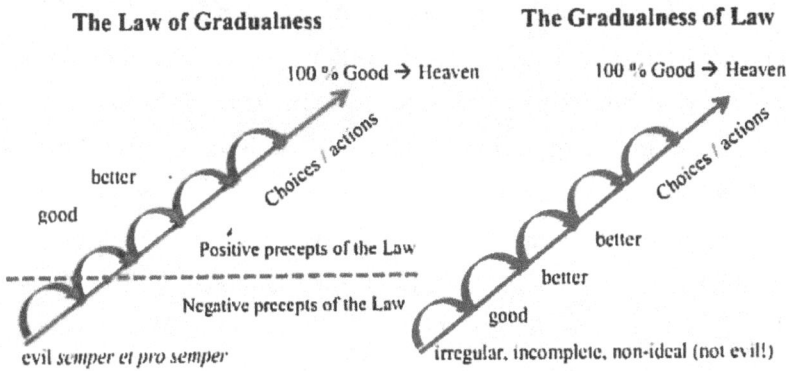

On the one hand, the "law of gradualness" entails that the Church must be sensitive to a man's moral progress, namely, that he is striving to become good by stages of moral growth. The former is, according to John Paul, a step-by-step moral advance in becoming good and realizing the standard of Christian holiness. In this context, we may speak of a man's moral immaturity, based on distinguishing between the "person-I-am" from the "person-I-ought-to-be."[189] Here, too, we should understand St. Paul pastoral admonition, "Brothers, if anyone is caught in any

---

[189] See the excellent digitally published article of Stanton L. Jones, "Sexual Orientation and Reason: On the Implications of False Beliefs about Homosexuality." https://media.focusonthefamily.com/fotf/pdf/channels/social-issues/sexual-orientation-and-reason-1-9-12.pdf. A shortened version of this article is published as, "Same-Sex Science, The Social Science Cannot Settle the Moral Status of Homosexuality," *First Things* February 2012. https://www.firstthings.com/article/2012/02/same-sex science. He appeals to this distinction, explicitly drawing on the anthropological thought of John Paul II, as cited in George Weigel, *Witness to Hope: The Biography of Pope John Paul II* (New York: HarperCollins, 1999), 8.

transgression, you who are spiritual should restore him in a spirit of gentleness" (Gal. 6:1).

John Paul II explains the pastoral implications of the "law of gradualness": "In this context, appropriate allowance is made both for God's mercy towards the sin of the man who experiences conversion and for the understanding of human weakness."[190] Indeed, "As Paul VI wrote: 'While it is an outstanding manifestation of charity toward souls to omit nothing from the saving doctrine of Christ, this must always be joined with tolerance and charity, as Christ himself showed by his conversations and dealings with men. Having come not to judge the world but to save it [John 3:17], he was uncompromisingly stern towards sin, but patient and rich in mercy towards sinners'."[191] Notwithstanding this compassion, John Paul adds, "Such understanding never means compromising and falsifying the standard of good and evil in order to adapt it to particular circumstances."[192] "In fact," the pope explains, "genuine understanding and compassion must mean love for the person, for his true good, for his authentic freedom. And this does not result, certainly, from concealing or weakening moral truth."[193] Again, "It is quite human," the pope adds, "for the sinner to acknowledge his weakness and to ask mercy for his failings; [but] what is unacceptable is the attitude of one who makes his own weakness the criterion of the truth about the good, so that he can feel self-justified, without even the need to have recourse to God and his mercy."[194] In other words, an individual will feel morally

---

[190] John Paul II, *Veritatis Splendor*, §104.

[191] John Paul II, *Veritatis Splendor*, §95, cites Pope Paul VI's Encyclical Letter, July 25, 1968, *Humanane Vitae*, §29.

[192] John Paul II, *Veritatis Splendor*, §95.

[193] John Paul II, *Veritatis Splendor*, §95.

[194] John Paul II, *Veritatis Splendor*, §95.

self-justified, indeed, self-absorbed, if he thinks that doing the best that he can in some situation is the only moral standard he is obliged to meet.

Significantly, the "law of gradualness" presupposes St. John's teaching, which is vitally important in pastoral practice when an individual falls short of doing the right thing: "If we say we have no sin, we deceive ourselves, and the truth is not in us. If we confess our sins, he is faithful and just to forgive us our sins and to cleanse us from all unrighteousness. If we say we have not sinned, we make him a liar, and his word is not in us" (1 John 1:8-10).

On the other hand, there is the idea of the "gradualness of the law." This understanding of the role of the moral law in the Christian life turns the obliging force of the law into an aspiring force, rendering the moral law an ideal. Furthermore, this view of the law holds that there are "in divine law various levels or forms of precept for various persons and conditions."[195] Contrary to this view, John Paul II argues, "They [those struggling to achieve moral good by stages of growth] cannot however look on the law as merely an ideal to be achieved in the future: they must consider it as a command of Christ the Lord to overcome difficulties with constancy." He explains, "And so what is known as 'the law of gradualness' or step-by-step advance cannot be identified with 'gradualness of the law', as if there were different degrees or forms of precept in God's law for different individuals and situations."[196] What this idea of the law means is, according to the late moral theologian Germain Grisez, that there are "gradations of the law," namely, "the whole of Christian morality—or, at least, many norms traditionally received as binding precepts—is [such] that willful violations are acceptable provided one looks forward to living according to the norm at some time in the future."[197]

---

[195] Grisez, *The Way of the Lord Jesus*, I, 687.
[196] John Paul II, *Familiaris Consortio*, §34.
[197] Grisez, The Way of the Lord Jesus, I, 687.

This view then legitimizes situation ethics in our pastoral care, and hence the relativization of morality.[198] This is the view of De Bruijne.

The pastoral practice entailed by the "gradualism of the law" is such that those individuals whose lives do not conform to the moral teaching of the Church are left in their objectively sinful condition. Of course, we should compassionately "enter into" the lives of people struggling to do the right thing. However, that does not mean that we should devise pastoral programs in which individuals are permitted to realize their so-called optimal ethical possibilities given their situation—divorced and civilly remarried people, cohabiting couples (whether heterosexuals or homosexuals), and clergy who have struggled with or violated continence. This way of approaching these individuals wrongly suggests that there is an ethically responsible way to live in these spiritually and morally problematic relationships.[199]

Biblically speaking, this approach is surely misguided. St. Paul would not say to the sinner: "We implore you on behalf of Christ, 'be reconciled to what is possible.'" Of course not. Otherwise, we would deny that our sinful condition from within is open to radical transformation. Indeed, St. Paul says, "We implore you on behalf of Christ, be reconciled to God" (Eph. 5:20, emphasis added). Elsewhere he proclaims, "My grace is sufficient for you, for my power is made perfect [or: brought to full measure] in weakness" (2 Cor. 12:9). In short, presupposing the "gradualism of the law" in our ethics of pastoral practice results in limiting individuals in morally problematic relationship to what is within the range of what is possible for them. Within the range of what is possible? Possible for whom? John Paul II pointedly asks, "Of man

---

[198] Contra Patrick Mullins, *Zorgen voor een eigenwijze kudde: Een pastorale ethiek voor een missionaire kerk* (Zoetermeer: Uitgeverij Boekcentrum, 2015), 126-130.

[199] John Paul II, *Veritatis Splendor*, §103.

dominated by lust or of man redeemed by Christ?" "This is what is at stake," he adds, "the reality of Christ's redemption. Christ has redeemed us! ... Only in the mystery of Christ's Redemption do we discover the 'concrete' possibilities of man.... This means that he has given us the possibility of realizing the entire truth of our being; he has set our freedom free from the domination of concupiscence. And if redeemed man still sins, this is not due to an imperfection of Christ's redemptive act, but to man's will not to avail himself of the grace which flows from that act."[200]

Furthermore, John Paul II correctly understands another implication of the "gradualness of the law" and its corresponding result of limiting individuals to what is possible for them. He says: "An attitude of this sort corrupts the morality of society as a whole, since it encourages doubt about the objectivity of the moral law in general and a rejection of the absoluteness of moral prohibitions regarding specific human acts, and it ends up by confusing all judgments about values."[201] Now, this view leads to moral laxity, indeed, to the sort of moral corruption the pope describes, and it is a matter of concern for the whole Church. St. Paul tells us that the Church must not succumb to a lax attitude toward sin (see 1 Cor. 5:6): "a little leaven leavens the whole lump"). He urges the believers at Corinth to take action against a man's sexual sin (i.e., incest) by removing him from the community. The community should mourn for him rather than become inflated with pride (5:2). As St. Paul says elsewhere in 1 Corinthians, we must "not rejoice at wrongdoing, but rejoice with truth" (13:6). The truth being that we in the Church are all sinners who are saved by grace: "For all have sinned and fall short of the

---

[200] John Paul II, *Veritatis Splendor*, §104.
[201] John Paul II, *Veritatis Splendor*, §104.

glory of God, and are justified by his grace as a gift, through the redemption that is in Christ Jesus, whom God put forward as a propitiation by his blood, to be received in faith" (Rom. 3:23-25).

Nevertheless, says St. Paul, the Church should take a stand against all sorts of sexual sin by warning the offending believers that if they continue in sexual immorality they will not inherit the Kingdom of God. Against this Pauline background, we should also ask proponents of this pastoral approach how they propose to help these offending believers to be "saved" from judgment "on the day of the Lord" (1 Cor. 5:5). What about St. Paul's teaching that serial and unrepentant immoral sexual practices put one at the risk of not inheriting God's eternal kingdom (1 Cor. 6:9-10; 2 Cor. 12:21; Gal. 5:19-21; Rom. 1:24-27; 6:19-23; Col. 3:5-10; Eph. 5:3-6, 4:17-19; 1 Thess. 4:2-8).

Moreover, how then does a person who is actively and unrepentantly engaged in same-sex sexual practice change his life, radically reorient his whole life, put an end to sin, turn away from evil, "with repugnance toward the evil actions [he has] committed,"[202] if no one, least of all the Church, calls him to interior repentance, conversion, that is, "the conversion of the heart, interior conversion"[203] and a holy life? As the Catechism of the Catholic Church teaches, "This endeavor of conversion is not just a human work. It is the movement of a 'contrite heart', drawn and moved by grace to respond to the merciful love of God who loved us first" (Psalm 51:17; John 6:44; 12:32; 1 John 4:10).[204]

St. Paul expressed this interior struggle pointedly, "For I do not do the good I want, but the evil I do not want is what I keep on doing" (Rom. 7:19). The solution to this interior struggle, he urges, is only union with the person of Christ, governed by moral guidelines—the authentic moral

---

[202] *Catechism of the Catholic Church*, §1431.
[203] *Catechism of the Catholic Church*, §1430.
[204] *Catechism of the Catholic Church*, §1428.

life flowing from the transformed life in Christ. This personal relationship with Christ through the work of the Holy Spirit effects a real transformation from within, establishing a harmony between what is right and my inclinations. "[P]ut off your old man, which belongs to your former manner of life and is corrupt through deceitful desires, and…be renewed in the spirit of your minds, and…put on the new man, created after the likeness of God in true righteousness and holiness" (Eph. 4:22-24).

St. Paul cautions us not to underestimate the seriousness of sin's power to enslave us and the power of the death and resurrection of Jesus Christ to liberate us from its stranglehold. Indeed, human nature is truly renewed by the redemptive power of Jesus Christ's finished work. St. Paul describes his own experience of sin trapping him, of a power at work within him, from which he is unable to break free (see Rom. 7:13-23). "Wretched man that I am! Who will deliver me from this body of death?" His answer: "Thanks be to God, through Jesus Christ our Lord!" (Rom. 7:24-25) [205]"For this is the will of God, your sanctification" (1 Thess. 4:3). So urges Vatican II in its timely and challenging presentation of the call to holiness of the whole Church.[206] "The Lord Jesus, the divine Teacher and Model of all perfection, preached holiness of life to each and every one of His disciples, regardless of their situation: 'You therefore must be perfect, as your heavenly Father is perfect' (Matt. 5:48). He Himself stands as the Author and Finisher of this holiness of life." At the head of all biblical motivations for holiness there is God's love. "God's love has been poured into our hearts through the Holy Spirit who has been given to us" (Rom. 5:5). The Council Fathers add, "For He sent the Holy Spirit upon all men that He might inspire them from within to love

---

[205] On sin being like an enslaving force, see Alister E. McGrath, *Intellectuals Don't Need God & other Modern Myths* (Grand Rapids: Zondervan, 1993), 136.
[206] *Lumen Gentium*, §§39-42.

God with their whole heart and their whole soul, with all their mind and all their strength (cf. Mark 12;30) and that they might love one another as Christ loved them (cf. John 13:34; 15:12)."[207]

Symptomatic, then, of the rejection of moral foundationalism is the abandonment of revealed moral truths—that is, a genuine moral norm expressing absolute and universally valid moral content in a true proposition—as Christian ethics' points of reference for justifying certain moral judgments and choices. De Bruijne's rejection of moral foundationalism entails the rejection of objective moral truths, moral absolutes, and hence of moral realism. Consider that his framing of the so-called central ethical hermeneutical question as it bears upon the relationship between ethics and Scripture does *not* include moral norms as expressing a true moral proposition constitutive of God's purposes for advancing the realization of his Kingdom, but only attitudes and practices. speaking, but rather of doing what optimally moves you in the direction of the Kingdom of God. That is, as I said above, it is about doing the "responsible" thing, the "better" thing, when dealing "with genuine choice options in real human lives in *real-life* contexts."[208] Hence, De Bruijne rejects the binary distinction between absolute good and absolute evil entailed by a moral absolute, which is an exceptionless moral norm.[209] He says, in contrast, "What *attitude* or *practice* within the given circumstances will do optimal justice to the aims of the work of the Triune God, which ultimately can be summarized as the coming of his kingdom?"[210] What about St. Paul's vital point that the moral law is, as he teaches, holy, just, and good (Rom 7:12), and hence there are moral

---

[207] *Lumen Gentium*, §40.
[208] De Bruijne, *Verbonden voor het Leven*, 45.
[209] De Bruijne, *Verbonden voor het Leven*, 44-45.
[210] De Bruijne, "Christian Ethics and God's Use of the Bible," 175, 178.

norms formulated in Scripture not only having the status of fundamental revealed moral truth but also are in themselves relevant for salvation (see 1 Cor 6:9-11)?

No, the Sexual Revolution is not a Renewal Movement

Back to de Bruijne's claim that the sexual revolution is at its core a renewal movement in the Christian tradition, he holds not only that this understanding of the affirmations of the tradition may be expressed differently, but also that these new re-formulations by the sexual emancipators, which involve, according to de Bruijne, corrections and a deepening in our understanding of those affirmations, preserve the same meaning and judgment of truth (*eodem sensu eademque sententia*) regarding freedom, etc., and hence the material continuity, identity, and universality of these affirmations in those formulations. Is that true? Or does de Bruijne's justification amount to little more than a sophistic justification of the values represented by the cultural impact of the sexual revolution?

Is there, then, a material continuity in conceptual understanding between the secularist concept of autonomous freedom that motivates the sexual liberationist ideology and the biblical concept of freedom? Regarding the former concept of freedom, autonomous freedom is exalted to an absolute such that there are no demands emanating from beyond the self and rooted in creation and culture, which includes the bonds of solidarity with my fellow man, nature, God, or human reason that man must heed. Rather, freedom creates moral values and norms, implying a denial of the participation of human reason in the wisdom of the divine

Creator and Lawgiver. In fact, this absolute freedom, or expressive individualism, is such that "man would not even have a nature."[211] On this view, for example, biologically-structured bodies, sexual difference, are outright ignored, if not dismissed as irrelevant. "Biology has nothing to do, we are told, with being a man or a woman.... Today we witness the intrinsic link between biology and sexual identity (gender) being put asunder."[212] This view denies the unity of the human person, leaving us with a dualism of soul and body.

At the root of anthropological dualism between soul and body and the corresponding contemporary Gnosticism—transgenderism!—is the ground motive of nature and freedom, according to both Dooyeweerd and John Paul II. On the one hand, explains Dooyeweerd, "The impulse to dominate nature by an autonomous scientific thought required a deterministic image of the world, construed as an uninterrupted chain of functional causal relations. . . . The mechanistic world-image constructed under the primacy of the nature-motive, aiming at the sovereign domination of the world, left no room for the autonomous freedom of human personality in its practical activity. Nature and freedom appeared to be opposite motives in the Humanistic starting-point."[213] In sum, the uniformity of natural causes in a closed system of unbreakable laws has no room for human freedom. The domination motive of human freedom views nature as an object to be dominated by autonomous science. On the other hand, explains Dooyeweerd, "The Humanist freedom-motive does not allow the acceptance of a given structural order of creation within the temporal horizon of experience." John Paul II elaborates that on this view nature is "reduced to raw material for human

---

[211] John Paul II, *Veritatis Splendor*, §46.

[212] Paul Gondreau, "Thomas Aquinas on the Metaphysical Biology of Sexual Difference," *Pro Ecclesia* 30, no. 2 (2021), 177-215.

[213] Dooyeweerd, *In the Twilight of Western Thought*, 35.

activity and for its power: thus, nature needs to be profoundly transformed, and indeed overcome by freedom, inasmuch as it [nature] represents a limitation and denial of freedom."[214] Not only is the human body, its make-up and its processes, included in nature, indeed even human nature, but also the full spectrum of culture. He concludes, "This ultimately means making freedom self-defining and a phenomenon creative of itself and its values. Indeed, when all is said and done man would not even have a nature; he would be his own personal life-project. Man would be nothing more than his own freedom!"[215] These are the roots and triumph of the modern self—to echo the title of Carl Trueman's book—shaping and informing the cultural—indeed, spiritual!—battles of the first quarter of the twenty-first century.[216]

By contrast, a biblical concept of freedom is, according to John Paul II, a *"participated theonomy,* since man's free obedience to God's law effectively implies that human reason and human will participate in God's wisdom and providence." He adds, "Law must therefore be considered an expression of divine wisdom: by submitting to the law, freedom submits to the truth of creation."[217] Although the law here is one beyond man's own making, it is not, as John Paul II correctly notes,

> *heteronomy,* as if the moral life were subject to the will of something all-powerful, absolute, extraneous to man and intolerant of his freedom. If in fact a heteronomy of morality were to mean a denial of man's self-determination or the imposition of norms unrelated to his good, this would be . . . nothing but a form of

---

[214] John Paul II, *Veritatis Splendor,* §46.

[215] John Paul II, *Veritatis Splendor,* §46.

[216] Carl Trueman, *The Rise and Triumph of the Modern Self: Cultural Amnesia, Expressive Individualism, and the Road to Sexual Revolution.*

[217] John Paul II, *Veritatis Splendor,* §41.

alienation, contrary to divine wisdom and to the dignity of the human person.[218]

The heteronomy of the moral law is not unrelated to man's good, because man freely interiorizes the truth of the law, which consists of norms related to his good; otherwise, there would be nothing but a form of self-alienation. Thus, the moral law is not only written on the heart of man (Romans 1:14ff), bearing witness in the inmost recesses of the heart, but also it must be effectually at work in man himself so that "the whole man must be good," as Herman Bavinck put it, "in intellect and will, heart and conscience."[219] He adds, therefore, "The heteronomy of the law and the autonomy of man are reconciled only by this theonomy."[220]

It is difficult to see how any conceptual continuity can exist given that autonomous freedom purports to be absolute freedom such that man's expressive individualism has the freedom to make the nature of sexuality open-ended—on this view of freedom a reality that cannot be manipulated by the human will does not exist—and the freedom to make whatever he chooses right. Alvin Plantinga describes this view:

> [I]t is we ourselves—we human beings—who are responsible for the basic structure of the world. This notion goes back to Prothagorus, in the ancient world, with his claim that man is the measure of all things; it finds enormously more powerful expression in modern times in Immanuel Kant's *Critique of Pure Reason*. Call it "enlightenment humanism," or "enlightenment

---

[218] John Paul II, *Veritatis Splendor*, §§40–41.

[219] Herman Bavinck, *The Philosophy of Revelation: The Stone Lectures for 1908-1909, Princeton Theological Seminary* (New York: Longmans, Green, and Co., 1909), 262.

[220] Bavinck, *The Philosophy of Revelation*, 263.

subjectivism," or, more descriptively, "creative anti-realism."²²¹

Such a view is clearly at odds with a Christian theistic view of the world in which the human sexual design has embedded principles and inbuilt meanings in the order of creation.

Furthermore, de Bruijne suggests that this notion of secularized freedom finds its roots in the Christian idea of human dignity and man's central place in reality, along with "the biblical emphasis on the value of the individual person and their specific gifts."²²² However, the notion of freedom in creative anti-realism is at odds with another culturally dominant worldview, namely, naturalism and its attendant materialism and determinism. Naturalism holds that "there is no God, and we human beings are insignificant parts of a giant cosmic machine that proceeds in majestic indifference to us, our hopes and aspirations, our needs and desires, our sense of fairness or fittingness."²²³ Plantinga elaborates:

> From this perspective, there is no God, and human beings are properly seen as parts of nature. The way to understand what is most distinctive about us, our ability to love, to act, to think, to use language, our humor and playacting, our art, philosophy, literature, history, our morality, our religion, our tendency to enlist in sometimes unlikely causes and devote our lives to them—the fundamental way to understand all this is in terms of our community with (non human) nature. We are best seen as parts of nature and are to be understood in terms of our place in

---

²²¹ Alvin Plantinga, "On Christian Scholarship," http://www.veritas-ucsb.org/library/plantinga/ocs.html.

²²² De Bruijne, "Seksualiteit en cultuurstrijd: Een theologische voorstel tot dialog," 277.

²²³ Plantinga, "On Christian Scholarship."

the natural world.[224]

Moreover, materialistic anthropology sees man as a chance product of impersonal matter in motion. There is, consequently, no reason to see man as objectively more valuable than animals. Furthermore, everything about man is explainable in terms of the uniformity of natural causes in a closed system, and hence he is not free to do something because there is an antecedent set of events and circumstances that causally determine us. Again, where is the underlying continuity between naturalistic secular freedom and the Christian tradition, once the creative anti-realist and naturalistic presuppositions are exposed?

Materialistic Anthropology, Sexual Disenchantment, and Its Implications

A materialistic anthropology is at the root of the reductionist claim that the finality of the sexual drive in man is nothing more and nothing less than a physical/biological need and a means of pleasure. The implications of this anthropology is elaborated by John Paul II. Within this anthropology, he explains:

> The body is no longer perceived as a properly personal reality, a sign and place of relations with others, with God and with the world. It is reduced to pure materiality: it is simply a complex of organs, functions and energies to be used according to the sole criteria of pleasure and efficiency. Consequently, sexuality too is depersonalized and exploited: from being the sign, place and language of love, that is, of the gift of self and acceptance of an-

---

[224] Plantinga, "On Christian Scholarship."

other, in all the other's richness as a person, it increasingly becomes the occasion and instrument for self-assertion and the selfish satisfaction of personal desires and instincts. Thus the original import of human sexuality is distorted and falsified, and the two meanings, unitive and procreative, inherent in the very nature of the conjugal act, are artificially separated: in this way the marriage union is betrayed and its fruitfulness is subjected to the caprice of the couple.[225]

However, if we view the sexual drive from the perspective of the whole man as a unified totality that is the body-person, rather than as a mere biological aspect, we can argue that this natural human dynamism is ordered per se to the specific end of man's existence, its extension, procreation. In other words, the existential meaning of this sexual drive is properly grasped only when we see its connection with existence. Karol Wojtyla argues:

Existence is, in fact, the first and fundamental good of every being. The existence of the species *Homo sapiens* is the first and fundamental good of that species. All other goods proceed from this fundamental one. I can act only insofar as I am. Various works of man, creations of his genius, fruits of his holiness, are possible only insofar as this man, this genius, this saint, exists. In order to be, he must have come into being. The natural path for man to come into existence passes through the sexual drive.[226]

---

[225] John Paul II, *Evangelium Vitae*, §23.
[226] Karol Wojtyla, *Love and Responsibility*, Translation, Endnotes, and Foreword by Grzegorz Ignatik, New Translation (Boston, MA: Pauline Books & Media, 2013 [1960]), 35.

By contrast, a materialistic anthropology locates the sexual drive "below the person and below love."[227] It turns this drive toward the psycho-physiological structure of the other person; sex is sought after for its own sake, and procreation is no longer the purpose of the sexual act; procreation is now rendered marginal and optional. So, one of the implications of a materialistic anthropology is that it misses out on the "objective greatness and meaning of the sexual drive." Louis Perry hits the nail on the head. "Sex has been disenchanted," which is a "natural consequence of the liberal privileging of freedom over all other values, because you want to be utterly free." But the disenchantment of sex means that "sex means nothing."[228] Contrary to the disenchantment of sex, Wojtyla explains that sex has objective greatness and meaning:

> Precisely this connection with the very existence of man and of the species *Homo sapiens* confers on the sexual drive its objective greatness and meaning. But this greatness appears in the consciousness only when with his love man takes up what is contained in the natural finality of the drive. . . . [T]he love of persons, of a man and a woman, is formed within this finality, in its bedrock, as it were; it is formed as if out of this material, which is provided by the drive. So, this love can be correctly formed only inasmuch as it is formed in close harmony with the proper finality of the drive. . . . The order of human existence, the order of being, does not remain in conflict with the love of persons, but is closely harmonized with it.[229]

---

[227] Wojtyla, *Love and Responsibility*, 36.
[228] Perry, *The Case Against the Sexual Revolution*, 11.
[229] Wojtyla, *Love and Responsibility*, 36–37.

De Bruijne misses seeing the intrinsic connection between human sexuality and existence because he fails to be critical of this materialistic anthropology, and the implication of sexual disenchantment.

On this anthropology, the sexual act of one person to the person of the other sex is instrumentalized such that the other person is used as a means to an end, a vehicle of self-realization. This means-end relation raises not only an ethical question about how people treat each other but also the objection that, as Karol Wojtyla argues, "treating the person as a means to an end, and even to the end that is pleasure—the maximization of pleasure—will always stand in the way of love."[230] Wojtyla raises the ethical question, "For a person should not be merely a means to an end for another person. This is excluded due to the very nature of the person, due to what every person simply is."[231] That is, "the person is a kind of good that is incompatible with using, which may not be treated as an object of use and, in this sense, as a means to an end." In other words, "the person is a kind of good to which only love [not using] constitutes the proper and full-mature relation."[232] The central commandment of love is unrestricted love for God, firstly, and then, secondly, to love one's neighbor as one loves oneself. In its fullest sense, argues Wojtyla, love for neighbors is grounded in love for persons. In this connection, Wojtyla reflects on the biblical commandment, the personalistic norm, as he calls it, and Christian anthropology.

The Love Commandment and the Personalistic Norm

The commandment to love and the attendant object of this love is the person. In other words, "Love persons." This love is grounded in the

---

[230] Wojtyla, *Love and Responsibility*, 25.
[231] Wojtyla, *Love and Responsibility*, 10.
[232] Wojtyla, *Love and Responsibility*, 25.

personalist principle. This principle negatively formulated demands, "The person is a kind of good that is incompatible with using, which may not be treated as an object of use and, in this sense, as a means to an end." In short, "Love is a union of persons," and this means-end relation with the end being pleasure, reflects a subjectivism, indeed, adds Wojtyla, "an egoism that is most rapacious, using another person for one's own sake, for one's 'maximum pleasure'."[233] A positive formulation of this principle states that the person is a kind of good to which only love constitutes the proper response. "And this positive content of the personalistic norm is precisely what the commandment to love brings out."[234] Furthermore, since love is a union of persons, of male and female, Wojtyla explains, "love . . . is the distinct opposite of using the person in the role of a means to an end."[235] The personalistic norm is grounded in the value of the person rather than in the value of pleasure, and hence "the person cannot be subordinated to pleasure; he cannot serve as a means to the end which is pleasure."[236] Therefore, Wojtyla explains, "The affirmation of the value of the person as such is contained in the essence of love. [In other words,] the love of the person must consist in affirming his supra-material and supra-consumer (supra-utilitarian) value. . . . Therefore, we must seek the proper solutions for sexual morality within the scope of the personalistic norm if these solutions are to be Christian. They must be based on the commandment to love."[237]

How then does love secure the objective union of persons, of a man and a woman, such that they constitute one common subject of action? The brief answer to this question here must be:

---

[233] Wojtyla, *Love and Responsibility*, 23.

[234] Wojtyla, *Love and Responsibility*, 23.

[235] Wojtyla, *Love and Responsibility*, 12.

[236] Wojtyla, *Love and Responsibility*, 12.

[237] Wojtyla, *Love and Responsibility*, 26–28.

Love is conditioned by the common relation of persons to the same good that they choose as an end and to which they subordinate themselves. Marriage is one of the most important areas for realizing this principle. For in marriage, two persons, a woman and a man, unite in such a way that they become in a sense "one flesh" (to use the words of the Book of Genesis [2:24], that is, so to speak, *one common subject of sexual life*. How can it be ensured that a person does not then become for the other— a woman for a man, and a man for a woman—merely a means to an end, that is, an object used to attain only one's own end? In order to exclude this possibility, both of them must then have a common end. Concerning marriage, this end is procreation, progeny, the family, and at the same time the whole constantly growing maturity of the relationship between both persons in all the spheres brought by the spousal relationship itself.[238]

Hence, this common subject of sexual life is unattainable by partners in sodomy. As Grisez rightly states, "the coupling of two bodies of the same sex cannot form one complete organism and so cannot contribute to a bodily communion of persons." Sodomy, therefore, "lacks the unitive significance of heterosexual intercourse which makes a couple a single reproductive principle."[239] Thus, when the *Catechism* states that homosexual acts "close the sexual act to the gift of life that is because only a unitive act can be generative."[240]

Furthermore, Wojtyla, too, rejects the idea that marriage is a means to an end. In his 1960 work, *Love and Responsibility*, Wojtyla rejects what he calls the "rigorist and puritan interpretation" of the conjugal

---

[238] Wojtyla, *Love and Responsibility*, 14. Emphasis added.
[239] Germain Grisez, *The Way of the Lord Jesus*, II, 654.
[240] *Catechism of the Catholic Church*, §2357.

life and sexual intercourse that sees the latter as instrumental goods serving the purpose of procreation.[241] Wojtyla carefully distinguishes this interpretation from the Manichean tradition because "this view does not reject marriage as something evil that in itself is evil and unclean due to being 'bodily' as was maintained by the Manicheans." Rather, it "contents itself with stating the permissibility of marriage for the sake of the good of the species."[242] Against this view, Wojtyla argues, "By joining in sexual intercourse, a man and a woman join themselves as rational and free persons, and their union has a moral value when it is justified by true conjugal love." He explains:

> For the Creator, by giving man and woman a rational nature and the ability to determine consciously their acts, gave them thereby the power to choose by themselves the end to which sexual intercourse leads in a *natural* way. And where two persons can choose together a certain good as an end, there the possibility of love also exists. Therefore, the Creator does not use persons merely as means or tools of his creative power, but opens before them the possibility of a particular realization of love. It depends on them whether they will place their sexual intercourse on the level of love, on the level proper to persons, or below this level. And the Creator wills not only the preservation of the species through sexual intercourse, but also its preservation based on love that is worthy of persons.[243]

Wojtyla regards procreation to be the primary end of marriage be-

---

[241] Wojtyla, *Love and Responsibility*, 43.
[242] Wojtyla, *Love and Responsibility*, 44.
[243] Wojtyla, *Love and Responsibility*, 44–45.

cause "procreation is objectively, ontologically, a more important purpose than that man and woman should live together, complement each other and support each other (*mutuum adiutorium*), just as this second purpose is in turn more important that the appeasement of natural desire."[244] He clarifies here that each of the traditional reasons for marriage, namely, the having and raising of children, mutual help, and *remedium concupiscentiae*, which is a legitimate orientation for desire, are all expressions of "love as a virtue." He adds, "However, opposing love to procreation or indicating a primacy of procreation over love is out of the question."[245] Wojtyla elaborates:

> Besides, the realization of these ends is a complex fact. A complete, positive exclusion of the possibility of procreation undoubtedly diminishes or even eliminates the possibility of durable, mutual co-education of the spouses themselves. Procreation unaccompanied by this co-education and co-striving for the highest good would also be in a certain sense incomplete and incompatible with the love of the person. Indeed, the point here is not only and exclusively the material multiplication of the headcount within the human species, but also education—whose natural substratum is the family based on marriage—cemented by *mutuum adiutorium*. If an interior cooperation between a woman and a man exists in marriage, and if they know how to educate and complement . . . each other, then their love matures to become the basis of the family. However, marriage is not identified with family and always remains, above all, an intimate union of two people.[246]

---

[244] Wojtyla, *Love and Responsibility*, 52; see also, 51.
[245] Wojtyla, *Love and Responsibility*, 52.
[246] Wojtyla, *Love and Responsibility*, 52–53.

Thus, significantly, for Wojtyla, love is not an end of marriage; rather, love is the single integrating principle of marriage as an ethical, or covenantal, community grounded in the sexual differentiation between a man and a woman, and expressed and fulfilled in the unitive and procreative ends marriage. Wojtyla's position emphasizes the centrality of conjugal love in Christian marriage, but without opposing love to procreation, rendering it marginal or optional, nor yet suggesting that procreation takes precedence over love.

The Roots of Sexual Promiscuity, Hedonism, and Self-transcendence

One must note here, furthermore, that this reductionist claim of a materialistic anthropology—reducing the sexual drive to a mere physical or biological need—has spawned a sexual promiscuity that has led to the fear of commitment and constancy in the quest for enduring interpersonal relationships rather than to sexual fulfillment. At the root of this promiscuity is the profound change in our sexual consciousness brought about by the sexual revolution with its concomitant hedonism, resulting in a consequent inability to defer sexual gratification, and hence a "using" that blocks the way to love, which, as Wojtyla claims, is a union of persons. In other words, a materialistic anthropology blocks self-transcendence and hence makes it impossible for the individual to be fulfilled in relationality in which the individual can "fully find himself only through a sincere gift of himself" to the other person.[247] What is the cause of this blockage?

Lillian Rubin correctly remarks, "Such change in consciousness, however, cannot have taken place without a concomitant transformation in the very structure of desire itself, in when and how desire is

---

[247] Vatican II, *Gaudium et Spes*, §24.

activated, experience and acted upon."[248] De Bruijne seems to recognize the point that Rubin is making when he suggests that perhaps the classical Christian vision was wise in claiming "that a healthy interaction with sexuality requires the regulating and controlling of the passions."[249] Rubin adds, "[R]easonable ideas of self-awareness and self-actualization soon became corrupted by a narcissistic involvement with self and a feverish search for instant gratification."[250] Furthermore, preoccupation with self-egoism generates a contradiction between our individual self-affirmation and being fulfilled in a relationship. "To become a couple, to be able to commit to being 'we', means we must be willing to give over some part of the 'I'—a need that soon comes into conflict with the quest for personal gratification and self-actualization."[251] If absolute freedom is at the root of the sexual revolution and its call for sexual emancipation, and this has led to self-enslavement to the self, this raises the question whether human nature is such that the meaning and purpose of human sexuality is grounded in embedded principles and inbuilt meanings of man's sexual design.

Yes, de Bruijne disagrees with this notion of absolute freedom at the root of the sexual revolution because it is destructive, resulting in new forms of self-enslavement, such as pornography and the commodification of sex, i.e., prostitution.[252] This is why he asks a couple of times at crucial points whether the model of sexuality in which sexuality receives its meaning and purpose from a Creator is more in keeping with the na-

---

[248] Rubin, *Erotic Wars*, 156.

[249] Ad de Bruijne, "Seksualiteit en cultuurstrijd: Een theologische voorstel tot dialog," 283.

[250] Rubin, *Erotic Wars*, 158.

[251] Rubin, *Erotic Wars*, 159–160.

[252] De Bruijne, "Seksualiteit en cultuurstrijd: Een theologische voorstel tot dialog," 282.

ture of human sexuality and man's dignity. Again, he raises this question, too, in light of man's sexual self-enslavement:

> That can give rise to the question whether, in connection with sexuality, there is nevertheless the element of meaning that is predicated on the basis of the phenomenon itself and transcends what people in their freedom are seeking to do with it and which does not tolerate being ignored (even regardless of what that meaning is).[253]

Still, de Bruijne remains non-committal regarding the embedded principles and inbuilt meanings of human sexuality that precede men's choices. So then, where is the underlying conceptual continuity?

Significantly, de Bruijne mentions the acceptance of contraception as a mark of the sexual revolution but does not pause to consider its effects on our understanding of the sexual act. That revolution was fueled largely by the effective technological resources that modern science had devised in the 1950s to separate the sexual act from reproduction. Procreation was thus taken to be at the discretion of a married or unmarried couple, in other words, an optional extra, that could "control" by technical means the number of their children and the time interval between them. Separating the sexual act from reproduction led to the public acceptance of sexual activities that were infertile by nature, such as masturbation or same-sex acts, or separated from marriage, and hence cohabitation became largely accepted. The culture lost the understanding of marriage as humanity has understood it since ancient times: the lifelong union of man and woman with the essential purpose of giving birth to new life and thus ensuring the future of society. Thus, it is not too

---

[253] De Bruijne, "Seksualiteit en cultuurstrijd: Een theologische voorstel tot dialog," 282.

much to say that contraception changed the sex act itself by separating sex and babies, separating sex and childbearing from each other. In the contraceptive morality, consequently, the sexual act became a self-sterilizing act, and once the idea took hold in our culture that there is nothing intrinsically wrong with contraceptive sex, there was no longer any reason to deny homosexual sex that by its very nature is sterile.[254] This understanding of the root-significance of contraception is not just a Catholic view, or, for that matter, a Christian view.

Anthony Giddens, for one, identifies contraception as the creation of what he called *"plastic sexuality."* It "severed [the sexual act] from its age-old integration with reproduction, kinship and the generations, [and this] was the precondition of the sexual revolution of the past decades."[255] Sex became what Giddens calls a "pure relationship," that is, "a social relation . . . entered into for its own sake, for what can be derived by each person from a sustained association with another; and which is continued only in so far as it is thought by both parties to deliver enough

---

[254] Joseph Cardinal Ratzinger, with Vittorio Messori, *The Ratzinger Report, An Exclusive Interview on the State of the Church*, trans. Salvator Attanasio and Graham Harrison (San Francisco, CA: Ignatius Press, 1985), on the section, "Against 'trivialized' sex," where the same argument is made. See also, "Gomorrah in the 21st Century. The Appeal of a Cardinal and Church Historian," http://magister.blogautore.espresso.repubblica.it/2018/11/05/gomorrah-in-the-21st-century-the-appeal-of-a-cardinal-and-church-historian/. For the whole article in Italian, Walter Cardinal Brandmüller, "Omosessualità e abusi - Affrontare la crisi: le lezioni della storia," Vatican Magazine, November 2018. http://magister.blogautore.espresso.repubblica.it/2018/11/03/affrontare-la-crisi-le-lezioni-della-storia/.

[255] Anthony Giddens, *The Transformation of Intimacy, Sexuality, Love & Eroticism in Modern Societies* (Stanford, CA: Stanford University Press, 1992), 27. The next few paragraphs are adapted here from Echeverria, *Pope Francis: The Legacy of Vatican II*, Second Edition (Hobe Sound, FL: Lectio Publishing, 2019), 363–364.

satisfactions for each individual to stay within it."²⁵⁶ Sex is nothing more and nothing less than a physical need and a means of pleasure. Procreation is marginal and optional. Furthermore, as Elizabeth Anscombe noted, "If you can turn intercourse into something other than the reproductive *type* of act . . . then why, if you can change it, should it be restricted to the married?"²⁵⁷ Or for that matter to heterosexuals? Consequently, the sex act is separated from marriage, leading to the widespread acceptance of non-marital cohabitation, which in turn has led to the practice that sex and childbearing can be separated from marriage. One of the consequences of this change is that it also transformed our attitude to children, in particular, children became extrinsically related to sex. Furthermore, transforming the sex act by separating it from procreation through contraception resulted in the contraceptive mentality that justified abortion; children were not intrinsically related to the sexual act, and hence they were disposable consequences if unwanted. Giddens writes, "Sexuality came into being as part of a progressive differentiation of sex from the exigencies of reproduction. With the further elaboration of reproductive technologies, that differentiation has today become complete." Children became a man-made product rather than a gift, a fruit of the conjugal act.

> Now that conception can be artificially produced, rather than only artificially inhibited, sexuality is at last fully autonomous. Reproduction can occur in the absence of sexual activity; this is a final "liberation" for sexuality, which thence can become

---

²⁵⁶ Giddens, *The Transformation of Intimacy*, 58.

²⁵⁷ Elizabeth Anscombe, "Contraception and Chastity," 1972, http://www.orthodoxytoday.org/articles/AnscombeChastity.php. She tells us what she means by a reproductive type of sex act, "I don't mean of course that every act is reproductive any more than every acorn leads to an oak-tree but it's the reproductive type of act."

wholly a quality of individuals and their transactions with one another.[258]

Moreover, Giddens also shows that this transformation led to considering gender/sex apart from the body's natural determinations, a sexually differentiated body, even to the extent of dissolving the meaning of the masculine/feminine difference, and hence for the "moral insignificance of sexual difference."[259] As Giddens correctly maintains, "the changes now affecting sexuality are indeed revolutionary, and in a very profound way."[260]

Finally, contraception also transformed the relationship between men and women. In particular, wrote Harvey Cox, "Sex becomes one of the items of leisure activity that the knowledgeable consumer of leisure handles with his characteristic skill and detachment. The girl becomes a desirable—indeed an indispensable—'Playboy accessory.'" On this view, "sex must be contained, at all costs, within the entertainment-recreation area. . . . [This view] is basically anti-sexual. [It] dilutes and dissipates authentic sexuality by reducing it to an accessory, by keeping it at a safe

---

[258] Giddens, *The Transformation of Intimacy*, 27.

[259] Christopher C. Roberts, *Creation & Covenant, The Significance of Sexual Difference in the Moral Theology of Marriage* (New York: T&T Clark, New York, 2007), 186.

[260] Giddens, *The Transformation of Intimacy*, 3. Abraham Kuyper was prescient in his anticipation of not only the eradication of sexual difference but of what is now called "trans-genderism" in his 1898 Stone Lectures on Calvinism. "Modernism, which denies and abolishes every difference, cannot rest until it has made woman man and man woman, and, putting every distinction on a common level, kills life by placing it under the ban of uniformity," *Lectures on Calvinism* (Eerdmans, 1931), 27.

distance."²⁶¹ Indeed, on this view, sexual disenchantment has left us thinking that sex has no intrinsic meaning; it's nothing more than a leisure activity, only having the meaning that people choose to give it.²⁶² Last but not least, Paul VI wrote:

> Another effect that gives cause for alarm [from the use of contraception] is that a man who grows accustomed to the use of contraceptive methods may forget the reverence due to a woman, and, disregarding her physical and emotional equilibrium, reduce her to being a mere instrument for the satisfaction of his own desires, no longer considering her as his partner whom he should surround with care and affection.²⁶³

However, the problems raised here regarding the presuppositions of sexual liberation make abundantly clear that there is no conceptual relation between orthodox Christianity and proponents of sexual emancipation. Consequently, human sexuality cannot be reduced to a physical or biological need and a mere source of pleasure, but is something of deeper importance because how we live our sexual lives has a deep impact on our relationship with God, on our capacity to love other persons, the stability of marriage and family life, which includes the good of children, and each person's internal harmony and well-being. In short, sex has a moral center that cannot be eradicated.²⁶⁴

---

[261] Harvey Cox, *The Secular City* (New York: The MacMillan Press, 1965), 201, 204. See also, Mark Regnerus, *Cheap Sex, The Transformation of Men, Marriage, and Monogamy* (Oxford: Oxford University Press, 2017).

[262] Perry, *The Case Against the Sexual Revolution*, 11.

[263] Pope Paul VI, *Humanae Vitae*, §17.

[264] Thomas Joseph White, *The Light of Christ, An Introduction to Catholicism* (Washington, DC: Catholic University of America Press, 2017), 239.

Ch. 3: Culture Wars, The Sexual Revolution, Ethics, Hermeneutics

Cardinal Eijk summarizes the teaching of the Church on homosexual acts.

"Homosexual acts are intrinsically evil because they are incompatible with marriage as God established it at creation [Gen 1:27; 2:24]... The Tradition of the Church and the Magisterium have always regarded homosexual acts as intrinsically disordered."[265] In a long passage that repays reflection, he writes:

> Therefore, from the perspective of Church teaching, homosexual acts cannot be justified.
>
> 1. First, what applies to homosexuals is the same as for all unmarried individuals—that they are called to live in sexual abstinence.
> 2. Like everyone, homosexuals have a natural inclination toward unity with a partner through sexual union. However, according to Grisez, [[266]] their experience of intimacy remains incommunicable for intrinsic reasons. Sexual union is an integral part of the total mutual self-giving that marriage between a man and a woman is, as God established at creation. The reason, according to Church teaching, is that the totality of this gift also includes the potential for the gift of parenthood. Because this potential is absent in homosexual unions, they cannot, for intrinsic reasons, authentically express the total mutual self-giving that is the essence of marriage.

---

[265] Eijk, *De Band van de Liefde*, 288, 289.
[266] "Sodomites use their bodies in a self-defeating attempt at intimacy," Grisez, *The Way of the Lord Jesus* II, 653.

3. According to the order of creation, man and woman are complementary to each other and can only fully express the image of God, which humanity bears, together within marriage. A sexual relationship between two people of the same sex cannot be an image of the communion of the three Divine Persons within the Trinity, who differ in their relationships yet are complementary and are one, and whose love becomes fruitful outwardly in creation. It is telling in this regard that Paul associates homosexual behavior with the rejection of God.
4. With the expression "acts against nature" (*para phusin*, Rom 1:24), Paul means that homosexual acts go against God's order of creation—that is, they go against the moral natural law. They contradict the inherent nature of marriage, which is a total mutual self-giving of the spouses to each other. This gift can be fully realized physically only if their sexual union is open to procreation.[267]

Four points deserve highlighting. One, the unity attained in becoming "two-in-one-flesh" between a man and a woman in marriage is grounded in the order of creation (Gen 1:27; 2:24). It is precisely the embodiment of human persons, as man and woman, which has been lost in our culture, even among Catholics, that is necessary for a proper understanding of marriage. These creation texts are normative for human sexual relations. Two, real bodily oneness, a one-flesh union between a man and a woman, *actualizes* marital unity, and hence only a unitive act

---

[267] Eijk, *De Band van de Liefde*, 288, 289.

can be generative. Three, following Germain Grisez, Cardinal Eijk argues that sodomites, which involves two bodies of the same sex, cannot experience real unity and hence cannot constitute a bodily communion of persons."[268]

In response to the question regarding the criteria of marriage, Robert George distinguishes the "comprehensive union" view from the view of marriage as an "emotional union." Concerning the former he writes: "As to (a), the union of mind and body: What bodily (biologically) unites two people is much like what unites the parts of an individual. One's organs form a unity by coordinating for the biological good of the whole (one's bodily life). Likewise, a male and female form a biological unity by mating—that is, by coordinated activity of the type that causes reproduction when its nonbehavioral conditions obtain. This understanding accounts for the historic legal norm of consummation of marriage by coition—a norm developed entirely apart from any questions regarding same-sex or multiple partner bonds. Of course, it presupposes—rightly in my view—that our bodies are part of our personal reality as human beings, not subpersonal extrinsic instruments at the service of the conscious and desiring aspect of the self."[269]

He continues, "While other sexual acts may be regarded by those desiring them as fostering emotional attachment, so can many non-sexual activities, which clearly involve nothing like the sort of bodily union integral to marriage (not only in my personal view, but across time and diverse cultures). So if—contrary to the historic understanding—sex acts

---

[268] Grisez, *The Way of the Lord Jesus* II, 653.
[269] Robert P. George, "Contrasting Views of Marriage: The Need for a Defining Principle," *Public Discourse,* July 22, 2014, http://www.thepublicdiscourse.com/2014/07/13526/.

of any type can seal a marriage, there is no reason of principle that marriage should be a sexual relationship at all."[270]

Furthermore, the gendered bodiliness of this two-in-one-flesh union—that union as one body is truly bodily, meaning thereby biologically or organically one body—has increasingly been denied by our culture by rejecting outright the significance of the human body, indeed of sexual differentiation for marriage.[271]

He continues: "As to (b), marriage's inherent orientation to procreation, family life, and thus a comprehensive range of goods: what explains this is the fact that the act that makes marital love is also the kind of act that makes new life. So marriage, the bond so embodied, would be fulfilled by family life, and is always fulfilled by the all-around domestic sharing uniquely apt for it. If it is rather the choice to adopt that makes a bond oriented to family life, and hence marital, then any group of individuals can form one—romantic partners, to be sure, but also two sisters in a platonic partnership which no one considers inherently oriented to procreation, as marriage is. As to (c), the fact that marriage calls for total commitment: because marriage is comprehensive in senses (a) and (b), it inherently calls for a commitment that is comprehensive, through time (permanent) and at each time (exclusive).

---

[270] George, "Contrasting Views of Marriage."

[271] "From the distinction between sex, or biological sexuality, and gender, or the social-cultural shaping of sex, some positions derive a fundamental equality and thereby the arbitrariness of different configurations of sexuality, whether as monogamous, polygamous, heterosexual, homosexual, or transsexual. Behind such positions stands a neo-Gnostic body-soul dualism, which fails to recognize the unity and holism of the human body (see 1 Cor 1:12-20). According to Christian conviction, the body, even in its sexuality, is a real symbol of the soul and the soul is the body's defining life-form. It is important to add that establishing the fact of differentiation in no way entails or justifies discrimination (see *CCC* 2357-59)," Walter Cardinal Kasper, *The Gospel of the Family*, 39n7.

In other bonds, there is no basis for such norms, apart from partners' subjective preferences. Of course, two men or two women can choose sexual exclusivity, but if emotional intimacy is what makes a marriage, there is no reason of principle that they should not practice sexual openness (if they happen to prefer that) or forgo a pledge of permanence.

Finally, if emotional bonding is what makes a marriage, why can't three people form a marriage, as poly-activists argue? And why, if marriage is fundamentally about intimacy, should the state recognize and regulate marriages at all?"[272]

In sum, the "comprehensive union" view of marriage can—but the "emotional union" view[273] cannot—explain at the level of principle these critical features of marriage:

1) Marriage is inherently a sexual partnership.
2) Marriage inherently calls for a pledge of sexual exclusivity.
3) Marriage calls for a pledge of permanence, not a term of years or "as long as love lasts."
4) Marriage can unite only two persons, not multiple-partner groups (of whatever combination of sexes).
5) Marriage should be legally recognized and regulated (unlike other friendships).

---

[272] George, "Contrasting Views of Marriage."

[273] Pope Francis also rejects marriage as a mere emotional union: "The family is experiencing a profound cultural crisis, as are all communities and social bonds. In the case of the family, the weakening of these bonds is particularly serious because the family is the fundamental cell of society, where we learn to live with others despite our differences and to belong to one another; it is also the place where parents pass on the faith to their children. Marriage now tends to be viewed as a form of mere emotional satisfaction that can be constructed in any way or modified at will," *Evangelii Gaudium*, §66, Nov 24, 2013.

"This *reductio* of the revisionist view—that it eliminates any principled difference between marriage and simple companionship—is not just of academic interest. If the law promotes and our culture absorbs a view of marriage that undermines the principled basis for its stabilizing norms, those norms will decline (even more) in practice."[274] Here is a summary of the argument against same-sex marriage by virtue of being unable to achieve bodily union.

1. If X and Y can realize bodily unity, then there must be some single bodily activity, Z, in which X and Y mutually participate (this is the source of their bodily unity, that is, the something else that is one through they are unified).
2. An action is a single bodily action if it (all its steps and levels of complexity) has a single telos/goal/good (this is the source of the unity of the activity, Z, through which X and Y are unified).
3. A bodily action, Z, is an action in which X and Y can mutually participate, iff neither X nor Y is individually complete/self-sufficient with respect to Z (this establishes the conditions under which mutual participation in an action is possible).
4. Human beings are individually complete/self-sufficient with respect to all bodily activities except for reproductive activities.
5. X and Y can realize bodily unity if they can engage in reproductive [type] activities.
6. If X and Y are of the same-sex they cannot engage in reproductive [type] activities.

---

[274] George, "Contrasting Views of Marriage."

7. If X and Y are of the same sex, they cannot realize bodily unity.[275]

Furthermore, man becomes the image of God by the communion of persons, and this communion reflects the union and distinctness of the divine persons.[276] The rejection of the image of God in this sense constitute the rejection of God. We can add here God's general revelation (Rom 1: 18ff) is open resistance and hence to distortion, misinterpretation, and rejection of the truth (see John 1:9-11; Rom 1:24-27). Robert Gagnon gives us a contemporary example of the suppression of truth and its substitution for something else.

Idolatry and same-sex intercourse together constitute an assault on the work of the Creator in nature. Instead of recognizing their creation in God's image [Gen 1:27] and dominion over animals, humans worshipped statues in the image of humans and animals. Similarly, instead of acknowledging that God made them "male and female," some humans went so far as to deny the transparent sexual complementarity of males and females by engaging in sex with the same sex. Those who had suppressed the truth about God visible in creation went on to suppress the truth about themselves in nature.[277]

Creation, Sexual Difference, and its Eschatological Significance

Against this background, particularly troublesome is de Bruijne's

---

[275] For a critique of the claim that bodily union is a morally significant aspect of the marital relation, see Rebekah Johnston, "Marriage and the Metaphysics of Bodily Union: Framing the Same-Sex Marriage Debate," *Social Theory and Practice*, 39, no. 2 (April 2013): 288-312. Although I find Johnston's argument unpersuasive, her summary of the argument against same-sex marriage, as founded on claims about bodily union, is clarifying (299).

[276] Vatican II, *Gaudium et Spes*, §24.

[277] Via and Gagnon, *Homosexuality and the Bible*, 78.

contradictory perspective on the relation between creation and eschatology. On the one hand, De Bruijne stresses the open-ended, future-oriented meaning, nature, and structure of human sexuality that he claims is derived from the Christian eschatological perspective of the new creation. De Bruijne seeks an eschatological perspective that justifies ontic novelty for human interrelations such that transsexuality, intersexuality, and homosexuality would just be instances of sexual variety. On the other hand, De Bruijne's recognizes the normative order of creation and the nature of things with its embedded principles and the inherent meanings of the human sexual design. He claims that his view doesn't contradict or reject that ordered creation, leaving nothing lost, but rather brings it to completion and fulfillment, with all the positive reality and goods of human nature, the good of marriage and its one-flesh communion of two sexes. But this is not the case. De Bruijne acknowledges that his proposal is speculative in claiming that "transsexuality, intersexuality, and homosexuality" may receive new positive meaning and moral legitimacy even here and now in light of the eschaton, rather than in relation to the ontology of creation for which de Bruijne sees no ontological and necessary relation.[278] Nonetheless, although I reject his proposal, his claim raises the legitimate question regarding the eschatological significance of embodied sexual difference of male and female that belongs ontologically to creation (Genesis 1:27).

Of course, the ontology of creation revelation in which God created man male and female does receive an eschatological orientation—Jesus said, "in the resurrection they neither marry nor are given in marriage" (Matthew 22:30; cf. Mark 12:25, Luke 20:34–36)—in the perspective of the resurrection. Yet, in this eschatological perspective, John Paul II correctly states:

---

[278] Roberts, *Creation & Covenant*, 207.

[H]ere we are with a development of the *truth about the same man*. Christ points out man's identity, although this identity *is realized in a different way in eschatological experience than* in the experience of the very "beginning" and of all history. And nevertheless, man will always be the same, just as he came forth from the hand of his Creator and Father.[279]

Indeed, John Paul II underscores the ontological identity of man created male and female even in light of Jesus's eschatological declaration. "[B]ut he [Jesus] does not affirm that this man of the 'future world' will no longer be male and female as he was 'from the beginning'."[280] On the one hand, the redemptive work of Christ is continuous with the restoration of the original intent of creation because sexual difference is not redundant. However, on the other hand, the eschatological fullness of that redemption is more than restoring or recovering that original intent. John Paul II explains:

One can say that St. Paul sees the future resurrection as a certain *restitution in integrum*, that is, as the reintegration and at the same time as the attainment of the fullness of humanity. It is not only a restitution, because in this case the resurrection would be, in a certain sense, a return to the state the soul shared in before sin, outside the knowledge of good and evil (see Gen 1–2). Yet, such a return does not correspond to the inner logic of the whole economy of salvation, to the deepest meaning of the mystery of redemption. *Restitutio in integrum*, linked with the resurrection and the reality of the "other world," can only be *an introduction to a new fullness*. It will be a fullness that presupposes man's

---

[279] John Paul II, *Man and Woman He Created Them*, 3.69.3.
[280] John Paul II, *Man and Woman He Created Them*, 3.69.3.

whole history, formed by the drama of the tree of the knowledge of good and evil (see Gen 3) and at the same time permeated by the mystery of redemption.[281]

Furthermore, the understanding of creation and the eschaton relies upon a correct grasp of the relation of nature and grace. The Anglican neo-Thomist Eric L. Mascall gives a correct interpretation of the Thomist maxim, "Grace does not destroy nature but perfects it," giving us a right reading of two complementary principles in Aquinas' thought. He states, "'Grace does not destroy nature but perfects it', and this is from within because nature always lies open to God." "Grace presupposes nature," not in the sense that grace is a mere superstructure erected on top of nature and needing nature only to prevent it from falling through the floor, *but that nature is the very material in which grace works and for whose ultimate perfection grace itself exists.*"[282] On this view, then, of the relation between nature and grace, the relation is such that grace restores nature rather than abolishes or leaves it untouched, and hence grace presupposes nature in order to build on it since nature is the "very material in which grace works and for whose ultimate perfection grace itself exists." Grace does not make nature superfluous because sexual difference is a material presupposition that it builds upon. Moreover:

> In his preaching Jesus unequivocally taught the original [i.e., creational, from the order of nature] meaning of the union of man and woman as the Creator willed it from the beginning. . . . By coming to restore the original order of creation disturbed

---

[281] John Paul II, *Man and Woman He Created Them*, 3.72.3.

[282] E.L. Mascall, *The Openness of Being, Natural Theology Today*, 153 (italics added). These two maxims are derived from St. Thomas Aquinas, *Summa Theologiae*, I, q. 1, a. 8, ad 2, and I, q. 2., a. 2, ad 1, respectively.

by sin, [Jesus] himself gives the strength and grace to live marriage in the new dimension of the Reign of God (*CCC*, §§1603, 1606–9, 1614–15).

Grace restores nature to function properly according to its divinely intended ends.

On the one hand, then, Jesus calls us back to the law of creation (Mark 10:6–7) that grounds an inextricable nexus of permanence, twoness, and sexual differentiation for marriage. In particular, marriage is such that it requires sexual difference, the bodily-sexual act, as a foundational prerequisite, indeed, as *intrinsic* to a one-flesh union of man and woman, "So they are no longer two but one flesh" (Mark 10:8). On the other hand, inasmuch as grace's restoration of the creation's fullness is not a mere recovery of the deepest foundations of created reality, in some sense those foundations are raised to a "higher level" in the eschatological consummation of God's plan of salvation for the whole creation. The exact sense in which "the redemption by grace of created reality, the reformation of nature, is not merely a recovery, *but raises the natural to a higher level than it originally occupied*"[283] is a hotly disputed matter, especially in Reformed and Catholic thought. Berkouwer summarizes this issue clearly in a long paragraph that repays reflection:

> This eschaton also, then, will lay to rest the familiar discussions of natural versus supernatural and the eschatological elevation of human nature. The problem of creatureliness has always been central to these discussions; and many have tried to define and do full justice to this "elevation" while consciously avoiding the pitfalls of pantheism.

---

[283] Jan Veenhof, "Nature and Grace in Bavinck," *Pro Rege* (June 2006): 10–31, especially 22.

Furthermore, Berkouwer explains the crux of this discussion:

> The meaning and extent of redemption [vis-à-vis creation] are the heart of the issue. Is God's Kingdom something more than just a *restoration* of what has been lost? Is not the deepest meaning of the eschatological mystery this, that it will supersede and transcend the original created nature of man? The peculiar thing about this line of thought is that those who want to attribute so much to redemption are driven to describe it with mundane analogies that remind one anew of renewal and restoration. It is as if according to God's intention the glory of creatureliness sets up certain boundaries that cannot be transgressed, and any effort to attribute something more to man in the eschaton runs against these boundaries. Those who defy these boundaries [because they regard them as outdated will always grope for the reality of the eschaton, but they must] be reminded that "it does not yet appear what we shall be" (1 John 3:2). This remark by John sets the limits to our penetration of the eschatological mystery. When we speak of that mystery, however, then, we cannot, *in the very nature of the case,* make a simple identification of end-time [Endzeit] and original-time [Urzeit]. The fact that the eschaton is *filled* with the mystery of history—the *Lamb* in the Book of Revelation—warns us against both over-simplification and speculation.[284]

Three points deserve highlighting. First, although redemption is more than a renewal and recovery of what was lost in the fall, describing the eschatological mystery of creation in earthly analogies (1 Cor 15:25–

---

[284] G.C. Berkouwer, *The Return of Christ*, trans. Kames van Oosterom, ed. Marlin J. van Elderen (Grand Rapids, MI: Eerdmans, 1972), 449–450.

53) suggests certain boundaries of creation that will not be transcended, hence renewed, and restored even while fulfilled. This perspective of creation receives support from Christ in Matthew 19:3–8 and Mark 10:6–9, given that His words refer back to the Genesis texts of 1:27 and 2:24. "Back-to-creation" is the *leitmotif* in Jesus's teaching. In His own teaching regarding marital monogamy and indissolubility, creation texts in Genesis 1–2 have foundational importance, in particular Genesis 1:27 and 2:24, "Male and female He created them" and "for this reason . . . a man will be joined to his wife and the two will become one flesh." These texts are normative for marriage, indeed, for sexual and conjugal ethics. Jesus unites into an inextricable nexus the concepts of permanence, twoness, and sexual complementarity. Yes, Genesis 2:24 is about the permanence of marriage; it is also about the exclusivity of the relationship, "twoness," and which "two": male and female. Hence, it is also about the fundamental prerequisite of complementary sexual differentiation for effecting the "two-in-one-flesh" union of man and woman. "So then they are no longer two but one flesh" (Mark 10:8).

Second, there is also the eschatological mystery that prohibits us from simply identifying the original creation with the eschatological fulfillment of creation. In this light, it cuts off speculation—such as de Bruijne's attempt to legitimize sexual diversity from an eschatological perspective—about what we shall be with resurrected bodies. Yes, the body will be raised, indeed, the totality of our human nature will be raised.

Third, in this connection, Jesus says, "in the resurrection they neither marry nor are given in marriage" (Matthew 22:30; cf. Mark 12:25, Luke 20:34–36). Similarly, St. Paul asks, "'How are the dead raised? With what kind of body do they come?'" (1 Corinthians 15:35). In light, then, of these passages, the late Catholic theologian Germain Grisez rightly asks, "How, then, can the one-flesh communion of marriage endure forever?" One thing is for sure, according to Jesus, it will not eschatologically endure within the limits of a two-in-one-flesh union being fulfilled by the having and raising of children. Christ states that "in the resurrection they will take neither wife nor husband" (Mark 12:25; cf. Matthew 22:30). Still, John Paul II adds, "man will always be the same, just as he came forth from the hand of his Creator and Father."[285] Thus, there is a development of the truth about the same man such that in the eschatological experience of the resurrection he will still be male and female as he was "from the beginning." In other words, grace renews nature from within such that the transfigured one-flesh communion is already, here and now, a concrete anticipation of the Kingdom of God, that communion cannot be abolished in the new creation. So, Jesus does affirm that this man of the new creation will be male and female as he was "from the beginning" (Matthew 19:8; Mark 10:6).

> It is thus evident that the meaning of being, with respect to the body, male or female in the "future world" should be sought outside of marriage and procreation, but there is no reason to seek it outside of that which (independently from the blessing of procreation) derives from the very mystery of creation and thereafter also forms the deepest structure of man's history on earth.[286]

In other words, redemption, eschatologically viewed, is not simply a return or recovery of an original state of creation. The one-flesh communion of man and woman of the new creation is perfected by and united specifically with the divine persons (John 14:23), through knowledge and love. Still, although redemption is not merely recovery,

---

[285] John Paul II, *Man and Woman He Created Them*, 69.3.
[286] John Paul II, *Man and Woman He Created Them*, 69.3.

it is so much more, that is, it is a supernatural perfecting of created nature, by a transforming fellowship with the triune God. Says Wojtyla, "those who will participate in the 'future world,' that is, in the perfect communion with the living God, will enjoy a perfectly mature subjectivity." He adds:

> If in this perfect subjectivity, while keeping masculinity and femininity in their risen (that is, glorious) bodies, ... then *this is explained* not only by the end of history, but also—and above all—by the eschatological *authenticity of the response* to that "self-communication" of the Divine Subject that will constitute the beatifying experience of God's gift of self, an experience absolutely superior to every experience proper to earthly life.[287]

In short, the position of John Paul II accounts both for continuity and discontinuity. That is, sexually differentiated embodiedness is ontologically constitutive of human identity (Genesis 1:27), such that, as John Paul II argues, Christ affirms

> at one and the same time, that human bodies, which are recovered and also renewed in the resurrection, will preserve their specific masculine or feminine character and that *the meaning of being male or female in the body* will be *constituted and understood differently* in the "other world" than it had been "from the beginning" and in its whole earthly dimension.[288]

There is substantial continuity between creation and the eschaton.

---

[287] John Paul II, *Man and Woman He Created Them*, 3.68.2.
[288] John Paul II, *Man and Woman He Created Them*, 3.66.4.

However, there is also discontinuity regarding the eschatological significance of sexually differentiated embodiedness. Still, the risen and manifested Lord had a body and that guarantees our creational identity, that "I" will remain, indeed the totality of our human nature of which sexual differentiation is an ontological fact.

Four Foundational Presuppositions to Sexual Ethics[289]

In Wojtyla's Introduction to the Second Polish Edition (1965) of *Love and Responsibility*, he identifies the primary authoritative sources that provide "an impetus for philosophical reflections concerning sexual problems."[290]

> That superior source is the Gospel together with its extension, the teaching of the Church. This source fostered reflections, whereas experience provides facts for confrontation with doctrine. The Gospel contains relatively few texts that speak directly about sexual and conjugal ethics, for example Matthew 5:27–28, Matthew 19:1–13, Mark 10:1–12, Luke 20:27–35, John 8:1–11, 1 Corinthians 7 (the entire chapter), and Ephesians 5:22–33, not to mention extremely significant texts in the Old Testament, especially in Genesis [1:27, 2:24].[291]

Then Wojtyla states the crucial hermeneutical principle of canonical criticism, attending to the unity and content of all of Scripture. "All the

---

[289] Portions of this section are adapted from Echeverria, *Pope Francis: The Legacy of Vatican II*, Second Edition, 367–369.

[290] Wojtyla, *Love and Responsibility*, xxvi.

[291] Wojtyla, *Love and Responsibility*, xxvi.

above mentioned passages organically inhere in the whole of the Gospel and must be in this whole as in their essential context. Read in this way, they give an incentive for philosophical reflection."[292] In this section, I will explain the four foundational presuppositions to sexual ethics, according to Wojtyla/John Paul II.

In *Familiaris Consortio*, the 1981 Post-Synodal Apostolic Exhortation of St. John Paul II, the pope writes, "God created man in His own image and likeness: calling him to existence *through love*, He called him at the same time *for love*. . . . Love is therefore the fundamental and innate vocation of every human being." In particular, he says, "God inscribed in the humanity of man and woman the vocation, and thus the capacity and responsibility, *of love* and communion" (§11). One might say that being created in and for love, man in his freedom is unintelligible without love. For the Christian faith, love is the supreme value and goal (end) not only of the sexual relationship but of *all* personal relationships, whether sexual, in the whole of their bodily life, or otherwise. Indeed, morality itself is fulfilled when it becomes true love of God and of man.

There is more to say about this love-ethics nature. For one, it is not opposed to universally valid moral precepts. In other words, this ethics has a normative character; it has a *deontological* basis, involving, then, a morality of duty, making judgments about duty in respect of the question: What ought I to do? What is good and what is evil in human acts and why? De Bruijne denies ethic's deontological basis. "God's will does not consist of abstract loose duties, with which you as a human being must unquestioningly comply, even if it is not clear why this is good."

---

[292] Wojtyla, *Love and Responsibility*, xxvii.

He calls this view "deontological voluntarism."[293] Wojtyla refutes this objection.[294]

Wojtyla's anthropology is such that he recognizes the person as the self-conscious cause of action, as a real being and a cause of its own action, but also the efficacy or causation that is proper to man in his becoming good or bad.[295] In other words, Wojtyla says that "in apprehending and investigating lived [ethical] experience as a phenomenological fact, we focus only on what happens in the person while performing an action. Although we then perceive the lived experience of efficacy and ethical value, these phenomenological elements do not present us with the actual whole [of a concrete human being] so long as we do not apprehend what happens to the person through the act that person consciously performs. What happens to the person is that the person himself . . . *becomes* good or bad depending on the act performed. . . . This becoming of the person also belongs to the totality of experience: the person *experiences* his . . . ethical becoming."[296] Phenomenological analysis of this ethical becoming of the person must be subordinated to metaphysical norms of potency and act as developed by Aquinas in his view that persons actualize themselves through actions.[297] Wojtyla uses the concept of *actualization* to refer to the transition from potency to act. He says, "it indicates some sort of becoming, not in the absolute sense—

---

[293] De Bruijne, *Verbonden voor het Leven*, 27.

[294] The next few paragraphs are adapted from Echeverria, *"In the Beginning"...A Theology of the Body*, 169-172-173.

[295] Echeverria, *"In the Beginning"...A Theology of the Body*, 79, 98.

[296] Karol Wojtyla, "The Problem of the Will in the Analysis of the Ethical Act," in *Person and Community: Selected Essays*, trans. Theresa Sandok, OSM (New York: Peter Lang, 1993 [1965]), 20.

[297] Karol Wojtyla, *Person and Act*, 63-64, 98-99.

this is possible only when something comes into being out of nonexistence—but in the relative sense, that is to say, becoming based on an already existing being and from within its inner structure."[298]

In this light we can see why Wojtyla understands man's acts to be the actualization of potentiality, its fulfillment, becoming good or bad depending on the action being performed. He argues: "Fulfillment reaches all the way to the potentiality of the person, as does unfulfillment. In relation to this potentiality essential to the human person, fulfillment is a good and unfulfillment is an evil—the lack of a good to which the person is 'by nature' disposed. In any case, the fulfillment of oneself in action, or self-realization, is also the attainment of the end proper to a human being as a person (a human being as a human being), and herein lies the essence of moral good. The essence of evil, on the other hand, consists in failing to achieve this end that is proper to a human being as a person (a human being as a human being)."[299] Wojtyla distinguishes Aquinas' view from a phenomenological one. "A conscious human act is for St. Thomas not merely a stage upon which ethical experience is enacted."[300] Aquinas does not divorce ethical becoming from the objective human *being*. Wojtyla explains this point—persons are actualized through actions—in a passage worth citing in full:

> The statement that moral value is also an end for human beings and human actions is verified even more fully when we take a different concept of end, when we view it not simply as the object of a particular aim but as that which fulfills—is conductive

---

[298] Wojtyla, *Person and Act*, 64.

[299] Karol Wojtyla, "The Problem of the Theory of Morality," in *Person and Community: Selected Essays*, 149.149.

[300] Wojtyla, "The Problem of the Will in the Analysis of the Ethical Act," 20.

to the fulfillment of—the subject and its activity. I should add that the concept of fulfillment perhaps most properly corresponds to the Latin *actus*. We know how important *actus* is in Aristotelian and Thomistic philosophy and ethics. In this regard, it seems that moral value determines the fulfillment of actions proper to persons and also determines the fulfillment of the persons themselves in such actions. In acting, we either fulfill ourselves or do not fulfill ourselves. This depends precisely on moral value. Moral good is that through which we fulfill ourselves in action, and evil the opposite. In this view, morality appears as something proper to the human person, corresponding to the person's dynamic sphere of fulfillment and unfulfillments. . . . As can be seen, the teleological interpretation is a dynamic development of the proper meaning of moral value. We have grasped this meaning in strict connection with the human being as a human being—as a person—becomes and is good, and moral evil that through which the human being as a human being—as a person—becomes and is evil. The teleological interpretation refers directly to this becoming, this *fieri*, [which is] proper to the human being as person. In this *fieri* is also contained the whole dynamic of auto-teleology that corresponds to the human being by reason of being a person.[301]

Furthermore, Wojtyla insists that such experiences cannot be divorced from, or be independent of, the existence of an objective hierarchy of goods, which is a normative order grounded in divine reason. "God is the supreme, transcendent measure of all beings through the unconditional perfection of [his] own being, through the unconditional

---

[301] Wojtyla, "The Problem of the Theory of Morality," 148-149.

fullness of existence that God is."[302] In Wojtyla's moral epistemology, "cognition does not in any way create 'reality' (cognition does not create its own content), but arises within the context of the different kinds of content that are proper to it; in other words, cognition arises thanks to the various kinds of *esse*, thanks to the enormous richness and complexity of reality." Without this transcendent reality in relation to moral cognition, he adds, "one would thereby rule out the realism of ethics."[303]

Against this background, we can understand why Wojtyla's love-ethic is also *axiological*, because duty possesses deontic dynamism, that is, duty "always arises in strict connection with the deeper, ontic reality of the person: 'to be good or evil'. Man is 'good or evil' through his acts—he is, or rather 'becomes' such because the act itself not so much 'is' as each time 'becomes'. Duty—not as an abstraction but as a reality—always enters into just that dynamic structure. Moral duty is dynamically connected with moral good and evil—and that this connection is both strict and exclusive. *Duty* arises 'because of' good or evil; it is always a *specific actualization of the spiritual potentiality of a person in act*; that actualization comes out 'for good' and 'against' evil." Furthermore, this love-ethic is also *praxiological* because "*a man, as a man, becomes good or evil through the act.*" This is, therefore, a reality that is thoroughly anthropological and personalistic.[304]

Thus, Christian anthropology must consider the reality of the human person in the order of love. Why? Because the "person finds in love

---

[302] Karol Wojtyla, "The Problem of Experience in Ethics," in *Person and Community: Selected Essays,* 116-117.

[303] Wojtyla, "The Problem of Experience in Ethics," 116-117.

[304] On the various aspects of morality, see Karol Wojtyla (Pope John Paul II), *Man in the Field of Responsibility*, trans. Kenneth W. Kemp & Zuzanna Maślanka Kieroń (South Bend, IN: St. Augustine's Press, 2011). See also Chapter 4 of this book where these various aspects of Wojtyla/John Paul II's theory of morality—axiological, praxiological, and deontological—are explored.

the greatest fullness of his being, of his objective existence. Love is such action, such an act, which most fully develops the existence of the person. Of course this has to be true love. What does true love mean?"[305] Since man—male and female—is created in and for love, accordingly, sexual ethics is, too, unintelligible without love. Hence, this crucial point about finding in love the greatest fullness of his being must also be applied to love between a man and a woman.

> In this field also, true love perfects the being of the person and develops his existence. False love, on the other hand, causes quite contrary effects. False love is a love that either turns to an apparent good or—as usually happens—turns to some true good, but in a way that does not correspond to the nature of the good, in a way contrary to it. At times this happens to be the love between a man and a woman either in its assumptions or—even despite (apparently) good assumptions—in its particular manifestations, in its realizations. False love is, in fact, evil love.[306]

A Christian approach to sexual ethics[307] appeals to the most elementary and undeniable moral truths and to the most fundamental values or goods to which the human person is ordered. For instance, the transcendent and objective value of the human person. Karol Wojtyla explains, "Such a good is the person, and the moral truth most clearly connected to the world of persons in particular is the 'commandment to love'—for love is the good proper to the world of persons. And therefore,

---

[305] Wojtyla, *Love and Responsibility*, 66.
[306] Wojtyla, *Love and Responsibility*, 66.
[307] On sexual ethics, Karol Wojtyla, "The Problem of Catholic Sexual Ethics, Reflections and Postulates," in *Person and Community: Selected Essays*, 279–299.

the most fundamental grasp of sexual morality is to grasp it on the basis of 'love and responsibility.'"[308] In other words, there exists responsibility in love, that is, responsibility for the person, for the person's true good.

> The human person, who is the most perfect being in the visible world, also, therefore, has the highest value. The value of the person is, in turn, the basis of the norm that should govern actions that have a person as their object. This norm may be called *personalistic* to distinguish it from other norms, which are based on the various natures of beings lower than the human being—nonpersonal natures. . . . All norms, including the personalistic norm, as based on the essences, or natures, or beings, are expressions of the order that governs the world. This order is intelligible to reason, to the person. Consequently, only the person is a *particeps legis aeternae et conscia legis naturae*, which means that the person is conscious of the normative force that flows from the essences, or natures, of all beings. In particular, the person is conscious of the normative force that flows from humanity, and this humanity in its individual form always appears as a person.[309]

Love separated from responsibility is a denial of itself, and, as a rule, is always egoism. "The more the sense of responsibility for the person, the more true love there is."[310] Wojtyla explains:

> For the choice of a person is a process in which the sexual value

---

[308] Wojtyla, *Love and Responsibility*, "Author's Introduction to the First Polish Edition (1960)," xxii.
[309] Wojtyla, "The Problem of Catholic Sexual Ethics," 287.
[310] Wojtyla, *Love and Responsibility*, 113.

cannot play a role of the only motive or even—in the ultimate analysis of this act of the will—the primary motive. This would contradict the very notion of the "choice of a person." If the only, or least, the primary motive of this choice were the sexual value itself, then we would not be able to speaks of choosing a person, but only of choosing the other sex connected with some "man" or even with some "body that is a possible object of use." It is clear that if we are to speak of choosing a person, the primary [although not the only] motive must be the very value of the person. . . . And only then, when each of them [choosing a woman by a man or a man by a woman] in this way, is the act of choice interiorly mature and complete. For only then is the proper integration of the object accomplished in it: the object of choice—the person—was grasped in his whole truth.[311]

Thus, sexual ethics is concerned with an "introduction of love into [sexual] love."[312] In the first case, love signifies the central commandment of love—"You should love the Lord, your God, with all your heart, with all your soul, and with all your mind. This is the greatest and the first commandment. The second is like it: You shall love your neighbor as yourself. The whole law and the prophets depend on these two commandments" (Matthew 22:36–40). The central commandment of love demands from us the responsibility that we love our neighbor. Indeed, the command is about responsible love for persons because the person is a good towards which the only proper and adequate response is love. "For if Jesus Christ commanded us to love those beings who are persons, then love is the proper form of relating to persons; it is the form of behavior for which we should strive when our behavior has a person as its

---

[311] Wojtyla, *Love and Responsibility*, 114–115.
[312] Wojtyla, *Love and Responsibility*, xviii.

object, since this form is demanded by that person's essence, or nature."[313]

In the second case, love refers to sexual love, and hence to sexual ethics. Wojtyla states, "To justify the norms of morality means to give reasons for their rightness. In performing this task, moral theologians should have before their eyes, as far as possible, the complete theoretical vision of reality contained in revelation, especially those elements of it that are indispensable for justifying the respective normative judgments. Normative judgments are based on value judgments, which, in turn, presupposes theoretical knowledge of the reality evaluated."[314] In this connection, I make explicit four presuppositions that are foundational to sexual ethics.

First, there is a distinctive sexual ethics rather than just a general ethics governing interpersonal relationships. On this view, sometimes called the "responsible-relational" (H. Richard Niebuhr)[315] position, moral norms that prohibit lying, deception, and exploitation are sufficient to render sexual acts morally good. This is how Margaret Farley describes the norms for what she calls sexual justice: refusal to do unjust harm, free consent, mutuality, equality, commitment, fruitfulness, and social justice, promote flourishing, and avoid harm and coercion.[316]

Whatever its undeniable merits—surely all interpersonal relationships should be free of deception, noncoercive, and nonexploitative—this ethics leaves us without a specific *sexual* ethics. The question here that needs attention is: what is the proper end of our sexual powers and their relationship to the nature of marriage? On this view, according to Philip Turner, "sexual acts, like all others, have no particular goods or

---

[313] Wojtyla, "The Problem of Catholic Sexual Ethics," 289.
[314] Wojtyla, "The Problem of Catholic Sexual Ethics," 280.
[315] Lawler, Boyle, and May, *Catholic Sexual Ethics*, 14.
[316] Farley, *Just Love: A Framework for Christian Sexual Ethics*, 231.

ends that are proper to them, and for this reason, and for this reason, like all acts, are to be assessed only on the basis of intention on the one hand and results on the other. There is," therefore," no act that is 'inherently right or wrong.'"[317] By contrast, there are "special moral responsibilities that flow from concern for the human goods [the interpersonal unity that is marital communion and its natural fulfillment in procreation] toward which sexuality itself is ordered [?]."[318] In other words, there can only be special moral responsibilities if sexual acts are uniquely distinct from other bodily acts because they are ordered to real human goods—the natural meanings and ends of man's sexual powers: union and procreation—that are intrinsic aspects of the well-being and fulfillment of human persons. Patrick Lee rightly states:

> It seems that there is something special about sex, and it seems that we can be aware of this point whether we accept revelation or not. For example, it seems clear to most people that a punch in the nose is far less serious than rape, although both involve violence. And it seems that this can be true only if sexual acts have some feature or features making them significantly different from other bodily acts.[319]

---

[317] Philip Turner, "Sex and the Single Life," *First Things* May 1993, 15–21.

[318] William E. May, et al., *Catholic Sexual Ethics*, 14.

[319] Patrick Lee, "The Human Body and Sexuality in the Teaching of Pope John Paul II," in *John Paul II's Contribution to Catholic Bioethics,* ed. Christopher Tollefsen (Dordrecht, Netherlands: Springer, 2004), 108. Available online: http://www.patrickleebioethics.com/jp2_on_sex_and_the_body.pdf. Similarly, Perry, *The Case Against the Sexual Revolution*, "The new sexual culture. . . push[es] a particularly radical idea about sex," namely, "the idea that sex is nothing more than a leisure activity, invested with meaning only if the participants choose to give it meaning. Proponents of this idea argue that sex has no

What then is it about sexual acts that make them different from other bodily acts? And if they are uniquely distinct, because they are ordered by their very nature to marital communion and procreation, marital love and children, in short, to the unitive and procreative ends of sexuality, doesn't that mean that there is a distinctive sexual ethics?

Second, one of the central reasons why a distinctive sexual ethics is denied by many is that there is no room, on their view, for a moral law, grounded in the one human nature, willed by God, and known as the natural law.[320] The reason for the rejection of a moral law derives from the view that the meaning of the body is no longer rooted in the very nature of man as an embodied person, male or female; this nature possessing a creational teleology ordering the body-soul person to the sexual "other" and hence to procreation and union.[321] Put differently, this view seems to be denying that there are meanings and ends embedded in the human sexual design that are grounded in the order of creation (*GS* §48). In other words, since sex is merely a biological category ("interesting external equipment") and gender is a socially and culturally constructed category, this view entails the rejection of the historic Church teaching, indeed of Vatican II, that "the principles of the moral order . . . spring from human nature itself."[322]

In contrast to this view, Benedict XVI argues that there is an ecology of man, language, and order of nature. Benedict says:

Man too has a nature that he must respect and that he cannot

---

intrinsic specialness, that it is not innately different from any other kind of social interaction, and that it can therefore be commodified without any trouble" (11).

[320] Benedict XVI, *Caritas in Veritate*, §59.

[321] Matthew Levering, "Knowing What is 'Natural': Thomas Aquinas and Luke Timothy Johnson on Romans 1–2," *Logos* 12, no. 1 (Winter 2009): 135.

[322] *Dignitatis Humanae*, §14.

manipulate at will. Man is not merely self-creating freedom. Man does not create himself. He is intellect and will, but he is also nature, and his will is rightly ordered if he respects his nature, listens to it and accepts himself for who he is, as one who did not create himself. In this way, and in no other, is true human freedom fulfilled.[323]

In short, this fundamental anthropology rejects the dualism between person and nature, as well as freedom and nature. Unsurprisingly, this too is the view of John Paul II:

And since the human person cannot be reduced to a freedom which is self-designing, but entails a particular spiritual and bodily structure, the primordial moral requirement of loving and respecting the person as an end [in the medium of its unity as body and soul] and never as a mere means also implies, by its very nature, respect for certain fundamental goods [toward which sexuality itself is ordered], without which one would fall into relativism and arbitrariness.[324]

In sum, one might conclude that in addition to the denial of a distinctive sexual ethics, the problem with contemporary thinking about human sexuality is that "it flouts the embedded principles and the inbuilt meanings of the human sexual design,"[325] or as *Gaudium et Spes* §51 puts it, "objective criteria ... drawn from the nature of the human person and human action."

---

[323] Pope Benedict XVI, Christmas Address to the Roman Curia, Friday, December 21, 2012.

[324] John Paul II, *Veritatis Splendor*, §48.

[325] Budziszewski, *On the Meaning of Sex*, 35.

Third, a key to understanding Catholic sexual ethics is the truth that the human person is a bodily being.[326] This view rejects a dualistic view of the human person—"dualistic in the sense of viewing the self as something which *has* or *inhabits* a body, rather than being a living, bodily entity."[327] But if the "human person is essentially a bodily being, a unity of body and soul, and that therefore the masculinity or femininity of the human being is internal to his or her personhood (rather than just interesting external 'equipment')," as John Paul II has argued, then it seems likely that this view does not do justice to the embodiment of human persons as man and woman and hence to sexual differences between them. By assuming the *in*significance of sexual difference for making a sexual act morally right, this view fails to grasp the unified totality that is the body-person and hence the human meaning of the body, especially but not only for sexual acts.[328] Says John Paul II, "The body can never be reduced to mere matter: it is a *spiritualized body*, just as man's spirit is so closely united to the body that he can be described as *an embodied spirit*."[329]

A basic example of a typical structure of an individual whole is Wojtyla's treatment of the body-person. This individual whole is sexed in its totality as not merely an abstract material body, as if sexual difference is located merely in one particular part of the body, but rather as the whole of man's temporal existence.[330] The essence of the problem

---

[326] Patrick Lee and Robert P. George, "Sex and the Body," in *Body-Self Dualism in Contemporary Ethics and Politics* (New York: Cambridge University Press, 2008), 176–217. See also, Lawler, Boyle, and William May, *Catholic Sexual Ethics: A Summary, Explanation and Defense*, 2nd edition (Huntington, IN: Our Sunday Visitor, 1998).

[327] Lawler, Boyle, and May, *Catholic Sexual Ethics*, 107.

[328] John Paul II, *Veritatis Splendor*, §50.

[329] John Paul II, *Letter to Families*, §19.

[330] See Rachel Lu, "Woman, Defined," *Law & Liberty*, January 19, 2023.

before us, according to Wojtyla, is "to grasp the relation between body and person."[331] In fact, Wojtyla says, "It is the body that gives man his concreteness," meaning thereby, in Dooyeweerd's words, "the one and ontically unique person."[332] Wojtyla adds, "[T]he human body in its visible dynamic is *the terrain and, in a sense, even the means of expression for the person.*"[333] This requires a brief—all too brief—explanation here.

Explains Wojtyla, "The human person is not just a conscious-ness prolific in experiences of various content, but is basically a highly organized being, an individual of a spiritual nature composed into a single whole with the body (hence, a *suppositum humanum* [that is a person]."[334] Indeed, "The human body shares in the dignity of the image of God."[335] John Paul II's theology of the body is central to understanding the basic issues in sexual ethics, in my judgment, because that theology emphasizes the bodily nature of the human person, meaning thereby that the body is intrinsic to human beings as bodily persons. Given that my body is intrinsic to myself, there is a unitary activity such that, as the pope says, "[t]he *person, including the body, is completely entrusted to himself, and it is in the unity of body and soul that the person is the subject of his own moral acts.*"[336] In short, since the human person is bodily, then sexual moral choices are exercised in and through an act in which my bodily "activity is as much the constitutive subject of what one does as

---

[331] Wojtyla, *Person and Act*, 312.

[332] Dooyeweerd, *Reformation and Scholasticism in Philosophy*, vol. 3, *Philosophy of Nature and Philosophical Anthropology*, ed. D.F.M. Strauss, trans. Magnus Verbrugge and D.F.M. Strauss (Ancaster, ON: Paideia Press, 2011), 186.

[333] Wojtyla, *Person and Act*, 212.

[334] Wojtyla, "The Problem of Catholic Sexual Ethics," 287.

[335] *Catechism of the Catholic Church*, §364.

[336] John Paul II, *Veritatis Splendor*, §48.

one's act of choice is."³³⁷ In short, our bodies can be the subject of virtues, in particular, love of the person in the ethical sense, and therefore as a virtue, that is, "as a concretization (and also, of course, a realization) of the personalistic norm . . . in light of the commandment of love."³³⁸

Wojtyla's anthropology regarding the structural whole that is the body-person is really a contemporary expression of Aquinas's anthropology, namely, the soul is the form of the body (*anima forma corporis*), and of the Church's teaching on the unity of the human person as body and soul.³³⁹ The then Joseph Cardinal Ratzinger explains:

> [T]he material elements from out of which human physiology is constructed receive their character of being "body" only in virtue of being organized and formed by the expressive power of soul. Distinguishing between "physiological unit" and "bodiliness" now becomes possible. . . . The individual atoms and molecules do not as such add up to the human being. . . . The physiology becomes truly "body" through the heart of the personality. Bodiliness is something other than a summation of corpuscles.³⁴⁰

---

³³⁷ Finnis, "Personal Integrity, Sexual Morality and Responsible Parenthood," in *Why Humanae Vitae Was Right: A Reader*, ed. Janet E. Smith (San Francisco: Ignatius Press, 1993), 171–192, particularly 177.

³³⁸ Wojtyla, "The Problem of Catholic Sexual Ethics," 289.

³³⁹ John Paul II develops the moral and anthropological significance of the unity of the human person as body and soul is *Veritatis Splendor*, §§46–50.

³⁴⁰ Joseph Ratzinger, *Eschatology, Death and Eternal Life*, 179–181. Ratzinger is persuaded that Aquinas' philosophical understanding of the "formula *anima forma corporis*: the soul is the form of the body" embodies a "complete transformation of Aristotelianism." He writes, "Thomas' twofold affirmation that the spirit is at once something personal and also the 'form' of matter would simply have been unthinkable for Aristotle. . . . And so we come at last

That is, in light of considering the human person as a unity of body and soul, we can understand why the *body is personal*. Rather than bodily existence being a mere instrument or extrinsic tool of man's personal self-realization, the body is the indispensable medium, argues Wojtyla, in and through which I reveal myself. In other words, Wojtyla's basic point is that the body and bodily action is in some sense communicative activity that reveals the person as a whole. As John Paul II says in *The Person and Act*, "For us action *reveals* the person, and we look at the person through his action."[341] Later he says, "man manifests himself . . . through his body. . . . It is generally recognized that the human body is in its visible dynamism the territory where, or in a way even the medium whereby, the person expresses himself."[342] And in the theology of the body, we find a sample of statements expressing the same point: "the body reveals man," "the body is an expression of man's personhood," and "the body *manifests* man and, in manifesting him, acts as an intermediary that allows man and woman from the beginning, to 'communicate' with each other according to that *communio personarum* willed for them in particular by the Creator."[343] In sum, "In this sense, the body is the territory and in a way the means for the performance of action and

---

to a really tremendous idea: the human spirit is so utterly one with the body that the term 'form' can be used of the body and retain its proper meaning. Conversely, the form of the body is spirit, and this is what makes the human being a person. . . . What seemed philosophically impossible has thus been achieved. . . . The soul belongs to the body as 'form', but that which is the form of the body is still spirit. It makes man a person and opens him to immortality. Compared with all the conceptions of the soul available in antiquity, this notion of the soul is quite novel. It is a product of Christian faith, and of the exigencies of faith for human thought" (148-149).

[341] Wojtyla, *Person and Act*, 11.

[342] Wojtyla, *Person and Act*, 203–204.

[343] Pope John Paul II, *Man and Woman He Created Them*, 1.9.4, note 18, and 1.12.5.

consequently for the fulfillment of the person."[344] Herman Dooyeweerd nicely puts this point, "The human body is man himself in the structural whole of his temporal appearance."[345]

Furthermore, human bodily existence has the character of a subject. In other words, given man's anthropological unity of body and soul, he exercises the capacity for ethical self-determination as a whole man, meaning thereby in and through his body.[346] John Paul II writes, "Man is a subject not by his self-consciousness and by self-determination, but also based on his own body. *The structure of this body is such that it permits him to be the author of genuine human activity.* In this activity, the body expresses the person."[347] Elsewhere the pope develops the moral significance that the human person is bodily, namely, that his body is not extrinsic to who he really is, and hence to his moral acts. "The person, including the body, is completely entrusted to himself, and it is in

---

[344] Wojtyla, *Person and Act*, 205.

[345] Herman Dooyeweerd, *A New Critique of Theoretical Thought*, vol. 3, 89. This, too, is the view of Herman Dooyeweerd's philosophical anthropology, *Reformation and Scholasticism in Philosophy*, vol. 3, *Philosophy of Nature and Philosophical Anthropology*, Part II, chapters 1–3, "[T]he human spirit cannot carry out any real acts outside its temporal corporal individuality-structure. For that reason, we said: it is the *individual human being* in the integral unity of 'body' and 'soul' who accomplishes the acts. The full person as a totality is the subject of the act.... In the acts, the 'soul' is actually operative in the entire enkaptic structure of the body, and only in the body does the soul have the capacity to do so, insofar as the acts are included in the temporal order of the body. In other words, we can take the 'acts' neither to be purely 'corporal' nor purely 'spiritual'. They are *both* inseparably connected and precisely for that reason they bear a *typically human* character. Only the act-structure in *its fundamental dependence upon the spirit* stamps the body as human" (162–163).

[346] Eberhard Schockenhoff, *Natural Law & Human Dignity, Universal Ethics in an Historical World*, trans. Brian McNeil (Washington, D.C., Catholic University of America Press, 2003), 208.

[347] Pope John Paul II, *Man and Woman He Created Them*, 1.7.2.

the unity of body and soul that the person is the subject of his own actions."[348] As John Paul says in *Person and Act*, "For us action *reveals* the person, and we look at the person through his action."[349] Later he says, "man manifests himself . . . through his body. . . . It is generally recognized that the human body is in its visible dynamism the territory where, or in a way even the medium whereby, the person expresses himself."[350] And in the theology of the body, we find a sample of statements expressing the same point. "The body reveals man," "the body is an expression of man's personhood," and "the body *manifests* man and, in manifesting him, acts as an intermediary that allows man and woman, from the beginning, to 'communicate' with each other according to the that *communio personarum* willed for them in particular by the Creator."[351] In sum, "In this sense, the body is the territory and in a way the means for the performance of action and consequently for the fulfillment of the person."[352]

This view of the relationship between the person and his body implies, as Schockenhoff rightly argues, "the body is freedom's boundary." That is, he explains, "We can respect each other as subjects capable of moral action only when we respect each other in the expressive form of our bodily existence. Only so do we make it possible for each other to unfold a personal existence which is a goal in itself."[353] Respecting another person's bodily life unconditionally is to respect that person himself because the "representation of his person . . . is accessible to us . . .

---

[348] John Paul II, *Veritatis Splendor*, §48.

[349] Wojtyla, *Person and Act*, 11.

[350] Wojtyla, *Person and Act*, 203-204.

[351] Pope John Paul II, *Man and Woman He Created Them*, 9.4; also note 18, and 12.5.

[352] Wojtyla, *Person and Act*, 205.

[353] Schockenhoff, *Natural Law & Human Dignity*, 208.

only in the medium of its unity as body and soul."[354]

A human person's body is not a mere extrinsic tool, an instrument, to be used for providing him with subjective states of consciousness, such as giving and obtaining pleasure. Rather, the body is intrinsic to one's self as a unified bodily person; in other words, as a unified whole the one and ontically unique person. This implies that the subject of one's own moral actions is the unified bodily person so that "bodily activity . . . is," as John Finnis says, "as much the constitutive subject of what one does as one's act of choice is."[355] This emphasis on the body being intrinsic to one's own self is rooted in the Church's teaching on the unity of the human person. As John Paul II says, "In fact, *body and soul are inseparable*: in the willing agent and in the deliberate act *they stand or fall together*."[356] Therefore, he adds, we can easily understand why separating "the moral act from the bodily dimensions of its exercise is contrary to the teaching of Scripture and Tradition."[357]

Such a separation occurs when the biological dimension of the human person is reduced to a "raw datum, devoid of any [intrinsic] meaning and moral values until freedom has shaped it in accordance with its design."[358] We saw such a separation in the materialistic anthropology I criticized earlier. That freely chosen design confers on sexual union the personal meaning of casual fun, of spousal commitment, or of procreative openness, and so forth. Significantly, any one of these meanings may be conferred by persons, as well as revoked by them. For sexual union as

---

[354] Schockenhoff, *Natural Law & Human Dignity*, 208.
[355] John Finnis, "Personal Integrity, Sexual Morality and Responsible Parenthood," 177.
[356] John Paul II, *Veritatis Splendor*, §49.
[357] John Paul II, *Veritatis Splendor*, §49.
[358] John Paul II, *Veritatis Splendor*, §48.

such does not by its very nature have any definite personal meaning.[359] "Consequently," John Paul II adds, "human nature and the body appear as [mere] *presuppositions or preambles*, materially *necessary*, for freedom to make its choice, yet extrinsic to the person, the subject and the human act."[360] On this view, given that sexual union is devoid of any intrinsic meaning, not having by its very nature any definite personal meaning, and because we can in freedom confer on it an instrumental meaning that is more than merely physiological, sexual union is, therefore, an extrinsic sign or symbol of personal communion, fostering marital love and friendship by signifying it. But on John Paul II's view, the sexual act is much more than a natural bodily symbol; indeed, it embodies marital union, becoming bodily, or organically complete, and thus one, expresses total self-giving and makes it bodily present in the sense that, as Lee says, "this expression is not extrinsic to what it expresses, but is the visible and tangible embodiment of it."[361]

In other words, given man's anthropological unity of body and soul, he exercises the capacity for ethical self-determination as a whole man, meaning thereby in and through his body.[362] This implies, as Schockenhoff rightly argues, that "the body can be called the concrete limit of freedom." That is, he explains, "the body and physical life are not 'goods' external to human personal realization, standing in a purely

---

[359] John F. Crosby, "The Estrangement of Persons from their Bodies," *Logos* 1, no. 2 (1997): 125–139, particularly 130–131.

[360] John Paul II, *Veritatis Splendor*, §48.

[361] Patrick Lee, "The Human Body and Sexuality in the Teaching of Pope John Paul II," 114.

[362] Eberhard Schockenhoff, "A Consistent Ethic of Life (with a Few Blemishes): Moral-Theological Remarks on *Evangelium Vitae* and on Some Protestant Questions about It," ed. Reinhard Hütter and Theodor Dieter (Grand Rapids, MI: Eerdmans, 1998), 237–261, and particularly at 249.

instrumental relation to the person's authentic determination as a subject. The body is rather the irreducible means of expression in which human persons in all their acts . . . are represented."[363] Respecting another person's bodily life unconditionally is to respect that person himself because a person shows himself only in and through his own body. So, "respect for the personal worth of persons relates not only to their inner convictions or moral values but must also include the inviolability of their bodily existence."[364] If the body is, then, freedom's boundary, such that respecting one's own body as well as others' bodies is both to respect our own person and other persons, this raises the question regarding the conditions under which a sexual act is morally right.[365]

Fourth, a rehabilitation of the "culture of the person" is necessary because the objective good of the person constitutes the essential core of all human culture. To promote that culture requires a whole nexus of fundamental goods that together determine marriage and family life. Marriage is grounded in God's purpose for creation. It is the two-in-one-flesh union of a man and a woman, with conjugal love being the integrating principle of the whole communion of marriage and family life. *Gaudium et Spes* §50 stated it this way, "Marriage and conjugal love are by their nature ordained toward the begetting and educating of children. Children are really the supreme gift of marriage." The question of what is the proper end of our sexual powers and their relationship to the nature of marriage is crucial for considering the issue of why giving oneself in sexual intercourse to the other person is fully justified only in mar-

---

[363] Schockenhoff, "A Consistent Ethic of Life," 249.
[364] Schockenhoff, "A Consistent Ethic of Life," 249.
[365] Wilhelmus Luijpen, *Existential Phenomenology*, fourth impression, translated from the Dutch edition (Pittsburgh, PA: Duquesne University Press, 1965 [1959]), 187–188.

riage. "[Marriage] corresponds to the truth of love and mutually safeguards the dignity of the person, only if both a man and a woman perform it [sexual intercourse] as spouses, as husband and wife."[366] This, too, has been lost sight of by sexual liberationist ideology and by those Christians who have accommodated themselves to this ideology.

There is an Appendix to the Second Edition of Wojtyla's *Love and Responsibility*.[367] This is his 1974 article, "On the Meaning of Spousal Love," which continues the discussion concerning the problems of conjugal morality begun in *Love and Responsibility*.[368] In this article, Wojtyla addresses the moral problem of premarital relations. Here's a passage from the article that makes clear the problem that Wojtyla is addressing.

> *Marriage as an institution is not something merely "external" in relation to the whole truth of persons*, of a man and a woman, when their love and self-giving are to be expressed with the "*right to such a gift.*" Marriage as an institution does not only proceed from the juridical-social order or a religious order as "external" in relation to the person and his love. Indeed, as an element of this order, marriage proceeds from the very "interiority" of this love, for the shape of the reciprocal self-giving of a man and a woman demands it.[369]

In other words, on the one hand, if marriage as an institution is essentially viewed from the juridical or canonical viewpoint, then the inner

---

[366] Wojtyla, *Love and Responsibility*, 293.

[367] The following paragraphs are from Eduardo Echeverria, "Guarino's Prolegomena of Systematic Theology," *Homiletics and Pastoral Review*, October 27, 2022.

[368] Wojtyla, *Love and Responsibility*, 275–294.

[369] Wojtyla, *Love and Responsibility*, 292–293.

nature of marriage is external to conjugal love, that is, it is the imposition of an extrinsic form upon the relation between a man and a woman. This marks the institution "with juridicism and signifies the primacy of an institution over man with his 'interior truth'."[370] On the other hand, if conjugal love, which is the reciprocal self-giving of a man and a woman, is the qualification of the inner nature of a marriage bond, then how do we avoid a subjectivism of love, which is a variable and subjective feeling, unsuitable to substantiate not only a permanent life-companionship, of indissolubility, but also the ethical demands for justifying sexual intercourse between a man and a woman?

Wojtyla avoids subjectivism because love is not merely a feeling. His ontology of love expressed in his anthropology involves attraction, need love, which is love that longs for the good of oneself, benevolent love, which is altruistic, friendship, and, most importantly, reciprocal love, which is inter-personal love such that it is something two-sided, something "between" persons, such that love between persons becomes one "we." "Reciprocity is decisive precisely for this 'we' to come into existence."[371] Wojtyla adds, "For love can survive only as a unity in which the mature 'we' is manifested.... Love has a structure of interpersonal community." It is a union of persons such that a man and a woman "constitute, in a sense, one common subject of action." This union of persons is grounded in a common good, which is the objective good of the person, and a common end, which is procreation, children, family, that binds a man and a woman.

> Love ... is conditioned by the common relation of persons to the same good that they choose as an end and to which they sub-

---

[370] Wojtyla, *Love and Responsibility*, 292.
[371] Wojtyla, *Love and Responsibility*, 69.

ordinate themselves. Marriage is one of the most important areas for realizing this principle. For in marriage, two persons, a woman and a man, unite in such a way they become in a sense "one flesh" (to use the words of the Book of Genesis [2:24]), that is, one common subject of sexual life.[372]

Finally, his ethical anthropology finds it perfection in spousal love. "The essence of spousal love is giving oneself, giving one's 'I'." This love is to be realized as a virtue such that the full ethical rectitude of a man and woman is realized in the deepening of spousal love as an interpersonal fact. This fact constitutes the "objective situation, the state, in which sexual intercourse—conjugal in its essence—can be the true and reciprocal gift of the person for another person. Because this intercourse is in its essence conjugal, this objective situation and state is called and is marriage."[373]

The "law of the gift" is fundamental to Wojtyla's anthropology and hence to spousal love, so we need to define it. Wojtyla explains:

> The *"law of the gift,"* which God as the Creator inscribed in the being of the human person, of a man and a woman, and the meaning of which was confirmed and deepened by him as the Redeemer in the consciousness of every man, *constitutes the proper basis of that "communio personarum."* From the very beginning, the Creator wills that marriage is this *"communio personarum"* in which a man and a woman realize day by day and

---

[372] Wojtyla, *Love and Responsibility*, 14.
[373] Wojtyla, *Love and Responsibility*, 293.

in the dimension of their whole life the ideal of the personal union by "giving and receiving each other." Spousal love can be understood as the realization of this ideal.[374]

Sexual intercourse between a man and a woman is substantiated in light of "the full ethical rectitude of a man and a woman's union and intercourse in marriage, which for Christians is a sacrament of faith, [and it] requires spousal love."[375] Spousal love is the full ethical rectitude or the whole truth of persons such that a man and a woman "give themselves to each other in sexual intercourse, such self-giving is fully justified; [such self-giving] corresponds to the truth of love and mutually safeguards the dignity of the person, only if both a man and a woman perform it as spouses, as husband and wife. Otherwise, an abuse of the 'law of the gift' takes place."[376]

---

[374] Wojtyla, *Love and Responsibility*, 287–288.
[375] Wojtyla, *Love and Responsibility*, 285–286.
[376] Wojtyla, *Love and Responsibility*, 293.

Chapter 4

Ethics in Search of Its Experiential Point of Departure

The Philosophical Ethics and Moral Theology of Margaret A. Farley and Karol Wojtyla/John Paul II

> One can say that the experience of morality possesses, as it were, different layers and different aspects. The layer to which the experience of morality at first points, in a way, is moral good or evil as a certain person or society (this is in a way, therefore, the *axiological* layer). At the same time that very "moral good or evil" always manifests itself in acts, is connected with them, and is their characteristic fruit (this is thus, as it were, the *praxiological* layer of the experience of morality). Nevertheless, while including both of these layers in the experience, we must always arrive ultimately at the element of moral duty as the element which constitutes every moral fact, both when we conceive human action in its purely personal dimension ("a man acts") and in its communal dimension ("a man acts together with other people"). One can define that layer of the experience of morality as the *deontological* layer.
>
> —Karol Wojtyla[1]

---

[1] Karol Wojtyla, *Man in the Field of Responsibility*, Translation by Kenneth W. Kemp and Zuzanna Maślanka Kieroń, Introduction by Fr. Alfred Wierzbicki (South Bend, Indiana: St. Augustine Press, 2011), 10.

If theology is about reality, then it must accept the authority of experience so defined. For to say that experience has authority is only another way of saying that it is a disclosure of reality, of being.... Thus, a sound theory of experience requires not only a sound epistemology but also a sound metaphysics.

—Aidan Nichols, OP[2]

A Sound Epistemology and a Corresponding Sound Metaphysics

This chapter is about the philosophical ethics and moral theology of Margaret A. Farley, RSM (1935-) and Karol Wojtyla (1920-2005; the future Pope John Paul II). In this article, I will argue that Karol Wojtyla's theory of experience provides not only a sound epistemology but also a sound metaphysics for Christian ethics. What is a sound epistemology and a corresponding sound meta-physics?

Chiefly, it distinguishes ontological and epistemological questions, that is, what there is, what reality is like, on the one hand, and how we can know reality on the other.[3] In other words, it distinguishes the conditions under which we are justified in knowing that something is true from the conditions that make something true; the former concerns justification, the latter is about truth. In short, it affirms epistemic realism and a realist view of truth ,i.e., alethic realism. The former means that reality is knowable, while the latter means that "true theories are true *in*

---

[2] Aidan Nichols, OP, *The Shape of Catholic Theology* (Collegeville, MN: The Liturgical Press, 1991), 236.

[3] Roger Trigg, *Reality at Risk: A Defence of Realism in Philosophy & the Sciences* (Sussex: The Harvester Press, 1980), vii, xii.

virtue of the nature of objective reality. Truth has its source in reality."[4] A realist about truth holds that a proposition is true if and only if what that proposition asserts is in fact the case about objective reality; otherwise, it is false. John Paul II writes regarding a philosophy of knowledge that a scripturally directed epistemology, one that can be of service to the Gospel, is one that affirms the "human capacity to *know the truth*"—that is, "to come to a knowledge which can reach objective truth by means of the *correspondence between thing and intellect (adaequatio rei et intellectus)*."[5] This is a realist theory of truth, a nonepistemic one, because truth depends not on justification but on the world, reality. Given this distinction, John Paul's concept of truth should be located with respect to the distinction between epistemic and nonepistemic conceptions of truth. The former holds that a proposition is true if and only I am epistemically justified in holding that proposition to be true; the latter position denies that truth depends on justification.[6] In other words, what makes the proposition true—a proposition is true in virtue of the

---

[4] Trigg, *Reality at Risk*, xiv. Raeburne S. Heinbeck rightly explains this distinction, "If we admit, therefore, that it is one thing for something *to be the case* (or not be the case) and another for us *to know or have reason for believing* that it is the case (or not the case), and if we admit that it is one thing for a statement *to be true* (or false) and quite another thing for us *to know or have reason for believing* that it is true (or false), then we have *ipso facto* acknowledge the validity of the distinction between criteria and evidence. For the gist of that distinction, to repeat, is simply the difference between the conditions which would have to be fulfilled for a statement to be true (or false) and the conditions which would have to be fulfilled for us to know or have reason for believing it to be true (or false)," *Theology and Meaning, Critique of Metatheological Scepticism* (London: George Allen and Unwin Ltd., 1969), 48.

[5] John Paul II, *Fides et Ratio*, §82.

[6] Lambert Zuidervaart, "Holistic Alethic Pluralism: A Reformational Research Program," in *Philosophia Reformata* 81 (2016): 156–78, and at 166, where he clearly states the issue at stake here.

nature of objective reality—is a different matter from how I know the proposition is true. This concept of truth is nonepistemic, verification-transcendent, as it were, because it distinguishes conditions of truth from conditions of epistemic justification—that is, the distinction between the conditions under which I come to know that *p* is true and the conditions that make *p* true. Wojtyla draws the correct implication here regarding the distinction between justification and truth:

> It is not the strength, the power of conviction, or the authenticity of belief with which the given subject passes a judgment that determines whether or not it is true, but rather its conformity with that to which or to whom the given judgment pertains. The subject is the exclusive author of the judgment, but is not, however, the author of its truth. This distinction is often forgotten, especially when the pertinent judgments or assessments are accompanied by strong affective reactions.[7]

In short, as I understand John Paul, truth in principle is distinguishable from what one is justified in holding to be true, and yet he explains how the two are connected.[8]

The failure to make these distinctions puts objective reality at risk because it limits what is real to what is real for human beings, treating reality to be "totally irrelevant to questions of truth."[9] We find such a view in liberal Catholic theologian, David Tracy. He states:

---

[7] Wojtyla, *Love and Responsibility*, 136.

[8] See my essay, "The Splendor of Truth in *Fides et Ratio*," in *Quaestiones Disputatae*, 9, no. 1, Fall 2018: 49-78.

[9] Trigg, *Reality at Risk*, vii, xiv.

Ch. 4: Ethics in Search of Its Experiential Point of Departure

> Reality is what we name our best interpretation. Reality is constituted, not created or simply found, through the interpretations that have earned the right to be called relatively adequate or true. . . . Reality is neither out there nor in here. Reality is constituted by the interaction between a text, whether book or world, and a questioning interpreter. The interaction called questioning can produce warranted assertions through relevant evidence.[10]

This is alethic anti-realism. Throughout his writings, Karol Wojtyla/John Paul II presupposes, on the contrary, epistemic realism and an alethic realist view of truth.

By contrast, Margaret Farley is not an alethic realist; rather, she is an alethic anti-realist because truth depends on justification, seeking to achieve reflective equilibrium, that is, an acceptable coherence among our beliefs, or how well the propositions pragmatically work. On her view, the evidence of experience "do not give actual access to 'reality', but only a pragmatic way of dealing with the world and ourselves."[11] She explains,

> The supposed bedrock of evidence that experience provides disappears in the endless circles of social construction. Nonetheless, and perhaps ironically, it is experience itself that has taught us: the worldviews that shape experience can be challenged and

---

[10] David Tracy, *Plurality and Ambiguity: Hermeneutics, Religion, and Hope* (San Francisco: Harper & Row, 1987), 48.

[11] Farley, *Just Love: A Framework for Christian Sexual Ethics*, 189.

in some respects modified and even overturned. The hermeneutical circle is not so tightly shut that we are denied a critical edge or opening.¹²

Despite her disclaimer in the concluding sentence of this passage, namely, that the "hermeneutical circle," the circle of interpretation, the idea that we always understand, experience, or interpret out of some presuppositions, doesn't close us off from reality, Farley puts the term 'reality' in scare quotes. Farley follows Tracy who writes, "'Reality' is the one word that should always appear within quotation marks."¹³ Why would she put term in such quotes? This is not a direct quotation. What she is doing is "distancing [herself] from the term in quotes."¹⁴ She denies, on the one hand, that our justified beliefs give us actual access to reality because of the "endless circles of social construction." John Paul II challenges this imprisonment in the hermeneutical circle. He writes, "The interpretation of this word [that is, the Word of God] cannot merely keep referring us to one interpretation after another, without ever leading us to a statement which is simply true."¹⁵ As the then Cardinal Ratzinger comments on this passage from *Fides et Ratio* and the hermeneutical position that Farley seems to endorse:

> Man is not trapped in a hall of mirrors of interpretations; he can and must look for the way out to the reality that stands behind

---

¹² Farley, *Just Love: A Framework for Christian Sexual Ethics*, 192.

¹³ Tracy, *Plurality and Ambiguity*, 47. Tracy is quoting Vladimir Nabokov (1899-1977), a Russian born American novelist.

¹⁴ "Scare Quotes," University of Sussex, Department of Informatics, accessed November 12, 2024, https://www.sussex.ac.uk/informatics/punctuation/quotes/ scare.

¹⁵ John Paul II, *Fides et Ratio*, 84.

the words and manifests itself to him in and through the words.[16]

Since we are not trapped in a hall of mirrors, "rationality requires more than endless deferrals of meaning,"[17] deferrals that keep referring us from one interpretation to another, according to John Paul, with reality eventually receding behind these interpretations, as it does in Farley's hermeneutical epistemology. We can know the truth about reality. Contrary to this alethic realism, Farley claims, "Postmodern ways of thinking have so subverted and destabilized notions of the human body and gender that there is no longer any room for a moral 'law'."[18] By contrast, Wojtyla argues that interpretation does not go all the way down, as if to say that "there is no ready-made reality, no way things are apart from how we construe them, only ways of construing them."[19] Farley doesn't deny the significance of human embodiment. In fact, she affirms that "our bodies . . . are intrinsic to ourselves," that is, "at the heart of Christian belief is the affirmation that not only is the human body good, but it is intrinsic to being human."[20] Still, given her hermeneutical epistemology, where she claims that we are trapped in an endless circle of social construction, we can understand her sympathy for postmodernism, that is, a metaphysical anti-realism. That is why she professes to be

---

[16] Ratzinger, *Truth and Tolerance: Christian Belief and World Religions*, 189.

[17] Aidan Nichols, O.P., *From Hermes to Benedict XVI: Faith and Reason in Modern Catholic Thought* (Herefordshire: Gracewing, 2009), 241.

[18] Farley, *Just Love: A Framework for Christian Sexual Ethics*, 136.

[19] Nicholas Wolterstorff, *Religion in the University* (New Haven: Yale University Press, 2019), 121.

[20] Farley, *Just Love: A Framework for Christian Sexual Ethics*, 110, 129, 131, respectively.

agnostic regarding "conflicting metaphysical analyses of human embodiment."[21] Farley's hermeneutical epistemology leads her to deny that there is a distinctive sexual ethics. Thus, it is not surprising that she rejects all the offenses against chastity described in the *Catechism of the Catholic Church*, §§2331-2400, and thus her position on masturbation, homosexuality, homosexual coupling, indissolubility of marriage, and divorce and remarriage, not to mention her anthropology and understanding of the natural law, is in contradiction to the constant teaching of the Magisterium.[22] Regarding the latter, the CDF states, "Sr. Farley also manifests a defective understanding of the objective nature of the natural moral law, choosing instead to argue on the basis of conclusions selected from certain philosophical currents or from her own understanding of 'contemporary experience'."[23] In particular, rather than a distinctive sexual ethics, she embraces the "responsible-relational" position in which the morally decisive factor in a sexual relationship is conformity to general moral norms governing relationships as such. This is how Farley describes the norms for what she calls sexual justice, and hence "just love": norms that prohibit lying, deception, and exploitation refusal to do unjust harm, free consent, mutuality, equality, commitment, fruitfulness, and they are sufficient to render sexual acts morally good.[24]

---

[21] Farley, *Just Love: A Framework for Christian Sexual Ethics*, 110.

[22] See the 2012 Notification from the Congregation for the Doctrine of the Faith on Farley's book, 2012: Notification on the book *Just Love. A Framework for Christian Sexual Ethics* by Sr. Margaret A. Farley, R.S.M. (vatican.va).

[23] CDF Notification on Farley's *Just Love*, §1.

[24] Farley, *Just Love: A Framework for Christian Sexual Ethics*, 231: "Sex should not be used in ways that exploit, objectify, or dominate; rape, violence, and harmful uses of power in sexual relationships are ruled out; freedom, wholeness, intimacy, pleasure are values to be affirmed in relationships marked by mutuality, equality, and some form of commitment; sexual relations like

On the other hand, Farley qualifies this point about a hermeneutical trap, which denies one access to reality, by stating in a footnote, "The point is that we never have full access to reality; our knowledge is always partial, in some way provisional."[25] What this means is that we know something truly, determinately, even if not exhaustively; there is always more to know. Inadequacy of expression doesn't mean inexpressibility of truth, however. So, which is it, according to Farley? She suggests something like this interpretation when she refers to "two basic features of human personhood: features that can be called *autonomy and relationality*." She explains the meaning of basic:

> "Basic" here does not imply that we can understand fully what the "essence" of the human person is. There is a wariness in contemporary Western thought about even acknowledging that there are "essences" to be known, let alone essences that *we* can know. My attempt to delineate features of what it means to be a human person recognizes the partiality of our knowledge, the historical changeability of knowledge and the variations of human self-understandings from culture to culture. *Nonetheless*, it seems to me that we cannot reasonably assert either that we know nothing at all about the human person as person, or that we have nothing of a shared knowledge in this regard.[26]

---

other profound interpersonal relations can and ought to be fruitful both within and beyond the relationship; the affections of desire and love that bring about and sustain sexual relationships are all in all genuinely to affirm both lover and beloved." See Eijk, *De Band van de Liefde*, 33-34.

[25] Farley, *Just Love: A Framework for Christian Sexual Ethics*, 189n34.
[26] Farley, *Just Love: A Framework for Christian Sexual Ethics*, 211.

By contrast, Karol Wojtyla/John Paul II is neither a "metaphysical anti-realist," nor is his philosophical position sympathetic to it. Reality is not socially constructed. Indeed, John Paul adumbrates a metaphysical analysis of human embodiment, that is, the sexually differentiated bodily dimensions of a moral act. Farley is right in stating that the basic issue in sexual ethics "is the question of whether, or to what extent, our bodies provide a basis, or even small clues, for determining acceptable practices of human sexuality."[27] She answers: embodiment, emotions, pleasure, language and social communication, procreative aim, and union.[28] In determining acceptable practices of human sexuality, embodiment, according to Farley, doesn't essentially consist of sexual differentiation.

John Paul II disagrees with Farley because he understands sexual differentiation, maleness and femaleness, as foundational to the human body, and hence to marriage, having then *the meaning of a gift of the person to the person.*[29] Indeed, he elaborates, "[T]he *original* [i.e., creational] and fundamental *meaning of being a body*, as also of being, as a body, male and female ... *is united to the fact that man is created as a person and is called to a life 'in communione personarum'*."[30] And as to the structure of the sacramental sign of marriage and what it signifies, John Paul argues, "The sacramental sign is constituted in the intentional order inasmuch as it is simultaneously constituted in the real order."[31] By the intentional order, John Paul means that the sign of the sacrament of marriage is constituted by the words intentionally spoken "on the level of intellect and will, of consciousness and the heart," by both the man and the woman, words that must then correspond to the reality,

---

[27] Farley, *Just Love: A Framework for Christian Sexual Ethics*, 111.

[28] Farley, *Just Love: A Framework for Christian Sexual Ethics*, 161-164.

[29] John Paul II, *Man and Woman He Created Them*, 61.1.

[30] John Paul II, *Man and Woman He Created Them*, 69.4.

[31] John Paul II, *Man and Woman He Created Them*, 103.3.

that is, the real order, of the full and real visible sign of the sacrament itself, of the human subjectivity of the man and woman. "Thus, from the words with which the man and the woman express their readiness to become 'one flesh' according to the eternal truth established in the mystery of creation [Gen 1:27; 2:24], we pass *to the reality* that corresponds to these words. Both the one and the other element are important *with regard to the structure of the sacramental sign*."[32] Otherwise, the words spoken by the man and the woman would not correspond to the sexual differentiation that is a fundamental prerequisite for the two to become one flesh.

This position on embodiment follows from John Paul II's anthropology of the body. He writes:

> *The person, including the body, is completely entrusted to himself, and it is in the unity of body and soul that the person is the subject of his own moral acts.* The person, by the light of reason and the support of virtue, discovers in the body the anticipatory signs, the expression and the promise of the gift of self, in conformity with the wise plan of the Creator. It is in the light of the dignity of the human person — a dignity which must be affirmed for its own sake — that reason grasps the specific moral value of certain goods towards which the person is naturally inclined. And since the human person cannot be reduced to a freedom which is self-designing, but entails a particular spiritual and bodily structure, the primordial moral requirement of loving and respecting the person as an end and never as a mere means also implies, by its very nature, respect for certain fundamental

---

[32] John Paul II, *Man and Woman He Created Them*, 103.4.

goods, without which one would fall into relativism and arbitrariness.[33]

Thus, Wojtyla argues, "Natural law points to the need for penetration into . . . . ontic structure[s] and to the need *to understand natures, i.e., the essence of things*, essences which enter into the object of human action."[34] Thus, justification is possible because the structural order of the world is binding on every theoretical judgment, meaning thereby that there is a ready-made reality. This makes his theory of truth a version of alethic realism.

I will turn to Farley's grounding of ethics in experience now, followed by Wojtyla's position. But first I begin with an analysis of their respective views of divine revelation.

Meaning of Divine Revelation

A Thin versus a Thick Idea of Revelation

Farley has a thin view of revelation. For one thing, she states, "The presupposition here [regarding tradition] is that a community's beliefs and moral insights through time not only are a fund of wisdom for each generation but are revelatory of God's presence and action in the life of the community."[35] What is the nature of that presence? She doesn't say, but we can surmise that it is an experiential presence. For another, then, she espouses an experiential expressivism. "Scripture, for example, is the

---

[33] John Paul II, *Veritatis Splendor*, §48.
[34] Wojtyla, *Man in the Field of Responsibility*, 72.
[35] Farley, *Just Love: A Framework for Christian Sexual Ethics*, 188.

record of some persons' experience of God."³⁶ As Calvin Seerveld describes this view, it is the "witness of Spirit-empowered humans." But "the Bible is *God speaking*."³⁷ This thin view of revelation eliminates the mediating role of propositions both from God's self-revelation to man and from man's faith in God. Thus, for example, she actually denies, in the words of John Paul II, "that there exist, in Divine Revelation, a specific and determined moral content, universally valid and permanent."³⁸ In Farley's view, there isn't "a systematic code of sexual ethics but occasional responses to particular questions in particular situations."³⁹ There are at best "guidelines" (Farley's word) "gleaned from an overall command to love God and neighbor."⁴⁰ But surely there are there moral norms formulated in Scripture not only having the status of fundamental revealed moral truth but also are in themselves relevant for salvation. The New Testament moral teaching affirms not only the continuing validity of the Decalogue but also its perfection and superabundant fulfillment. As Germain Grisez correctly emphasizes, "In the Sermon on the Mount, Jesus broadens and deepens several of the commandments and demands their interiorization (see Mt 5:21-37). All the synoptics, moreover, present Jesus as affirming the commandments as a necessary condition for entering eternal life (see Mt 19:16-20; Mk 10:17-19; Lk 18:18-21)."⁴¹ St. Paul, too, adds Grisez "assumes the truth of the Decalogue and its permanent ethical relevance."⁴² Indeed, following the pattern of

---

³⁶ Farley, *Just Love: A Framework for Christian Sexual Ethics*, 190.

³⁷ Calvin G. Seerveld, *How to Read the Bible to Hear God Speak* (Sioux Center, IA: Dordt College Press, 2003), 79.

³⁸ John Paul II, *Veritatis Splendor*, §37.

³⁹ Farley, *Just Love: A Framework for Christian Sexual Ethics*, 184.

⁴⁰ Farley, *Just Love: A Framework for Christian Sexual Ethics*, 184.

⁴¹ Grisez, *The Way of the Lord Jesus*, 1, 838.

⁴² Grisez, *The Way of the Lord Jesus*, 1, 838.

Christ, St. Paul urges us to avoid self-deception regarding the inseparability of the moral choices we make that are worthy of the calling we have received in Christ and eternal life. Thus, he links fundamental moral decisions with admission to, as well as exclusion from, the Kingdom of God (see 1 Cor 6:9-11).[43] In short, Farley does not embrace Catholic teaching on divine revelation, namely, a thick view of divine revelation.

A Thick Idea of Revelation

General revelation is God's revelation of himself in, by and through the works of creation (Rom 1:19-20).[44] That is, God makes himself and his divine plan known to us, not only through the Holy Scripture, but also through his right ordering of everything in creation—nature, history, culture, society, and human existence in the world. As the *Catechism of the Catholic Church* succinctly states, "Because God creates through wisdom, his creation is ordered.... The universe, created in and by the eternal Word, the 'image of the invisible God', is destined for and addressed to man, himself created in the 'image of God', and called to a personal relationship with God."[45] The divine wisdom which orders and

---

[43] Joseph Ratzinger, "The Church's Teaching Authority—Faith—Morals," *Principles of Christian Morality* (San Francisco: Ignatius Press, 1986), 95-105.

[44] Francis Martin, "Revelation as Disclosure: Creation." In: *Wisdom and Holiness, Science and Scholarship*, Essays in Honor of Matthew L. Lamb, edited by M. Dauphinais & M. Levering (Naples, Florida: Sapientia Press, 2007), 205-247.

[45] *Catechism of the Catholic Church*, §299. In *Caritas in Veritate*, Benedict XVI makes an important point about God's creation revelation: "*Nature expresses a design of love and truth.* It is prior to us, and it has been given to us by God as the setting for our life. Nature speaks to us of the Creator (cf. *Rom* 1:20) and his love for humanity. It is destined to be 'recapitulated' in Christ at the end of time (cf. *Eph* 1:9-10; *Col* 1:19-20). Thus it too is a 'vocation'. Nature is at our

shapes human existence in the world is inseparably tied in with the preserving and providentially governing activity of God in the totality of relationships within cosmic reality. Since God has made this creation revelation to be known, corresponding to this divine wisdom through which the creation is ordered is "our human understanding, which shares in the light of the divine intellect, [and] can understand what God tells us by means of his creation, though not without great effort and only in a spirit of humility and respect before the Creator and his work."[46] In sum, as Albert M. Wolters puts it, "Creation makes itself known; there is a revelation in and through the created order."[47] General revelation regarding the orders of creation is particularly relevant for criticizing Farley's cultural and moral relativism and the "overwhelming determination of moral norms by historical and cultural contingencies."[48] By contrast, John Paul II argues, "The great concern of our contemporaries," I would add, such as Farley, "for historicity and for culture has led some to call into question *the immutability of the natural law* itself, and thus the existence of 'objective norms of morality' valid for all people of the present and the future, as for those of the past. Is it ever possible, they ask, to consider as universally valid and always binding certain rational determinations established in the past, when no one

---

disposal not as 'a heap of scattered refuse', but as a gift of the Creator who has given it an inbuilt order, enabling man to draw from it the principles needed in order 'to till it and keep it' (*Gen* 2:15)" (§48).

[46] *Catechism of the Catholic Church*, §299.

[47] Albert M. Wolters, "Creation Order: A Historical Look at Our Heritage," in *An Ethos of Compassion and the Integrity of Creation*, eds., Brian J. Walsh, Hendrik Hart, and Robert E. Vander Vennen (Lanham: University Press of America, Inc., 1995), 33-48, and at 40.

[48] Farley, *Just Love: A Framework for Christian Sexual Ethics*, 62.

knew the progress humanity would make in the future?"[49] Yes, argues John Paul II.

Against the background of the idea that God's creation is ordered, we can consider as an example of this ordered creation reflecting the immutability of the natural law and the God-ordained limits and responsibilities of marriage. According to the Catholic tradition, God himself is the author of marriage and hence marriage is grounded in the order of creation.[50] Marriage is not a mere cultural or social artifact. Rather, there are essential and permanent characteristics attached to the institution of marriage "despite the many variations it may have undergone through the centuries in different cultures, social structures, and spiritual attitudes." In addition, "Although the dignity of this institution is not transparent everywhere with the same clarity, some sense of the greatness of the matrimonial union exists in all cultures." One important factor that contributes to this lack of clarity is sin. In other words, marriage is also under the regime of sin. "As a break with God, the first sin had for its consequence the rupture of the original communion between man and woman." "Nevertheless, the order of creation persists, though seriously disturbed." Jesus Christ reveals to us the truths about marriage by referring us back to the creation texts of Gen 1:27 and 2:24. "Male and female he created them" and "for this reason . . . a man will be joined to his wife and the two [male and female] will become one flesh." These texts are absolutely normative for marriage, indeed, for the Christian anthropology that ungirds sexual ethics, according to the *Catechism of the Catholic Church* (§§2331-2345). Marriage is a two-in-one-flesh union between a man and a woman. The truth of this judgment is grounded in objective reality, according to the order of creation – the way things really are. Its contact with reality is the basis of this teaching's validity. Jesus unites

---

[49] John Paul II, *Fides et Ratio*, §53.
[50] *Catechism of the Catholic Church*, §1603.

into an inextricable nexus the concepts of indissolubility, twoness, and sexual differentiation. Furthermore, Jesus Christ's redemptive work "restores the original order of creation disturbed by sin, [for] he himself gives the strength and grace to live marriage in the new dimension of the Reign of God."[51]

Doctrinal Development

There remains to say something briefly about the charge that all natural-law morality of the sort that John Paul II affirms in *Veritatis Splendor* cannot do justice to man's historical actuality, and to doctrinal development. That is simply not the case. There is doctrinal development. For instance, John Paul II explicitly states a foundational principle of Christian anthropology: "In fact, *body and soul are inseparable*: in the willing agent and in the deliberate act *they stand or fall together.*"[52] This principle has been developed in John Paul's philosophical anthropology of the body by affirming sexual differentiation and hence the bodily nature of the human person as constitutive of marriage. The sexually differentiated bodily sexual act is such that, as a foundational prerequisite, it is intrinsic to a one-flesh union; and hence the form of love that is marriage is not detachable from its foundation in a bodily sexual union of man and woman.

Development here is by way of clarification, says John Paul,

> Certainly, there is a need to seek out and to discover *the most adequate formulation* for universal and permanent moral norms in the light of different cultural contexts, a formula-tion

---

[51] The quotation in this paragraph is from the *Catechism of the Catholic Church*, §§1603, 1607-1608, and 1615.

[52] John Paul II, *Veritatis Splendor*, §49.

most capable of ceaselessly expressing their historical relevance, of making them understood and of authentically interpreting their truth. This truth of the moral law — like that of the "deposit of faith" — unfolds down the centuries: the norms expressing that truth remain valid in their substance, but must be specified and determined *"eodem sensu eademque sententia"* [keeping the same meaning and the same judgment] in the light of historical circumstances by the Church's Magisterium, whose decision is preceded and accompanied by the work of interpretation and formulation characteristic of the reason of individual believers and of theological reflection.[53]

In line, then, with the thought of Vincent of Lérins (d. 450), John Paul follows Vatican II by distinguishing between truth and its historically conditioned formulations, truth-content and context, in sum, propositions and sentences. John XXIII alluded to these distinctions in his opening address at Vatican II, *Gaudet Mater Ecclesia*:

For the deposit of faith [2 Tim 1:14], the truths contained in our sacred teaching, are one thing; the mode in which they are expressed, but with the same meaning and the same judgment [*eodem sensu eademque sententia*], is another thing."

The subordinate clause here – *eodem sensu eademque senten-tia* – is part of a larger passage from Vatican I's *Dei Filius*, and this passage is, in

---

[53] John Paul II, *Veritatis Splendor*, §53, and §29. See also Karol Wojtyla who writes, "[W]e can distinguish, in the whole vast world of norms [as the truth of the good] which combine to direct human activity, those norms which can be characterized as *norms of adaptation* to the various conditions in which man happens to perform his actions" (*Man in the Field of Responsibility*, 31).

turn, from the *Commonitórium* (23) of Vincent of Lérins: "Therefore, let there be growth and abundant progress in understanding, knowledge, and wisdom, in each and all, in individuals and in the whole Church, at all times and in the progress of ages, but only with the proper limits, i.e., within the same dogma, the same meaning, the same judgment." We must always determine whether those new re-formulations are preserving the same meaning and judgment (*eodem sensu eademque sententia*), and hence the material continuity, identity, and universality of those truths.[54]

Special Divine Revelation

The main point I want to make here now is about the prominent role of the special revelation of Holy Scripture: sin has also affected the human knower's capacity to grasp the original order of creation and God rectifies that fallen knower through Holy Scripture, bringing, in consequence, that ordered creation to clarity.[55] Thus, we now need to address the question of special revelation: chiefly, revelation in Scripture, but

---

[54] See Echeverria, "Vincent of Lérins: The Development of Christian Doctrine," 171–98. See also, Echeverria, *Revelation, History, and Truth: A Hermeneutics of Dogma*.

[55] St. Bonaventure writes, "The world was like a damaged *[deletes]* book which God brought to perspicacity *[illuminavit]* and rectified by the book of Scripture" (as cited in Francis Martin, "Revelation as Disclosure: Creation," 206n3). Bonaventure's view is shared by John Calvin, *Institutes of the Christian Religion*, Book 1, chapter VI, §1, "Just as old or bleary-eyed men and those with weak vision, if you thrust before them a most beautiful volume, even if they recognize it to be some sort of writing, yet can scarcely construe two words, but with the aid of spectacles will begin to read distinctly; so Scripture, gathering up the otherwise confused knowledge of God in our minds, having dispersed our dullness, clearly shows us the true God."

also the relation between Scripture and Tradition.[56] Special revelation is historical, verbal, and salvific.

The schema (S) I propose to use here to give an account of special revelation claims is as follows: (S) m reveals a to n by means of (through, etc.) k.[57] This schema is about the origin, content, manner, and purpose of God's special revelation.[58] In other words, the agent of the revelation is represented by m; a represents the content of the revelation, and n the recipient; k represents the manner or means of the revelation. I turn now to look at each of the elements in the schema.

The *agent* (m) of the revelation is God himself because revelation originates with God. "It pleased God, in his goodness and wisdom, to reveal himself and to make known the mystery of his will (cf. Eph. 1:9)."[59] Furthermore, he is the essential foundation (*principium essendi*), the source, the primary efficient cause, of our knowledge of him. Without his divine self-communicative acts, his personal self-disclosures, we would not know anything of God at all. As Herman Bavinck, the neo-Calvinist master of dogmatic theology, concisely put it, "He is knowable only because and insofar as he himself wants to be known."[60]

Moving on to the next item (a) in this schema, what is the content of revelation? Put differently, what is it that is revealed? In a fundamental sense, God reveals *himself*, and so we may say that the content of revelation is God's own proper reality, his own self, the gift of himself "as a

---

[56] The following paragraphs on special revelation are adapted from Echeverria, *"In the Beginning..." A Theology of the Body*, 26-31.

[57] I am indebted to George I. Marvrodes here for this schema: *Revelation in Religious Belief* (Philadelphia: Temple University Press, 1988), 88-94.

[58] J. van Genderen & W.H. Velema, *Concise Reformed Dogmatics*, translated by Gerrit Bilkes, edited by M. van der Mass (Phillipsburg, NJ: Presbyterian & Reformed, 2008 [1992]), 24-26.

[59] *Dei Verbum*, §2; see also §6.

[60] Bavinck, *Gereformeerde Dogmatiek*, I, 183 (ET: 212).

communion of persons inviting human persons to enter into communion."[61] In the words of *Dei Verbum*, "His will was that men should have access to the Father, through Christ, the Word made flesh, in the Holy Spirit, and thus become sharers in the divine nature (cf. Eph. 2:18; 2 Pet. 1:4). By this revelation, then, the invisible God (cf. Col. 1:15; 1 Tim. 1:17), from the fullness of his love, addresses men as his friends (cf. Ex. 33:11; Jn. 15:14-15), and moves among them (cf. Bar. 3:38), in order to invite and receive them into his own company."[62] Indeed, *Dei Verbum* discloses that the purpose of God's self-revelation is coming to know him. "Now this is life eternal: that they may know you, the only true God, and Jesus Christ, whom you have sent" (John 17:3). We are invited, therefore, to Trinitarian communion with the Father, through the Son, Jesus Christ, the Word made flesh, in the power of the Holy Spirit. Revelation is, then, not the *mere* communication of truths but rather "the life-bestowing self-communication of the Trinitarian God, in which he addresses humans as friends," as *Dei Verbum* states.[63] This is the variable n in the schema above. It refers to the recipient of special revelation.

Yet, there is more to the content of revelation: God reveals himself in the economy of special revelation in his words and actions. *Dei Verbum* holds that the economy of revelation in Sacred Scripture consists of a pattern of deeds of God in history and words, of divine actions and divinely-given interpretations of those actions, that are inextricably bound together in that revelation.[64] That is, God's redemptive revelation

---

[61] Germain Grisez, "On Interpreting Dogmas," *Communio: International Catholic Review* 17 (1990): 120-126, and at 120.

[62] *Dei Verbum*, §2.

[63] Hermann J. Pottmeyer, "Tradition," in *Dictionary of Fundamental Theology*. Edited by René Latourelle and Rino Fisichella, English Language edition ed. by René Latourelle. (New York: Crossroad, 1994), 1119-1126, and at 1123.

[64] See also, Helm, *The Divine Revelation*, 32-35.

of himself is accomplished through historical events as well as through written words. Thus: "the works performed by God in the history of salvation show forth and bear out the doctrine and realities signified by the words; the words, for their part, proclaim the works, and bring to light the mystery they contain."[65] In sum, "the most intimate truth which this revelation gives us about God and the salvation of man shines forth in Christ, who is himself both the mediator and the sum total of Revelation [see Matt 11:27; John 1:14, 17; 14:6; 17:1-3; 2 Cor 3:16, 4:6; Eph 1:3-14]."[66] This important emphasis on the *history* of salvation reaching its absolute zenith in the person and work of Christ, since God's revelation in him is perfect and definitive, means that there is a history of revelation, with revelation progressing through the history of salvation in phases.[67]

Moreover, God not only reveals himself, giving us himself in Trinitarian communion. Rather, at one and the same time, Holy Scripture is not only God's gift of himself, inviting humanity to share in his life, but also a disclosure of *revealed truths,* that is, propositional revelation. In other words, revelation, while involving a profound personal engagement with the revealing God, "also and necessarily has an irreducibly cognitive dimension."[68] The *Catechism of the Catholic Church* correctly captures both the personal and the propositional in its understanding of faith and revelation. "Faith is first of all a personal adherence of man to God. At the same time, and inseparably, it is a *free assent to the whole truth that God has revealed.*"[69] In this connection, we should heed Paul

---

[65] *Dei Verbum,* §2.

[66] *Dei Verbum,* §2.

[67] J. van Genderen & W.H. Velema, *Concise Reformed Dogmatics,* (Phillipsburg, NJ: P&R Publishing, 2008), 25-26.

[68] Thomas G. Guarino, *Vattimo and Theology* (London: T&T Clark, 2009), 115.

[69] *Catechism of the Catholic Church,* §150.

Helm's point: "There is no antithesis between believing a proposition and believing a person if the proposition is taken to be the assertion of some person."[70] Thus, we must reject the dichotomy between God revealing propositions and revealing himself, between the propositional and the personal, if the propositions are understood to be assertions of God's self-communicative acts.[71] Indeed, Richard Swinburne is correct: "It is in this case very hard to see how God could reveal himself in history (e.g. in the Exodus or the life, death, and resurrection of Jesus) without at the same time revealing some propositional truth about himself. For events are not self-interpreting. Either God provides with the historical events its interpretation, in which there is a propositional revelation; or he does not, in which case how can anyone know that a revelatory event has occurred?"[72] As I have already shown above, this too is the view of *Dei Verbum* in affirming the inextricable connection between words and deeds in the economy of divine Revelation.

---

[70] Paul Helm, "Revealed Propositions and Timeless Truths," *Religious Studies* 8 (1972): 127-36, and at 135-36.

[71] This core certitude of the Christian faith does not exclude affirming that language has a variety of functions in revelation other than asserting: commanding, questioning, invitations, promising, praising, confessing, exhorting, and many others. There are also various literary genres: historical narrative, law, prophecy, poetry, proverb, romance, letter, apocalypse, and much else. Yet, the major point is that all these other ways that God uses language in the special revelation of Holy Scripture "logically presupposes the straight propositional account," Helm, *The Divine Revelation*, 35.

[72] Richard Swinburne, *Revelation* (Oxford: Clarendon, 1992), 4. Similarly, Avery Cardinal Dulles, "The Orthodox Imperative," *First Things* August 2006: 31-35, and at 33: "A non-propositional understanding of revelation contradicts the tenor of Holy Scripture and the earliest confessions of faith, which describe particular historical events of crucial importance for faith."

Briefly, tradition and the church are intrinsically and necessarily related to Scripture, that is, co-inhere as a network of interdependent authorities, and that means that the Magisterium of the Church can justify, or adequately certify, no truth from Scripture alone, but for that matter neither from tradition alone nor from the magisterium alone. Yes, these authorities function together (each in its own way) differing in degree of authority, with Scripture being the supreme rule of faith, the *norma normans non normata* (the norm with no norm over it), such that Scripture is not subservient to tradition or to the teaching office of the Church. Furthermore, the Church does not hold that the teaching office of the Church operates on its own, that is, without reference to any superior norm.

> But the task of authentically interpreting the word of God, whether written or handed on, has been entrusted exclusively to the living teaching office of the Church, whose authority is exercised in the name of Jesus Christ. *This teaching office is not above the Word of God*, but serves it, teaching only what has been handed on, listening to it devoutly, guarding it scrupulously and explaining it faithfully in accord with a divine commission and with the help of the Holy Spirit, it draws from this one deposit of faith everything which it presents for belief as divinely revealed.[73]

---

[73] *Dei Verbum*, 10, emphasis added. See my article, "Solum Magisterium?" *Crisis Magazine,* September 15, 2023, https://crisismagazine.com/opinion/solum-magisterium.

Ch. 4: Ethics in Search of Its Experiential Point of Departure 369

Sources of Christian Ethics

Since we are now discussing the sources of Christian ethics, or moral theology, I would like to say something briefly about two forms of moral theology referred to by Wojtyla. One form is positive theology. "This form of theology is an *exegesis* of the doctrine of Christian morality contained in revelation (scripture and tradition), in keeping with the magisterium of the Church."[74] A second form is "speculative theology, or theological ethics; this form is an *interpretation* of scripture and tradition in keeping with the magisterium of the Church *by means of a particular philosophical system.*"[75] Wojtyla asks, "What is the significance of this 'philosophization' that occurs in speculative theology?" This is an "interpretation that throws light on the data of revelation and insightfully arranges them by means of metaphysical categories."[76] First, man has the propensity to inquire into the causes of things, that is, says Wojtyla, "to understand reality *per ultimas causas.*"[77] Second, to understand man's ultimate end, which entails not only a particular concept of good, but also a particular concept of the selfhood of the human person, as with "giving an ultimate justification of the norms of morality."[78] Furthermore, to examine certain concepts, such as, "the moral law, conscience, freedom, personal responsibility, guilt, and so forth, all of which

---

[74] Karol Wojtyla, "The Problem of Catholic Sexual Ethics," in *Person and Community: Selected Essays*, 279-299.

[75] Karol Wojtyla, "Ethics and Moral Theology," in *Person and Community: Selected Essays*, 101-106, and at 101. See John Paul II, *Fides et Ratio*, §64-91, on the necessity of philosophy.

[76] Wojtyla, "Ethics and Moral Theology," 103.

[77] Wojtyla, "Ethics and Moral Theology," 102. Wojtyla, *Man in the Field of Responsibility*, 58-9.

[78] Wojtyla, "Ethics and Moral Theology," 103. Wojtyla, *Man in the Field of Responsibility*, 59.

are defined with reference to philosophical ethics."[79] We mustn't forget here philosophical anthropology, an "enriched concept of the human person [that] can and should be brought into the interpretation of revelation as well."[80] In sum, says Wojtyla,

> I favor defining moral theology in general as follows: Moral theology is a science that, in the light of revelation, makes justified statements concerning the moral value, or goodness and badness, of human actions. . . . Moral theology, as a normative science, deals with the norms of morality contained in divine revelation and proclaimed by the magisterium of the Church in solemn and ordinary teachings. The task of moral theologians is to scientifically interpret these norms and, above all, to justify them in the light of reason and revelation. A justification of the norms of morality is more than an interpretation of them. This might also be expressed more clearly by saying that a complete and ultimate scientific (theological [and philosophical]) interpretation of the norms of revealed (Catholic) morality is a justifying interpretation. To justify the of morality means to give reasons for their rightness.[81]

Sources of moral theology are the "superior source" of "the Gospel together with its extension, the teaching of the Church." Wojtyla explains, "This source fostered reflections, whereas experience provided facts for confrontation with doctrine. The Gospel contains relatively few

---

[79] John Paul II, *Fides et Ratio*, §66. In §68, he states "moral theology must employ a correct philosophical standpoint, with regard either to human nature and society or to the universal principles of ethical discourse."

[80] Wojtyla, "Ethics and Moral Theology," 104.

[81] Wojtyla, "The Problem of Catholic Sexual Ethics," 279-280.

Ch. 4: Ethics in Search of Its Experiential Point of Departure

texts that speak directly about sexual and conjugal ethics, for example, Matthew 5:27-28, Matthew 19:1-13, Mark 10:1-12, Luke 20:27-35, John 8:1-11, 1Corinthians 7 (the entire chapter), and Ephesians 5:22-33, not to mention extremely significant texts in the Old Testament, especially in Genesis [Genesis 1:27, 2:24]."[82] In accordance with *Dei Verbum* §11, Wojtyla anticipates the hermeneutical golden rule of canon criticism, namely, "to attend to the unity and content of the whole of Scripture." "All of the above-mentioned passages organically inhere in the whole of the Gospel and must be read in this whole as in their essential context. Read in this way, they give an incentive for philosophical reflection. After all, it is well known that not only theology, which employed philosophy as a tool of intellectual speculation, came to be on the basis of Revelation. Revelation also provided a powerful impetus for philosophy—it is sufficient only to mention the conception of being that St. Thomas developed.[83] So it seems that in a somewhat similar manner the Gospel

---

[82] Karol Wojtyla, *Love and Responsibility*, Translation, Endnotes, and Foreword by Grzegorz Ignatik, New Translation (Boston: Pauline Books & Media, 2013 [1960]), xxvii.

[83] Gilson, *The Spirit of Medieval Philosophy*, 50-51: Gilson writes of the "laborious gropings" (alluding to Acts 17: 27) of Plato and Aristotle, as they sought to say something about God. Compared with their efforts, he adds, "how straight forward is the method of the Biblical revelation, and how startling its results." And then, famously, Gilson adds: "In order to know what God is, Moses turns to God. He asks His name, and straightway comes the answer: *Ego sum qui sum, Ait: sic dices filiis Israel; qui est misit me ad vos* (Exod 3:14). No hint of metaphysics, but God speaks, *causa finite est*, and Exodus lays down the principle from which henceforth the whole of Christian philosophy will be suspended. From this moment it is understood once and for all that the proper name of God is Being and that, according to the word of St. Ephrem, taken up again later by St. Bonaventure, this name denotes His very essence." See also, 433n9: "Of course we do not maintain that the text of Exodus [3:14] is a revealed metaphys-

provides an impetus for philosophical reflection concerning sexual [ethical] problems."[84]

We turn now to Farley's reflections on the sources of Christian ethics. Although she regards experience as one of the four sources of Christian sexual ethics, the others being the Bible, tradition, and secular disciplines of knowledge, experience is "not just one source among many. Experience is at the root of all the other sources.[85] Epistemologically speaking, I would call her position a version of "reflective equilibrium," which is a coherence view of justification among one's beliefs.

> The method of reflective equilibrium consists in working back and forth among our considered judgments (some say our "intuitions") about particular instances or cases, the principles or rules that we believe govern them, and the theoretical considerations that we believe bear on accepting these considered judgments, principles, or rules, revising any of these elements wherever necessary in order to achieve an acceptable coherence among them.[86]

Farley will go on to make considered judgments about sexual acts, governed by principles or rules, and supported by theoretical considerations that bear on the justification of these considered judgments, with

---

ical definition of God; but if there is no metaphysics *in* Exodus there is nevertheless a metaphysics *of* Exodus; and we shall see it developed in due course by the Fathers of the Church, whose indications on this point the mediaeval philosophers merely follow up and exploit."

[84] Wojtyla, *Love and Responsibility*, xxvi.

[85] Farley, *Just Love: A Framework for Christian Sexual Ethics*, 190.

[86] "Reflective Equilibrium," *Stanford Encyclopedia of Philosophy*, online: Reflective Equilibrium (Stanford Encyclopedia of Philosophy/Spring 2004 Edition).

Ch. 4: Ethics in Search of Its Experiential Point of Departure 373

the aim of seeking acceptable coherence. We have already considered the theoretical considerations informing Farley's ethics. I only add here what she refers to as the "obligating [or basic] features of personhood."[87] She explains:

> "Obligating features" of persons constitute the basic of requirement to *respect* persons, in whatever way we relate to them, sexually or otherwise. Autonomy and relationality in particular are "obligating features" because they *ground* an obligation to respect persons as *ends in themselves* and forbid, therefore, the use of persons as mere means.[88]

Despite her disclaimer that she is not an essentialist about the basic features of the human person, these surely look like essences constitutive of the human person *qua* person. But what she seems to give with the right hand, as it were, she takes away with the left. "Experience is no incontestable, foundational, immediate, and direct 'deposit' for insight in a fund of experience. Experience does not explain everything else without needing to be explained itself. Not only does it not automatically yield full-blown ethical universals, it also cannot be understood as an

---

[87] Farley, *Just Love: A Framework for Christian Sexual Ethics*, 211.

[88] Farley, *Just Love: A Framework for Christian Sexual Ethics*, 212. It would take us too far afield critically to compare Karol Wojtyla's "personalist principle," its roots in Immanuel Kant's third Categorical imperative, in *Love and Responsibility*, Chapter 1, Part I, 2-28. As Fr. Alfred Marek Wierzbicki puts it in the Introduction to Wojtyla's study, *Man in the Field of Responsibility*, "Wojtyla's critique of Utilitarianism, like Kant's, is based on presenting the person as the source of moral law. While for Kant the principle of autonomy is sufficient to ground the positive content of the categorical imperative, Wojtyla looks for the metaphysical foundations of the personalistic norm, foundations which reside in the being and good of the person" (xi).

'anything goes' approach based on rival experiences of seemingly equal instructive value."[89] In order to avoid a hermeneutical subjectivism, Farley appeals to some guiding criteria, such as, "coherence of the insights from experience with general moral norms; intelligibility of accounts of experience in relation to fundamental beliefs; mutual illumination when measured with other sources of moral insight; harmful or helpful consequences of interpretations of experience; confirmation in a community of discernment and integrity in the testimony of those who present their experience. All of these may be tests for the validity and usefulness of given experiences in a process of moral discernment."[90] The question we address now is what sort of evidence does experience provide such that it provides a "critical edge or opening" to reality?

By "experience" Margaret Farley means the "actual living of events and relationships, along with the sensations, feelings, images, emotions, insights, and understandings that are part of this lived reality. Experience in this sense is a given, something providing data to be interpreted; but it is also something that is already interpreted, its content shaped by previous understandings in a context of multiple influences." In particular, experience is a "source of moral insight, a factor in moral judgment, a test of the rightness, goodness, and wisdom of moral decision."[91] Farley holds that there are other sources for moral discernment in theological ethics: Scripture, tradition, secular disciplines, and contemporary experience.[92] Taken as a descriptive and analytical thesis, and not a purely normative proposal, I agree with her that a comprehensive and coherent

---

[89] Farley, *Just Love: A Framework for Christian Sexual Ethics*, 194.

[90] Farley, *Just Love: A Framework for Christian Sexual Ethics*, 193.

[91] Margaret A. Farley, "The Role of Experience in Moral Discernment," in *Changing Questions: Explorations in Christian Ethics*, Edited and with an Introduction by Jamie L. Manson (Maryknoll, NY: Orbis Books, 2015), 47-68, and at 49.

[92] Farley, *Just Love: A Framework for Christian Sexual Ethics*, 190.

Ch. 4: Ethics in Search of Its Experiential Point of Departure 375

Christian theological ethics must be adequate with reference to those "criteria" (or, in my terms, the sources of "Scripture and Tradition" and the aid that experience may provide to discerning the Word of God). But she means her thesis to be taken as a normative proposal, her so-called "quadrilateral approach," and hence she assumes an absolute equality between these sources. Thus, in my judgment, her normative proposal is incompatible with the dogmatic tradition of the Catholic faith in which Sacred Scripture is the primary and supreme normative source ("the highest authority," in John Paul II's words[93]) for faith and practice, and Sacred Tradition is indispensable to the interpretation of the Word of God. This also means that other aids to discernment can be used, such as experience, insofar as they cohere with the primary and normative source of Sacred Scripture and the living Tradition of the Church.

Yet, Farley's "quadrilateral approach" eventually gives way to "experience" as "an authority that modifies the prior norms that would order it."[94] It seems that experience has in some sense priority over Scripture, because in some sense Scripture itself grows out of human experience. This the experiential expressivist view of revelation. Farley says, "Experience is also potentially misleading as a named source for Christian insight, for it is not just one source among many. It is an important part of the content of each of the other sources, and it is always a factor in interpreting the others. Scripture, for example, is the record of some persons' experience of God; tradition is the lived experience of a faith community through time; and secular disciplines, too, are shaped by the experience of those who engage in them."[95] But what guiding criteria does one employ to determine the authority of experience? We answered this

---

[93] John Paul II, *Ut Unum Sint*, §70.
[94] Farley, *Just Love: A Framework for Christian Sexual Ethics*, 194.
[95] Farley, *Just Love: A Framework for Christian Sexual Ethics*, 190.

question above. And yet, significantly, experience trumps all these guiding criteria: "experience may challenge its own tests and assert an authority that modifies the prior norms that would order it. Something deeper is at stake."[96]

The authority of experience trumps even the Bible's own authority. In particular, women's experience, more accurately, the experience and consciousness of feminists, claims Farley, serves precisely as a "negative limit" in the interpretation of Scripture. This experience and consciousness expresses "deep convictions" and, Farley adds, "whatever contradicts those convictions cannot be accepted as having the authority of an authentic revelation of truth. It is simply a matter of there being no turning back."[97] Thus, on the question of Scripture and experience, it is an understanding of authority that is the basic question. "It is impossible," says Farley, "to separate the question of authority from the question of the content or meaning of what is presented as authoritative."[98] And in order to decide the question of, say, the authority of the Scriptures, whether you ought to accept its claims, the Bible "must 'make sense' to the one who accepts it."[99] Therefore, according to Farley, "The . . . authority . . . of any source is ultimately contingent on a 'recognition' of the truth it offers. . . . No source has real and living authority in relation to our moral attitudes and choices unless it can elicit from us a responding recognition."[100] In particular, the Bible "cannot be believed unless it

---

[96] Farley, *Just Love: A Framework for Christian Sexual Ethics*, 190.

[97] Margaret A. Farley, "Feminist Consciousness and the Interpretation of Scripture," in *From Christ to the World: Introductory Readings in Christian Ethics*, edited by Wayne G. Boulton, Thomas D. Kennedy, and Allen Verhey, (Grand Rapids, MI: Eerdmans, 1994), 51-57, and at 56.

[98] Farley, *Just Love: A Framework for Christian Sexual Ethics*, 194.

[99] Farley, *Just Love: A Framework for Christian Sexual Ethics*, 194.

[100] Farley, *Just Love: A Framework for Christian Sexual Ethics*, 194-95.

Ch. 4: Ethics in Search of Its Experiential Point of Departure   377

'rings true' to our deepest capacity for truth and goodness."[101] In that case, however, isn't that to reduce the authority of the Bible "to a measure that is outside of it?"[102] Aren't we dealing here with a subjectification of biblical authority, meaning thereby that the Bible only becomes the authoritative Word of God through acknowledgement? It certainly seems so. For it is within the negative limit established by the deep convictions of feminist consciousness and experience that the "biblical witness as a whole is experienced as authentic," meaning thereby that, according to Farley, "some religious authority is given to Scripture."[103]

Does Farley then leave it up to human understanding to decide which biblical texts are authoritative and revelatory? Doesn't this mean that biblical authority is, on her view, founded on human reasoning and the authority of man's own power of conviction, rather than on divine authorship and inspiration, which is the deep foundation of all scriptural faith? Is her view an experiential or existential view that holds the Bible to be authoritative "only in those parts that are existentially engaging and compelling—that give grounding and meaning to existence [?]"[104] Farley is, however, quick to assure us, "This does not mean that sources are completely subjectified, that there is—for example—no revelation in the Bible unless everyone perceives it."[105] Still, she adds,

> It does mean that not every interpretation of every verse or text of the Bible can be "authoritative" or normative by itself for

---

[101] Farley, *Just Love: A Framework for Christian Sexual Ethics*, 195.

[102] Farley, *Just Love: A Framework for Christian Sexual Ethics*, 195.

[103] Farley, "Feminist Consciousness and the Interpretation of Scripture," 56.

[104] This is how Dan O. Via, Professor Emeritus of New Testament at Duke University Divinity School, describes his own view of biblical authority in dialogue with Robert A.J. Gagnon, *Homosexuality and the Bible: Two Views*, 2.

[105] Farley, *Just Love: A Framework for Christian Sexual Ethics*, 195, and note 38.

every person. Nonetheless, a subjective "recognition" of a text (of whatever sort) as "making sense" is in some way inevitable."[106]

Given this inevitability, I am left wondering whether her claim brings with it the very real danger that the authority of biblical truth is tailored to suit human needs. In other words, the claim that biblical truth is authentically authoritative because it elicits from us a responding recognition so easily turns into its opposite, namely, that it is only biblical truth and hence authoritative because it elicits that response from us.[107]

Farley's disclaimer, then, notwithstanding, I still wonder whether we are dealing with a subjectification of authority in her proposal. Admittedly, the content of Scripture is essential to the proclamation of the Gospel and hence biblical authority cannot be completely severed from man's coming to recognize that content as a revelation of truth. Let me make my position clear by distinguishing objective revelation and subjective illumination.[108] We spoke above of special revelation as an act of God by which he communicates himself and the mystery of his will to man. In this connection, we need to understand that this communicative act of God reaches us in two ways, and hence I will distinguish between the external and the internal principle of knowing (*principium cognoscendi externum* and *internum*), the external and the internal word, objective revelation and subjective illumination. Francis Martin gives an account of these two ways:[109]

---

[106] Farley, *Just Love: A Framework for Christian Sexual Ethics*, 195n38.

[107] Bavinck, *Gereformeerde Dogmatiek*, I, 524 (ET: 552-553).

[108] These paragraphs are adapted from Echeverria, "In the Beginning... " *A Theology of the Body*, 55-6.

[109] Martin's account is based on *Dei Verbum*, particularly §§2-6.

There is first God's activity in history that is accomplished through intimately connected words and deeds, culminating in Jesus Christ, who is both the mediator and fullness of revelation [*principium cognoscendi externum*]. Second, there is the activity, also historical and also mediated by Jesus Christ, by which God moves and assists someone to believe, that is to commit himself . . . to God, yielding to and accepting the divine self-communication [*principium cognoscendi internum*]. While the first activity was brought to completion by the resurrection of Jesus Christ, the second is still continuing. This second dimension is always present as the Holy Spirit brings each person into living contact with the Father's self-revelation in Jesus Christ from the dead. In a mysterious interaction of divine initiative and human freedom, the Holy Spirit leads those who assent to his action from the first act of yielding in faith to its consummation in a transforming vision of God. Only then does God completely manifest and communicate himself, which allows us to obtain a clear knowledge of the eternal mystery of his will. Revelation actually exists only when both dimensions of the divine activity are present: the words and deeds culminating in Christ and the personal appropriation of these realities.[110]

---

[110] Francis Martin, *The Feminist Question: Feminist Theology in the Light of the Christian Tradition* (Grand Rapids, MI: Eerdmans, 1994), 2-23. Similarly, Bernard Lonergan states in rejecting a pure non-propositional view of revelation, "[T]he word of religious expression is not just the objectification of the gift of God's love; in a privileged area it also is specific meaning, the word of God himself. . . . [Thus] there is a further and far deeper sense in which a religion may be named historical. The dynamic state of being in love has the character of a response. It is an answer to a divine initiative. The divine initiative is not just a creation. It is not just God's gift of his love. There is a personal entrance

Everything hangs inseparably together in this doctrine of revelation: corresponding to the objective revelation of God occurring outside of ourselves in acts, in historical events culminating in the person and work of Christ, who is the fullness and mediator of all revelation, there is the subjective illumination of the Spirit working in order than man may acknowledge and accept that revelation. In sum, corresponding to this external principle of knowing there is an internal principle, to this objective revelation there is a subjective revelation or illumination—all are part of the one activity we call revelation. Undoubtedly, Fr. Martin agrees that objective revelation, which consists in acts, in the events of history culminating in the person and work of Christ, but also in words, in the communication of truth, *exists independently* of the believer's personal appropriation of those realities. Of course, he is correct to insist on an internal revelation or illumination of the Spirit.

Briefly, how does the Catholic tradition address the question regarding the reasonable of assenting to biblical authority? Unlike Farley who holds that biblical authority is no longer acceptable on the basis of a judgment of credibility, or motive of credibility,[111] "the truth of authority," as the German Lutheran theologian, Wolfhart Pannenberg (1928-2014) insightfully puts it, "becomes a function of a more or less arbitrary subjective decision."[112] This is Farley's position since the guiding criteria she lists for moral discernment may be trumped by experience. Pannenberg adds, "The divine truth, then, that faith relies upon falls back on the

---

of God himself into history, a communication of God's word into the world of religious expression. Such was the religion of Israel. Such has been Christianity" (*Method in Theology*, [New York: Herder and Herder, 1972], 118-19).

[111] Denzinger, §3013.

[112] Wolfhart Pannenberg, "History and Meaning in Bernard Lonergan's approach to theological method," in *Looking at Lonergan's Method*, ed. Patrick Corcoran, SM (Dublin: The Talbot Press, 1975), 88-100.

decision of the subject itself."¹¹³ This is fideism. The Catholic alternative to this modern trend where the subjective decision lacks a judgment of credibility makes a distinction between the motive of credibility and the motive of real faith. In answering "the question why something is believed" there is an appeal to "the motive of credibility (the reason for holding that the witness is sufficiently credible and that he in fact testifies to something)."¹¹⁴ Since the Catholic tradition does not support rationalism, this is distinguished from "the real motive of faith, that is, the sole authority of God, who is truth itself, incapable of deceiving anyone when he reveals himself."¹¹⁵

There remains to ask, if the normative Scriptures and the dogmatic tradition is countercultural, or seems no longer meaningful, by the standards of contemporary human experience, then are the Scriptures and/or doctrinal tradition to be abandoned, adulterated, or radically reinterpreted?

Finally, positions like Farley's are entirely unsustainable from the standpoint of a thick doctrine of divine revelation. For one thing, her position represents "an excessive privileging of Christian experience over against the witness of Scripture and tradition, and over against the Church's magisterium as their interpreter."¹¹⁶ In Christian theology, experience is an *aid* to discernment of revealed truth as found in revelation's sources, Scripture and tradition, rather than being itself a living *source* of enlightenment.¹¹⁷

---

¹¹³ Pannenberg, "History and Meaning in Bernard Lonergan's approach to theological method," 98.

¹¹⁴ Karl Rahner and Herbert Vorgrimler, *Theological Dictionary*, editor, Cornelius Ernst, OP, translated by Richard Strachan (New York: Herder & Herder, 1965), 168.

¹¹⁵ Rahner and Vorgrimler, Theological Dictionary, 168.

¹¹⁶ Nichols, *The Shape of Catholic Theology*, 241.

¹¹⁷ Nichols, *The Shape of Catholic Theology*, 246.

The basic theological reason for this distinction is stated by Aidan Nichols:

> For Catholic theology, after the apostles, more precisely with the death of the last apostle, revelation is closed. In terms of Scripture this means that the canon of the New Testament is completed in the moment when the apostolic Church understands herself as the Church of these Scriptures and no other. In terms of Tradition, it means that the *regula fidei* and *institutio christiana* of the Church are constituted in all essentials in the apostolic period, all else being crystallization and reformation. *But does this mean that from that point on, experience can provide no elements of novelty to an understanding of specifically Christian revelation?*[118]

The brief answer to the question in the last sentence of this quotation is, "not at all." Although not a source of revelation, there is another kind of experience that counts. As Richard B. Hays nicely puts it, "experience must be treated as a hermeneutical lens for reading the New Testament rather than as an independent, counterbalancing authority."[119] That experience is a *corrective* of an already established understanding of revelation, such as the view of some Christians on slavery. But the authority that experience has lies not in the experience itself but in the truth of revelation it lays hold of more fully. In other words, our increased experience of the brotherhood of all men – guided by the revelation that we

---

[118] Nichols, *The Shape of Catholic Theology*, 240 (italics added to last sentence).

[119] Richard B. Hays, *The Moral Vision of the New Testament: Community, Cross, New Creation—A Contemporary Introduction to New Testament Ethics* (San Francisco: HarperSanFrancisco, 1996), 399.

are all made in the image and likeness of God – was instrumental in changing our thinking of slavery. Our increased experience of the abilities of women has led us to admit women to more kinds of influence and authority. I think experience does help us interpret Scripture but that experience must be one that accords with objective truth, not subjective distortions, such as the experiences had by many homosexuals and even by women who claim to be called to the priesthood. In other words, in this kind of faith-experience the individual is changed *not* by the experience itself, but through becoming united with Truth itself. Thus, in order to determine whether an experience is authoritative, we "must appeal in the last analysis to some sort of discernment of spirits."[120] And without revealed truth, propositional revelation, which is God's verbal revelation, consisting in the disclosure of truths about himself and his redemptive acts in history, there would be no way to ensure that our faith-experience in fact unites us to the True God, the God who is our happiness and salvation.

Ethics as a Philosophical Theory of the Experience of Morality

What are Science and Experience?

"The point of departure in ethics is . . . the experience of morality."[121] What does Wojtyla mean by ethics? Briefly, ethics is a normative science (*Wissenschaft*), not just descriptive, such as a psychology or sociology of

---

[120] Nichols, *The Shape of Catholic Theology*, 237.
[121] Wojtyla, "The Problem of Experience in Ethics" (1969), 107-127, and at 112.

morality; nor is an apriorism in which "immediate and self-evident primary [moral] judgments have their source in reason alone."[122] Regarding apriorism, Wojtyla rejects "[Kantian] formalism" which "means an escape from teleology." This normative science "aims at 'objectifying' norms, and thus above all at ultimately justifying them, and not just presenting them."[123]

Furthermore, what does Wojtyla mean by experience? To understand Wojtyla's epistemological reflections on experience it is crucial to understand his reliance on Edmund Husserl's distinction between "*Erfahrung*" and "*Erlebnis*." "*Erfahrung* . . . refers to the objective content of a person's contact with some reality, whereas *Erlebnis* . . . refers to the subjective dimension reflected in consciousness."[124] Wojtyla's translators refer to the latter as *"lived experience."* It refers to the concrete experience of agent causation and efficacy that is the experiential basis for connecting ethical value with the ethical becoming of the person as its proper subject, namely, *"to be good or evil."*[125] Regarding the former, Wojtyla argues that human experience already has a preunderstanding of that which is experienced. This preunderstanding is, says Wojtyla, "characterized by a distinct realist conviction. *Morality* is a kind of reality."[126] And this particular conviction about morality rests on a "more general *conviction about the correctness of a realist position in cognition*,

---

[122] Wojtyla, "The Problem of Experience in Ethics," 108, 109.

[123] Wojtyla, "Ethics and Moral Theology," 100.

[124] Wojtyla, *Man in the Field of Responsibility*, 8n2. See Edmund Husserl, *Experience and Judgment*. Translated by James S. Churchill and Karl Ameriks (Evanston, Ill.: Northwestern University Press, 1973). For an instructive account of Husserl's epistemology, see Henry Pietersma, *Phenomenological Epistemology* (New York: Oxford University Press, 2000), 36-84.

[125] Wojtyla, *Man in the Field of Responsibility*, 17.

[126] Wojtyla, *Man in the Field of Responsibility*, 13.

in philosophy and in science."¹²⁷ Thus, this preunderstanding is about "the essential content of the reality given in experience as morality."¹²⁸ It is not about the experience of morality, but rather "the content of *morality* as given in experience."¹²⁹ Hence, the very essence of morality "is not primarily an abstract system," says Wojtyla, "but a distinctive mode of human life and existence."¹³⁰ This givenness involves a cognition about something real. "Cognition does not in any way create 'reality' (cognition does not create its own content)."¹³¹ The objective content of the judgment is not about an "idea" or "*a priori*." Rather, "The fact of experience reveals that morality is a form of reality, a form of *esse*."¹³² In sum, Wojtyla's sound epistemology is a version of epistemic realism. He explains:

> The first element of experience can be defined as a "sense of reality," placing the accent on *reality*—on the fact that something exists with an existence that is real and objectively independent of the cognizing subject and the subject's cognitive act, while at the same time existing as the object of that act. Because of this, the structural whole of experience also contains a second element, which can be defined as a sense of knowing. This is a sense of a distinctive kind of relation to what exists in a real and objective way, together with a sense of a distinctive kind of contact or union with what exists and exists in such a way.¹³³

---

[127] Wojtyla, *Man in the Field of Responsibility*, 12.
[128] Wojtyla, "The Problem of Experience in Ethics," 134.
[129] Wojtyla, "The Problem of Experience in Ethics," 134.
[130] Wojtyla, "The Problem of the Theory of Morality," 129-161, and at 134.
[131] Wojtyla, "The Problem of Experience in Ethics," 116.
[132] Wojtyla, "The Problem of Experience in Ethics," 116.
[133] Wojtyla, "The Problem of Experience in Ethics," 115.

Different Aspects and Layers of the Moral Life: axiology, praxeology, and deontology

In the epigraph to this essay, Wojtyla states, "the experience of morality possesses, as it were, different layers and different aspects."[134] These aspects and their corresponding approaches are as follows. There are objective values which reflect the teleological interpretation of human action in which such values "become real 'in action', within the dynamic structure of action as an *actus personae*," and by means of which the human person becomes good or evil. Wojtyla adds, "As a result, moral value somehow 'makes its abode" in the person: it roots itself in the person and becomes a quality of the person."[135] A man, *qua* man, "becomes good or evil through the act."[136] There is a metaphysical foundation to the "experience of being [man as a being] and becoming good or evil through one or another act." For it is "the subject itself, the 'I'— the person [who] becomes morally good or evil."[137] Hence, the *axiological* and the *praxiological* layers, and thoroughly anthropological, personalistic, and metaphysical reality, of the experience of morality, of becoming and being. Chiefly, however, there is the *deontological* layer, which, according to Wojtyla, is the "*proper element* of morality [that] is contained in the experience of *duty*."[138] There is a deontic dynamism here, too, because the normative principles that constitute duty, which is an objectification of the truth of the good, are also about making the person good. The element of duty, says Wojtyla, is "the distinctive *constitutivum* of the lived experience to which we ascribe a moral character in the

---

[134] Wojtyla, *Man in the Field of Responsibility*, 10.
[135] Wojtyla, "The Problem of the Theory of Morality," 137.
[136] Wojtyla, *Man in the Field of Responsibility*, 17.
[137] Wojtyla, *Man in the Field of Responsibility*, 22.
[138] Wojtyla, *Man in the Field of Responsibility*, 8.

proper sense of the term. Duty is more decisive for morality than is value," [139] namely, "*what* exactly *ought* I to do?" and "*why ought I to do what I ought to do?*" He adds, "This is an understanding of duty not only as a lived *experience*, but at the same time as an objective *fact*."[140] In sum:

> The existence proper to a person is an existence in truth, an existence in dynamic relation to truth. And that is why persons exist and act, actualizing their *esse* and their *operari*, not just on the level of values, but also on the level of principles. Morality is the essential coordination of these levels.[141]

This claim that experience possesses different layers and different aspects is a reflection of the starting-point, according to Wojtyla, for ethics. "Every experience is also a primordial understanding, and so it can serve as a point of departure for subsequent understandings and as a kind of provocation toward them."[142] Wojtyla aims to "objectify" (his word) the objective content of the experience of morality. He explains, "to objectify means to stand beyond experience, to pull away from the subjective context that the experience of morality always involves. . . . The transposition of this content to the theoretical order must not obliterate its existential expression, but must accentuate it in a special way."[143] The understanding and interpretation of this theoretical order is dependent, says Wojtyla, "*on one's overall conception of philosophy*, on

---

[139] Wojtyla, "The Problem of the Theory of Morality," 150.
[140] Wojtyla, *Man in the Field of Responsibility*, 15.
[141] Wojtyla, "The Problem of the Theory of Morality," 139.
[142] Wojtyla, "The Problem of Experience in Ethics," 117.
[143] Wojtyla, "The Problem of the Theory of Morality," 134-35.

one's gnoseological, epistemological principles, which, as is known, fundamentally condition the relation to metaphysics."[144] Regarding metaphysics, it is about a peculiar union of axiology and ontology, of deontic norms, duties, and ontology, that is, natural law, which is the fundamental structure of the normative foundation, but also about the justification of the norms of human morality.[145]

In this experience of morality, there arises the question of moral good and evil. That is, "What is morally good and what is morally evil in human actions?" and "What makes human actions morally good or evil?"[146] Objectifying the essential content of morality in the experience of morality reveals an axiological content, a sphere of objective values differentiated into good and evil, "a differentiation that, moreover, has its roots in a norm of morality."[147] This objective content is, then, *axiological-normative*. The second question above raises the question regarding the ultimate basis of this good and evil. What makes them so is their relation to norms. Says Wojtyla, "When we ask the further question 'Why?' we are then inquiring into the ethical foundation of the norms upon which the moral good or evil of human actions rests." That is, we are inquiring into the foundations of the norms themselves. Wojtyla adds, "The form of ethics that emerges from these questions by means of interpretation will be a *normative* form."[148] The norm determines the end because the "conceptualized ethical norm is nothing other than an objectivization of the truth of the good." The truth of the good is, says Wojtyla, "the primary content of each of these norms. What justifies a given moral decision is the fact that it contains the "truth of the good

---

[144] Wojtyla, *Man in the Field of Responsibility*, 19.
[145] Wojtyla, *Man in the Field of Responsibility*, 71.
[146] Wojtyla, "The Problem of the Theory of Morality," 130.
[147] Wojtyla, "The Problem of the Theory of Morality," 135.
[148] Wojtyla, "The Problem of the Theory of Morality," 131.

and it is wrong if it does not correspond to it."¹⁴⁹ We have before us now the deontological dimension of the moral life: "I ought to do *x*, I ought not to do *y*." Here, too, in these concrete judgments regarding the truth of the good, we find a dynamism that Wojtyla refers to as "*deontic dynamism* that draws its force from the elementary axiology of the being of the person." That is, "I want to be good—I do not want to be evil," which is the "very reason for being the person in the axiological order."¹⁵⁰ In sum, Wojtyla explains,

> Duty is unquestionably linked to autoteleology—the element of fulfillment or unfulfillment—that we discovered at the core of the reality of morality. It arises from the structure of a personal being, a being capable of self-realization, and is based on a potentiality proper to such a being. This potentiality is the spiritual potentiality of the will, the potentiality of freedom, which in a rational being—and the person is such a being—reveals a dynamic ordered to truth.¹⁵¹

The Necessity of Metaphysics: the normative order of Natural Law

Wojtyla argues that metaphysics is necessary as a foundation for realist ethics; not only the metaphysics of the human person, but also the created order of things. His realist ethics require undergirding philosophical principles that possess "metaphysical authority."¹⁵² Wojtyla states that the phenomenological analysis of the lived experience of good and evil can only play a subsidiary role because it says "nothing about what is good and what is evil, [and why] but merely asserts that upon the

---

[149] Wojtyla, *Man in the Field of Responsibility*, 60.
[150] Wojtyla, *Man in the Field of Responsibility*, 45.
[151] Wojtyla, "The Problem of the Theory of Morality,"
[152] Nichols, *The Shape of Catholic Theology*, 346.

occasion of a certain thing (some value), 'good' or 'evil' is experienced."[153] Wojtyla insists that such experiences cannot be divorced from, or be independent of, the existence of an objective hierarchy of goods, which is a normative order grounded in divine reason. "God is the supreme, transcendent measure of all beings through the unconditional perfection of [His] own being, through the unconditional fullness of existence that God is. . . . Herein lies the very heart of the normative order."[154] This order pertains not only to the transcendental character of the natural law, as Wojtyla states above, but also to its "*immanence* in man and in the world." That is, says Wojtyla, "Immanence is embodied in the fact that the natural law is inscribed in the very being of man and of the world, in the fact that natural law is in some way identical with that very being."[155] Traditionally stated, the natural law is human participation in the eternal law of God. In Wojtyla's own words, "By knowing it [the objective order of nature] with reason and preserving it in his actions, man becomes a partaker of God's thought, *particeps Creatoris*; he has a share in the law which God eternally imparted to the world by creating it."[156] This is a realist theology that attends to the structures of creation in which an immanent wisdom is embodied, reflecting the law of creation. Says John Paul II pointedly, "Law must therefore be considered an expression of divine wisdom." He explains, "by submitting to the law, freedom submits to the truth of creation."[157]

Wojtyla elaborates, "Natural law points to the need for penetration into. . . ontic structure[s] and to the need *to understand natures, i.e., the*

---

[153] Wojtyla, "On the Metaphysical and Phenomenological Basis of the Moral Norm," 73-94, and at 84-85.

[154] Wojtyla, "On the Metaphysical and Phenomenological Basis of the Moral Norm," 77.

[155] Wojtyla, *Man in the Field of Responsibility*, 71-72.

[156] Wojtyla, *Love and Responsibility*, 232-33.

[157] John Paul II, *Veritatis Splendor*, §41.

essence of things, essences which enter into the object of a human action."[158] This includes also the particular position of man as a person, whose reality is not separated from nature. "Quite the contrary, the personalistic norm signifies a deeper penetration into the world of natures in order, on the normative plane, to extract more fully the 'nature of man' who, by his very nature, is a person."[159] John Paul II argues that the moral order flows from human nature itself.[160] God created persons with a design. That is, he understands a human being as one who possesses a permanent nature or, as Jacques Maritain puts it, "an ontological structure which is a locus of intelligible necessities," meaning thereby, "man possesses ends which necessarily correspond to his essential constitution and which are the same for all."[161] Maritain calls this the ontological element of natural law.[162] But there is also a second element, namely, the gnoseological element in natural law, which is "natural law *as known*."[163] This epistemic element is particularly important for giving an account of the growth of moral knowledge of the natural law.[164] The known natural law is not a codex, that is, a written law; there is always more to

---

[158] Wojtyla, *Man in the Field of Responsibility*, 72.

[159] Wojtyla, *Man in the Field of Responsibility*, 74. For an extensive discussion of the "personalist norm" in Wojtyla's sexual ethics, see Wojtyla, *Love and Responsibility*, Chapter 1, Part I, 2-28. We see this personalism at work in Wojtyla's pre-papal philosophical writings, "Thomistic Personalism," "On the Dignity of the Human Person," "The Human Person and Natural Law," and "The Person: Subject and Community," to name just a few of his most significant essays. All these essays are in Karol Wojtyla, *Person and Community: Selected Essays*, trans. Theresa Sandok, O.S.M. (New York: Peter Lang, 1993), 165–86, 219–62.

[160] John Paul II, *Veritatis Splendor*, §51.

[161] Jacques Maritain, *Man and the State*, 86.

[162] Maritain, *Man and the State*, 85.

[163] Maritain, *Man and the State*, 89.

[164] Maritain, *Man and the State*, 90.

know. Ontologically speaking, "the natural law makes up," says Wojtyla, the foundation for all codification, make it possible, and verify it." Furthermore, adds Wojtyla, "The natural law is the 'codex' of the Creator himself, inscribed into the very being of man and of the world—and kept accessible to man as a rational being: knowable for and realizable by him."[165]

What is Just Love?

These reflections on the natural law and ontic structures of creation bring us back, in conclusion, to Margaret Farley's hermeneutical epistemology and its affinity with postmodern skepticism, namely, "Postmodern ways of thinking have so subverted and destabilized notions of the human body and gender that there is no longer any room for a moral 'law'."[166] Contrary to Farley's understanding of "just love," which denies the legitimacy of a distinctive sexual ethics, and which only speaks of "justice in the horizontal direction," Wojtyla, indeed, John Paul II, takes his "point of departure" in reflecting on "just love," on "justice [to be] the fact of creation."[167] This is what Wojtyla states as "justice in the vertical direction—a need to justify all conduct in the sexual sphere with respect to God."[168] Wojtyla explains:

> God is the Creator, which means that all beings in the universe, all creatures and among them man in particular, owe their existence to him. God is not only the Creator, i.e., the unceasing Giver of existence, but the very essences of individual creatures

---

[165] Wojtyla, *Man in the Field of Responsibility*, 71.
[166] Farley, *Just Love: A Framework for Christian Sexual Ethics*, 136.
[167] Wojtyla, *Love and Responsibility*, 232.
[168] Wojtyla, *Love and Responsibility*, 231.

come from him as well; they constitute a reflection of the eternal thought and plan of God. In this way, the whole order of nature has its source in God, for this order is based directly on the essences (i.e., natures) of beings existing in the world; hence proceed all dependencies, relations, and connections between them.[169]

In this light, we can understand why the Church judges that marriage is a two-in-one-flesh union between a man and woman because that judgment is true to an objective reality, according to the order of creation. This is a Christian realism: marriage is grounded in the order of creation, of an independently existing reality, and therefore has an objective structure judged by the Church to be the case or the way things really are. Vatican II's *Gaudium et Spes* §48, states, "The intimate partnership of married life and love has been established by the Creator and qualified by His laws." The *Catechism of the Catholic Church* adds, "The vocation to marriage is written in the very nature of man and woman as they came from the hand of the Creator."[170]

Consequently, the starting point of the philosophical anthropology undergirding John Paul II's theology of the body is that sexual difference is grounded in an ontology of creation. In other words, the sexual difference between male and female is a creational given such that all mankind is bound to the structures of creation. It is also creational given that, at one and the same time, mankind is one and a bi-unity: male and female. John Paul explains:

> Let us enter into the setting of the biblical "beginning." [i.e., from the order of creation] In it the revealed truth concerning

---

[169] Wojtyla, *Love and Responsibility*, 232.
[170] *Catechism of the Catholic Church*, §§1603, 1614-15.

man as "the image and likeness" of God constitutes the immutable *basis of all Christian anthropology*. "God created man in his own image, in the image of God he created him; male and female he created them" (Gen 1: 27). This concise passage contains the fundamental anthropological truths: man is the high point of the whole order of creation in the visible world; the human race, which takes its origin from the calling into existence of man and woman, crowns the whole work of creation; *both man and woman are human beings to an equal degree*, both are created *in God's image*.[171]

Indeed, the pope imitates Christ (see Matt 19:3-9; Mark 10: 1-10) by appealing to the "beginning," to the creational structure for marriage, drawing on Genesis 1 and 2 for his understanding of the normative intent of a biblical ontology of creation, the objective structures of creation, as they pertain to a bi-unity of husband and wife, united as complementary, bodily persons, in a two-in-one-flesh communion. Jesus calls us back to the law of creation (Mark 10:6-7) that grounds an inextricable nexus of permanence, twoness, and sexual differentiation for marriage. In particular, marriage is such that it requires sexual difference, the bodily-sexual act, as a foundational prerequisite, indeed, as *intrinsic* to a one flesh union of man and woman: "So then they are no longer two but one flesh." (Mark 10:8)

John Paul's treatment of these foundational texts is ultimately theological, because it is grounded in an historical-redemptive dialectic of creation, fall (sin), redemption, and fulfillment. But it is also philosophical – it articulates a philosophical anthropology of the body-person, which in its broadest sense is man himself in the temporal form of

---

[171] John Paul II, Apostolic Letter, 1988, *Mulieris Dignitatem: On the Dignity and Vocation of Women*, §6.

existence of human life. Most significantly, the pope is arguing that, in the totality of the personal structure of man, his body is a basis, a substructure forming part of the unity of man and thus of the person. Indeed, the meaning of the human body is an integral part of the structure of the personal subject, rather than being "extrinsic to the person, the subject and the human act." John Paul then argues, "the human body is not only the field of reactions of a sexual character, but [rather] it is at the same time the means of the expression of man as an integral whole, of the person, which reveals itself through the 'language of the body'." Indeed, he says, "Man is *in some sense unable to express* this singular language [fundamental to the communion of persons] of his personal existence and vocation *without the body.*"[172]

"This 'language' has an important interpersonal meaning," he adds, "especially in the area of the reciprocal relations between man and woman." This shows that the "'language of the body' should *express*, at a determinate level, *the truth of the sacrament*," namely, a one-flesh union. "So then they are no longer two but one flesh." (Mark 10:8) The foundation of the form of love that is marriage is a bodily sexual union of man and woman as *one flesh*. But since the body is intrinsic to personhood, the nature of marriage is such that it requires sexual difference, the bodily-sexual act, as a foundational prerequisite, indeed, as also *intrinsic* to a one-flesh sacramental union. In his philosophical anthropology, John Paul II develops the sacramental importance of the bodily-sexual act as intrinsic to a one-flesh union.

The *sacramental sign* of marriage is constituted by the couple, by the "word" they exchange – "I take you as my wife/as my husband, and I promise to be faithful to you always, in joy and in sorrow, in sickness and in health, and to love you and honor you all the days of my life."

---

[172] John Paul II, *Man and Woman He Created Them*, 104.7.

And in their reciprocal "fidelity," they commit themselves to "living" a reality of grace. John Paul comments, "This reality (the *copula conjugale*), moreover, has been defined from the very beginning by institution of the Creator. 'A man will leave his father and his mother and unite with his wife, and the two will be one flesh'." (Gen. 2:24)

Why the sacrament of marriage presupposes sexual differentiation is made clear in the realization of what is meant by the "sacramental sign": "The words [*form*] spoken by them would not of themselves constitute the sacramental sign if the human subjectivity of the engaged man and woman and at the same time the consciousness of the body linked with the masculinity and the femininity of the bride and the bridegroom did not correspond to them [*matter*]."

John Paul explains: "What determines it [the sacramental sign of marriage] is *in some sense 'the language of the body'*, inasmuch as the man and the woman, who are to become one flesh by marriage, express in this sign the reciprocal gift of masculinity and femininity as the [creational] foundation of the conjugal union of the persons. The sign of the sacrament of Marriage is constituted by the fact that the words spoken by the new spouses take up again the same 'language of the body' as at the 'beginning' [from creation] and, at any rate, give it a concrete and unrepeatable expression.... In this way the perennial and ever new 'language of the body' *is not only the 'substratum', but in some sense also the constitutive content of the communion of persons*."[173]

Pace Farley, without this creational perspective, and its corresponding philosophical anthropology, we shall not have an understanding of just love, and, consequently, human sexuality and sexual ethics will be uprooted from reality.

---

[173] John Paul II, *Man and Woman He Created Them*, 103.3.4.5.

Chapter 5

Mercy and Truth

Pastoral Care of Individuals in Spiritually and Morally Problematic Relationships

The good of the person lies in being in the Truth and doing the Truth.[1]

The pastoral policy of truth can hurt and be uncomfortable. But it is the way to healing, peace, and interior freedom. A pastoral policy that truly seeks to help people must always be based on the truth; only what is true can ultimately be pastoral. Then you will know the truth, and the truth will set you free (John 8:32).[2]

Truth has such a clear and calm power. My aim in pastoral work is this: to help by the power of the truth.[3]

What is the nature and purpose of pastoral care for individuals in spiritually and morally problematic relationships? The latter includes

---

[1] John Paul II, "Discorso Di Giovanni Paolo II Ai Partecipanti Al Congresso Internazionale Di Teologia Morale," §1. http://w2.vatican.va/content/john-paul-ii/it/speeches/1986/april/documents/hf_jp-ii_spe_19860410_teologia-morale.html.

[2] Benedict XVI, "La pastorale del matrimonio deve fondarsi sulla verità." http://www.osservatoreromano.va/it/news/la-pastorale-del-matrimonio-deve-fondarsi-sulla-ve.

[3] Romano Guardini, *Wahrheit des Denkens und Wahrheit des Tuns*, ed. J. Messerschmid, 3d ed. (Paderborn, 1980), 85; as cited by Joseph Ratzinger in "Pluralism as a Problem for Church and Theology," in *Church, Ecumenism, & Politics* (San Francisco: Ignatius Press, 2008 [1987]), 92 n20.

not just the divorced and civilly remarried and cohabiting couples (either heterosexuals or homosexuals) but also clergy who are violating continence. I will answer this question in this chapter. I follow this up with a brief discussion of homosexuality. I consider, not the ethics of homosexuality, but rather the "anthropological meaning of homosexuality in terms of what the Church calls a 'disordered tendency'." [4] In this connection, I raise the question regarding the legitimacy of claiming that "homosexual orientation" grounds human identity. The Christian anthropology of the Catholic tradition with good reason rejects this claim, and hence we should reject any pastoral approach predicated on that presupposition.

---

[4] Monsignor Livio Melina, "Homosexual Inclination as an 'Objective Disorder': Reflections on Theological Anthropology," in *Living the Truth in Love: Pastoral Approaches to Same-Sex Attraction*, edited by Janet E. Smith and Father Paul Check (San Francisco: Ignatius Press, 2015), 129-140, and at 132. See the Church's teaching in *Persona Humana* (1975), Declaration on Certain Questions Concerning Sexual Ethics (http://www.vatican.va/roman_curia/congregations/cfaith/documents/rc_con_cfaith_doc_19751229_persona-humana_en.html); *Homosexualitatis problema* (1986), Letter to the Bishops of the Catholic Church on the Pastoral Care of Homosexual Persons (http://www.vatican.va/roman_curia/congregations/cfaith/documents/rc_con_cfaith_doc_19861001_homosexual-persons_ en.html); and the *Catechism of the Catholic Church* on Christian anthropology and sexual ethics, §§2331-2359, (http://www.vatican.va/archive/ENG0015/_INDEX.HTM).

Ch. 5: Mercy and Truth

The Nature and Purpose of Pastoral Care[5]

Pope Benedict XVI writes in his encyclical *Caritas in Veritate*, "Charity, in fact, 'rejoices in the truth' (1 Cor 13:6)."[6] He adds, "*Only in truth does charity shine forth*, only in truth can charity be authentically lived. Truth is the light that gives meaning and value to charity."[7] Yes, expressing truth without compassion, kindness, patience, and understanding turns cold, harsh, ugly, and judgmental, and hence, in short, truth without love is nothing (1 Cor 13:2). Vice-versa: Love without truth is, however, blind, sentimental, and empty. Says Benedict XVI, "In a culture without truth, this is the fatal risk facing love. It falls prey to contingent subjective emotions and opinions, the word 'love' is abused and distorted."[8] Rather than overlooking truth or love, however, in the context of the Church's pastoral practice, we need to show the *interdependency* of love and truth. Authentic expressions of charity are not possible outside of or in opposition to the truth. This is a constant theme in Benedict's theology. As then Fr. Ratzinger wrote in 1973, "Love is of no avail. It serves no purpose if truth is not on its side. Only when truth and love are in harmony can man know joy. For it is truth that makes man free."[9] Returning to Benedict:

---

[5] Some paragraphs in this article are adapted from Echeverria, *"In the Beginning. . ." A Theology of the Body* (Eugene, Oregon: Pickwick Publications, 2010), Chapter 6-7.

[6] Pope Benedict XVI, *Caritas in Veritate*, §3. http://w2.vatican.va/content/benedict-xvi/en/encyclicals/documents/hf_ben-xvi_enc_20090629_caritas-in-veritate.html.

[7] *Caritas in Veritate*, §3.

[8] Benedict XVI, *Caritas in Veritate*, §3.

[9] Joseph Ratzinger (Benedict XVI), *Principles of Catholic Theology*, 80. On the corollary of love and truth, see also, John Paul II, "Canonization of Edith Stein and Homily," §6: "St. Benedicta of the Cross says to us all: Do not accept

Hence the need to link charity with truth not only in the sequence, pointed out by Saint Paul, of *veritas in caritate* (Eph 4:15), but also in the inverse and complementary sequence of *caritas in veritate*. Truth needs to be sought, found and expressed within the "economy" of charity, but charity in its turn needs to be understood, confirmed and practiced in the light of truth.[10]

Speaking the truth in charity (Eph 4:15) is the context in which I consider the question of the pastoral care of individuals in spiritually and morally problematic relationships.

This question must deal directly with the eternal significance of the moral choices that people make, indeed, with their eternal salvation. In this light, we can understand why St. Paul consistently urges us to make choices that are worthy of the calling that we have received in Christ (Eph 4:1; Phil 1:27; Col 1:9). In particular, he identifies the risk posed by, especially *but not only*, sexual offenses: "Do you not know that the unrighteous will not inherit the kingdom of God? Stop deceiving yourselves: Neither sexually immoral persons [*pornoi*, i.e., like the incestuous man], nor idolaters, nor adulterers, nor 'soft men' [*malakoi*, i.e., men who feminize themselves to attract male sex partners], nor men who lie with a male [*arsenokoitai*, a term formed from the Levitical prohibition of male homosexual practice] . . . shall inherit the kingdom of God (1 Cor 6:9-10)."[11] The *Catechism of the Catholic Church* instructs us that

---

anything as the truth if it lacks love. And do not accept anything as love which lacks truth! One without the other becomes a destructive life."

[10] Benedict XVI, *Caritas in Veritate*, §2.

[11] See also Gal 5:19-21; Eph 5:3-5; 1 Thess 4:2-8. I am using Robert Gagnon's translation of 1 Cor 6:9-11. For a thorough exegetical justification of this translation of the passive and active partners in homosexual acts, see his *The Bible and Homosexual Practice*, 303-339.

certain choices result "in the loss of charity and the privation of sanctifying grace, that is, of the state of grace." The *Catechism* adds, "If it is not redeemed by repentance and God's forgiveness, it causes exclusion from Christ's kingdom and the eternal death of hell." How is that so? Because, the *Catechism* concludes, "our freedom has the power to make choices for ever, with no turning back."[12] This focus makes the Church's pastoral practice a life-and-death matter. Clearly, then, our pastoral practice should be informed by the sense of urgency for the lives of people and that of their eternal salvation.

I think it is necessary to begin my reflections on the pastoral care of individuals in spiritually and morally problematic relationships by defining the meaning of "pastoral" in the notion of pastoral care. I know of no better attempt to describe this meaning than the one given by Joseph Ratzinger in his explanation of what it means to speak of Vatican II as a pastoral council. He explains: "'Pastoral' should not mean nebulous, without substance, merely 'edifying'—meanings sometimes given to it. Rather what is meant is positive care for the man of today who is not helped by condemnations and who has been told for too long what is false and what he may not do. Modern man really wishes to hear what is true. He has, indeed, not heard enough truth, enough of the positive message of faith for our time, enough of what the faith has to say to our age."[13] Christianity has a life-affirming message grounded in the truth.

We find precisely this interdependency in the pastoral approach of John Paul II. He emphasizes "the coexistence and mutual influence of two equally important principles."

---

[12] *Catechism of the Catholic Church*, §1861,

[13] Joseph Ratzinger, *Theological Highlights of Vatican II*, trans. Henry Traub, S.J., et al. (New York: Paulist Press, 1966), 23.

> The first principle is that of compassion and mercy, whereby the Church, as the continuer in history of Christ's presence and work, not wishing the death of the sinner but that the sinner should be converted and live, and careful not to break the bruised reed or to quench the dimly burning wick, ever seeks to offer, as far as possible, the path of return to God and of reconciliation with him. The other principle is that of truth and consistency, whereby the Church does not agree to call good evil and evil good. Basing herself on these two complementary principles, the Church can only invite her children who find themselves in these painful situations to approach the divine mercy by other ways, not however through the sacraments of penance and the Eucharist until such time as they have attained the required dispositions.[14]

In the light of the Church's ecclesiology, we can see that these two equally important principles of mercy and truth are grounded in the Church's nature as both Mother and Teacher.[15] John Paul II explains:

> The Church's teaching, and in particular her firmness in defending the universal and permanent validity of the precepts prohibiting intrinsically evil acts, is not infrequently seen as the sign of an intolerable intransigence, particularly with regard to the enormously complex and conflict-filled situations present in the moral life of individuals and of society today; this intransigence

---

[14] John Paul II, *Reconcilatio et Paenitentia*, Apostolic Exhortation, December 2, 1984, §34. http://w2.vatican.va/content/john-paul-ii/en/apost_exhortations/ documents/hf_jp-ii_exh_02121984_reconciliatio-et-paenitentia.html.

[15] John Paul II, *Familiaris Consortio*, §33. http://w2.vatican.va/content/john-paul-ii/en/apost_exhortations/documents/hf_jp-ii_exh_19811122_familiaris-consortio.html.

is said to be in contrast with the Church's motherhood. The Church, one hears, is lacking in understanding and compassion. But the church's motherhood can never in fact be separated from her teaching mission, which she must always carry out as the faithful Bride of Christ, who is the Truth in person. "As Teacher, she never tires of proclaiming the moral norm... The Church is in no way the author or the arbiter of this norm. In obedience to the truth which is Christ, whose image is reflected in the nature and dignity of the human person, the Church interprets the moral norm and proposes it to all people of good will, without concealing its demands of radicalness and perfection."[16]

In fact, genuine understanding and compassion must mean love for the person, for his true good, for his authentic freedom. And this does not result, certainly, from concealing or weakening moral truth, but rather from proposing it in its most profound meaning as an outpouring of God's eternal Wisdom, which we have received in Christ, and as a service to man, to the growth of his freedom and to the attainment of his happiness.

In the matter, then, of the coexistence and mutual influence of the two equally important principles of mercy and truth, John Paul II provides us with a set of conceptual distinctions to understand the dynamics of moral progress, namely, the "law of gradualness" and the "gradualness of the law."[17] I have discussed this distinction in Chapter 3 and so I will not return to it fully here. In sum, on the one hand, the "law of gradual-

---

[16] John Paul II, *Familiaris Consortio*, §34, as cited in John Paul II, *Veritatis Splendor*, §95.

[17] John Paul II, *Familiaris Consortio*, §34.

ness" entails that the Church must be sensitive to a man's moral progress, namely, that he is striving to become good by stages of moral growth. The former is, according to John Paul, a step-by-step moral advance in becoming good and realizing the standard of Christian holiness. In this context, we may speak of a man's moral immaturity, based on distinguishing between the "person-I-am" from the "person-I-ought-to-be."[18] Here, too, we should understand St. Paul pastoral admonition, "Brothers, if anyone is caught in any transgression, you who are spiritual should restore him in a spirit of gentleness." (Gal 6:1)

On the other hand, there is the idea of the "gradualness of the law." This understanding of the role of the moral law in the Christian life turns the *obliging* force of the law into an *aspiring* force, rendering the moral law an ideal. Furthermore, this view of the law holds that there are "in divine law various levels or forms of precept for various persons and conditions."[19] Contrary to this view, John Paul II argues, "They [those struggling to achieve moral good by stages of growth] cannot however look on the law as merely an ideal to be achieved in the future: they must consider it as a command of Christ the Lord to overcome difficulties with constancy."[20] He explains, "And so what is known as 'the law of gradualness' or step-by-step advance cannot be identified with 'gradualness of the law', as if there were different degrees or forms of precept in God's law for different individuals and situations." What this idea of the law means is, according to the late moral theologian Germain Grisez, that there are "gradations of the law," namely, "the whole of Christian

---

[18] See Jones, "Sexual Orientation and Reason: On the Implications of False Beliefs about Homosexuality." He appeals to this distinction, explicitly drawing on the anthropological thought of John Paul II, as cited in George Weigel, *Witness to Hope: The Biography of Pope John Paul II* (New York: HarperCollins, 1999), 8.

[19] Grisez, *The Way of the Lord Jesus*, I, 687.

[20] John Paul II, *Familiaris Consortio*, §34.

Ch. 5: Mercy and Truth 405

morality—or, at least, many norms traditionally received as binding precepts—is [such] that willful violations are acceptable provided one looks forward to living according to the norm at some time in the future."[21] This view then legitimizes situation ethics in our pastoral care.

Christian Anthropology, Homosexuality, and Objectively Disordered Inclination

In Chapter 3, I was critical of Ad de Bruijne's arguments for justifying sexual diversity in his study *Verbonden voor het Leven: Een theologisch-ethisch voorstel rond homosexualiteit en seksuele diversiteit*. His aim was to transcend the erotic cultural wars but his proposal is an utter failure. His argument resembles a "theology of compromise,"[22] that is, a revisionist theology best described as expressing the pathos liberal theology. His proposal to transcend these wars between orthodox Christianity's traditional sexual morality and the sexual liberationist ideology by arguing that the latter is really a correction of the former, and hence that we can see the latter as a renewal movement within orthodox Christianity's understanding of the nature, meaning, and purpose of human sexuality, is mistaken on all counts. His understanding of the sexual revolution, its presuppositions regarding the nature of the sexual urge, its materialistic anthropology, absolutizing of freedom, rejection of nature, and its impact on our culture is not really probed to its depth by de Bruijne in order to see why it is at odds with orthodox Christianity's traditional sexual morality and the fundamental presuppositions that undergird this morality.

Confusion. Division. Chaos. Heresy. These terms describe the effects of the serious flirtations with the *Zeitgeist* currently afflicting to a

---

[21] Grisez, *The Way of the Lord Jesus*, I, 687.
[22] Eijk, *De Band van de Liefde*, 34.

lesser or greater degree the Catholic Church—see the German and Belgian episcopacy—and other Protestant churches—Dutch Reformed, Episcopal, Methodist, Presbyterian Church (USA)—regarding the basics of traditional Christian sexual morality, especially homosexuality, and Christian anthropology.[23]

Thankfully, there are voices of sanctified reason in this spiritual and cultural war over sexual morality. For one, the Catholic Church's normative teaching from the Congregation for the Doctrine of the Faith, *Persona Humana* (1977), *Homosexualitatis Problema* (1987), the universal *Catechism of the Catholic Church* (1992), John Paul II, *Man and Woman He Created Them: A Theology of the Body* (2006), and the Congregation for Education, *"Male and Female He Created Them": Towards a Path of Dialogue on the Question of Gender Theory in Education* (2019). For another, there is the recent study by Willem Jacobus Kardinaal Eijk of the Netherlands, *De Band van de Liefde: Katholieke Huwelijksmoraal en Seksuele Ethiek*. Still another is the just-approved 175-page report to the Christian Reformed Church (CRC) Synod 2022 from the *Committee to Articulate a Foundation-Laying Biblical Theology of Human Sexuality*. Both the Catholic Church, furthermore, and this report understand that Christian sexual morality is grounded in basic Christian truths about God, man, and the world, such that you cannot change the former without undoing the latter.

The overarching hermeneutical framework for understanding normative sexual morality is creation, fall, redemption, consummation. For example, Genesis 1:27 and 2:24 are paradigmatic texts for a creational sexual ethic. As the CRC report puts it, "What God has *proscribed* as his normative will for men and women [is] rooted in creation." The 1986

---

[23] Echeverria, "Male and Female He Created Them: Ecumenical Reflections," in *Homiletics and Pastoral Review*, December 23, 2020.

letter *Homosexualitatis problema* to the Bishops of the Catholic Church by the Congregation for the Doctrine of the Faith makes this very point.

> Providing a basic plan for understanding this entire discussion of homosexuality is the theology of creation we find in Genesis. God, in his infinite wisdom and love, brings into existence all of reality as a reflection of his goodness. He fashions mankind, male and female, in his own image and likeness. Human beings, therefore, are nothing less than the work of God himself; and in the complementarity of the sexes, they are called to reflect the inner unity of the Creator. They do this in a striking way in their cooperation with him in the transmission of life by a mutual donation of the self to the other. In Genesis 3, we find that this truth about persons being an image of God has been obscured by original sin. There inevitably follows a loss of awareness of the covenantal character of the union these persons had with God and with each other. The human body retains its "spousal significance" but this is now clouded by sin.[24]

The biblical revelation has epistemic priority over God's creation revelation, but what these texts assert about the structure of creation grounds "the church's teaching on premarital sex, extramarital sex, adultery, polyamory, pornography, and homosexual sex," and others, such as gender dysphoria and disorders of sexual development, the Report rightly argues throughout. Rather than being creational, these sexual matters, for example, same-sex attraction, reflect the brokenness of our sinful world, the disordered creation that exists since the fall. A hermeneutical framework that takes seriously creational structures, as leading

---

[24] Letter to the Bishops of the Catholic Church on the Pastoral Care of Homosexual Persons (vatican.va), §6.

Catholic Dominican theologian Romanus Cessario puts it, "seeks to contemplate an immanent wisdom in the universe . . . reflecting the ordering wisdom of the divine plan for creation."[25] Significantly, this realist emphasis on the objective structures of creation aligns Roman Catholicism with the tradition of Reformed Christianity, in particular, the CRC Report.

Genesis 1:27 asserts that God made man in His image, male and female He created them. This assertion is true to objective reality such that it *excludes* a state of affairs, according to the Report, in which "God created sexuality as a spectrum, with some human beings falling somewhere *in between* male and female. . . . [This] is not only foreign to the text but also contradicts the obvious meaning and significance of sexuality in the text. To read the notion of sexuality as a spectrum into Genesis 1:27 is to isolate that verse and rip it from its context." This, too, is the view of Reformed Baptist American theologian Gregg Allison urging that the account in Genesis 1:27 is binary and not a spectrum.[26] "Important to consider is the language of 'separation': (1) 'And God *separated* the light from the darkness' (Gen. 1:4), (2) 'And God said. Let there be an expanse in the midst of the waters, and let it *separate* the waters from the waters'" (1:6 ESV). (3) And God said, 'Let there be lights in the expanse of the heavens to *separate* the day from the night . . . to *separate* the light from the darkness'" (1:6 ESV). In sum, concludes Allison, "My conclusion is that the language of the creation narrative emphasizes disconnection and distinction, not the intermediate notion [of spectrum]."[27] To his credit, De Bruijne doesn't go this exegetical route. But, as I have shown

---

[25] In John Paul II, *Man and Woman He Created Them* 18.3, and the *Catechism of the Catholic Church*, §§ 2331–2400, we explicitly find this realism.

[26] Gregory R. Allison, *Embodied: Living as a Whole People in a Fractured World* (Grand Rapids, MI: Baker Books, 2021), 44n7.

[27] Allison, *Embodied*, 44n7.

Ch. 5: Mercy and Truth

in Chapter 3, he does seek to justify eschatologically "ontic novelty" in the realm of human interrelations, such that the sexual variation of so-called LGBTQ+ may be affirmed. I have criticized his view in that chapter so I won't return to it now.

When asked about divorce (Mark 10:6–7; Matthew 19:3–9), Jesus calls us back to the law of creation affirmed in those texts, rather than beginning with man's fallen state and its "fallen sexual desires and intimate experiences as sinful human beings." As the Report states, "He grounds the ethic of marriage in the purposes of God from creation." The unity attained in becoming "two-in-one-flesh" in marriage is grounded in the order of creation (Genesis 1:27; 2:24), persists through the regime of sin, and is affirmed and simultaneously renewed by grace through the redemptive sacrament of marriage in Christ.[28] Real bodily oneness, a one-flesh union between a man and a woman, *actualizes* marital unity.

There is an inextricable creational nexus of permanence, twoness of male and female, and sexual differentiation for marriage, such that the latter is a fundamental prerequisite for the two to become one flesh. In particular, Genesis 2:24 affirms that marriage requires sexual difference of man and woman, with the bodily-sexual act as a foundational prerequisite, indeed, as *intrinsic* to a two-in-one-flesh union of man and woman: "So then they are no longer two but *one flesh*" (Mark 10:8).

Furthermore, the moral and sacramental, that is, redemptive, significance of the two-in-one-flesh *bodily* unity as foundational to the marital form of love is constitutive of this framework. However, it is precisely the embodiment of human persons, as man and woman, which has been lost in our culture, even amongst some Catholic and Reformed Christians, for a proper understanding of marriage and, more generally, for a

---

[28] See *Catechism of the Catholic Church*, §§1601–1666.

creational sexual ethic. According to the Report, "At the heart of the biblical understanding of humanity is the teaching that our bodies matter. The Bible does not pit the soul against the body." Contrary to the anthropological dualism of soul and body, the Catholic tradition also affirms that the body is intrinsic to selfhood because the human person *is* bodily.[29] Cardinal Eijk states this point well:

> The Catholic view is opposed both to an exaggerated individualism and to a dualistic view of man. According to the Catholic view of man, the human person is a substantial unity of soul and body. The body, including one's biological sex, belongs essentially to the human person and is therefore an intrinsic value.[30]

Elsewhere, John Paul II explains that the body is intrinsic to self-identity: "Man is a subject not only by his self-consciousness and by self-determination, but also based on his own body. *The structure of this body is such that it permits him to be the author of genuinely human activity.* In this activity, the body expresses the person."[31] The body is intrinsic to one's own self and, indeed, it "shares in the dignity of 'the image of God'."[32]

The Report correctly concludes from the idea that the body is intrinsic to selfhood that "this means that we cannot treat a person's subjectively experienced gender as a fact of their existence independent of their biological nature. We cannot claim that a person's true identity resides in their subjective sense of self, as distinct from the body with which they were born." Furthermore, the Report also concludes, "Due to the fall,

---

[29] *Catechism of the Catholic Church*, §§362–368.
[30] Eijk, *De Band van de Liefde*, 110-111.
[31] See John Paul II, *Man and Woman He Created Them*, 7.2.
[32] *Catechism of the Catholic Church*, §364.

Ch. 5: Mercy and Truth   411

through no fault of their own, some people experience a disconnect between their gender identity and their sex. Nevertheless, there is no redemption in embracing this disconnect as a sign of God's good intent." The Congregation for Education argues this crucial point in its 2019 document.

Regarding homosexuality, the Catholic tradition in 1977, 1987, and 1992 distinguishes being same-sex attraction and acting on those attractions. "[H]omosexual acts are *intrinsically disordered* and can in no case be approved of." Why? "For according to the objective moral order, homosexual relations are acts which lack an essential and indispensable finality." The *Catechism* later explains: "They are contrary to the natural law. They close the sexual act to the gift of life [because they are not unitive, and only a unitive act can be procreative]. They do not proceed from a genuine affective and sexual complementarity. Under no circumstances can they be approved."[33]

The Church's Magisterial teaching about homosexuality is expressed in two ways: both as a *condition* (expressive of an inclination, attraction, or desire) and as an *activity*.[34] The Church rightly understands that Holy Scripture's condemnation of homosexuality pertains

---

[33] *Catechism of the Catholic Church*, §2357.

[34] See Magisterial documents of the Catholic Church's teaching on homosexuality, such as *Persona Humana* (1975), *Homosexualitatis problema* (1986), and the relevant paragraphs from the *Catechism of the Catholic Church* on sexual ethics (§§2357-2359). I refrain from using the term "orientation" in order to avoid the implication that some persons are "constitutionally" homosexual in a biological or genetic sense. On the question of whether same-sex attraction is genetically determined before birth, and on the possible causes of that attraction, see the document of the Catholic Medical Association, *Homosexuality and Hope: Questions and Answers about Same-Sex Attraction* (2008). http://www.cathmed.org/issues_resources/publications/position_papers/homosexuality_and_hope/. Furthermore, Benedict Ashley, OP, and Kevin D.

not only to outward acts but also to the inward condition, to homosexual actions as well as to the desires or inclinations constitutive of the homosexual condition itself. First, as condition, "Homosexuality refers to relations between men or between women who experience an exclusive or predominant sexual attraction toward persons of the same sex."[35] Furthermore, as activity, "Basing itself on Sacred Scripture, which presents homosexual acts as acts of grave depravity, tradition has always declared that 'homosexual acts are intrinsically disordered'. They are contrary to the natural law. They close the sexual act to the gift of life. They do not proceed from a genuine affective and sexual complementarity. Under no circumstances can they be approved."[36] Same-sex attraction may come "from a false education, from a lack of normal sexual development, from habit, from bad example, or from other similar causes."[37] In addition, there may be other causative factors for homosexuality from a person's

---

O'Rourke, OP, are, in my judgment, right: "Even if it is eventually proven that homosexuality is genetic in origin, this defect, like other genetic defects, would not excuse aberrant behavior, but would call for continuing efforts to find a remedy. It remains probable that homosexuality has multiple causes of which the principal are a dysfunctional family and early masturbatory or homosexual experiences. Thus the popular stereotype of genetically gay and lesbian persons is a social construct developed in recent years that greatly distorts the historical, biological, psychological, and social facts (Catholic Medical Association, 2004). The Church urges health professionals to treat homosexuals with respect and compassion and to encourage them to get help from psychiatrists and psychologists who regard this condition as a disorder that may be remediable. It strongly encourages objective scientific research to gain greater certainty about its etiology and possible methods of treatment" (*Health Care Ethics: A Theological Analysis*. Fifth Edition. Washington, D.C.: Georgetown University Press, 2006. 68).

[35] *Catechism of the Catholic Church*, §2357.
[36] *Catechism of the Catholic Church*, §2357.
[37] *Persona Humana*, §8.

developmental environment: they include indirect congenital influences, postnatal biological influences, macro- and micro-cultural influences from one's familial environment, and personal psychological predispositions.[38] Thus, in this light, we can understand that the condition of homosexuality is not one that is merely chosen; it is experienced as a given, not as something freely chosen. The latter is essential for the choice to be considered a sin.

Since it is not necessarily something freely chosen, some have wrongly concluded that the so-called "homosexual condition" is not only not sinful but is also something "natural." Indeed, *Homosexualitatis problema* explicitly rejects this kind of "overly benign interpretation" that some theologians give to the "homosexual condition itself, some going so far as to call it neutral or even good." Contrary to this conclusion, Monsignor Livio Melina correctly argues that the homosexual condition is experienced as "natural" by the individual "because of the disordered disposition of his being." He adds, "Saint Thomas points this out in relation to unnatural pleasures: 'What is contrary to the nature of the species becomes natural to this individual *per accidens*'." Melina concludes, "In the case of homosexuality, as in other cases, the complaint 'that's the way I am' expresses many things: the frustrating realization that one cannot change, a way of blaming nature and perhaps God for one's condition, even the unwillingness to reconsider one's attitude toward reality."[39]

---

[38] Paul Sullins, "The gay gene myth has been exploded," in *Mercatornet*, September 3, 2019. https://www.mercatornet.com/conjugality/view/the-gay-gene-myth-has-been-exploded/22824. Sullins' article is a commentary on the recent findings in a study of the genetic basis of homosexuality published in the journal Science: https://science.sciencemag.org/content/365/6456/eaat7693.

[39] Melina, "Homosexual Inclination as an 'Objective Disorder'," 132. Melina is citing, *Summa Theologiae* I-II, q. 31, a. 7.

Furthermore, I think that this "overly benign interpretation" in part derives from characterizing the "choice" as if it were a bare choice, lacking context, and other causal factors for the homosexual condition, as described above. Robert Gagnon rightly states, "Choices . . . involving response to socio-cultural stimuli [from a person's developmental environment]. . . may, down the end of a long road, lead to greater or lesser likelihood of homosexual identification."[40] In this light, we can understand why it is not inconsistent to hold that a person freely chooses to engage in homosexual practice in light of a "plurality of elements and factors in the personality that are meant to make up a unified tendency upon which the subject constructs his own sexual identity and recognizes his place in relation with others and the surrounding world."[41] This means, as *Homosexualitatis problema* puts it (§11), that we must reject the "unfounded and demeaning assumption that the sexual behavior of homosexual persons is always and totally compulsive and therefore in- culpable."

Furthermore, the Church's teaching on homosexuality does not accept the homosexual condition itself. How could she accept that condition when embedded in that condition "is a more or less strong tendency ordered toward an intrinsic moral evil [?]" Since the Church regards the "inclination itself . . . as an objective disorder," then it is not solely ho- mosexual acts that are intrinsically disordered and thus objectively evil,

---

[40] Robert Gagnon, "Sexual Orientation," email correspondence, July 8, 2005.

[41] Melina, "Homosexual Inclination as an 'Objective Disorder'," 132.

Ch. 5: Mercy and Truth

but the inclination itself is equally disordered as the source of man's sinful homosexual activities.[42] In other words, as Mansini and Welch correctly state the teaching of the Church in *Homosexualitatis problema*, "if homosexual activity itself is always intrinsically immoral, and homosexual tendencies are therefore always objectively disordered because they incline to what is always intrinsically immoral, then it makes good sense to say that his [homosexual's] sexual affections, as such, are not good. They do not bear on the feminine, which is the target of mature male psychosexual desire. And therefore, since they are deep seated, they prevent 'affective maturity', which means, if it means anything, having good desires rightly ordered."[43]

Clearly, then, the act/orientation distinction is morally relevant only insofar as it allows us to distinguish between culpable homosexual acts and the interior source of those acts in an individual's same-sex attraction for which he may not be morally culpable. However, it should be abundantly clear that the act/orientation distinction, as the Church understands it, explicitly rejects the interpretation of that orientation as morally neutral—rather the homosexual desire itself is an objectively disordered inclination or propensity to evil. What, then, is the origin of that inclination if not the choices that men make?

Theologically, the ultimate origin of this condition, and hence those homosexual tendencies that incline an individual to what is always intrinsically immoral, is the Fall. John Finnis, Aidan Nichols[44], Helmut

---

[42] *Homosexualitatis problema*, §3.

[43] Guy Mansini, O.S.B., and Lawrence J. Welch, "In Conformity to Christ," *First Things*, April 2006. https://www.firstthings.com/article/2006/04/in-conformity-to-christ. The article is an exposition and interpretation of the November 29, 2005, instruction concerning the admission of men with homosexual tendencies to seminaries released by the Congregation for Catholic Education in Rome.

[44] Nichols, *Epiphany: A Theological Introduction to Catholicism*, 423.

Thielicke[45], and others are right that the intrinsically disordered inclination of this objectively evil condition, which reflects the brokenness of our sinful world, the disordered creation that exists since the Fall, should be seen as a specific manifestation of the concupiscence that comes from original sin and leads to sin but is itself not, necessarily, consciously chosen sin.

Furthermore, theologically, if the ultimate origin of the homosexual condition is our fallen human nature, then there would be no justification for seeing homosexuality from the order of creation as a creational given, a normal variant of sexuality, and hence there would be no parity between homosexuality and heterosexuality in light of that order. Therefore, Scripture's condemnation of homosexuality pertains not only to outward acts but also to the inward desires and inclinations constitutive of the condition itself. For, according to the Scriptures, it is not only actions that are wrong, but also the desire to do such actions (see Matt 5:27-29; Rom 13:14; Col 3:5-6; 1 Pet 2:11). This point should be clear from the fact that Jesus interiorizes the demands of the moral law, condemning not only the outward acts of adultery but also the "adultery of mere desire."[46] "And Jesus said, 'What comes out of a person is what defiles him. For from within, out of the heart of man, come evil thoughts, sexual immorality, theft, murder, adultery, coveting, wickedness, deceit, sensuality, envy, slander, pride, foolishness. All these evil things come from within, and they defile a person'." (Mark 7: 20-23).[47]

---

[45] Helmut Thielicke, *The Ethics of Sex*, trans. John W. Doberstein (New York: Harper & Row, 1964), 282.

[46] *Catechism of the Catholic Church*, §2380.

[47] See Chapter 3 in Echeverria, *Pope Francis: The Legacy of Vatican II*, second edition 2019, 108-154.

Briefly, what this means is that the desire for sex with a person of the same sex is a sinful desire. This desire is contrary to the moral law of creation, and hence a desire God expressly forbids.

In 1987, the then-Cardinal Ratzinger critically observed, "An overly benign interpretation was given to the homosexual condition itself, some going so far as to call it neutral, or even good." The CRC Report suggests evidence of this benign interpretation in failing to grasp the intrinsically disordered nature of same-sex attraction. This is puzzling since, according to the CRC report, the ultimate origin of the homosexual condition, and hence same-sex attraction, is our fallen human nature. On the one hand, the Report states, "[T]here is no sin in being attracted to the same sex. We only sin if we act on our sexual attraction." It also acknowledges that St. Paul's argument in Romans 1:24–27 is clear: "sexual acts between a female and another female or between a male and another male are 'unnatural' and wrong, because such conduct goes against one's *created* nature." But here the CRC Report conflates two things. One, desiring sex with a person of the same sex is a sinful desire, as I argued above, because it contradicts the moral law of creation. Two, giving into a homosexual desire in thought life and acting on that desire in behavior.

Therefore, the crux here is the question whether the Scripture condemns same-sex attraction, despite the Report's demurral. On its face, according to the Scriptures, it is not only actions that are wrong, but also the desire to do such actions (see Matthew 5:27–29; Romans 13:14; Colossians 3:5–6; 1 Peter 2:11). This point should be clear from the fact that Jesus interiorizes the demands of the moral law, condemning not only the outward acts of adultery but also the "adultery of mere desire."[48]

---

[48] *Catechism of the Catholic Church*, §2380; see Mark 7:20–23.

Thus, as Ratzinger explains, "Although the particular inclination of the homosexual person is not a sin, it is a more or less strong tendency ordered toward an intrinsic moral evil; and thus the inclination itself must be seen as an objective disorder." The Report's overly benign interpretation of same-sex attraction is in tension with the logic of its sexual orthodoxy. Since the Catholic Church regards the "inclination itself . . . as an objective disorder," then, *pace* the CRC Report, it is not *solely* homosexual acts that are intrinsically disordered and thus objectively evil, but the inclination itself is equally disordered as the source of man's sinful homosexual activities. Then, we must acknowledge that the desire itself must be sinful.

Through these documents from both traditions, may Catholic and Reformed Christians committed to sexual orthodoxy find new ways to reach out to Christians from other traditions and to the culture.

The Legitimacy of Homosexual Identity?

The controverted book by James Martin, SJ, presupposes the legitimacy of homosexual identity.[49] Notwithstanding his claim, Fr. Martin's presupposition is *not* "well within church teaching,"[50] particularly when we consider the anthropological orthodoxy of the Church's teaching—man's creation as male and female (Genesis 1:27; Roman 1)—in light of referring to the condition of homosexuality as an "objective disorder."[51] Thus, it is my contention that Fr. Martin implicitly presupposes that "same-sex" attraction is good from the order of creation. That is, he asks

---

[49] James Martin, SJ, *Building a Bridge*, Revised and Expanded (New York: HarperCollins, 2018 [2017]).

[50] Martin, *Building a Bridge*, 9.

[51] *Catechism of the Catholic Church*, §2358.

a homosexual to reflect on himself in light of Psalm 139 in order to affirm his identity, that as a homosexual *qua* homosexual he is "wonderfully made."[52] In this connection, it follows that he holds it to be legitimate to ground human identity in homosexual "orientation," which encompasses an individual's personal and social identity. How does Fr. Martin justify the legitimacy of this self-description—indeed, insisting on it? The only criterion that he suggests that legitimizes it is individual experience. Individual experience becomes a supreme court for adjudicating the gospel, the teachings of the Church. This leads him to the conclusion that a person's homosexuality is a *creational given* rather than being in itself inherently disordered. However, as Aidan Nichols correctly states, "It is not experience we should trust but the transmutation of experience by Scripture and Tradition."[53] One would then take as normative the truth that God made man, our created nature, as male and female for each other (Gen 1:27), and that this nature is savagely wounded by sin, broken, but, thanks be to God, it is redeemed in Christ through his atoning work.

In between the first and second edition of his book, Fr. Martin responded in an article to the criticism that he rejected the Church's teaching on the ethics of homosexuality by supposedly laying out clearly and accurately "official church teaching."[54] I contend that Fr. Martin misunderstands magisterial teaching regarding homosexuality. As I will show below, he is not alone in this misunderstanding.

---

[52] Martin, *Building a Bridge*, 134-137.

[53] Nichols, *Christendom Awake: On Reenergizing the Church in Culture*, 41-52 and at 41.

[54] James Martin, SJ, "What is the official church teaching on homosexuality? Responding to a commonly asked question," *America*, April 6, 2018. https://www.americamagazine.org/faith/2018/04/06/what-official-church-teaching-homosexuality-responding-commonly-asked-question.

He claims that, as a Catholic priest, he has never challenged nor will he ever challenge those teachings.[55] However, that claim is grossly unclear, not only intellectually but also practically. First, despite his disclaimer that he would never challenge those teachings, that claim is surely not the same thing as saying that he affirms the *truth* of the Church's teachings as the "lights along the path of faith." There is no evidence that Fr. Martin holds that teaching to be true, especially because he makes no reference to the organic connection between the teaching and one's spiritual life such that this teaching is necessary for authentic human flourishing. He never draws on that teaching to "illuminate it [the spiritual life] and make it secure." He leaves same-sex attracted people alienated from that teaching such that neither their "life is upright, [nor there] intellect and heart [and hence it] will [not] be open to welcome the light shed by the dogmas of faith."[56] As I show below, this is especially the case with respect to the Catholic tradition's Christian anthropology. Practically speaking, furthermore, given Fr. Martin's enthusiastic and vocal support for "Pride" events, for pro-homosexual organizations, such as New Ways Ministry and Out at St. Paul's, he leaves no doubt that his statements and activity regarding same-sex related issues have caused and continue to cause great confusion.[57]

I now will focus on the foundational presupposition of his controverted book, namely, the legitimacy of homosexual identity. In other

---

[55] Martin, "What is the official church teaching on homosexuality?"

[56] *Catechism of the Catholic Church*, §89.

[57] Archbishop Charles J. Chaput, O.F.M. Cap., "Fr. James Martin and Catholic belief," in *CatholicPhilly*, September 19, 2019. http://catholicphilly.com/2019/09/archbishop-chaput-column/father-james-martin-and-catholic-belief/. See also, Robert P. George, "Fr. James Martin, Friendship and Dialogue, and the Truth about Human Sexuality," *Public Discourse*, June 17, 2018. https://www.thepublicdiscourse.com/2018/06/21846/.

words, Fr. Martin affirms, without any arguments, that same-sex attraction is a valid basis for establishing one's human identity. Indeed, given its alleged legitimacy, he is doubtful about referring to a person's sexuality [as] "objectively disordered."[58] Is this only a matter of linguistic formulation or a matter of rejecting the claim that being sexually attracted to people of the same sex is wrong? He explains:

> Our sexuality, in a sense, touches everything we do, including the way we love, even when the sexual expression of that love is neither involved nor even contemplated. So to call a person's sexuality "objectively disordered" is to tell a person that all of his or her love, even the most chaste, is disordered. For many LGBT Catholics, that seems unnecessarily cruel.

Now, Fr. Martin makes clear that he understands this phrase to relate "to the orientation, not the person."[59] Furthermore, since it does not refer to the person *qua* person, the phrase "objective disorder" . . . "does not detract from the inherent dignity of any human being, since God created all human beings equal and good."[60] This is correct. Still, Fr. Martin calls for an amendment of the Church's language calling a person's sexuality "objectively disordered" as found in the *Catechism of the Catholic Church*. Is he simply objecting to the language used to describe the homosexual condition as "inherently disordered"? Does he object because many experience that language as needlessly hurtful and cruel? Fr. Martin cites the statement of an Australian bishop, Vincent Long Van Nguyen, who in 2016 at the Synod on the Family states:

---

[58] Martin, *Building a Bridge*, 74.
[59] Martin, *Building a Bridge*, 73.
[60] Martin, "What is the official church teaching on homosexuality?"

> We cannot talk about the integrity of creation, the universal and inclusive love of God, while at the same time colluding with the forces of oppression in the ill-treatment of racial minorities, women, and homosexual persons. . . . It won't wash with young people, especially when we purport to treat gay people with love and compassion and yet define their sexuality as "intrinsically disordered."

This objection is hard to fathom. The fall into sin, original sin, has corrupted the image of God in all men. "The harmony . . . thanks to original [holiness and] justice is now destroyed: the control of the soul's spiritual faculties over the body is shattered; the union of man and woman becomes subject to tensions, their relations henceforth marked by lust and domination. Harmony with creation is broken: visible creation has become alien and hostile to man."[61] And so the same question could be asked, indeed, has been asked throughout the history of the Church and Christian theology: does my fallen human nature undercut the *imago Dei* and, if so, in what sense? Put differently, how are we to understand the central question of man's humanity *in* his sinfulness? Does the Fall literally dehumanize man, depriving him of his essential nature?

We are all children of Adam and by virtue of this unity we are all implicated in his sin.[62] St. Paul affirms: "By one man's disobedience many [that is, all men] were made sinners": "sin came into the world through one man and death through sin, and so death spread to all men

---

[61] *Catechism of the Catholic Church*, §400. Furthermore, "Because of man, creation is now subject 'to its bondage to decay' [Rom 8:21]. Finally, the consequence explicitly foretold for this disobedience will come true: man will 'return to the ground' [Gen 3:19], for out of it he was taken. *Death makes its entrance into human history* [see Rom 5:12]" [Ibid.] See also, *Catechism*, § 405.

[62] *Catechism of the Catholic Church*, §402.

Ch. 5: Mercy and Truth

because all men sinned" (Rom 5:12, 19). This original sin is the state or underlying condition of man's alienation from God that is the source of visible acts of sin. It affects human nature, resulting in a deep flaw in that nature and hence a fallen state. Helmut Thielicke correctly remarks in his gloss on Romans 5:18 ("one man's trespass led to condemnation for all men"): "We are all under the same condemnation and each of us has received his 'share' of it." He then draws this implication: "In any case, from this point of view the homosexual share of that condemnation has no greater gravity which would justify any Pharisaic feelings of self-righteousness and integrity on the part of us 'normal' persons."[63]

Of course, God didn't create man flawed. John Paul II rightly says, "The splendor of truth shines forth in all the works of the Creator and, in a special way, in man, created in the image and likeness of God (cf. Gen 1:26)."[64] Thus, we must distinguish between his nature as created by God and the crisis effected by original sin itself. This fallen state affects the whole of man's nature, every aspect of human existence—personal, social, cultural, and the like. In the history of Christian thought sin has been likened to an illness, moral guilt, an enslaving force, as well as the antithesis between two comprehensive ways of living (death and life [Rom 6: 3-8], darkness and light [John 1: 5; 1 Pet 2: 9], flesh and spirit [Gal 5: 16-26], being lost and being found [Luke 15]).[65]

Against this background, Fr. Martin could still make clear that being sexually attracted to people of the same sex is, then, a sign of one's brokenness, an expression of man's fallen condition, and hence contrary to the Church's anthropology in which "sexuality is ordered to the conjugal

---

[63] Thielicke, *The Ethics of Sex*, 283.

[64] John Paul II writes these words in the opening sentence of *Veritatis Splendor*.

[65] On this, see McGrath, *Intellectual Don't Need God & Other Modern Myths*, 134-137.

love of man and woman"[66] given that God created man, male and female (Gen 1:27). If that were solely it, then, he would acknowledge the distinction between the normative order of creation in which God created man and the order of the fall, followed by the order of redemption. He would then take as normative the truth that God made man, our created nature, as male and female for each other (Gen 1:27), and hence that "sexuality is constitutively relative to the gender difference of male and female] and is thus in and of itself 'normally' heterosexual."[67] He would add that this nature is savagely wounded by sin, broken, but, thanks be to God, it is redeemed in Christ through his atoning work. However, it is clear from the passage cited above that he does not think that there is anything wrong as such with being sexually attracted to people of the same sex. He infers this simply from the claim that being a homosexual is not a sin because it is not one that is merely chosen. Fr. Martin states:

> [I]n the eyes of the church simply being gay or lesbian is not a sin—contrary to widespread belief, even among educated Catholics. That may be one of the most poorly understood of the church's teachings. Regularly I am asked questions like, "Isn't it a sin to be gay?" But this is not church teaching. Nowhere in the catechism does it say that simply being homosexual is a sin. As any reputable psychologist or psychiatrists will agree, people do not choose to be born with any particular sexual orientation.[68]

Fr. Martin misunderstands this teaching. He is not alone. It has often been misunderstood even by its supporters, or misrepresented, at times, by those who do not expressly deny the Church's teaching about

---

[66] *Catechism of the Catholic Church*, §2360.
[67] Melina, "Homosexual Inclination as an 'Objective Disorder'," 131.
[68] Martin, "What is the official church teaching on homosexuality?"

either homosexual tendencies or homosexual practice, but whose understanding of this teaching is such that they cannot consistently assert it. Indeed, some critics of the Church's teaching insist that if the individual in a homosexual condition is morally blameless, they ask, why is that individual morally blameworthy if he acts upon it? Is the Church's teaching contradictory? To avoid this charge, we must make explicit, in stating that the homosexual condition is objectively disordered, that a fallen human nature is the source of man's sinful acts. In other words, even though we may have wounds in our being for which we are not responsible, it is not correct at all to claim that that woundedness is natural and thus a legitimate source for human moral action.

The most common misunderstanding of the Church's teaching is found in the 1998 USCCB pastoral document, *Always Our Children, A Pastoral Message to Parents of Homosexual Children and Suggestions for Pastoral Ministers*. Twice the pastoral states that the homosexual condition is not sinful or immoral in itself, because an individual does not freely choose it. It refrains from speaking of the condition itself as objectively disordered because these deeply ingrained impulses incline to what is always intrinsically wrong. This leaves us with the impression that it is, therefore, morally neutral, benign, or good. However, this is clearly not the case. For example, an infertile woman did not freely choose that condition, but no one suggests that infertility is a good. Thus, denying that it is a personally chosen sin does not mean that it is not a disorder.

Another example representative of this misunderstanding, indeed, misrepresentation is the earlier statement by the "Core Council for Gay and Lesbian Students" at the University of Notre Dame, "Homosexuality and Sexual Orientation: Common Questions."[69] In reply to the question, "What does the Catholic Church say about homosexuality?" the Council replied, "Homosexual orientation in and of itself is morally neutral, but genital homosexual relations are sinful, in the same way that genital heterosexual relations outside marriage are immoral." In a more recent statement, "Beloved Friends and Allies: A Pastoral Plan for the Support and Holistic Development of GLBTQ and Heterosexual Students at the University of Notre Dame,"[70] invokes the "distinction commonly drawn between the homosexual condition or tendency and individual homosexual actions."[71] It adds, "With the American Bishops' Committee on Marriage and Family, the University defends that 'Generally, homosexual orientation is experienced as a given, not as something freely chosen. By itself, therefore, a homosexual orientation cannot be considered sinful."

There are several major things wrong with this answer, according to the Church's teaching on homosexuality that I have explained above.

First, homosexual tendencies are not morally neutral, but rather objectively disordered, as such, because they incline a man to homosexual practice that is itself intrinsically immoral. Something can be bad in some sense other than being morally sinful, for instance, the condition of infertility, or being born blind, without it being something that is

---

[69] The website of the Core Council for Gay and Lesbian Students at the University of Notre Dame does not post It only posts the 1998 document, *Always Our Children*, as well as interpretations of that teaching. http://corecouncil.nd.edu/church_response/index.shtml. This website has been taken down and replaced with another: "Beloved Friends and Allies: A Pastoral Plan for the Support and Holistic Development of GLBTQ and Heterosexual Students at the University of Notre Dame," accessed November 21, 2024, https://friendsandallies.nd.edu/.

[70] "Beloved Friends and Allies."

[71] The pastoral plan is citing from *Homosexualitatis problema*, §3.

knowingly and explicitly chosen. Still, as I argued above, it is not inconsistent to hold that a person chooses to engage in homosexual practice in light of a "plurality of elements and factors in the personality that are meant to make up a unified tendency upon which the subject constructs his own sexual identity and recognizes his place in relation with others and the surrounding world."[72]

Second, the claim that heterosexual and homosexual sexual relations are sinful *in the same way* because they manifest sins against chastity fails to recognize that homosexuality, unlike heterosexuality, is a fundamental problem because homosexual tendencies are objectively disordered. As two critics of the view represented by the Notre Dame Council recently wrote, "if homosexual activity itself is always intrinsically immoral, and homosexual tendencies are therefore always objectively disordered because they incline to what is always intrinsically immoral, then it makes good sense to say that his sexual affections, as such, are not good. They do not bear on the feminine, which is the target of mature male psychosexual desire."[73] Furthermore, this pastoral plan contradicts itself: it denies that the homosexual orientation is a disorder but simultaneously affirms that "the longstanding position of the natural law tradition of the Church that, 'sexuality is ordered to the conjugal love of man and woman' [*Catechism of the Catholic Church* §2360]."[74]

Third, the Council is, therefore, mistaken in claiming that "the Church does not say that the *homosexual orientation* is wrong; rather, it is *sexual activity between same sex persons* that is 'objectively disordered' and therefore sinful." This statement is inaccurate, giving us only a half-truth. Actually, the Church says that the source of objectively disordered homosexual activity is the homosexual condition that is itself therefore

---

[72] Melina, "Homosexual Inclination as an 'Objective Disorder'," 132.
[73] Mansini, and Welch, "In Conformity to Christ."
[74] "Beloved Friends and Allies."

always objectively disordered because it inclines to what is always intrinsically immoral. And although the Notre Dame Council and the subsequent pastoral plan of "Beloved Friends and Allies" is right to insist that the homosexual inclination is not a disease, nonetheless, it is an objective disorder, a sexual deviance, as it were, because it is unable to meet the natural goods of sexuality, of the body-soul person's creational ordering to the sexual "other."[75]

So, to say that the condition itself is not sinful is not to say, or to imply, moral neutrality. Homosexual desires are wrong in the sense of not being good, and this is not the same thing as making a moral judgment about the personal moral guilt of an individual who engages in homosexual activity. He is morally blamable for such activity only if the act was freely and knowingly chosen. Furthermore, homosexual and heterosexual genital relations are not morally wrong *in the same way*, as if to say that those engaging in both types of relations have similarly failed to be chaste. This equates the problem of homosexual and heterosexual sexual activity, leaving us with the impression that the homosexual condition itself is not a moral problem in any sense whatsoever, which suggests parity between homosexuality and heterosexuality on the order of creation. However, heterosexuality is not in itself objectively disordered because it does not incline, unlike homosexual tendencies, to intrinsically wrong sex acts. The orientation/act distinction implies, as it is used by the Notre Dame Council, and others like Fr. Martin, that there exists parity between heterosexual and homosexual orientation on the order of creation, and the Church's teaching on human sexuality rejects that claim. In conclusion, there is no basis in the Church's teaching to claim human identity on the ground of homosexual inclination since the latter is intrinsically disordered.

---

[75] Levering, "Knowing What is 'Natural'," 13.

Fr. Martin's pastoral strategy proceeds from the assumption that homosexual orientation grounds human identity, and this strategy is contrary to the Church's anthropology. Thus, in all likelihood those who follow it will fall into the danger of what Pope Francis calls therapeutic self-absorption. He writes in *Evangelii Gaudium*, §170. "Although it sounds obvious, *spiritual accompaniment must lead others ever closer to God, in whom we attain true freedom.* . . . To accompany them would be counterproductive if it became a sort of therapy supporting their self-absorption and ceased to be a pilgrimage with Christ to the Father" (emphasis added). We need a pastoral approach that is consistent with the Christian anthropology that is grounded in the truth that God made man, our created nature, as male and female for each other (Gen 1:27), and that this nature is savagely wounded by sin, broken, but, thanks be to God, it is redeemed in Christ through his atoning work.

Chapter 6

The Triumph of the Therapeutic Mentality

It is not experience we should trust but the transmutation of experience by Scripture and Tradition.

—Aidan Nichols, OP[1]

Truth has such a clear and calm power. My aim in pastoral work is this: to help by the power of truth.

—Romano Guardini[2]

To defend the truth, to articulate it with humility and conviction, and to bear witness to it in life are . . . exacting and indispensable forms of charity.

—Benedict XVI[3]

By the triumph of the therapeutic mentality, indeed way of life, I mean a gospel of personal happiness in which happiness rests on the justification of self-authenticating experiences. This therapeutic way of life is pervasive throughout the domain of, for example, homosexual sexual

---

[1] Aidan Nichols, "Reviving Doctrinal Consciousness," in *Christendom Awake: On Reenergizing the Church in Culture*, 41-52 and at 41.

[2] Romano Guardini, *Wahrheit des Denkens und Wahrheit des Tuns*, ed. J. Messerschmid, 3d ed. (Paderborn, 1980), 85; as cited by Joseph Ratzinger in "Pluralism as a Problem for Church and Theology," in *Church, Ecumenism, & Politics* (San Francisco: Ignatius Press, 2008 [1987]), 92 n20.

[3] Benedict XVI, *Caritas in Veritate*, § 1.

experiences in which "no criteria of validity [for those experiences is offered] other than the therapeutic experience of conviction."[4] In response to the question, by what standards are these experiences to be judged, the therapeutic mentality presupposes that a person's life-experience is self-validating. Experience is granted an authority that sometimes even for Christians trumps the Bible's own moral authority;[5] indeed, an individual's experience is taken to be "a final arbiter of truth and falsehood in the Church."[6] But I shall argue that this turn to individual experience as self-validating or authenticating is "no more acceptable that any of the other historically recurring attempts to make of private inspiration a supreme court for adjudicating the gospel."[7] In the epigraph to this article, Aidan Nichols correctly affirms, "It is not experience we should trust but the transmutation of experience by Scripture and Tradition."

---

[4] Philip Rieff, *The Triumph of the Therapeutic*, 40th Anniversary Edition (Wilmington, Delaware: Intercollegiate Studies Institute, 2006 [1966]), 98.

[5] Fr. James Martin, SJ, suggested in a tweet (citing a remark posted by Fr. Richard Rohr, OFM, which cites a passage from a book by the late Methodist writer Walter Wink) that there exists an analogy between slavery and homosexuality vis-á-vis the moral authority of Scripture. He seemed to imply that not unlike the view of Christians who came to reject Scripture's stance on slavery so too we now may possibly do the same with its stance on homosexual practice: "Interesting: "Where the Bible mentions [same-sex sexual] behavior at all, it clearly condemns it. I freely grant that. The issue is precisely whether the biblical judgment is correct. The Bible sanctioned slavery as well and nowhere attacked it as unjust. . . . Are we prepared to argue today that slavery is biblically justified?" Now, this is all implied but it is clear what he wants to say. Since we are not prepared to justify the biblical stance on slavery, so too let us consider rejecting the Bible's stance on homosexuality. I refute this argument in my article, "No, @JamesMartinSJ, the analogy between slavery and homosexuality does not hold," *Catholic World Report*, October 26, 2019, https://www.catholicworldreport.com/2019/10/26/no-jamesmartinsj-the-analogy-between-slavery-and-homosexuality-does-not-hold/.

[6] Nichols, "Reviving Doctrinal Consciousness," 41.

[7] Nichols, "Reviving Doctrinal Consciousness," 41.

Ch. 6: The Triumph of the Therapeutic Mentality

By contrast to the therapeutic mentality, Cardinal Eijk makes clear that the starting point of pastoral practice is the "teaching of the Church, namely, "that homosexual acts are intrinsically evil."[8] The 1975 CDF document, *Persona Humana*, states this starting point:

> In the pastoral field, these homosexuals must certainly be treated with understanding and sustained in the hope of overcoming their personal difficulties and their inability to fit into society. Their culpability will be judged with prudence. But no pastoral method can be employed which would give moral justification to these acts on the grounds that they would be consonant with the condition of such people. For according to the objective moral order, homosexual relations are acts which lack an essential and indispensable finality. In Sacred Scripture they are condemned as a serious depravity and even presented as the sad consequence of rejecting God.[9]

In response to the teaching of the Church on homosexuality, some revisionist moral theologians have proposed, says John Paul II, "a kind of double status of moral truth. Beyond the doctrinal and abstract level, one would have to acknowledge the priority of a certain more concrete existential consideration." In other words, explains John Paul,

> The latter, by taking account of circumstances and the situation, could legitimately be the basis of certain *exceptions to the general rule* and thus permit one to do in practice and in good conscience what is qualified as intrinsically evil by the moral law. A

---

[8] Eijk, *De Band van de Liefde*, 291.

[9] *Persona Humana* - Declaration on Certain Questions Concerning Sexual Ethics, Sacred Congregation Doctrine of the Faith, 29 December 1975 (vatican.va). Cited by Eijk, *De Band van de Liefde*, 291.

separation, or even an opposition, is thus established in some cases between the teaching of the precept, which is valid in general, and the norm of the individual conscience, which would in fact make the final decision about what is good and what is evil. On this basis, an attempt is made to legitimize so-called "pastoral" solutions contrary to the teaching of the Magisterium, and to justify a "creative" hermeneutic according to which the moral conscience is in no way obliged, in every case, by a particular negative precept.[10]

A good example of the therapeutic mentality is found throughout the book by James Martin, SJ, *Building a Bridge: How the Catholic Church and the LGBT Community can Enter into a Relationship of Respect, Compassion, and Sensitivity*, Revised and Expanded (New York: HarperOne, 2017; 2018; hereafter, *BB*).[11] Significantly, Fr. Martin does not argue for the authority of experience as self-justifying; rather, it is a presupposition of his work. There are two other presuppositions that play an important role in Fr. Martin's work: his understandings of dialogue and of respect.

Experience, Dialogue, and Respect

Against the background of the presupposition of the therapeutic mentality that grants such authority to experience that it renders it self-

---

[10] John Paul II, *Veritatis Splendor*, §56.

[11] This chapter is a revised and expanded version of my June 16, 2017 article, "Fr. James Martin, 'Bridges', and The Triumph of the Therapeutic Mentality," *Catholic World Report*, https://www.catholicworldreport.com/2017/06/16/fr-james-martin-s-j-and-the-triumph-of-the-therapeutic-mentality/.

justifying, we can understand why Fr. Martin does not argue but implicitly presupposes that "same-sex" attraction is good from the order of creation and even finds justification for this in scripture. That is, a homosexual *qua* homosexual is "wonderfully made" (Psalm 139), as Martin suggests in asking a SSA attracted person to reflect on himself and his experience in light of that psalm (*BB*, 134-137). In this connection, it follows that Martin holds it to be legitimate to ground human identity in so-called homosexual orientation, which encompasses an individual's personal and social identity. How does Fr. Martin justify the legitimacy of the self-description of a person's identity, indeed, insisting on it? The only criterion that he suggests legitimizes it is individual experience. Individual experience becomes a supreme court for adjudicating the gospel, the teachings of the Church. This leads him to the conclusion that a person's homosexuality is a creational given rather than being in itself inherently disordered, a sign of brokenness, an expression of man's fallen condition. For example, Fr. Martin portrays the fact that persons with SSA find happiness in their SSA relationships, and can be caring and loving to each other as self-justifying experiences; that is, because they find their same sex sexual relationships satisfying in many ways, they must be good. But since God is the source and end of all blessings, the anthropological question regarding the particularity of God's will and purpose in creating man as male and female arises here (Gen 1:27; 2:24), namely, whether individual experience legitimizes SSA.

No, it does not. The creation of male and female receives the judgment of goodness by God, which is his blessing. The Church has always understood same-sex intercourse to be inconsistent with Scripture, tradition, natural law reasoning – and, in particular, with Christian anthropology, which teaches sexual morality and hence marriage to be an intrinsically male-female union. Martin holds that there are "goods" in same-sex relationships – "love," "commitment," "fidelity," "mutuality."

But we must not treat them as *neutral* goods abstracted from particular sexual behavior, which the Church unequivocally rejects, and from the larger culture of homosexuality – to say nothing of the worldview (the sexual revolution!) underpinning the interpretation of these goods.

In contrast to Fr. Martin, the *Catechism of the Catholic Church* (§2357; hereafter, *CCC*) teaches: "Basing itself on Sacred Scripture, which presents homosexual acts as acts of grave depravity, tradition has always declared that 'homosexual acts are intrinsically disordered'." Martin comments on the phrase found in *CCC*, §2358, namely, the homosexual inclination is "objectively disordered:" "The phrase relates to the orientation, not the person, but it is still, as countless LGBT people have told me, needlessly hurtful to them. . . . So to call a person's sexuality 'objectively disordered' is to tell a person that all of his or her love, even the most chaste, is disordered. For many LGBT Catholics, that seems unnecessarily cruel" (*BB*, 73-74).

Fr. Martin does not say that the problem with the term "objectively disordered" is solely with the language used that otherwise correctly describes the homosexual condition. Indeed, if that were the problem, he would just suggest a change in the language used to describe an expression of human brokenness because of man's fallen state. Fr. Martin, however, does not consider the individual in the homosexual condition to be in a fallen state. Thus, he does not consider whether the term is true to reality and hence morally right about homosexual practice; or even whether it is, however inadequately, getting at the reality of the homosexual condition. Rather, he only considers how the term leaves the individual feeling about himself, hurt or abused verbally. That is it.

Again, Fr. Martin does not just object to the formulation of the homosexual condition as "objectively disordered." If that were solely it, he would acknowledge the distinction between the normative order of creation and the order of the fall, followed by the order of redemption. One

Ch. 6: The Triumph of the Therapeutic Mentality

would then take as normative the truth that God made man, our created nature, as male and female for each other (Genesis 1:27), and that this nature is savagely wounded by sin, broken, but, thanks be to God, it is redeemed in Christ through his atoning work. It is not Fr. Martin's view to convey the Church's understanding of SSA; rather, he is concerned solely with the feelings of those who experience SSA.

In Fr. Martin's view, causing a person to feel hurt or abused verbally shows a lack of respect. On Martin's view, what is respect? He says this about respect: "*respect* means, at the very least, recognizing that the LGBT community *exists*, and extending to it the same recognition that any community desires and deserves because of its presence among us" (*BB*, 32). What exactly is involved in respect other than the recognition of a community's existence? Fr. Martin seems to be suggesting something more than merely tolerating this community's existence. But he seems to want people to "respect" the same-sex desires of people with SSA and the concomitant beliefs they hold that their desires are innate and good. But it is wrong to ask people to express respect for what they think is immoral, false, and harmful. As Simon Blackburn puts it,

> We can respect, in the minimal sense of tolerating, those who hold false beliefs. . . But once we are convinced that a belief is false, or even just that it is irrational, we cannot respect in any thicker sense those who hold it—not on account of their holding it. We may respect them for all sorts of other qualities, but not that one. We would prefer them to change their minds.[12]

Hence, the old adage, "Love the sinner but hate the sin."

---

[12] Simon Blackburn, "Religion and Respect," in *Philosophers without Gods*, ed. Louise M. Anthony (New York: Oxford University Press, 2010), 179-193, and at 180.

Of course, all men deserve respect in a more specific sense. It seems to me that Fr. Martin confuses two things in his understanding of respect: how we relate to people, on the one hand, and evaluating their beliefs and practices on the other. The former relation should be ethical: honoring the dignity of a person qua person, relating to that person in the context of "encounter, accompaniment, and friendship" (*BB*, 64). But the latter relation calls us to assessment, critical judgment, discerning the difference between good and evil, embracing the former and rejecting the latter (Rom 12: 9; 1 Thess 5: 21-22). This distinction between relating to people and evaluating their beliefs and practices is affirmed by Vatican II: "But it is necessary to distinguish error, which always merits repudiation, and the person in error, who never loses the dignity of being a person even when he flawed by false or inadequate religious [or moral] notions."[13] (*Gaudium et spes*, §28). This distinction is lost to Fr. Martin. He wants the Church to make "an unabashedly positive statement" about people with SSA "without including a critique."[14]

But critics, such as Fr. Martin, of this distinction raise the following objection. On the one hand, the Church teaches that the individual who experiences SSA is a person of dignity, created in God's image, and that he should be shown respect, compassion, and sensitivity. On the other hand, if my sexual identity is at the core of my personal identity—as these critics of the Church's position claim—how then can my dignity be honored if that core is objectively disordered, and is regarded as an objective evil? Isn't then the affirmation of being in God's image just an

---

[13] *Gaudium et Spes*, §28.

[14] Fr. Martin's tweet of May 2013 as cited by Michael O'Loughlin, "Fr. James Martin & Others Are Saying Something Positive," https://www.newwaysministry.org/2013/06/05/fr-james-martin-others-are-sayingsomethingpositive/.

abstraction that is undercut, as one objector put it, "if not by logic, then by psychological experience [?]."¹⁵

This objection is hard to fathom. The fall into sin, original sin, has corrupted the image of God in all men. *CCC* teaches (§400): "The harmony... thanks to original [holiness and] justice is now destroyed: the control of the soul's spiritual faculties over the body is shattered; the union of man and woman becomes subject to tensions, their relations henceforth marked by lust and domination. Harmony with creation is broken: visible creation has become alien and hostile to man." And so the same question could be asked, indeed, has been asked throughout the history of the Church and Christian theology: does the fallen human nature of every person undercut the *imago Dei* and, if so, in what sense? Put differently, how are we to understand the central question of man's humanity *in* his sinfulness? Does the Fall literally dehumanize man, depriving him of his essential nature?

The brief but nonetheless correct answer here to this question must be no. On the one hand, there is the Church's biblical teaching that the heart of sin is the alienation from God that produces spiritual death, that manifests itself in "hardness and impenitent heart" (Rom 2: 5), in "ungodliness and unrighteousness" (Rom 1: 18), in "vanity and darkness" (Rom 1: 21), and "foolishness and uncleanness (Rom 1: 22, 24). Clearly, this biblical perspective undercuts Fr. Martin's presupposition regarding the justification of self-authenticating experiences, for some of our experiences are clearly the result of our inherited sinfulness, disorderedness, brokenness.

On the other hand, however, the Church also teaches that *in* this alienation from God, man still remains man: man's nature, his fundamental identity, has not been annihilated or extinguished by sin, and

---

¹⁵ Stephen Pope, "The Vatican's Blunt Instrument," *The Tablet*, August 9, 2003. https;//www.clgs.org/marriage/history_pope.html.

since all substantializing of sin is rejected, man's nature after the Fall is still the work and creature of God, intrinsically religious, that is, intrinsically ordered to the knowledge of God, and hence the deepest foundation of human nature is still what God made it. We find this distinction expressed, for example, in the *Catechism of the Catholic Church*: "According to faith the disorder [in marriage] we notice so painfully does not stem from the *nature* of man and woman, nor from the nature of their relations, but from sin. As a break with God, the first sin had for its first consequence the rupture of the original communion between man and woman" (§1607). So, the essential feature of human nature remains the same, being substantial, or primary, and hence sin is a secondary element such that it is accidental to human nature. What has been called the Augustinian Principle affirms that the *nature* of man persists in the regime of man's fallen state. Augustine writes, "The natures in which evil exists, in so far as they are natures, are good. And evil is removed, not by removing any nature, or part of a nature but by healing and correcting that which had been vitiated and depraved."[16]

The good news is that Jesus Christ renews and regenerates the fallen man from sin, reconciling him to God the Father, in Christ, and through the power of the Holy Spirit. The restorative and saving grace of God, through the saving death and resurrection of Christ, renews the meaning of God's creation, breaks the power of sin, cancels our moral guilt, and offers us new life in Christ as a gift.

The key evidence for my contention that Fr. Martin is confused about what respect involves is, then, that he nowhere presents the so-called LGBT community with the Church's life-giving teaching toward homosexuality. Fr. Martin ignores the following principle: "There is an organic connection between our spiritual life and the dogmas. Dogmas

---

[16] Augustine, *City of God*, book 14, chapter 11.

Ch. 6: The Triumph of the Therapeutic Mentality 441

are lights along the path of faith; they illuminate it and make it secure. Conversely, if our life is upright, our intellect and heart will be open to welcome the light shed by the dogmas of faith" (*CCC*, §89).

In this connection, it is important to see that his view of dialogue is almost exclusively about listening. In the words of the Congregation for Education: "The Church, mother and teacher, does more than simply listen. Remaining rooted in her original mission [of proclaiming the gospel], and at the same time always open to the contribution of reason, she puts herself at the service of the community of peoples, offering it a way of living."[17] In addition,

> The methodology in mind is based on three guiding principles seen as best suited to meet the needs of both individuals and communities: *to listen, to reason and to propose.* In fact, listening carefully to the needs of the other, combined with an understanding of the true diversity of conditions, can lead to a shared set of rational elements in an argument, and can prepare one for a Christian education rooted in faith that "throws a new light on everything, manifests God's design for man's total vocation, and thus directs the mind to solutions which are fully human."[18]

Fr. Martin makes a disclaimer which he believes absolves himself from presenting the Church's teaching. His book is "not a treatise on moral theology, nor is it a reflection on the sexual morality of LGBT people.... This is a book primarily about dialogue and prayer" (*BB*, 6). But what are we engaged in dialogue about if not the beliefs and allegedly

---

[17] Congregation for Catholic Education, *"Male and Female He Created Them": Towards a Path of Dialogue on the Question of Gender Theory in Education* (Vatican City, 2019), §30.

[18] *"Male and Female He Created Them": Towards f Path of Dialogue*, §5.

self-authenticating desires of people in a homosexual condition? John Paul II is correct, "Dialogue is a means of seeking after truth and sharing it with others. For truth is light, newness, and strength."[19] Furthermore, Martin implies that Catholics who experience SSA know what the Church teaches and hence there is no need to present that teaching. But do they understand the rationality of the Church's teaching? Fr. Martin leaves us with the impression that their rejection of the Church's teaching—same sex attraction, blessing, and marriage—is responsible and justified. He makes no mention of the kind of reasoning that led them to hold these false beliefs, for example, negligent reasoning, ideological rationalization, or wishful thinking. Except for the phrase, "respect, compassion, sensitivity" (*CCC*, §2358), being the sole basis on which he builds his position, Fr. Martin completely ignores the entire normative context of Christian anthropology that is the prolegomena in the Church's teaching on the sixth commandment (*CCC*, nos, 2331-2336), the vocation of the human person that follows from that anthropology (§§2337-2347), and the sexual morality of man's vocation to chastity (§§2348-2356). Having ignored that normative context, he never discusses the teaching of the Church regarding the relationship between chastity and homosexual practice. (*CCC*, §2357).[20] In fact, Fr. Martin claims that his position "builds on the *Catechism of the Catholic Church*,

---

[19] John Paul II, "On the Occasion of Meeting with the Exponents of Non-Christian Religions," February 5, 1986, http://www.vatican.va/content/john-paul-ii/en/speeches/1986/february/documents/hf_jp-ii_spe_19860205_religioni-non-cristiane.html.

[20] I refute his claims in my article, which is now Chapter 5 of this book, "Mercy and Truth: Pastoral Care of Individuals in Spiritually and Morally Problematic Relationships," *Clerical Sexual Misconduct: An Interdisciplinary Analysis*, ed Jane F. Adolphe and Ronald J. Rychlak (Providence: Rhode Island: CLUNY Media, 2020), 365-381, 477-480.

and is well within church teaching" (*BB*, 9). Neither claim is true: he ignores not only the full teaching of the Church, its Christian anthropology and its corresponding sexual ethics, but also proceeds from the assumption that homosexual orientation grounds human identity, and this strategy is contrary to the Church's anthropology. What is the Church's view of man?

Christianity is Life-Affirming[21]

More than thirty years ago, the future Pope Benedict XVI, then Fr. Joseph Ratzinger, gave the answer to this question by suggesting one reason more than any other why so many unbelievers are put off from the Christian faith. "The most telling refutation of what Christianity claims to be," wrote Ratzinger, is "this feeling that Christianity is opposed to joy, this impression of punctiliousness [showing great attention to correct behavior] and unhappiness." Furthermore, he adds, Christians are perceived to be obsessed with the "fourth [parental authority] and sixth commandments [sexual morality] that the resultant complex with regard to authority and purity renders the individual so incapable of free self-development that his selflessness degenerates into a loss of self and a denial of love, and his faith leads, not to freedom but to rigidity and an absence of freedom."[22] Of course, this alleged malady is our culture's distorted vision of the Christian life.

This distorted vision of Christianity is found in thinkers, such as Friedrich Nietzsche, who attacked Christianity, not as a doctrinal system

---

[21] Adapted from Echeverria, *Pope Francis: The Legacy of Vatican II*, 219-222.

[22] Joseph Ratzinger, *Principles of Catholic Theology*, 75-80, and at 76-77. This view of Ratzinger, now Pope Emeritus Benedict XVI, has remained unchanged almost thirty-five years later in *Without Roots: The West, Relativism, Christianity, Islam* (New York: Basic Books, 2006), 124-26.

with truth claims, but rather as a way of living. Nietzsche wrote: "Up to the present the assault against Christianity has not only been faint-hearted, it has been wide of the mark. So long as Christian *ethics* are not felt to be a *capital crime against* life, their defenders will have the game in their hand. The problem of the "truth" of Christianity—the existence of its God or the historicity of its legend, to say nothing of its astronomy and its natural science—is in itself a very subsidiary problem so long as the value of Christian ethics goes unquestioned."[23] According to Nietzsche and others, such as Albert Camus, the concept of value that informs Christian ethics is fundamentally anti-life, rather than life-affirming or life-fulfilling. These critics of Christianity seem to think that Christianity holds that "life in this world is nothing but a means to reach heaven."[24] In other words, "nothing one does in this life contributes directly to human fulfillment: the only human fulfillment is in enjoyment of God in heaven." Hence, "life in this world is only a means to reach heaven, and that heaven is an entirely other-worldly goal."[25] Is it any wonder that Camus expressed his revolt against this other-worldliness, parodying the words of Christ, "'My kingdom is not of this world,' with the statement '*Notre royaume est de ce monde*—our kingdom is of this world.'"[26] Ratzinger concludes regarding the anti-life worldview that is taken to be core Christianity, "it is surely a more likely explanation of why people leave the Church than are any of the [intellectual challenges or] problems the faith may pose today."[27]

---

[23] Cited in Henri de Lubac, SJ, *The Drama of Atheist Humanism* (San Francisco: Ignatius Press, 1995), 115.

[24] Grisez, *The Way of the Lord Jesus*, 1, 807.

[25] Grisez, *The Way of the Lord Jesus*, 1, 807.

[26] Cited in Ratzinger, *Principles of Catholic Theology*, 76.

[27] Ratzinger, *Principles of Catholic Theology*, 76.

Yet, Ratzinger quickly responds by stating that the dangers for the culture today seem to be not scrupulosity ("moralism") but laxity, not legalism but antinomianism ("lawlessness"), not a lack of freedom but license ("anything goes"), since, he correctly notes, "there are no longer any forbidden trees" (with an allusion to Gen 3:1-7). We seem to be living in a time when there are "those who call evil good, and good evil; who put darkness for light, and light for darkness; who put bitter for sweet, and sweet for bitter!" (Is 5:20). In this biblical light, Ratzinger asks whether mankind has become any healthier. Those who have eyes to see must conclude that it seems not. Thus, he observes, "morality," wrongly understood as a straightjacket, on the one hand, "and immorality," on the other, "seem to enslave man, to make him joyless and empty. Is there, in the last analysis, no hope for him?"

Ratzinger proceeds to ask more specifically: "What makes a man joyful? What robs him of joy? What puts him at odds with himself? What opens him to himself and to others?" The approach that Ratzinger takes to answering these questions is similar to Bergoglio's analysis briefly sketched above. That is, a man must come to terms with his own existence, accepting himself, rather than being at odds with who he is, in short, self-affirmation. Ratzinger makes clear that he is not talking about egoism: the theory of human nature affirming that one's own self is, or ought to be, the motivation or goal of all of one's actions. He insists that egoism is not the same as true self-acceptance or self-affirmation. Says Ratzinger, "The former must be overcome; the latter must be discovered." Unfortunately, however, Christians have all too often confused "egoism" with the call to self-acceptance, self-affirmation, and hence they wrongly assumed, argues Ratzinger, that to root out egoism is at the same time "exorcizing the affirmation of self." In reaction to this confusion, egoism has sought "to avenge such a betrayal [of oneself] by becoming all the more rampant—this, ultimately, is the root of what the

French have labeled the *maladie catholique*." This so-called malady can be easily understood in light of the points Nietzsche and Camus made above in revolt against an "other-worldly" view of Christianity. On this view, says Ratzinger, "one who wants to live only on the supernatural level and to the exclusion of self will be, in the end, without a self but not, for that reason, selfless."[28]

Defeating the "maladie catholique"

So the key to defeating the "maladie catholique" is to show that "the root of man's joy is the harmony that he enjoys with himself. He lives in this affirmation." But, adds Ratzinger, "how does one go about affirming, assenting to, one's *I*?" Intriguingly, he continues, "We cannot do so by our own efforts alone. Of ourselves we cannot come to terms with ourselves. Our *I* becomes acceptable to us only if it has first become acceptable to another *I*. We can love ourselves only if we have first been loved by someone else." In other words, the source of authentic self-love begins with someone else who not only says to you, "It is good that you exist," but also shows you the truth of that assertion with an "act of the entire being that we call love." "For it is the way of love to will the other's existence and, at the same time, to bring that existence forth again." But this act of loving the other for himself, of affirming him in his own self-existence, raises the question of truth. "Is it true, then, when someone says to me: 'It is good that you exist'? Is it really good? Is it not possible that that person's love, which wills my existence, is just a tragic error? If the love that gives me courage to exist is not based on truth, then I must, in the end, come to curse the love that deceives me, that maintains in existence something that were better destroyed."[29]

---

[28] Ratzinger, *Principles of Catholic Theology*, 79.
[29] Ratzinger, *Principles of Catholic Theology*, 80.

Ratzinger then takes an interesting turn in his argument by claiming that the question of my own existence, of being at one with myself, "actually raises the question of the whole universe." "Is it good that anything at all exists? Is the world good? How many persons today would dare to affirm this question from the heart—to believe it is good that they exist? That is the source of the anxiety and despair that incessantly affects mankind." And the latter cannot be resolved by love alone. Love is not all you need! Indeed, "only when truth and love are in harmony can man know joy. For it is truth that makes man free."[30] Here we come to the truth of the Gospel: The Yes of Jesus Christ.[31] "But as God is faithful, our word to you was not Yes and No. For the Son of God, Jesus Christ, who was preached among you by us... was not Yes and No, but in Him was Yes. For all the promises of God in Him are Yes, and in Him Amen, to the glory of God through us." Indeed, "The truth is that only in the mystery of the incarnate Word does the mystery of man take on light."[32] Ratzinger elaborates:

> The content of the Christian *evangelium* reads: God finds man so important that he himself has suffered for man. The Cross, which was for Nietzsche the most detestable expression of the negative character of the Christian religion, is in truth the center of the *evangelium*, the glad tidings: "It is good that you exist"— no, "It is necessary that you exist." The Cross is the approbation of our existence, not in words, but in an act so completely radical that it caused God to become flesh and pierced this flesh to the quick; that, to God, it was worth the death of his incarnate Son. One who is so loved that the other identified his life with this

---

[30] Ratzinger, *Principles of Catholic Theology*, 80.
[31] 2 Cor 1:18-20.
[32] *Gaudium et Spes* §22. See also, Joseph Ratzinger, *The Yes of Jesus Christ*.

love and no longer desires to live if he is deprived of it; one who is loved even unto death—such a one knows that he is truly loved. But if God so loved us, then we are loved in truth. Then love is truth, and truth is love. Then life is worth living. This is the *evangelium*. This is why, even as the message of the Cross, it is glad tidings for one who believes; the only glad tidings that destroy the ambiguity of all other joys and make them worthy to be joy. Christianity is, by its very nature, joy—the ability to be joyful... "Rejoice!" with which it begins expresses its whole nature.[33]

Pace Nietzsche and Camus, then, Christianity is life-affirming: the grace of the Cross neither destroys fallen human nature nor leaves it untouched but, rather, renews and transforms it from within, bringing about nature's fulfillment by ordering it to its proper ends.

Teaching Authority?[34]

Fr. Martin might respond to the charge that he never discusses the teaching of the Church regarding the relationship between chastity and homosexual practice by saying that he instructs the members of the so-called LGBT+ community to respect the authority of the Church's teaching, but, he is quick to add, "As Catholics, we believes in various levels of teaching authority in our church (*BB*, 99), and hence not all [teachings] have equal authority" (*BB*, 100, 78). As a general principle, this is of course correct. Still, Fr. Martin gives no examples of which teachings are authoritative, and in what sense. He never tells the so-called LGBT community which teachings, in respect to same-sex issues, are binding

---

[33] Ratzinger, *Principles of Catholic Theology*, 81.

[34] I discuss the question of teaching authority in Chapter 1.

in faith, on what grounds, and to what extent. Why binding in faith? "Faith is the theological virtue by which we believe in God and believe all that he has said and revealed to us, and that Holy Church proposes for our belief, because he is truth itself" (*CCC*, §1812). A call for some vague "respect" doesn't approximate what the assent of faith requires when we are speaking of teachings that are irreversible, definitive, indeed, infallible and hence possessing the highest degree of certainty—such as the teachings in *CCC*, §§2331-2359—and which therefore require the assent of faith, meaning thereby that they should be held to be true. Furthermore, even those truths that the Church teaches authoritatively but non-definitively require more than just respect. The assent here, too, is intrinsic to the logic of faith such that "the faithful are to accept their teaching and adhere to it with a religious assent," which is a "religious submission of mind and will."[35]

Is Fr. Martin suggesting that the Christian anthropology (Gen 1:27) that is the prolegomena to the Church's teaching on the sixth commandment (*CCC*, §§2331-2336), the vocation of the human person that follows from that anthropology (*CCC*, §§2337-2347), and the sexual morality of man's vocation to chastity (*CCC*, §§2348-2356), are non-definitive teaching? Yes, he says, "Catholics must prayerfully consider what [the Church is] teaching. To do that, we are called to listen. Their teaching deserves our respect" (*BB*, 78). This means, he adds, "LGBT Catholics are invited to challenge themselves to listen closely. . . . [to] consider, pray, and of course use their informed consciences as they discern how to lead their lives" (*BB*, 79). This advice falls far short of informing them that faith requires them to accept the Church's teaching on sexuality.

You would think in a book that deals with the Church's stance toward homosexuality, Fr. Martin would make a real effort to inform the

---

[35] *Lumen gentium*, §25.

members of the so-called LGBT+ community of the Church's teaching on the sixth commandment and all its implications for sexual morality and the moral life in Christ (*CCC*, §§2331-2359). But he never does. No, not one word in this book.

In sum, homosexual practice is morally unacceptable, because not only are such sexual acts not open to life but also, because sexual differentiation is a fundamental prerequisite for the two-in-one-flesh union between a man and a woman, they cannot realize unity. As Robert Reilly puts it, "only a unitive act can be generative, and only a generative act can be unitive—in that only it makes two 'one flesh'."[36] This one-flesh union is not just posited by ecclesiastical law. Rather, Jesus calls us back to the law of creation (Mark 10:6-7). "Law must therefore be considered an expression of divine wisdom: by submitting to the law, freedom submits to the truth of creation."[37] This law of creation grounds an inextricable nexus of permanence, twoness, and sexual differentiation for marriage. In particular, marriage is such that it requires sexual difference, the bodily-sexual act, as a foundational prerequisite, indeed, as intrinsic to a one-flesh union of man and woman. "So then they are no longer two but one flesh" (Mark 10:8). Elsewhere, *CCC* explains, "In his preaching Jesus unequivocally taught the original meaning of the union of man and woman as the Creator willed it from the beginning. . . . By coming to restore the original order of creation disturbed by sin, [Jesus] himself gives the strength and grace to live marriage in the new dimension of the Reign of God" (§§1614-1615).

---

[36] Robert Reilly, *Making Gay Okay, How Rationalizing Homosexual Behavior is Changing Everything* (San Francisco: Ignatius Press, 2014), 36.

[37] John Paul II, *Veritatis Splendor*, §41

Homosexual "Love" a Gift?

Fr. Martin seems to think homosexuals experience the gift of "love."[38] In what sense, if any, is homosexual "love" a gift?

The mind of the Church is that this "love" certainly cannot be a gift of God, neither natural, that is, creational, nor supernatural (sacramental). According to the *Catechism of the Catholic Church*, the ultimate source of love is God himself. Quoting John Paul II's 1981 Apostolic Exhortation, *Familiaris Consortio*, (§11),[39] the *Catechism of the Catholic Church* asserts:

> God is love and in himself he lives a mystery of personal loving communion [eternally united in being, relationship, and love]. Creating the human race in his own image . . . , God inscribed in the humanity of man and woman [Genesis 1:27] the vocation, and thus the capacity and responsibility, of love and communion.

Against this background, the *Catechism* (§§2332-2333) teaches:

> Sexuality affects all aspects of the human person in the unity of his body and soul. It especially concerns affectivity, the capacity to love and to procreate, and in a more general way the aptitude for forming bonds of communion with others. Everyone, man and woman, should acknowledge and accept his *sexual identity*.

---

[38] Pope Francis with Fabio Marchese Ragona, *Life: My Story Through History*, Translated from the Italian by Aubrey Botsford (Milano: HarperCollins Italia, 2024), 219.

[39] John Paul II, *Familiaris Consortio* (November 22, 1981).

And to make clear that this sexual identity is grounded in sexual differentiation between a man and a woman, the Catechism states:

> Physical, moral, and spiritual difference and complementarity are oriented toward the goods of marriage and the flourishing of family life. The harmony of the couple and of society depends in part on the way in which the complementarity, needs, and mutual support between the sexes are live out.

On its face, Francis does not think that homosexual "love" is an inherently disordered form of love. Does he think that the homosexual is able to live the vocation to chastity, and hence, of love in a same sex relationship? How could the homosexual do so since that vocation involves sexual differentiation between a man and a woman (Gen 1:27), which according to Christian anthropology, means, as the *Catechism* states, "the successful integration of sexuality within the person and thus the inner unity of man in his bodily and spiritual being." The *Catechism* explains, "Sexuality, in which man's belonging to the bodily and biological world is expressed, becomes personal and truly human when it is integrated into the relationship of one person to another, in the complete and lifelong mutual gift of a man and a woman." (§2337)

Referring to chastity as a virtue, an internal moral principle that takes root in a person's life, the Catechism states: "The virtue of chastity therefore involves the integrity of the person and the integrality of the gift." (*CCC*, §2337)

Chastity, therefore, presupposes the sexual differentiation of male and female, such that only a sexual union of male and female persons makes bodies in any real sense "one flesh" (Gen 2:24), with the latter organic bodily union being a necessary condition for the existence of authentic conjugal love. Homosexual love is not a gift, indeed, it is a false love, because it is incapable of fulfilling the vocation to chastity, of perfecting the being of the person and developing his existence, and hence of being ordered to the natural law, in other words, the order of creation, and hence to God. The Pontifical Biblical Commission makes the point: "The anthropological perspective that the Bible promotes recognizes in the loving relationship between a man and a woman the realization pf the *design willed by the Creator* [emphasis added] for the human being (Gen 1-2)."[40] Homosexual love, then, is a disordered form of love and hence it not only lacks integration but it is a counter-integration by virtue of being an offense against the vocation to chastity, making it unable to realize the integrity of the person and the integrality of the gift of self.

Christian anthropology must consider the reality of the human person, of man and woman, in the order of love. Why? Because, as Karol Wojtyla rightly states in his philosophical magnum opus, *Love and Responsibility*,[41] the "person finds in love the greatest fullness of his being, of his objective existence. Love is such action, such an act, which most fully develops the existence of the person. Of course, this has to be true love. What does true love mean?"[42]

Love is an analogical concept, meaning thereby that there are different kinds of love—paternal love, the love of brothers and sisters, friendship, and, last but not least, the love between a man and a woman. "The love of a man and a woman is a reciprocal relation of persons and possesses a personal character."[43] Briefly, love involves attraction to the sensory-sexual values, and spiritual or moral values, of the other person, for

---

[40] Pontifical Biblical Commission, *What is Man? A Journey through Biblical Anthropology*, translated by Fearghus O'Fearghail and Adrian Graffy (London: Darton, Longman & Todd, 2021), 166.

[41] Wojtyla, *Love and Responsibility*.

[42] Wojtyla, *Love and Responsibility*, 56.

[43] Wojtyla, *Love and Responsibility*, 58.

example, says Wojtyla, "to her intelligence or virtues of character." There is also "need love," or love as desire, and "benevolence." "Need love" desires "the person as a good for oneself." Love as benevolence is about desiring the other person's good. "Benevolence is simply disinterestedness in love: 'I do not long for you as a good', but 'I long for your good', 'I long for what is good for you'."[44]

Wojtyla then turns to the problem of reciprocity, which brings about a synthesis "of love of desire and of benevolent love." Reciprocity involves the relation of "I" and "we," and hence where an interpersonal community is formed. "Love finds its full being not merely in an individual subject only but in an inter-subjective, inter-personal relation. . . . The transition from 'I' to 'we' is for love no less essential than transcending one's 'I' as expressed through [attraction], love of desire, and love of benevolence." Being inherently disordered, homosexual love is unable to form an inter-personal community where unity is manifested in the mature "we." Finally, Wojtyla sees the fullness of love as gift love, or what he calls spousal love, which is giving oneself to the other person, entailing the reciprocal self-giving of persons. He adds, "The concept of spousal [gift] love possesses a key meaning for establishing the norm for all sexual morality."

Since man—male and female—is created in and for love, accordingly, sexual ethics is, too, unintelligible without love. Hence, this crucial point about finding in love the greatest fullness of his being must be applied to love between a man and a woman. "Love is a union of persons," says Wojtyla, "in which a man and woman have the sense that they constitute, in a sense, one common subject of action,"[45] an objective union in which this one subject constitutes "one flesh" (Genesis 2:24). This un-

---

[44] Wojtyla, *Love and Responsibility*, 66-7.
[45] Wojtyla, *Love and Responsibility*, 129.

ion may not be detached from its biotic foundation in the organic differences between the sexes. This objective union is born of "a common good," an "objective good," that is, the good of the human persons, and a common end," which binds [them]."[46] "This end is procreation, progeny, the family, and at the same time the whole constantly growing maturity of the relationship between both persons in all the spheres brought by the spousal relationship itself."[47]

Consequently, when the *Catechism* asserts that homosexual sexual acts are closed to the gift of life (*CCC*, §2357) that is because such acts do not have an objective union in the sexual differentiation of a man and a woman. "Under no circumstances can they be approved." Such acts are "sin gravely contrary to chastity." (*CCC*, §2357) Hence, homosexual love is not a gift.

Caritas in Veritate

In Chapter 5, I argued for the co-existence and mutual influence of charity and truth, in order to avoid watering down the Gospel and the teachings of the Church. St. Paul states the message that we have been entrusted with, namely, the message of reconciliation. "We beseech you on behalf of Christ, be reconciled to God" (2 Cor 5: 20). Why this urgency?

St. Paul consistently urges us to make choices that are worthy of the calling that we have received in Christ (Eph 4: 1; Phil 1: 27; Col 1:9). In particular, he identifies the risk posed by, especially *but not only*, sexual offenses: "Do you not know that the unrighteous will not inherit the kingdom of God? Stop deceiving yourselves: Neither sexually immoral

---

[46] Wojtyla, *Love and Responsibility*, 12.
[47] Wojtyla, *Love and Responsibility*, 14.

persons [*pornoi*, i.e., like the incestuous man], nor idolaters, nor adulterers, nor 'soft men' [*malakoi*, i.e., men who feminize themselves to attract male sex partners], nor men who lie with a male [*arsenokoitai*, a term formed from the Levitical prohibition of male homosexual practice] . . . shall inherit the kingdom of God (1 Cor 6:9-10)."[48] The *Catechism of the Catholic Church* (§1861) instructs us that certain choices result "in the loss of charity and the privation of sanctifying grace, that is, of the state of grace." The *Catechism* adds, "If it is not redeemed by repentance and God's forgiveness, it causes exclusion from Christ's kingdom and the eternal death of hell." How is that so? Because, the *Catechism* concludes, "our freedom has the power to make choices for ever, with no turning back."[49] This makes the Church's pastoral practice a life-and-death matter. Clearly, then, our pastoral practice should be informed by the sense of urgency for the lives of people and that of their eternal salvation.

Before turning to consider the objection to the Church's pastoral practice, I think it's absolutely necessary to define the meaning of "pastoral" in the notion of pastoral practice. I know of no better attempt to describe this meaning than the one given by then Fr. Joseph Ratzinger in his attempt to explain what it means to speak of Vatican II as a pastoral council. He explains: "'Pastoral' should not mean nebulous, without substance, merely 'edifying'—meanings sometimes given to it. Rather what was meant was positive care for the man of today who is not helped by condemnations and who has been told for too long what is false and what he may not do. Modern man really wishes to hear what is true. He

---

[48] See also Gal 5: 19-21; Eph 5: 3-5; 1 Thess 4: 2-8. I am using Robert Gagnon's translation of 1 Cor 6:9-11. For a thorough exegetical justification of this translation of the passive and active partners in homosexual acts, see his *The Bible and Homosexual Practice*, 303-339.

[49] *Catechism of the Catholic Church*, §1861.

Ch. 6: The Triumph of the Therapeutic Mentality 457

has, indeed, not heard enough truth, enough of the positive message of faith for our time, enough of what the faith has to say to our age."[50] The significance of the point that Ratzinger is making here for a pastoral practice is as follows: in an effort to show compassion take care not to dilute the truth of the Gospel regarding the meaning of man's body. "The human body shares in the dignity of 'the image of God': it is a human body precisely because it is animated by a spiritual soul, and it is the whole human person that is intended to become, in the body of Christ, a temple of the Spirit [Cf. 1 Cor 6:19; 15:44-45]."[51] (*CCC*, §364) Viceversa: truth without compassion turns cold, harsh, and ugly, and hence, in short, truth without love is nothing (1 Cor 13:2). Love without truth is, however, blind, sentimental, empty. Says Benedict XVI, "In a culture without truth, this is the fatal risk facing love. It falls prey to contingent subjective emotions and opinions, the word 'love' is abused and distorted."[52] Rather than overlooking truth or love, however, in the context of sketching the Church's practical practice, we need to show the interdependency of love and truth. As Ratzinger say, "Love is of no avail. It serves no purpose if truth is not on its side. Only when truth and love are in harmony can man know joy. For it is truth that makes man free."[53]

What, then, is the objection to the Church's pastoral practice regarding homosexuals?[54] There are those who are at odds with the vision of John Paul II. For instance, the twentieth century German Lutheran theologian. Helmut Thielicke (1908-1986), a distinguished theologian, prolific author, preacher, and professor, and others, such as Timothy Radcliff, OP (a recent speaker at the Synod on Synodality, and now recently

---

[50] Ratzinger, *Theological Highlights of Vatican II*, 23.
[51] *Catechism of the Catholic Church*, §364.
[52] Benedict XVI, *Caritas in Veritate*, §3.
[53] Ratzinger , *Principles of Catholic Theology*, 80.
[54] See Chapter 5 for a fuller account of that pastoral practice.

Cardinal designate by Pope Francis), suggest a pastoral strategy in which, says Thielicke, "the homosexual has to realize his optimal ethical potentialities *on the basis* of his irreversible situation."

For one, Fr. Timothy Radcliffe put this objection to the Church's pastoral practice succinctly as follows: the Church must be "with people where they are, not telling them where they ought to be." "It is no good telling people that they should not be divorced or remarried or living with a partner or gay. We begin where they are now."[55] This is Radcliffe's strategy where "there is an abyss between what the Church teaches and the way many members of the Church live."[56] What is then the point that he is making here?

Fr. Radcliffe is suggesting that there are "in divine law various levels or forms of precept for various persons and conditions."[57] The latter is described (and rejected) by John Paul II as the "gradualness of the law."[58] What this law means, according to Grisez, is that there are "gradations of the law," namely, "the whole of Christian morality—or, at least, many norms traditionally received as binding precepts—is [such] that willful violations are acceptable provided one looks forward to living according to the norm at some time in the future."[59] But this is ruled out by Radcliffe. Again, he insists that the Church must be "with people where they are, not telling them where they ought to be." "It is no good telling people that they should not be divorced or remarried or living with a partner or gay. We begin where they are now."[60] So by his own account the

---

[55] Timothy Radcliffe, **OP,** *What's the Point of Being a Christian?* (New York: Bloomsbury, 2005), 42.

[56] Radcliffe, *What's the Point of Being a Christian?*, 95.

[57] Grisez, *The Way of the Lord Jesus*, 687.

[58] John Paul II, *Familiaris Consortio*, §34. See Chapter 3 for a discussion of the "law of gradualism vs the gradualism of the law."

[59] Grisez, *The Way of the Lord Jesus*, 687.

[60] Radcliffe, *What's* the Point of Being a Christian?, 42.

"gradualness of the law" cannot even mean that "received moral norms characterizing various kinds of acts as grave matter merely mark out an ideal to be achieved in the future."[61] These norms do not have an aspirational force, let alone an obligatory one.

If the Church's teaching is clear, unambiguous, and absolute (i.e., exceptionless)—as is her teaching regarding adultery, same-sex intercourse, rape, murder, incest, for example—then the moral law is not an "ideal" that is realized in varying degrees in various persons and under differing conditions. For if morally obligatory then only one moral choice is the right one. Of course, "man is sometimes confronted by situations that make moral judgments less assured and decision difficult. But he must always seriously seek what is right and good and discern the will of God expressed in divine law."[62] Yet, the presumption is that when the Church has made her moral teaching clear, then it *isn't* a question of discovering what is right for me here and now, but rather of *doing* the right thing. So "the process of gradualness has no place unless one accepts divine law with a sincere heart and seeks the goods which protected and promoted by the moral truth clarified in Jesus and proposed to us in the Church's moral teaching."[63]

I am not sure Radcliffe agrees with the last sentence of the preceding paragraph. Indeed, the tenor of his pastoral proposal is such regarding those Catholics whose lives do not conform to the moral teaching of the Church that they are left in their sinful condition. Of course we should compassionately "enter into" the lives of people struggling *to do* the right thing. But does that mean that we should devise pastoral programs, such as Helmut Thielicke and others suggest, in which "the homosexual has to realize his optimal ethical potentialities *on the basis* of his irreversible

---

[61] Grisez, *The Way of the Lord Jesus*, I, 687.
[62] *Catechism of the Catholic Church*, §1787.
[63] Grisez, *The Way of the Lord Jesus*, I, 687.

situation."[64] Unlike Radcliffe, Thielicke, first, clearly explains that, biblically speaking, "homosexuality cannot simply be put on the same level with the normal created order of the sexes, but that it is rather a habitual or actual distortion or deprivation of it.... The homosexual must therefore be willing to be treated or healed so far as this is possible; he must, as it were, be willing to be brought back into the 'order'."[65] But what about the homosexual who is allegedly incurable, that is, whose condition is judged to be "constitutional" (as Thielicke puts it). In this case, Thielicke asks whether there is an *"ethically responsible* way" to live with homosexuality and "achieve an acceptable partnership."[66] Still, there is a difference between them explained by John Paul II. Radcliffe is sympathetic to an ethics of circumstance, where right and wrong is person and situation specific, whereas Thielicke's position highlights the tension between the moral law and the circumstance.

> Beyond the doctrinal and abstract level, one would have to acknowledge the priority of a certain more concrete existential consideration. The latter, by taking account of circumstances and the situation, could legitimately be the basis of certain *exceptions to the general rule* and thus permit one to do in practice and in good conscience what is qualified as intrinsically evil by the moral law. A separation, or even an opposition, is thus established in some cases between the teaching of the precept,

---

[64] Thielicke, *The Ethics of Sex*, 285. See also, for a similar pastoral strategy, Philippe Bordeyne, "Homosexuality, Seen in Relation to Ecumenical Dialogue: What Really Matters to the Catholic Church." *New Blackfriars* 87, no. 1012 (November 2006), 561-577.

[65] Thielicke, *The Ethics of Sex*, 283.

[66] Thielicke, *The Ethics of Sex*, 285, 287.

which is valid in general, and the norm of the individual conscience, which would in fact make the final decision about what is good and what is evil. On this basis, an attempt is made to legitimize so-called "pastoral" solutions contrary to the teaching of the Magisterium, and to justify a "creative" hermeneutic according to which the moral conscience is in no way obliged, in every case, by a particular negative precept.[67]

In the end, however, Thielicke's pastoral strategy dovetails with Radcliffe's own, and hence it suffers from the same limitations.[68] Central to Fr. Radcliff's pastoral proposal is urging the Church to take the stance of "friendship and proximity" so that she "can be with us as we face moral dilemmas and make choices." He adds, "The Church will only be a cradle of gospel freedom if we are seen to stand beside people, supporting them as they make moral decisions *within the range of what is possible*, rather than making decisions for them." This, too, is the position of Cardinal Blasé Cupich, the current archbishop of Chicago: "It's a lot easier to tell

---

[67] John Paul II, *Veritatis Splendor*, §56. By negative precept is meant (§52): The *negative precepts* of the natural law are universally valid. They oblige each and every individual, always and in every circumstance. It is a matter of prohibitions which forbid a given action *semper et pro semper,* without exception, because the choice of this kind of behavior is in no case compatible with the goodness of the will of the acting person, with his vocation to life with God and to communion with his neighbor. It is prohibited — to everyone and in every case — to violate these precepts. They oblige everyone, regardless of the cost, never to offend in anyone, beginning with oneself, the personal dignity common to all."

[68] In all fairness to Thielicke, I should add that he sees the homosexual subject to certain temptations that are so great that he does not "venture to credit the "minimal chances of being able to live ethically with homosexuality and achieve an acceptable partnership . . . with anything more than being a possible exception" (*The Ethics of Sex*, 287).

people what they are doing in black and white. The important thing in all of this as we move forward is to recognize that people's lives are very complicated. There are mitigating circumstances, psychological, their own personal history, maybe even biological. It's not a matter of detracting from what the ideal is." Therefore, he adds, homosexual couples may be led "through a period of discernment, to understand what God is calling them to *at that point*." We have a situation-ethic at work here. Under certain circumstances, acting contrary to the moral law, is good, justified, but not the highest good of attaining the ideal.

Thus, according to this pastoral strategy, the self-professed homosexual is called to make moral decisions "within the range of what is possible," as Radcliff puts it. But St. Paul would not say, "We implore you on behalf of Christ," as Thielicke states, "achieve the optimal ethical potential of sexual self-realization." Of course not. Otherwise, we would deny that our sinful condition is open to radical transformation, as John Paul stated above. Indeed, St. Paul says, "We implore you on behalf of Christ, *be reconciled to God*" (Eph 5:20; italics added). Elsewhere he proclaims, "My grace is sufficient for you, for my power is made perfect [or: brought to full measure] in weakness" (2 Cor 12: 9). Thus, St. Paul would not say to the self-professed homosexual: "We implore you on behalf of Christ, 'be *reconciled to what is possible*'." Within the range of what *is possible*? *Possible for whom?* John Paul II pointedly asks, "Of man *dominated* by lust or of man *redeemed by Christ*?" "This is what is at stake," he adds, "the *reality* of Christ's redemption. *Christ has redeemed us!* . . . Only in the mystery of Christ's Redemption do we discover the 'concrete' possibilities of man. . . .* This means that he has given us the possibility of realizing the *entire truth* of our being; he has set our freedom free from the *domination* of concupiscence. And if redeemed man still sins, this is not due to an imperfection of Christ's redemptive act, but to man's will not to avail himself of the grace which flows from that act."[69]

In this connection, we can understand why Cardinal Eijk argues that integral to pastoral practice is the sacrament of confession, of reconciliation. He writes:

> The path that someone must take to come to a life of sexual abstinence as a homosexual can be long and arduous, and requires much self-denial and asceticism. In this process, the priest must stand by them with great patience, understanding, and dedication. It is not excluded that those involved may occasionally fall in their striving towards a life of sexual abstinence. Therefore, it is of the utmost importance that they frequently take refuge in the sacrament of confession and learn to rely on prayer and the sacrament of the Eucharist as the primary sources of grace to acquire the virtue of chastity, the inner capacity to integrate sexual impulses and feelings into a state of life as an unmarried person living in sexual abstinence. Alongside participation in these sacraments, however, the personal effort to acquire the natural virtue of chastity remains necessary.[70]

Now, rather than the virtue of chastity, I think Radcliffe's position will lead, indeed, to moral laxity, indeed, to the sort of moral corruption the pope describes, and it is a matter of concern for the whole Church. St. Paul tells us that the Church must not succumb to a lax attitude toward sin (see 1 Cor 5:6: "a little leaven leavens the whole lump"). He urges the believers at Corinth to take action against a man's sexual sin (i.e., incest) by removing him from the community. The community

---

[69] John Paul II, *Veritatis Splendor*, §103.
[70] Eijk, *De Band van de Liefde*, 470.

should mourn for him rather than become inflated with pride (5:2). As St. Paul says elsewhere in 1 Corinthians, we must "not rejoice at wrongdoing, but rejoice with truth" (13:6). *The truth being that we in the Church are all sinners who are saved by grace*: "For all have sinned and fall short of the glory of God, and are justified by his grace as a gift, through the redemption that is in Christ Jesus, whom God put forward as a propitiation by his blood, to be received in faith" (Rom 3:23-25).

Nevertheless, says St. Paul, the Church should take a stand against all sorts of sexual sin by warning the offending believers that if they continue in sexual immorality they will not inherit the Kingdom of God. Against this Pauline background, we should also ask Radcliffe how he proposes to help these offending believers to be "saved" from judgment "on the day of the Lord" (1 Cor 5:5). What about St. Paul's teaching that serial and unrepentant immoral sexual practices puts one at the risk of not inheriting God's eternal kingdom (1 Cor 6:9-10; 2 Cor 12:21; Gal 5:19-21; Rom 1:24-27; 6:19-23; Col 3:5-10; Eph 5:3-6, 4:17-19; 1 Thess 4:2-8). Furthermore, if "our deepest freedom is to do the will of the Father," as Radcliffe rightly says, how then does a person who is actively and unrepentantly engaged in same-sex practice change his life, radically reorient his whole life, put an end to sin, turn away from evil, "with repugnance toward the evil actions [he has] committed"[71], if no one, least of all the Church, calls him to interior repentance, conversion, that is, "the conversion of the heart, interior conversion" and a holy life?[72] As the *Catechism of the Catholic Church* teaches, "This endeavor of conversion is not just a human work. It is the movement of a 'contrite heart', drawn and moved by grace to respond to the merciful love of God who loved us first" (Ps 51:17; John 6:44; 12:32; 1 John 4:10).[73]

---

[71] *Catechism of the Catholic Church*, §1431.

[72] *Catechism of the Catholic Church*, §1430.

[73] *Catechism of the Catholic Church*, §1428.

Now, then, if we begin where people are, as Radcliffe suggests, that is because we seek to bear witness to the truth of the integrity of the chaste person. "The chaste person maintains the integrity of the powers of life and loved place in him. This integrity ensures the unity of the person; it is opposed to any behavior that would impair it. It tolerates neither a double life nor duplicity in speech."[74] We bear witness to this truth in the power of God's love and mercy to and for them, hoping and praying that by his grace he will give them a new heart (see Ezek 36:26-27). Chastity is an infused moral virtue, a gift of God's grace, which takes root in a person's character, and helps him to become virtuous by refining, educating and disciplining his desires. Specifically, virtues properly order our desires to the good, and thus the transformation of morally corrupted desires, like same-sex attraction, takes place through true virtue.

Let us then follow the lead of Robert Sokolowski, who following Aristotle, distinguishes four possibilities of human character. Character has to do with a person's whole moral identity. A moral agent may be (1) virtuous, or (2) self-controlled, or (3) weak in self-control, or (4) vicious.[75] A virtuous man is one who not only knows what is right, but also is inwardly disposed to do it. A self-controlled man is one who knows what is right, but whose inward disposition is in conflict with reason. Says Sokolowski, "He does not exist in the harmony found in the virtuous man; he requires self-control. Since he possesses self-control, he generally masters his inclinations and usually does what is good. . . . Self-control, although good, is not the same as virtue."[76] Echoing Sokolowski,

---

[74] *Catechism of the Catholic Church*, §2338.
[75] Sokolowski, *The God of Faith and Reason*, 57-58.
[76] Sokolowski, *The God of Faith and Reason*, Ibid., 57.

Radcliffe claims that the interior freedom, or spontaneity, that characterizes virtue, is "the fruit of a deep travail or rebirth."[77] This interior freedom is ordered to the integral gift of the self.

A weak man is one who knows what is right but he often cannot do it. His inclinations are in conflict with reason but, unlike a person who has self-control, exhibiting self-mastery, he is not able to master his inclinations. "His reason is disposed correctly but it is often overcome by inclination; this kind of man," Sokolowski adds, "often repents for what he does." Finally, "a vicious man is one whose mind and inclinations both move toward what is bad."[78] There is no internal struggle with a vicious man; he is not overcome by his desires, doing what he knows to be wrong. Unlike the weak person, a vicious person "chooses what is wrong and consequently is not likely to repent."[79]

We all should strive to be virtuous persons. "It is not easy for man, wounded by sin, to maintain moral balance. Christ's gift of salvation offers us the grace necessary to persevere in the pursuit of the virtues."[80] And pursuing the virtues in order to become virtuous, that is, to develop a habitual and firm interior disposition to do the good, involves, in the wonderful words of the *Catechism*, "an apprenticeship in self-mastery which is training in human freedom."[81] This training is required because our desires or feelings can be unruly, possessing of life of their own, as it were, resulting in an inner struggle between what we know to be right and the sway of disordered emotions. "The alternative is clear: either

---

[77] Radcliffe, *What's the Point of Being a Christian?* 42.

[78] Robert Sokolowski, *The God of Faith & Reason, Foundations of Christian Theology* (Washington, DC: Catholic University of America Press, 1995 [1982]), 58.

[79] Sokolowski, *The God of Faith and Reason*, 58.

[80] *Catechism of the Catholic Church*, §1811.

[81] *Catechism of the Catholic Church*, §2339.

man governs his passions and finds peace, or he lets himself be dominated by them and becomes unhappy."[82]

St. Paul expressed this interior struggle pointedly, "For I do not do the good I want, but the evil I do not want is what I keep on doing" (Rom 7:19). The solution to this interior struggle, he urges, is only union with the person of Christ, governed by moral guidelines—the authentic moral life flowing from the transformed life in Christ. This personal relationship with Christ through the work of the Holy Spirit effects a real transformation from within, establishing a harmony between what is right and my inclinations. "[P]ut off your old man, which belongs to your former manner of life and is corrupt through deceitful desires, and . . . be renewed in the spirit of your minds, and . . . put on the new man, created after the likeness of God in true righteousness and holiness" (Eph 4:22-24). Wouldn't Radcliffe agree? Isn't this what he means when says, "Christ in us makes all our actions ours."[83]

Radcliffe's proposal seems to pull him in another direction. Central to his proposal is urging the Church to take the stance of "friendship and proximity" so that she "can be with us as we face moral dilemmas and make choices."[84] He adds, "The Church will only be a cradle of gospel freedom if we are seen to stand beside people, supporting them as they make moral decisions *within the range of what is possible*, rather than making decisions for them."[85] Within the range of what *is possible? Possible for whom?* John Paul II pointedly asks, "Of man *dominated* by lust or of man *redeemed by Christ?*"[86]

---

[82] *Catechism of the Catholic Church*, §2339.
[83] Radcliffe, *What's the Point of Being a Christian?* 42.
[84] Radcliffe, *What's the Point of Being a Christian?* 40.
[85] Radcliffe, *What's the Point of Being a Christian?* 37; italics added.
[86] John Paul II, *Veritatis Splendor*, §103.

Doesn't Radcliffe's pastoral proposal underestimate the seriousness of sin's power to enslave us and the power of the death and resurrection of Jesus Christ to liberate us from its stranglehold? Doesn't his proposal deny that human nature is truly renewed by the redemptive power of Jesus Christ's finished work? St. Paul describes his own experience of sin trapping him, of a power at work within him, from which he is unable to break free (see Rom 7:13-23). "Wretched man that I am! Who will deliver me from this body of death?" His answer: "Thanks be to God, through Jesus Christ our Lord!" (Rom 7:24-25).[87] "For this is the will of God, your sanctification" (1 Thess 4:3). So urges Vatican II in its timely and challenging presentation of the call to holiness of the whole Church.[88] "The Lord Jesus, the divine Teacher and Model of all perfection, preached holiness of life to each and every one of His disciples, regardless of their situation: 'You therefore must be perfect, as your heavenly Father is perfect' (Mt 5:48). He Himself stands as the Author and Finisher of this holiness of life." At the head of all biblical motivations for holiness there is God's love. "God's love has been poured into our hearts through the Holy Spirit who has been given to us" (Rom 5:5). The Council Fathers add, "For He sent the Holy Spirit upon all men that He might inspire them from within to love God with their whole heart and their whole soul, with all their mind and all their strength (cf. Mk 12;30) and that they might love one another as Christ loved them (cf. John 13:34; 15:12)."[89]

But, as Fr. Raniero Cantalamessa rightly notes, "there is no sanctity without obedience," and thus "to say that all those baptized are called to

---

[87] On sin being like an enslaving force, see Alister E. McGrath, *Intellectuals Don't Need God & other Modern Myths*, 136.

[88] *Lumen Gentium*, §§39-42. See also, John Webster, *Holiness*, (Grand Rapids: Eerdmans, 2003), 91.

[89] *Lumen Gentium*, §40.

Ch. 6: The Triumph of the Therapeutic Mentality

holiness," which Vatican II does, "is to say that all are called to obedience." He adds, "St Paul speaks of obedience to faith (Rm 1:5; 16:26), of obedience to the teaching (Rm 6:17), of obedience to the Gospel (Rm 10:16; 2 Th 1:8),of obedience to truth (Gal 5:7), of obedience to Christ (2 Cor 10:5)."[90] There is no sanctity without obedience, and there is no obedience without the gift of faith in Jesus Christ as Lord, trusting fully in his saving work, following him, dying to self, and living for him who loved me and gave himself for me on the Cross (Gal 2:20; cf. Mk 8:34-36).

Radcliffe's pastoral strategy is missing the call to holiness, to conversion, repentance, and the forgiveness of sins. But there is no sanctity without obedience, and no obedience without interior conversion of the heart. Of course, the Church consists of sinners who are saved by grace. Nevertheless, there is a spiritual battle being waged in our lives (see Eph 6:10-20). "This is the struggle of conversion directed toward holiness and eternal life to which the Lord never ceases to call us."[91] Jesus calls us to conversion. This is not only the initial response to the Gospel, which is the fruit of the regenerating grace of Baptism, of the new birth and gift of the Holy Spirit. This is "Christ's call to conversion [that] continues to resound in the lives of Christians."[92] "This second conversion is," the Catechism adds, "the movement of a 'contrite heart', drawn and moved by grace to respond to the merciful love of God who loved us first [in

---

[90] Raniero Cantalamessa, O.F.M. Cap. *Obedience: The Authority of the Word* (Slough, England: St. Pauls, 1985), 30-31, 34, respectively.
[91] *Catechism of the Catholic Church*, §1426.
[92] *Catechism of the Catholic Church*, §1428.

Christ]."⁹³ In short, this movement is "the conversion of the heart, interior conversion."⁹⁴ Indeed, that should be the aim of the Church's pastoral practice regarding the sexual sin of homosexuality.⁹⁵

"The Spirit of Truth"

Fr. Martin has recently written about the work of the Holy Spirit in the process of conversion involving an openness to change regarding the Church's teaching on homosexuality.⁹⁶ Missing from his recent reflection is an account of the relationship between the Holy Spirit and truth, as well as how emphasizing the experiential presence of the Spirit doesn't promote a hermeneutical individualism, subjectivism, and sectarianism.⁹⁷

"And it is the Spirit who bears witness, because the Spirit is truth" (1 John 5:6). This verse is just one of many in the Johannine literature where the Spirit is called by Jesus the Spirit of truth.⁹⁸ Thomas G. Weinandy explains why. "The Spirit is the Spirit of truth because he testifies

---

⁹³ *Catechism of the Catholic Church*, §1428.

⁹⁴ *Catechism of the Catholic Church*, §1430.

⁹⁵ Helpful in drawing out Scriptural principles for clinical practice is Robert A.J. Gagnon, "Scriptural Perspectives on Homosexuality and Sexual Identity."

⁹⁶ James Martin, SJ, "How James Martin SJ was converted at the Synod of Bishops," *Ignis* November 8, 2024. https://igniswebmagazine.nl/kerk/hoe-james-martin-sj-bekeerd-werd-op-de-bisschoppensynode/.

⁹⁷ The following paragraphs are adapted from Echeverria, *Dialogue of Love: Confessions of an Evangelical Catholic Ecumenist*, 118-120.

⁹⁸ Jesus refers to the Holy Spirit as the "Spirit of truth" in the following verses of the Gospel of John: "And I will pray the Father, and He will give you another Helper [Counsellor], that He may abide with you forever—the Spirit of truth" (John 14:16f.). "But when the Helper comes, whom I shall send to you from the Father, the Spirit of truth who proceeds from the Father, He will testify of Me" (John 15:26). Also in John we find Jesus saying, "I still have many things

Ch. 6: The Triumph of the Therapeutic Mentality

to the truth. God's word is truth. Jesus as the Word of God is the truth of God (the source of all truth) to which God's Spirit of truth bears witness."[99] In general, the Holy Spirit has a many-sided role. He was promised by Jesus as the Comforter, Advocate, Counselor,[100] indeed, the Spirit of truth, who leads the Apostles and the Church into the truth. He is the witness to Christ, glorifying him (John 14:17; 15:26; 16:14), convicting men of sin, righteousness and judgment (John 16:8-11), regenerating them (John 3:3), for with him who is the giver of life is the love and power of a "new creation" (Rom 8:22; 2 Cor 5:17; Col 3:10; Gal 6:15; Eph 2:15), and evoking from men the response that Christ is Lord (1 Cor. 12:3). Furthermore, the Spirit assures men of their adoption as sons of God and of their heavenly inheritance (Rom 8:14; 2 Cor 1:22; 5:5; Eph 1:13; 4:30). He also makes known all the things believers have received from God (1 Cor 2:12; 1 John 2:20; 3:24; 4:6-13), and in the Church is the source of all spiritual gifts and Christian virtues (1 Cor 12:8-11; Gal 5:22).[101] Furthermore, the Holy Spirit leads the Church toward a deepened understanding of revealed truth. This explains the significance of Jesus' words: "When the Spirit of truth comes, he will guide you into all the truth" (John 16:13. Commenting on this verse, John Paul II writes,

---

to say to you, but you cannot bear them now. However, when He, the Spirit of truth, has come, He will guide you into all truth; for He will not speak on His own *authority*, but whatever He hears He will speak; and He will tell you things to come" (John 16:12f.)

[99] Thomas G. Weinandy, OFM. Cap., *The Father's Spirit of Sonship:* Reconceiving the Trinity (Eugene, OR: Wipe & Stock, 1995), 48.

[100] Jesus calls the Spirit "another *paraclētos* (paraclete)" (John 14:6), another like himself. "The word *paraclētos* has often been translated as "comforter" or "counselor" here (the ESV prefers "Helper"), but there is no one word in English that accurately captures its meaning" (Robert Letham, *The Holy Trinity, In Scripture, History, Theology, and Worship*, 58). On the meaning of *paraclētos*, see also *Catechism of the Catholic Church*, §692.

[101] Bavinck, *Gereformeerde Dogmatiek*, I, 563. (ET: 593).

"He watches over the teaching of that truth, over its preservation and over its application to changing historical situations. He stirs up and guides the development of all that serves the knowledge and spread of that truth, particularly in scriptural exegesis and theological research. These can never be separated from the guidance of the Spirit of truth nor from the Magisterium of the Church, in which the Spirit is always at work."[102] If anything is missing from the reflections of Fr. Martin on openness to change is this crucial Catholic teaching of John Paul

In particular, however, the Holy Spirit has epistemological significance. For example, the Holy Spirit works, epistemically, not only as a witness to the truth of the Gospel (see, e.g., John 15:26-27; Acts 5:32; Rom 8:16), but also he makes a person inwardly certain of that truth (see, e.g., 1 Thess 1:5). In short, the Holy Spirit has an epistemic role to play: the truth of divine revelation known is known in faith not only by the Spirit's internal illumination or testimony but also he makes a man inwardly certain of that truth. The *Catechism of the Catholic Church* teaches, "'No one can say 'Jesus is Lord' except by the Holy Spirit' [1 Cor 12:3]. 'God has sent the Spirit of his Son into our hearts, crying, '*Abba! Father!*' [Gal 4:6]. This knowledge of faith is possible only in the Holy Spirit."[103] Elsewhere the *Catechism* states, "Believing is possible only by grace and the interior helps of the Holy Spirit."[104]

In this connection, it is important to recall that the Holy Scripture is God's gift to the church, which has been entrusted with the responsibility to teach faithfully and be its authoritative interpreter. Furthermore,

---

[102] John Paul II, *A Catechesis on the Creed*, Vol. III, *The Spirit, Giver of Life and Love*, 24; see also, 346-350. See *Dei Verbum*, §8: The apostolic faith "develops in the Church with the help of the Holy Spirit. For there is a growth in the understanding of the realities and the words which have been handed down."

[103] *Catechism of the Catholic Church*, §683.

[104] *Catechism of the Catholic Church*, §154.

the living understanding of the Catholic faith has an ecclesial structure.[105]

First, then, the Catholic tradition—indeed, Vatican I and II—affirms that the Lord himself has delivered the Scripture to the church. Though the Scriptures are canonical and hence authoritative because they have God as their author, are inspired, and have been delivered by the Spirit to the church, "the writings gathered in the Bible are [canonical], and can be, a 'Bible', 'Scripture', only within the church." Second, the Church's authority to teach is one of three functions that Christ conferred on the church, functions which he fulfilled and united in himself in the offices of prophet, priest, and king, namely, to teach, sanctify and govern. Briefly, the authority given by Jesus Christ to the apostles and hence to his successors, included the powers to bind and loose (Mt 16:9; Mt. 18:8), to forgive sins (John 20:21–23), to baptize (Mt 28:18–20), and to make disciples. (Mt 28:18–20)

Regarding the Church's responsibility to teach, explains Avery Dulles, "The Church . . . is commissioned by Christ to bear authoritative witness to God's revelation in Christ,"[106] and, significantly, not my individual experience, or the collective experience of a community, as some contemporary Catholics suggest. As Aidan Nichols states in the first epigraph to this chapter states, "It is not experience we should trust but the transmutation of experience by Scripture and Tradition." Furthermore, Dulles adds, "the term 'Magisterium' . . . designates the Church's function of teaching. More precisely, it means the authoritative teaching of those who are commissioned to speak to the community in the name of Christ, clarifying the faith that the community professes."[107] Moreover,

---

[105] The following paragraphs are adapted from my book, *Berkouwer and Catholicism*, 327-28, 332-34.

[106] Dulles, *Magisterium, Teacher and Guardian of the Faith*, 3

[107] Dulles, *Magisterium, Teacher and Guardian of the Faith*, 3

Dulles explains, "the Catholic Church believes and teaches that Christ delivered his revelation to the Church as a corporate body. Having received the Word of God, the Church has an inalienable responsibility to hand it on, explain it, and defend it against errors."[108] Disagreements about the truth of the gospel involve the discriminating responsibility of the Church's teaching office. This responsibility means "determining whether or not a particular teaching is identifiable or consistent with what is taught in the scriptures and the tradition of the church. This special teaching function is essentially the power to recognize sameness and difference between what was taught and what is being proposed."[109] There is more, the Church's special teaching function involves her being preserved from errors; otherwise, the saving teaching of Christ would no longer be available to men. As Dulles writes, "it is logical to suppose that if God deems it important to give a revelation, he will make provision to assure its conservation. If he did not set up reliable organs of transmission, the revelation would in a few generations be partly forgotten and inextricably commingled with human speculations."[110] Indeed, it is more than logical to argue for the necessity of a teaching office that speaks for the church in the name of the church. "God was moved by love to impart to men the fullness of his revelation through Christ and the apostles; was he also moved by love to guarantee the infallible teaching of this revelation until the end of time? Or did he leave men after the death of the apostles with a mute text which each could interpret as he

---

[108] Dulles, *Magisterium, Teacher and Guardian of the Faith*, 4-5.

[109] Sokolowski, *The God of Faith & Reason, Foundations of Christian Theology*, 26.

[110] Dulles, *Magisterium, Teacher and Guardian of the Faith*, 4-5. In essence, this is John Henry Newman's argument for a teaching office of the church in *An Essay on the Development of Christian Doctrine*, chapter II, Section II. See also Newman's *Apologia Pro Vita Sua*, chapter V.

saw fit?"[111] Of course, this latter alternative is unacceptable to a Catholic hermeneutics. It sees the Bible as the result of a communicative action, meaning thereby that the meaning of the text an intentional action of its human and divine authors. As Jeanine Brown correctly states, this intentional action is the "communicative act of the author that has been inscribed in the text and addressed to the intended audience for purposes of engagement."[112] Vatican II's *Dei Verbum* §§11-12 agrees:

> Those divinely revealed realities that are contained and presented in Sacred Scripture have been committed to writing under the inspiration of the Holy Spirit. . . . Therefore, since everything asserted by the inspired authors or sacred writers must be held to be asserted by the Holy Spirit, it follows that the books of Scripture must be acknowledged as teaching solidly, faithfully and without error that truth which God wanted put into sacred writings for the sake of salvation. . . . Since God speaks in Sacred Scripture through men in human fashion, the interpreter of Sacred Scripture, in order to see clearly what God wanted to communicate to us, should carefully investigate what meaning the sacred writers really intended, and what God wanted to manifest by means of their words.

In sum, the responsibility of the Church's teaching office, the Magisterium, is to keep faithfully, to judge authentically, distinguishing between true and false teaching, and to define infallibly the content of the deposit of the faith. The Church is called by the Lord Jesus to be a herald

---

[111] Charles Journet, *The Primacy of Peter*, translated from the French by John Chapin (Westminster, Maryland: The Newman Press, 1954), 41

[112] Jeannine K. Brown, *Scripture as Communication: Introducing Biblical hermeneutics* (Grand Rapids, MI: Baker Academic, 2007), 14.

of the apostolic faith, to defend the faith against opposed errors in its judgments, and, as Dulles puts it, "to clarify the faith by bringing forth from the treasury 'things new and old'."[113] He adds, "In answering new questions, as in refuting new errors, the Magisterium sometimes brings out hitherto unnoticed implications of the faith."

The second question I want to address pertains to stressing the work of the Holy Spirit in opening us up to change. Will invoking the work of the Spirit help to block the move to hermeneutical individualism or experiential subjectivism, and thus safeguard the objectivity and authority of Scripture, binding religious subjectivity to the Word of God itself, safe guarding interpretations from these cul-de-sacs and hence from the loss of the authority of Scripture? Karl Rahner gives a Catholic response to this question. Briefly, the Church has a place in its hermeneutics for the Holy Spirits epistemological significance, and so the issue here is not over whether the Spirit is at work in interpretations made in the light of faith. Rather, the issue concerns the question as to how the Spirit of God works concretely. According to the Catholic position of faith's living understanding of Scripture, says Rahner, that understanding has itself an ecclesial structure because faith lives on in the church in a way that makes Scripture a living reality in the power of the Spirit. He explains:

> This does not dethrone Scripture. It does not cease to be the *norma non normata* for the church and also for its teaching office. We did not discover the Bible somewhere by our own curiosity, but rather, as something which awakens faith and brings faith and communicates the Spirit, it comes to us only in the preaching of the concrete church. And this says to us: here is the Word of God, a word which it gives witness to in such a way that

---

[113] Dulles, *Magisterium, Teacher and Guardian of the Faith*, 62–63.

according to the Catholic understanding of the faith too it can manifest itself by its own power.... However, faith's living understanding of Scripture, and Scripture's transposition into faith's really pneumatic experience of the reality which Scripture means are processes whose place Scripture itself cannot take, and the process of faith's living understanding of Scripture has itself an ecclesial structure. It is not simply and merely an affair of the individual's religious subjectivity. Rather it is more originally an affair of the Church as such, an affair of the single community of believers within which the individual Christian acquires his concrete understanding of the faith. This community of faith is not only the sum of individual religious subjectivities, *but rather it really has a structure, a hierarchical constitution, and an authoritative leadership through which the church's single understanding of the faith receives its unambiguous meaning and its binding character.*[114]

In sum, Rahner states admirably well in the above passage, the formative process of faith's understanding of divine revelation, of salvation, of sin, the cross and grace, and so much more, is essentially an ecclesial one, namely, by being members of Christ's historic Church, the Catholic Church. And this ecclesial structure is hierarchically constituted with the official and public teaching of the church, the Magisterium, consisting of an authoritative leadership, of the pope and the bishops who are in communion with him. The experiential subjectivism entailed by the triumph of the therapeutic mentality leads to separating the Bible from the church—that has led to a crisis of authority, indeed, a crisis of faith in

---

[114] Karl Rahner, *Foundations of Christian Faith: An Introduction to the Idea of Christianity,* translated by William V. Dych (London: Darton Longman & Todd, 1978), 364–365. Emphasis added.

the authority off Scripture. This crisis cannot be resolved by reasserting orthodoxy alone or the Church's hierarchical teaching office alone. Rather what is needed is the teaching and practice of Vatican II's dogmatic constitution, *Dei Verbum*, namely, a trilateral conception of authority wherein Scripture, tradition and the church's teaching office, being intrinsically and necessarily related operating together, but exercising authority in a way that is unique to each one of them. In other words, to quote Dulles, "nothing is believed on the authority of tradition alone, Scripture alone, or the magisterium alone."[115] Concluding with *Dei Verbum* §10: "It is clear, therefore, that sacred tradition, Sacred Scripture and the teaching authority of the Church, in accord with God's most wise design, are so linked and joined together that one cannot stand without the others, and that all together and each in its own way under the action of the one Holy Spirit contribute effectively to the salvation of souls."

Call to Conversion and Holiness

Fr. Martin calls all Christians to conversion. He says, "What I mean by *conversion* is the conversion that *all of us* are called to by God and the conversion of minds and hearts that Jesus called for" (*BB*, 23). He adds, "LGBT people are called to be holy, as all of us are" (*BB*, 44). The crucial question I want to ask now is about the relationship between faith and morality in the context of the call to holiness. As Fr. Raniero Cantalamessa rightly notes, "there is no sanctity without obedience," and thus "to say that all those baptized are called to holiness," which Vatican II does, "is to say that all are called to obedience." He adds, "St Paul speaks of obedience to faith (Rm 1:5; 16:26), of obedience to the teaching

---

[115] Avery Cardinal Dulles, SJ, "Vatican II on the Interpretation of Scripture," *Letter & Spirit* 2 (2006): 17–26, and at 17.

Ch. 6: The Triumph of the Therapeutic Mentality

(Rm 6:17), of obedience to the Gospel (Rm 10:16; 2 Th 1:8), of obedience to truth (Gal 5:7), of obedience to Christ (2 Cor 10:5)."[116] There is no sanctity without obedience, and there is no obedience without the gift of faith in Jesus Christ as Lord, trusting fully in his saving work, following him, dying to self, and living for him who loved me and gave himself for me on the Cross (Gal 2:20; cf. Mk 8:34-36).

According to the Catholic Church, there is an intrinsic and unbreakable bond between faith and morality. Jesus said, "Abide in my love. If you keep my commandments, you will abide in my love, just as I have kept my Father's commandments and abide in his love" (John 15:10; 1 John 5: 2-3). This question about the bond between faith and morality must deal directly with the eternal significance of the moral choices that people make, indeed, with their eternal salvation. In this light, we can understand why St. Paul consistently urges us to make choices that are worthy of the calling that we have received in Christ (Eph 4: 1; Phil 1: 27; Col 1:9). In particular, he identifies the risk posed by, especially *but not only*, sexual offenses: "Do you not know that the unrighteous will not inherit the kingdom of God? Stop deceiving yourselves: Neither sexually immoral persons [*pornoi*, i.e., like the incestuous man], nor idolaters, nor adulterers, nor 'soft men' [*malakoi*, i.e., men who feminize themselves to attract male sex partners], nor men who lie with a male [*arsenokoitai*, a term formed from the Leviticus prohibition of male homosexual practice] . . . shall inherit the kingdom of God (1 Cor 6:9-10)."[117] The *Catechism of the Catholic Church* instructs us that certain choices

---

[116] Cantalamessa, *Obedience: The Authority of the Word*, 30-31, 34, respectively.

[117] See also Gal 5: 19-21; Eph 5: 3-5; 1 Thess 4: 2-8. I am using Robert Gagnon's translation of 1 Cor 6:9-11. For a thorough exegetical justification of this translation of the passive and active partners in homosexual acts, see his *The Bible and Homosexual Practice*, 303-339.

result "in the loss of charity and the privation of sanctifying grace, that is, of the state of grace." The *Catechism* adds, "If it is not redeemed by repentance and God's forgiveness, it causes exclusion from Christ's kingdom and the eternal death of hell." How is that so? Because, the *Catechism* concludes, "our freedom has the power to make choices for ever, with no turning back."[118]

Against this background, we are not surprised that Fr. Martin never addresses the question of morality let alone sexual morality,[119] and hence never presents the members of the so-called LGBT community with the call to chastity, namely, "to fulfill God's will in their lives and, if they are Christians, to unite to the sacrifice of the Lord's Cross the difficulties they may encounter from their condition" (*CCC*, §2358). In addition, "By the virtues of self-mastery that teach them inner freedom, at times by the support of disinterested friendship, by prayer and sacramental grace, they can and should gradually and resolutely approach Christian perfection" (*CCC*, §2359).

Yes, Fr. Martin generalizes by saying that "we are all imperfect people, struggling to do our best in the light of our individual vocations. We are all pilgrims on the way, loved sinners following the call we first heard at our baptism and that we continue to hear every day of our lives" (*BB*, 76). True enough. And yet, once again, one would think that in a book about human sexuality, an author writing from a Catholic perspective would identify the specific sexual struggles of the moral life in Christ as the sixth commandment bears upon them, and the corresponding sexual

---

[118] *Catechism of the Catholic Church*, §1861,

[119] Adding to the confusion regarding the moral authority of the Bible is that Fr. Martin never states whether "there exists, in Divine Revelation, a specific and determined moral content, universally valid and permanent" (John Paul II, *Veritatis Splendor*, §37).

Ch. 6: The Triumph of the Therapeutic Mentality

sins against chastity. But no, they receive no attention; they do not figure in this book at all.

In this connection, this is not the book's only flaw. I surmise that Fr. Martin is trying to diminish the importance of sexual sins relative to others by suggesting that all sins are equal before God, with none being worse than others. He insists on an egalitarian view of sin.[120] But is this true? There is a hierarchy of sins, such as is implied in the distinction between mortal and venial sins.[121] In short, all sins are equally covered by the atoning work of Christ, but they are not equal in all respects, and hence some sins are graver than others. Biblical scholar Robert Gagnon correctly identifies the reason why homosexual practice is more heavily weighted than other sins. "Homosexual practice, committed or otherwise, is the violation that most clearly and radically offends against God's intentional creation of humans as 'male and female' (Gen 1:27) and definition of marriage as a union between a man and a woman (Gen 2:24)."[122]

St. Paul tells us that the Church must not succumb to a lax attitude toward sin (see 1 Cor 5:6: "a little leaven leavens the whole lump"). He urges the believers at Corinth to take action against a man's sexual sin (i.e., incest) by removing him from the community. The community should mourn for him rather than become inflated with pride (5:2). As

---

[120] For an insightful critique of the egalitarian view of sin, See Robert Gagnon, "Is Homosexual Practice No Worse Than Any Other Sin?," January 7, 2015, http://www.robgagnon.net/articles/homosexAreAllSinsEqual.pdf.

[121] *Catechism of the Catholic Church*, §§1854-1864. See also, John Paul II, *Veritatis Splendor*, §§ 69-70.

[122] Robert A. J. Gagnon, "How Bad is Homosexual Practice According to Scripture and Does Scripture's Indictment Apply to Committed Homosexual Unions?," 1-11, and at 2; http://robgagnon.net/articles/HomosexHowBadIsIt.pdf.

St. Paul says elsewhere in 1 Corinthians, we must "not rejoice at wrongdoing, but rejoice with truth" (13:6). *The truth being that we in the Church are all sinners who are saved by grace*: "For all have sinned and fall short of the glory of God, and are justified by his grace as a gift, through the redemption that is in Christ Jesus, whom God put forward as a propitiation by his blood, to be received in faith" (Rom 3:23-25).

Nevertheless, says St. Paul, the Church should take a stand against all sorts of sexual sin by warning the offending believers that if they continue in sexual immorality they will not inherit the Kingdom of God. Against this Pauline background, we should ask Fr. Martin how he proposes to help these offending believers to be "saved" from judgment "on the day of the Lord" (1 Cor 5:5). What about St. Paul's teaching that serial and unrepentant immoral sexual practices puts one at the risk of not inheriting God's eternal kingdom (1 Cor 6:9-10; 2 Cor 12: 21; Gal 5:19-21; Rom 1:24-27; 6:19-23; Col 3:5-10; Eph 5:3-6, 4:17-19; 1 Thess 4:2-8)?

This Pauline teaching is stated clearly in *CCC*, §1861: "Mortal sin is a radical possibility of human freedom, as is love itself. It results in the loss of charity and the privation of sanctifying grace, that is, of the state of grace. If it is not redeemed by repentance and God's forgiveness, it causes exclusion from Christ's kingdom and the eternal death of hell, for our freedom has the power to make choices for ever, with no turning back. However, although we can judge that an act is in itself a grave offense, we must entrust judgment [regarding the eternal standing] of persons to the justice and mercy of God."

Furthermore, if sinners are called to follow their baptismal vocation throughout their lives, as Martin rightly says, how then does a person who is actively and unrepentantly engaged in same-sex practice change his life, radically reorient his whole life, put an end to sin, turn away from evil, if no one, least of all the Church, least of all Fr. Martin, calls him to

Ch. 6: The Triumph of the Therapeutic Mentality 483

interior repentance, conversion, that is, "the conversion of the heart, interior conversion" (*CCC*, §1430), and a holy life?

Moreover, how should we understand, as Fr. Martin holds, that "[we] are loved by God as [we] are" (10)? Yes, we come to the Lord just as we are, sinners who sins are under the mercy and justice of the cross. Is that what Fr. Martin means? Does he understand that "Christ died for the ungodly," and so "God demonstrates his own love for us in this: While we were still sinners, Christ died for us" (Romans 5: 6, 8). Indeed, "when we were God's enemies, we were reconciled to him through the death of his Son" (vs. 10).

Yes, God is rich in mercy (Eph 2:4). He forgave my sins out of love for me in Christ even while I was dead through my trespasses (Eph 2:5), even while I was still his enemy (Rom 5:10). In this light, we can easily understand the wideness of God's mercy, why mercy is inclusive, grounded in divine redemption, and hence neither discriminating nor relativizing—all men are sinners and are under the power of sin (see Rom 3:9-18). But "God so loved the world that He gave His only begotten Son, that whoever believes in Him should not perish but have eternal life" (John 3: 16). The Church welcomes all sinners, none are excluded.

But how shall they know that they are called by the Gospel to repentance and amendment of life, if they have not heard that call (cf. Rom 10: 14-17). But "how can they hear without someone preaching to them" (vs. 14). Paul VI affirms in his 1975 Apostolic Exhortation, *Evangelii Nuntiandi* §22, "All Christians are called to this witness, and in this way they can be real evangelizers." Nevertheless, Paul VI adds, "this [witness] *always remains insufficient*, because even the finest witness will prove *ineffective* in the long run if it is not explained, justified – what Peter called always having 'your answer ready for people who ask you the reason for the hope that you all have' [1 Peter 3:15] – and made explicit by a clear and unequivocal proclamation of the Lord Jesus. Thus, when proclaiming the Father's mercy in Christ and in the power of the Holy Spirit towards others it must be clear to them that our action is rooted in God's prior act of mercy shown to us in and through the finished work of Christ. Thus: "if we confess our sins he is faithful and just, and will forgive us our sins and cleanse us from all unrighteousness. If we say we have not sinned, we make him a liar and his word is not in us" (1 John 1: 9-10).

It is worth repeating what Pope Francis has written: "Although it sounds obvious, *spiritual accompaniment must lead others ever closer to God, in whom we attain true freedom*. . . . To accompany them would be counterproductive if it became a sort of therapy supporting their self-absorption and ceased to be a pilgrimage with Christ to the Father."[123] Fr. Martin's book does not tell the so-called LGBT+ community the truth, indeed, the gospel truth, and hence he cannot help people avoid the danger of what Francis calls here therapeutic self-absorption. This point undercuts Fr. Martin's presupposition justifying self-authenticating experiences. Chiefly, spiritual accompaniment calls for conversion, including moral conversion. As *CCC* teaches, "This endeavor of conversion is not just a human work. It is the movement of a 'contrite heart', drawn and moved by grace to respond to the merciful love of God who loved us first" (Ps 51:17; John 6:44; 12:32; 1 John 4:10). I conclude with the words of the *Catechism of the Catholic Church* (§§1785, 1802):

> In the formation of conscience, the Word of God is the light for our path. We must assimilate it in faith and prayer and put it into practice. We must also examine our conscience before the Lord's Cross. We are assisted by the gifts of the Holy Spirit,

---

[123] *Evangelii gaudium*, §§169-170.

aided by the witness or advice of others and guided by the authoritative teaching of the Church.

. . . . This is how moral conscience is formed.

Afterword

The Project of Redeeming Sex

The Battle for the Body

The human body shares in the dignity of the "image of God."

—*Catechism of the Catholic Church.*[1]

Responsibility in sexual development implies a responsibility to nature—to the ordered good of the bodily form which we have been given.... When God made mankind male and female, to exist alongside each other and for each other, he gave a form that human sexuality should take and a good to which it should aspire. None of us can, or should, regard our difficulties with that form, or with achieving that good, as the norm of what our sexuality is to be. None of us should see our sexuality as a mere self-expression, and forget that we can express ourselves sexually only because we participate in this generic form and aspire to this generic good.

—Oliver O'Donovan[2]

Surely, given the current penchant of the culture for pluralism, for celebrating difference, Christians need to celebrate sameness

---

[1] *Catechism of the* Catholic Church, §364.
[2] *Begotten or Made?* With a new introduction and afterword (Landrum, SC: Davenant Press, 2022), 34-5.

. . . . We cannot dodge our moral obligations by playing the cultural difference card. It is into this world of objective structures, though fallen and hence warped and bent, that the one Gospel comes. It is the Creator's Gospel . . . . The Gospel has the same kind of objectivity as the structures of creation do. It is the amazing grace of their Creator. Its claims are held to be true with the same kind of truth, not relative, subjective truth, but objective truth.[3]

—Paul Helm

This book has provided a philosophical, theological, and Catholic ecumenical exploration into the project of redeeming sex, namely, reclaiming the rich meaning and vocation of human embodiment, of the body-person, of the sexual difference of man and woman in light of the grand narrative of creation, fall into sin, redemption in Jesus Christ, oriented eschatologically. In this Afterword, I state six summative theses that capture the main emphases in this book on the battle for the body.

Six Theses

First, the late St. John Paul II, the philosopher-pope, issued a call to the new evangelization, that is, to the revitalization of the Christian faith at the heart of Western culture. This vital call for renewal is, in truth, an expression of the Church's missionary nature to proclaiming the gospel throughout the world, bringing the gospel to bear on the whole spectrum of human life, and transforming creation from within and making it new—the plan of creation, fall, redemption, and the consummation of

---

[3] Paul Helm, "Against Ideological Apologetics," *Reformation 21* (February 2007).

Afterword: The Project of Redeeming Sex 489

all creation in Christ. John Paul II urged us to carry out the new evangelization as integral evangelization—to use a term coined by Aidan Nichols that nicely captures the full scope of integral evangelization, of the redemption of the whole man, including human reason, and the full spectrum of culture. In a Catholic theology of culture, the question of the relationship between nature, sin, and grace—or among the orders of creation, fall into sin, redemption, and fulfillment—becomes the problem of faith and culture, and thus Christ and culture, Church and world. In addition, I show that, epistemologically speaking, the question of the relation between nature and grace, or between the order of creation and the order of redemption has implications for the problems of faith and reason. John Paul succinctly puts the thesis defended in this three-volume work: "A faith that does not become culture is a faith not fully accepted, not entirely thought out, not faithfully lived."[4] He sums up the call to integral evangelization:

> Indeed, the Church's mission of spreading the Gospel not only demands that the Good News be preached ever more widely and to ever greater numbers of men and women, but [also] that the very power of the Gospel should permeate thought patterns, standards of judgment, and the norms of behavior; in a word, it is necessary that the whole of human culture be steeped in the Gospel. The cultural atmosphere in which a human being lives has a great influence upon his or her way of thinking and, thus, of acting. Therefore, a division between

---

[4] John Paul II, Letter instituting the Pontifical Council for Culture, May 20, 1982, AAS LXXIV (1982), 683-88, as cited in *Towards a Pastoral Approach to Culture*, Pontifical Council for Culture, 1999, §1.

faith and culture is more than a small impediment to evangelization, while a culture penetrated with the Christian spirit is an instrument that favors the spreading of the Good News[5].

This thesis is at the heart of my three-volume work, *Creation Redeemed*, Vol. 1, *Redeeming Sex: The Battle for the Body*, Vol. 2, *Redeeming Reason: Faith, Rationality, and Truth*, and Vol. 3, *Redeeming Culture: Christ the Sign of Contradiction*.

Second, is there an orthodoxy regarding marriage and sexual ethics? This question is raised by James K.A. Smith in his discussion of the relationship between the fundamentals of orthodoxy, namely, the ecumenical councils and creeds of the Church that are grounded in the nature of God (Triune), the Incarnation, the means of our salvation, the church, and the life to come, on the one hand, and non-fundamentals, as he suggests, on the other, that reflect a "particular view of sexuality and marriage."[6] The issue here is, according to Smith, not whether one can be indifferent to the latter view since they are not a matter of creedal definition, but whether a standard of sexuality and marriage pertain essentially to orthodoxy, namely, "right beliefs" or "correct beliefs," "beliefs that are true rather than false."[7] Smith does not say what particular view of sexuality and marriage he has in mind, a view that he refers to as traditional, as the "historic teaching of the Church." I surmise that he means the idea that sexual difference between a man and woman is constitutive of our humanity (Gen 1:27), and hence of sexual morality such

---

[5] John Paul II, "A Deep Commitment to Authentic Christian Living," *The Whole Truth about Man*, ed. with intro. James V. Schall, S.J. (Boston: St. Paul Editions, 1981), 84–91, and at 89.

[6] James K.A. Smith, "On 'Orthodox Christianity': some observations and a couple of questions," *Fors Claviga*, Friday, August 4, 2017.

[7] Eleonore Stump, "Orthodoxy and Heresy, *Faith and Philosophy*, Volume 16, Issue 2, April 1999, 147-163.

Afterword: The Project of Redeeming Sex 491

that only a sexual union of male and female persons makes bodies in any real sense "one flesh" (Gen 2:24), with the latter organic bodily union being a necessary condition for the existence of authentic conjugal love; thus, in this light, marriage is the two-in-one-flesh union of a man and a woman.

Does rejecting this view about the nature of marriage as essential to orthodoxy presuppose that moral norms regarding sexual ethics are not part of the proper content of revelation, and hence for that reason are not matters of creedal definition? The question that arises is whether it is being denied, in the words of John Paul II, "that there exists, in Divine Revelation, a specific and determined moral content, universally valid and permanent."[8] Aren't there moral norms found in Scripture having not only the status of fundamental revealed moral truth constitutive of orthodoxy but also are in themselves relevant for salvation (1 Cor 6:9–11)?

The Catholic tradition rejects the sharp distinction made by Smith between creedal Christianity and the Church's historic teaching on sexuality and marriage. Fundamental *revealed* moral truth, and the revealed truth about marriage grounded in the creation order, both which are universally valid, holding for all times and places throughout the centuries, are constitutive of orthodoxy. For example, Jesus grounds sexual ethics and the corresponding ethic of marriage in the order of creation. Müller explains, "Sexuality can be contextualized only if a conjugal design exists."[9] Critics of this position call it confessionalism. Berkouwer defines confessionalism in his 1949 study, *Conflict met Rome*, "Confessionalism in effect takes the position that the Scriptures have been given their final form in the confession. The Bible lies behind; ahead of us is the 'extract'. The Scriptures have no longer any

---

[8] John Paul II, *Veritatis Splendor*, §37.
[9] Müller, *Vatican Confidential*, 67.

actuality."[10] Confessionalism, also called traditionalism, is allegedly opposed to "*ecclesia semper reformanda est*," the church reformed, always being reformed. In short, it absolutizes continuity of dogmatic truth without displaying any appreciation for the historical nature of those truths' human expression. As Jaroslav Pelikan describes the position that Berkouwer calls confessionalism or traditionalism: "Tradition without history has homogenized all the stages of development into one statically defined truth."[11]

In response, I argue that Church teaching has different levels of authority and certainty; while some are fundamental, definitive, indeed, infallible, and hence irreformable, others are not and so may be subject to reform, the possibility of reversals (e.g., the church's previous teachings on religious freedom, church/state relations, ecumenism have been reformed).[12] So not all church teaching carries the same weight or authority because the church has never held that every magisterial teaching is, ipso facto, infallible. The latter, however, are permanently valid, objectively, or absolutely true, and hence are not subject to rejection or correction or reversibility. Certainly the following biblical affirmations are of that sort: "Jesus is Lord" (1 Cor 12:3), "God was in

---

[10] *Conflict met Rome* (Kampen: Kok, 1949, 43; ET: *The Conflict with Rome*, 31.

[11] Pelikan, *The Christian Tradition*, I, *The Emergence of the Catholic Tradition* (100-600). (Chicago/London: The University of Chicago Press, 1971). 9.

[12] On the possibility of reversals, see Thomas G. Guarino, *Vincent of Lérins and the Development of Christian Doctrine* (Grand Rapids, MI: Baker Academic, 2013). on the various levels of magisterial authority, see Vatican Council II, Dogmatic Constitution, *Lumen Gentium* (1965), §25; "Profession of Faith," Congregation for the Doctrine of the Faith (1989); *Donum Veritatis*, Congregation for the Doctrine of the Faith (1990); "Commentary on the Profession of Faith's concluding paragraphs, Professio Fidei (1998). All of these documents may be found in appendices e–h, respectively, in Dulles, *Magisterium: Teacher and Guardian of the Faith*, 131–181.

Afterword: The Project of Redeeming Sex 493

Christ reconciling the world to himself" (2 Cor 5:19), and "the Word was made flesh and dwelt among us" (John 1:14), and many other biblical and creedal theological propositions as found, for instance, in the Nicene-Constantinople creed, but also in the Belgic Confession of Faith, the Heidelberg Catechism, and other Reformed and Lutheran confessions. In defending this claim, we need to see that doxological affirmations, such as these affirmations, contain propositions, that is, claims that things are such and such and so not their contradictories. All affirmations of the Christian faith, all dogmas, are such that being true propositions they can never become infected with error, with falsehood.[13]

Notwithstanding this fundamental point about irreformable statements, which are statements protected by infallibility, even teaching that is fundamental, definitive, and hence irreformable is such that it may require further thought and elucidation. Seeing the distinction here clearly requires us to distinguish between an unqualified fallibilism and qualified fallibilism. "Fallibilism does not challenge the claim that we can know the truth, but rather the belief that we can know that we have attained the final truth with absolute certainty."[14] There is an inconsistency generated by an unqualified fallibilism by virtue of implying the reversibility, in principle, at some later point, of all Christian doctrinal and dogmatic truths that are putatively irreversible or final, such as the examples given above. In contrast, a qualified fallibilism presupposes the distinction between the propositional truths of faith and their linguistic expressions, between truth-content and context, such

---

[13] George Lindbeck, "The Infallibility Debate," in *The Infallibility Debate*, edited by John J. Kirvan (New York: Paulist Press, 1971), 107–152, and at 111.

[14] This definition of fallibilism is by Richard Bernstein, "Philosophers respond to [John Paul II's] *Fides et Ratio*," *Books and Culture* 5 (July/August 1999): 30–32.

that those truths are "open to reconceptualization and reformulation, and that [is because] no statement comprehensively exhausts truth, much less divine truth."[15] As Avery Dulles also puts it, "Irreformable statements may, however, require completion, refinement, reinterpretation, and restatement in accordance with new conditions, which raise new questions and provide new information, new conceptual categories, new methods, and new vocabulary."[16] In this connection, the idea of doctrinal development rears its head. As Nichols puts it, "What we should look for is a theory which allows for genuine development in doctrine yet respects the substantial homogeneity of revealed truth."[17]

Yves Congar, for one, has argued that the distinction between the propositional truths of faith and their expression summarizes the meaning of the entire council.[18] Although the propositional truths of the faith may be expressed differently, we must always determine whether those new re-formulations are preserving the same meaning and judgment (*eodem sensu eademque sententia*), and hence the material continuity, identity, and universality of those truths.

Furthermore, the distinction between propositions and their varied expressions, between propositions and sentences, is relevant to understanding a famous statement made at the beginning of the Second Vatican council by Pope John XXIII regarding a faithful restatement of catholic teaching. As I understand the pope, the understanding of the content of faith can only be deepened without threatening its unchangeable

---

[15] Thomas G. Guarino, *Foundations of Systematic Theology* (New York/London: T&T Clark, 2005), 139n59.

[16] Dulles, *Magisterium, Teacher and Guardian of the Faith*, 60.

[17] Nichols, *From Newman to Congar*, 169.

[18] Yves Congar, OP, *A History of Theology*, Translated by Hunter Guthrie (Garden City, N. Y.: Doubleday, 1968), 18–19.

Afterword: The Project of Redeeming Sex

meaning and truth if we hold to the following distinction: "the deposit or the truths of faith, contained in our sacred teaching, are one thing, while the mode in which they are enunciated, keeping the same meaning and the same judgment, is another."[19] Yves Congar, for one, has argued that this distinction summarizes the meaning of the entire council.[20] Although the propositional truths of the faith may be expressed differently, we must always determine whether those new re-formulations are preserving the same meaning and judgment (*eodem sensu eademque sententia*), and hence the material continuity, identity, and universality of those truths.

Now, the claim that there are different ways of expressing these basic doctrinal truths of the Christian faith in different epistemic contexts, using different conceptualities to understand these truths more fully and to communicate them more effectively, has raised questions regarding their universality and normativity, indeed, regarding the unchangeability as such of the truths of the Christian faith. Of course, there is something undeniably positive in this claim about expressing the truth of Christian faith differently, given that the motive is, as then Joseph Cardinal Ratzinger put it, "to help understand faith afresh as something that makes possible true humanity in the world of today." Still, it is just as undeniable that some efforts to expound Christian faith have changed "it into the small coin of empty talk painfully laboring to hide a complete spiritual vacuum."[21] This is the pathos of liberal theology.

---

[19] Ioannes XXIII, "Allocutio habita d. 11 oct. 1962, in initio Concilii," 54. *Acta Apostolicae Sedis* [1962], 796, and for this quote, 792.

[20] Yves Congar, OP, *A History of Theology*, 18–19.

[21] Joseph Cardinal Ratzinger (Pope Benedict XVI), *Introduction to Christianity*, trans. J.R. Foster (San Francisco: Ignatius Press, 1990, Second German edition, published with a new preface, 2000; originally published in German, 1968), 32.

Third, given the neo-gnostic character of our contemporary culture's anthropology, particularly as it pertains to the body, sexual differentiation, and the bearing of the latter in sexual ethics and marriage, my book examines Christian anthropology in both Roman Catholicism and Neo-Calvinism, the unity of human nature, of the body/soul unity of man, and the bodily subjectivity of the human person. The body has a proper subjectivity that encompasses the whole man, writes the philosopher-pope John Paul II, a position shared by the Dutch Reformational philosopher Herman Dooyeweerd. The body is intrinsic to personhood. John Paul explains: "The person, including the body, is completely entrusted to himself, and it is in the unity of the body and soul that the person is the subject of his own moral acts."[22] Furthermore, the body's proper subjectivity encompasses the foundation of sexual difference between male and female, that is, the somatic constitution of the personal subject. It is here that sexual differentiation is the basis for reciprocal enrichment in the two-in-one-flesh-unity between a man and a woman. Similarly, Dooyeweerd argues in his social ontology of marriage that essential to marriage as such is sexual differentiation. The internal structural principle of marriage has an invariant transcendental character. In other words, the internal structural principle of the marital love-communion, the ethical aspect of this love-community being its qualifying function, may not be detached from, in Dooyeweerd's words, "its biotic foundation in the organic difference between the sexes."[23] Despite their polemics over substance ontology, both Dooyeweerd and John Paul II affirm in their anthropologies that the body is intrinsic to personhood, and hence they support not only, in John Paul's words. "the Church's teachings on the unity of the human person," but also that "body and

---

[22] John Paul II, *Veritatis Splendor*, §48.
[23] Dooyeweerd, *New Critique of Theoretical Thought*, III, 320.

soul are inseparable: in the person, in the willing agent and in the deliberate act they stand or fall together."[24]

Fourth, the neo-Calvinist hermeneutics of Dutch Reformed theologian, Ad L. Th. de Bruijne, a professor of ethics and spirituality at the Kampen Theological University, argues that the culture war between orthodox Christians and proponents of the sexual revolution, so-called, emancipatory liberals, and their sexual liberationist ideology, should be left behind. In general, De Bruijne stands in the line of the neo-Calvinism of Abraham Kuyper and Herman Bavinck by continuing to develop a hermeneutic of culture for the sake of renewal. But unlike his illustrious predecessors, De Bruijne suffers the pathos of liberal theology. His argument resembles a "theology of compromise,"[25] over sexual ethics, marriage, Christian anthropology, moral norms, that is, a revisionist theology committed, as David Tracy rightly states, to "the dramatic confrontation, the mutual illuminations and corrections, the possible basic reconciliation between the principal values, cognitive claims, and existential faiths of both a reinterpreted post-modern consciousness and a reinterpreted Christianity."[26] In short, this critical correlation between the "Christian tradition and contemporary understandings of human existence"[27] in revisionist theology is best described as the pathos of liberal theology. As the late American liberal theologian, Van A. Harvey (1923-2021) succinctly describes that pathos. "The pathos of the liberal is that, by adopting modernity and accommodating Christianity to it, he is confronted by a solution of his own making in which Christianity has lost its 'transcendence' over common experience and is simply a re-

---

[24] John Paul II, *Veritatis Splendor*, §§48-49.
[25] Cardinal Eijk, *De Band van de Liefde*, 34.
[26] David Tracy, *The Blessed Rage for Order: The New Pluralism in Theology* (New York: The Seabury Press, 1975), 32.
[27] David Tracy, *The Blessed Rage for Order*, 23.

presentation of its own self-understanding. On the other hand, if the theologian identifies himself with a faith that transcends and judges modernity, he must appear to that modernity and to himself, perhaps, as out of joint with the times."[28]

Unlike his illustrious predecessors, De Bruijne's revisionist theology is not a form of retrieval theology, namely, the project of *ressourcement*. In other words, the theological project of retrieval theology is a "mode or style of theological discernment that looks back [to authoritative sources of faith] in order to move forward."[29] As Kevin Vanhoozer correctly states, "*Ressourcement* describes a return to authoritative sources for the sake of revitalizing the present."[30] Indeed, adds Vanhoozer, on the one hand, "we ought not to confuse retrieval with either retrenchment or repristination." Rather, "the main purpose of retrieval is the revitalization of biblical interpretation, theology, and the church today. *To retrieve is to look back creatively in order to move forward faithfully.*"[31] On the other hand, moving faithfully forward involves "*aggiornamento*," the meaning of which is best captured in Vatican II's *Gaudium et Spes*, §4:

> To carry out such a task, the Church has always had the duty of scrutinizing the signs of the times and of interpreting them in the light of the Gospel. Thus, in language intelligible to each generation, she can respond to the perennial questions which

---

[28] Van A. Harvey, "The Pathos of Liberal Theology." *Journal of Religion* Vol. 56, No. 4, October 1976, 382-391, and at 391. This is Harvey's article review of David Tracy's book, *The Blessed Rage for Order: The New Pluralism in Theology*.

[29] W. David Buschart, and Kent D. Eilers, *Theology as Retrieval: Receiving the Past, Renewing the Church* (Downers Grove, IL: IVP Academic, 2015), 12

[30] Kevin Vanhoozer, *Biblical Authority After Babel* (Grand Rapids, MI: Brazos Press, 2016), 23.

[31] Vanhoozer, *Biblical Authority After Babel*, 24; italics are Vanhoozer's.

Afterword: The Project of Redeeming Sex

men ask about this present life and the life to come, and about the relationship of the one to the other. We must therefore recognize and understand the world in which we live, its explanations, its longings, and its often dramatic characteristics.

Significantly, as Oscar Cullman rightly stressed, "*aggiornamento* should be a consequence, not a starting point,"[32] of renewal, of *ressourcement*. Indeed, he adds, *aggiornamento* should not be understood as an "*isolated motive for renewal.*"[33] Therefore, in the interplay between *ressourcement* and *aggiornamento*, the former has normative priority.

Ressourcement, then, involves a "return to the sources" of Christian faith, for the purpose of rediscovering their truth and meaning in order to meet the critical challenges of our time. If *ressourcement* is about revitalization, then the oftmentioned *aggiornamento* is a question of finding new ways to rethink and reformulate the fundamental affirmations of the Christian faith in light of today's questions. As Berkouwer describes the project of retrieval theology, of *ressourcement*, in Neo-Calvinism:

> [I]ntegrity and truth compel the church, [Bavinck] said, to give an account to those outside the church as candidly as possible. *Continuity of faith within all the changes of time*—this is what Bavinck was concerned to express.... [This] was a common problem that Catholics and Protestants shared as they sought the right way for the church to travel "between the times." In all

---

[32] Oscar Cullman, "Have Expectations Been Fulfilled?" In: *Vatican II, The New Direction*. Essays Selected and Arranged by James D. Hester. New York: Harper & Row, 1968, 54–63, and at 57.

[33] Cullman, "Have Expectations Been Fulfilled?" 58.

this, it is no wonder that Bavinck became a model of how theology could be done with commitment to the truth combined with openness to problems, and carefulness to judgments against others. And we understand that this posture had nothing to do with relativism.[34]

Fifth, in a wide-ranging discussion of the philosophical ethics and moral theology of liberal/revisionist Catholic theologian, Margaret Farley and orthodox Catholic philosophical theologian, Karl Wojtyla/John Paul II, I examine in depth a theology of revelation, in particular the necessity of propositional revelation, doctrinal development, the sources of Christian ethics, as well as the nature of human experience and judgment, and how a theory of experience grounds a sound epistemology but also a sound metaphysics for Christian ethics.

The Catholic tradition affirms both cognitive and ontological realism. Gerhard Cardinal Müller makes the meaning of this affirmation clear: "The realistic view of God's revelation and saving will, which embraces the whole human being, implies a realistic epistemology and insight into the identity of truth and reality."[35] Here is the crux of the conflict between Margaret Farley and John Paul II. Accordingly, this tradition distinguishes ontological and epistemological questions, that is, what there is, what reality is like, on the one hand, and how we can know reality on the other. It distinguishes the conditions under which I know that something is true and the conditions that make something true. In other words, it distinguishes the conditions under which we are justified

---

[34] G. C. Berkouwer, *A Half Century of Theology: Movements and Motives*, trans. and ed. Lewis B. Smedes (Grand Rapids: Eerdmans, 1977), 17–18, emphasis added.

[35] Gerhard Cardinal Müller, *True and False Reform: What it Means to Be a Catholic*, Translated by Susan Johnson (Steubenville, OH: Emmaus Academic, 2023), 21.

Afterword: The Project of Redeeming Sex

in knowing that something is true from the conditions that make something true; the former concerns justification, the latter is about truth. In short, it affirms epistemic realism and a realist view of truth, i.e., alethic realism. The former means that reality is knowable, while the latter means "true theories are true in virtue of the nature of objective reality. Truth has its source in reality."[36] A realist about truth holds that a proposition is true if and only if what that proposition asserts is in fact the case about objective reality; otherwise, it is false.

The failure to make these distinctions puts objective reality at risk because it limits what is real to what is real for human beings, treating reality to be "totally irrelevant to questions of truth."[37] We find such a view in liberal Catholic theologian, David Tracy. He states:

> Reality is what we name our best interpretation. Reality is constituted, not created or simply found, through the interpretations that have earned the right to be called relatively adequate or true. . . . Reality is neither out there nor in here. Reality is constituted by the interaction between a text, whether book or world, and a questioning interpreter. The interaction called questioning can produce warranted assertions through relevant evidence.[38]

This is alethic anti-realism. Throughout his writings, Karol Wojtyla/John Paul II presupposes, on the contrary, epistemic realism and an alethic realist view of truth. By contrast, Margaret Farley is not

---

[36] Roger Trigg, *Reality at Risk: A Defence of Realism in Philosophy & the Sciences* (Sussex: The Harvester Press, 1980), xiv.

[37] Trigg, *Reality at Risk*, vii, xiv.

[38] David Tracy, *Plurality and Ambiguity: Hermeneutics, Religion, and Hope* (San Francisco: Harper & Row, 1987), 48.

an alethic realist; rather, she is an alethic anti-realist because truth depends on justification, seeking to achieve reflective equilibrium, that is, an acceptable coherence among our beliefs, or how well the propositions pragmatically work. On her view, the evidence of experience "do not give actual access to 'reality,' but only a pragmatic way of dealing with the world and ourselves."[39] She explains,

> The supposed bedrock of evidence that experience provides disappears in the endless circles of social construction. Nonetheless, and perhaps ironically, it is experience itself that has taught us: the worldviews that shape experience can be challenged and in some respects modified and even overturned. The hermeneutical circle is not so tightly shut that we are denied a critical edge or opening.[40]

Despite her disclaimer in the concluding sentence of this passage, namely, that the "hermeneutical circle," the circle of interpretation, the idea that we always understand, experience, or interpret out of some presuppositions, doesn't close us off from reality, Farley puts the term 'reality' in scare quotes. Farley follows Tracy who writes, "'Reality' is the one word that should always appear within quotation marks."[41] Why would she put the term in such quotes? This is not a direct quotation. What she is doing is "distancing [herself] from the term in quotes."[42] She

---

[39] Margaret A. Farley, *Just Love: A Framework for Christian Sexual Ethics*, 189.

[40] Farley, *Just Love: A Framework for Christian Sexual Ethics*, 192.

[41] Tracy, *Plurality and Ambiguity*, 47. Tracy is quoting Vladimir Nabokov (1899-1977), a Russian born American novelist.

[42] "Scare Quotes," University of Sussex, Department of Informatics, accessed November 12, 2024, https://www.sussex.ac.uk/informatics/ punctuation/quotes/ scare.

Afterword: The Project of Redeeming Sex

denies, on the one hand, that our justified beliefs give us actual access to reality because of the "endless circles of social construction." John Paul II challenges this imprisonment in the hermeneutical circle. He writes, "The interpretation of this word [that is, the Word of God] cannot merely keep referring us to one interpretation after another, without ever leading us to a statement which is simply true."[43] As the then Cardinal Ratzinger comments on this passage from *Fides et Ratio* and the hermeneutical position that Farley seems to endorse:

> Man is not trapped in a hall of mirrors of interpretations; he can and must look for the way out to the reality that stands behind the words and manifests itself to him in and through the words.[44]

Since we are not trapped in a hall of mirrors, "rationality requires more than endless deferrals of meaning,"[45] deferrals that keep referring us from one interpretation to another, according to John Paul, with reality eventually receding behind these interpretations, as it does in Farley's hermeneutical epistemology. We can know the truth about reality. Contrary to this alethic realism, Farley claims, "Postmodern ways of thinking have so subverted and destabilized notions of the human body and gender that there is no longer any room for a moral 'law.'"[46] By contrast, Wojtyla argues that interpretation does not go all the way down such that reality recedes behind differing interpretations. To suggest

---

[43] John Paul II, *Fides et Ratio*, 84.

[44] Joseph Cardinal Ratzinger, *Truth and Tolerance: Christian Belief and World Religions*, Translated by Henry Taylor (San Francisco: Ignatius Press, 2004), 189.

[45] Aidan Nichols, O.P., *From Hermes to Benedict XVI: Faith and Reason in Modern Catholic Thought* (Herefordshire: Gracewing, 2009), 241.

[46] Farley, *Just Love: A Framework for Christian Sexual Ethics*, 136.

otherwise would be to say that "there is no ready-made reality, no way things are apart from how we construe them, only ways of construing them."[47] Farley doesn't deny the significance of human embodiment. In fact, she affirms that "our bodies . . . are intrinsic to ourselves," that is, "at the heart of Christian belief is the affirmation that not only is the human body good, but it is intrinsic to being human."[48] Still, given her hermeneutical epistemology, where she claims that we are trapped in an endless circle of social construction, we can understand her sympathy for postmodernism, that is, a metaphysical anti-realism. That is why she professes to be agnostic regarding "conflicting metaphysical analyses of human embodiment."[49]

Sixth, what is the nature and purpose of pastoral care for individuals in spiritually and morally problematic relationships? The latter includes the divorced and civilly remarried and cohabiting couples (either heterosexuals or homosexuals). Rather than overlooking truth or love, however, in the context of the Church's pastoral practice, we need to show the *interdependency* of love and truth. Authentic expressions of charity are not possible outside of or in opposition to the truth. This is a constant theme in Benedict XVI's theology. As then Fr. Ratzinger wrote in 1973, "Love is of no avail. It serves no purpose if truth is not on its side. Only when truth and love are in harmony can man know joy. For it is truth that makes man free."[50] I follow this analysis up with a brief discussion of homosexuality. I consider, not the ethics of homosexuality,

---

[47] Nicholas Wolterstorff, *Religion in the University* (New Haven: Yale University Press, 2019), 121.

[48] Farley, *Just Love: A Framework for Christian Sexual Ethics*, 110, 129, 131, respectively.

[49] Farley, *Just Love: A Framework for Christian Sexual Ethics*, 110.

[50] Joseph Ratzinger (Benedict XVI), *Principles of Catholic Theology*, 80. On the corollary of love and truth, see also, John Paul II, "Canonization of Edith

Afterword: The Project of Redeeming Sex

but rather the "anthropological meaning of homosexuality in terms of what the Church calls a 'disordered tendency.'"[51] Speaking the truth in charity (Eph 4:15) is the context in which I consider the question of the pastoral care of individuals in spiritually and morally problematic relationships.

In critical dialogue with, *inter alia*, influential Jesuit theologian, James Martin, SJ, I examine his pastoral strategy towards homosexuals. It proceeds from the assumption that homosexual orientation grounds human identity. However, this strategy is contrary to the Church's anthropology. "But no pastoral method can be employed which would give moral justification to these acts on the grounds that they would be consonant with the condition of such people. For according to the objective moral order, homosexual relations are acts that lack an essential and indispensable finality. In Sacred Scripture they are condemned as a serious depravity and even presented as the sad consequence of rejecting God."[52] How then does Fr. James Martin justify the legitimacy of a person's self-description as a homosexual—indeed, insisting on it? The only criterion that he suggests that legitimizes it is individual experience. Individual experience becomes a supreme court for adjudicating the gospel, the teachings of the Church. This leads him to the conclusion that a person's homosexuality is a *creational given* rather than being in itself inherently

---

Stein and Homily," §6: "St. Benedicta of the Cross says to us all: Do not accept anything as the truth if it lacks love. And do not accept anything as love which lacks truth! One without the other becomes a destructive life."

[51] Monsignor Livio Melina, "Homosexual Inclination as an 'Objective Disorder': Reflections on Theological Anthropology," in *Living the Truth in Love: Pastoral Approaches to Same-Sex Attraction*, edited by Janet E. Smith and Father Paul Check (San Francisco: Ignatius Press, 2015), 129-140, and at 132.

[52] Sacred Congregation for the Doctrine of the Faith, *Persona Humana* (1975), §VIII.

disordered. However, as Aidan Nichols correctly states, "It is not experience we should trust but the transmutation of experience by Scripture and Tradition."[53] One would then take as normative the truth that God made man, our created nature, as male and female for each other (Gen 1:27), and that this nature is savagely wounded by sin, broken, but, thanks be to God, it is redeemed in Christ through his atoning work.

Thus, in all likelihood those who follow Martin's strategy will fall into the danger of what Pope Francis calls therapeutic self-absorption. He writes in *Evangelii Gaudium*, §170. "*Although it sounds obvious, spiritual accompaniment must lead others ever closer to God, in whom we attain true freedom.* ... To accompany them would be counterproductive if it became a sort of therapy supporting their self-absorption and ceased to be a pilgrimage with Christ to the Father" (emphasis added). We need a pastoral approach that is consistent with the Christian anthropology that is grounded in the truth that God made man, our created nature, as male and female for each other (Gen 1:27).

These theses that capture the main emphases of this book should help to give focus to the philosophical and theological issues regarding the redemption of the body.

---

[53] Aidan Nichols, OP, in *Christendom Awake: On Reenergizing the Church in Culture* (Grand Rapids, MI: Eerdmans, 1999), 41-52 and at 41.

Bibliography

Allison, Gregory R. *Embodied: Living as a Whole People in a Fractured World*. Grand Rapids, MI: Baker Books, 2021.

Anscombe, Elizabeth. "Contraception and Chastity." 1972. http://www.orthodoxytoday.org/articles/AnscombeChastity.php.

Aquinas, *Summa Theologiae*.

Ashenden, Gavin Ashenden. "The Archbishop of Canterbury's new position on sex and marriage: a 'journey' or a departure?" *Christian Today*. 26 October 2024.

Ashley, Benedict, OP. *Living the Truth in Love: A Biblical Introduction to Moral Theology*. New York: Alba House, 1996.

———, Jean Deblois, and Kevin D. O'Rourke, OP, *Health Care Ethics: A Theological Analysis*. 5th ed. Washington, D.C.: Georgetown University Press, 2006.

Augustine. *City of God*. newadvent.org.

Balthasar, Hans Urs von. "On the Tasks of Catholic Philosophy in Our Time." *Communio: International Catholic Review* 20 (Spring 1993): 147–87.

Banks, Robert, and R. Paul Stevens, eds. *The Complete Book of Everyday Christianity: An A-to-Z Guide to Following Christ in Every Aspect of Life*. Downers Grove: InterVarsity Press, 1997. S.v. "Consumerism," 220–22.

Baucham, Voddie T., Jr., *It's Not like Being Black: How Sexual Activists Hijacked the Civil Rights Movement*. Delaware: Regnery Faith, 2024.

Bauwens, Michael. "Synchronic Progress in the Understanding of Doctrine: A Marian Perspective," in *Progress in Theology: Does the Queen of the Sciences Advance?*, edited by Gijsbert van den Brink, Rick Peels and Bethany Sollereder (London/New York: Routledge, 2025), 64-83,

Bavinck, Herman. "Common Grace." Translated by R. C. van Leeuwen. *Calvin Theological Journal* 24, no. 1 (1989): 45–47, 60.

———. *Reformed Dogmatics, Vol. 1, Prolegomena*. Edited by John Bolt. Translated by John Vriend. 1895. Grand Rapids: Baker Academic, 2008.

———. *The Christian Family*. Translated by Nelson D. Kloosterman. Introduction by James Eglinton. Grand Rapids, MI: Christian's Library Press, 2012.

———. *The Philosophy of Revelation: The Stone Lectures for 1908-1909, Princeton Theological Seminary*. New York: Longmans, Green, and Co., 1909.

Beabout, Gregory R., and Eduardo J. Echeverria. "The Culture of Consumerism: A Catholic and Personalist Critique." *Journal of Markets & Morality* 5, no. 2 (Fall 2002): 339–83.

Benedict XVI. "La pastorale del matrimonio deve fondarsi sulla verità." http://www.osservatoreromano.va/it/news/la-pastorale-del-matrimonio-deve-fondarsi-sulla-ve.

———, and Jürgen Habermas. *Dialectics of Secularization: On Reason and Religion*. Edited by Florian Schuller. Translated by Brian McNeil, C.R.V. San Francisco: Ignatius Press, 2006.

———. Christmas Address to the Roman Curia, Friday, December 21, 2012.

———. "Communication and Culture." In *On the Way to Jesus Christ*, translated by Michael J. Miller, 42–52. San Francisco: Ignatius Press, 2005.

———. "La pastorale del matrimonio deve fondarsi sulla verità." http://www.osservatoreromano.va/it/news/la-pastorale-del-matrimonio-deve-fondarsi-sulla-ve.

———. *A Turning Point For Europe*. Second Edition. Translated by Brian McNeil, C.R.V. San Francisco: Ignatius Press, 2010.

Bibliography

———. *Caritas in Veritate*, §3. http://w2.vatican.va/content/ benedict-xvi/en/encyclicals/documents/hf_ben-xvi_enc_20090629_ caritas-in-veritate.html.

———. *Introduction to Christianity*. Translated by J. R. Foster. Communio Books. San Francisco: Ignatius Press, 1990.

———. *Truth and Tolerance: Christian Belief and World Religions*. Translated by Henry Taylor. San Francisco: Ignatius Press, 2003.

Berkouwer, G. C. *A Half Century of Theology: Movements and Motives*. Translated and edited by Lewis B. Smedes. Grand Rapids: Eerdmans, 1977.

———. *Conflict met Rome* (Kampen: Kok, 1949); ET: *The Conflict with Rome*, Translated by David Freeman. Grand Rapids, MI: Baker Book House, 1958.

———. *General Revelation*. Grand Rapids: Eerdmans, 1955.

———. *Holy Scripture*. Translated and edited by Jack B. Rogers as one volume. Grand Rapids, MI: Eerdmans, 1975.

———. *Man: The Image of God*. Translated by Dirk W. Jellema. Grand Rapids, MI: Eerdmans, 1962.

———. *Nabetrachting op het Concilie*. Kampen: J.H. Kok, 1968.

———. *The Church*. Translated by James E. Davison. Grand Rapids, MI: Eerdmans, 1976.

———. *The Conflict with Rome*. Translated by David Freeman. Grand Rapids, MI: Baker Book House, 1958.

———. *The Return of Christ*. Edited by Marlin J. Van Elderen. Translated by James Van Oosterom. Grand Rapids, MI: Eerdmans, 1972.

———. *The Second Vatican Council and the New Catholicism*. Translated by Lewis Smedes. Grand Rapids, MI: Eerdmans, 1965.

Bernstein, Richard. "Philosophers respond to [John Paul II's] *Fides et Ratio*." *Books and Culture* 5 (July/August 1999): 30–32.

Blackburn, Simon. "Religion and Respect." In *Philosophers without Gods*, edited by Louise M. Anthony, 179-193. New York: Oxford University Press, 2010.

Boer, Theo. "Waarom ik Katholieke Ethiek nodig heb." In *Flirten met Rome, Protestanten naderen Katholieke*, edited by Almatine Leene, 37–47. Amsterdam: Buijten & Schipperheijn, 2017.

Booth, Wayne. "Individualism and the Mystery of the Social Self," in *Freedom and Interpretation: The Oxford Amnesty Lectures, 1992*, edited by Barbara Johnson. New York: HarperCollins, 1993.

Bordeyne, Philippe. "Homosexuality, Seen in Relation to Ecumenical Dialogue: What Really Matters to the Catholic Church." *New Blackfriars*, November 2006, 561-577.

Brandmüller, Walter Cardinal. "Gomorrah in the 21st Century. The Appeal of a Cardinal and Church Historian." http://magister.blogautore.espresso.repubblica.it/2018/11/05/gomorrah-in-the-21st-century-the-appeal-of-a-cardinal-and-church-historian/. Original Italian: "Omosessualità e abusi - Affrontare la crisi: le lezioni della storia." *Vatican Magazine*. November 2018. http://magister.blogautore.espresso.repubblica.it/2018/11/03/affrontare-la-crisi-le-lezioni-della-storia/.

Brown, Robert McAfee. *Spirit of Protestantism*. Oxford: Oxford University Press, 1965.

Budziszewski, J. *Evangelicals in the Public Square*. Grand Rapids: Baker Academic, 2006.

———. *On the Meaning of Sex*. Wilmington, DE: ISI Books, 2012.

Buschart, W. David and Eilers, Kent D, *Theology as Retrieval: Receiving the Past, Renewing the Church*. Downers Grove, IL: IVP Academic, 2015.

Cahill, Lisa Sowle "Is Catholic Ethics Biblical?" Warren Lecture Series in Catholic Studies 20. University of Tulsa, 1992.

Calvin, J. 1960. *Institutes of the Christian Religion.* Edited by John T. McNeill. Translated by Ford Lewis Battles. 2 vols. Library of Christian Classics 20–21. Philadelphia: Westminster Press.

Cantalamessa, Raniero O.F.M. Cap. *Obedience: The Authority of the Word.* Translated by Francis Lonergan Villa. Boston: St. Paul, 1989.

Carlin, David R. *Three Sexual Revolutions: Catholic-Protestant-Atheist, A sociological & Historical Perspective.* Hobe Sound, Florida: Lectio Publishing, 2022.

Catechism of the Catholic Church. http://www.vatican.va/archive/ENG0015/_INDEX.HTM.

Catholic Medical Association. *Homosexuality and Hope: Questions and Answers about Same-Sex Attraction.* 2008. http://www.cathmed.org/issues_resources/publications/position_papers/homosexuality_and_hope/.

Chaput, Archbishop Charles J. O.F.M. Cap., "Fr. James Martin and Catholic belief." In *CatholicPhilly,* September 19, 2019. http://catholicphilly.com/2019/09/archbishop-chaput-column/father-james-martin-and-catholic-belief/.

Christian Reformed Church (CRC) Synod 2022 document *A Foundation-Laying Biblical Theology of Human Sexuality.*

Congar, Yves, O. P. *A History of Theology.* Translated by Hunter Guthrie. Garden City, N Y: Doubleday, 1968.

Congregation for Catholic Education. *"Male and Female He Created Them": Towards a Path of Dialogue on the Question of Gender Theory in Education* (Vatican City, 2019).

Congregation for the Doctrine of the Faith. Notification on the book *Just Love. A Framework for Christian Sexual Ethics* by Margaret A. Farley (vatican.va). 2012.

Core Council for Gay and Lesbian Students at the University of Notre Dame does not post It only posts the 1998 document, *Always Our*

Children, as well as interpretations of that teaching. http://corecouncil.nd.edu/church_response/index.shtml. This website has been taken down and replaced with another: https://friendsandallies.nd.edu/.

Cox, Harvey. *The Secular City*. New York: The MacMillan Press, 1965.

Crosby, John F. "The Estrangement of Persons from their Bodies." *Logos* 1, no. 2 (1997): 125–39.

Cullmann, Oscar. "Have Expectations Been Fulfilled?" In *Vatican II, The New Direction*, essays selected and arranged by James D. Hester, 54–63. New York: Harper & Row, 1968.

D'Costa, Gavin. *Vatican II: Catholic Doctrines on Jews & Muslims*. Oxford: Oxford University Press, 2014.

de Bruijne, Ad, and Hans Burger, eds. *Gereformeerde Hermeneutiek Vandag: Theologische Perspectieven* [Reformed Hermeneutics Today: Theological Perspectives]. Barneveld: De Vuurbaak, 2017.

———. "Christian Ethics and God's Use of the Bible." In *Correctly Handling the Word of Truth, Reformed Hermeneutics Today*, edited by Mees te Velde and Gerhard H. Visscher, 171–86. Eugene, OR: Wipf & Stock, 2014.

———. "Culture Wars About Sexuality: A Theological Proposal for Dialogue." In *Public Discourses About Homosexuality and Religion in Europe and Beyond*, edited by Marko Derks and Mariecke Van den Berg, 105–124. Cham: Palgrave MacMillan 2020.

———. "De kunst van het verstaan: Hermeneutiek in Kampen," *Gereformeerde hermeneutiek vandag: Theologische perspectieven*. Barneveld: De Vuurbaak, 2017).

———. "Ethiek en hermeneutiek." in *Gereformeetde hermeneutiek vandaag,*

Theologische perspectieven, eds. Ad de Bruijne en Hans Burger (Barneveld: De Vuurbaak, 2017).

---. "Homosexuality and Moral Authority: A Theological Interpretation of Changing Views in Evangelical Circles." In *Evangelicals and Sources of Authority*, edited by Miranda Klaver, Stefan Paas, and Eveline van Sataalduine-Sulman, 143–62. Amsterdam: VU Press, 2016.

---. "Homosexuality: Improving the Traditional Theory?" In *Familie: Verwandtschaft, die den Unterschied macht, Family: Kinship that Matters*, edited by Gerard den Hartog and Jan Roskovec, 103–112. Leipzig: Evangelische Verlagsanstalt, 2012.

---. "Seksualiteit en cultuurstrijd: Een theologische voorstel tot dialog" ["Sexuality and Cultural Conflict: A Theological Proposal for Dialogue"]. In *Religie en Samenleving* 11, nr. 2, September 2016.

---. "Seksualiteit in de laatste dagen." December 7, 2015. https://www.youtube.com/watch?v=QY66hisTfDI

---. *God, seks en politiek*, 271–87.

---. *Verbonden voor het Leven: Een theologisch-ethisch voorstel rond homosexualiteit en seksuele diversiteit*. Utrecht: KokBoekencentrum, 2022.

de Lubac, Henri. "Apologetics and Theology." In *Theological Fragments*, 91–104. San Francisco: Ignatius Press, 1989.

---. *A Brief Catechesis on Nature and Grace*. Translated by Richard Arnandez, F.S.C. San Francisco: Ignatius Press, 1984.

---. *At the Service of the Church: Henri de Lubac Reflects on the Circumstances That Occasioned His Writings*. Translated by Anne Englund. San Francisco, CA: Ignatius Press, 1993.

---. *Catholicism: Christ and the Common Destiny of Man*. Translated by Lancelot C. Sheppard and Sister Elizabeth Englund, O.C.D. 1938. Reprint, San Francisco: Ignatius Press, 1988.

---. *The Drama of Atheist Humanism*. Revised Edition. San Francisco: Ignatius Press, 1995.

———. *The Mystery of the Supernatural*. Translated by Rosemary Sheed. 1965. Reprint, New York: Crossroad, 1998

Denzinger, Heinrich. *Compendium of Creeds, Definitions, and Declarations on Matters of Faith and Morals*. Edited by Peter Hünermann. English edition edited by Robert Fastiggi and Anne Englund Nash. 43rd ed. San Francisco: Ignatius Press, 2012.

Dolan, Jay P. *In Search of an American Catholicism*.

Dooyeweerd, Herman. "Creation and Evolution." *Philosophia Reformata* 24 (1959): 113–59.

———. "The Significance of the Philosophy of the Law Idea for the Theory of Human Society," Philosophia Reformata 87 (2022): 108-21.

———. "Van Peursen's Critische Vragen Bij 'A New Critique of Theoretical Thought'." *Philosophia Reformata* 25 (1960): 97–150.

———. *A New Critique of Theoretical Thought*. 4 vols. Philadelphia: Presbyterian and Reformed Publishing Company, 1953-59.

———. *In the Twilight of Western Thought: Studies in the Pretended Autonomy of Philosophical Thought*. Nutley, NJ: Craig Press, 1968.

———. *Reformation and Scholasticism in Philosophy*, I-VI, *Philosophy of Nature and Philosophical Anthropology*. Edited by D. F. M. Strauss. Translated by Magnus Verbrugge and D. F. M. Strauss. Part II. Ancaster, ON: Paideia Press, 2011.

———. *The Crisis in the Humanistic Political Theory*. Collected Works, Series B, Vol. 7. Edited by D. F. M. Strauss. Grand Rapids, MI: Paideia Press, 2010 [1931].

———. *The Theory of Man: 32 Propositions on Anthropology*. https://jgfriesen.files.wordpress.com/2016/12/32propositions.pdf

———. *Roots of Western Culture*, trans. John Kraay, and edited by Mark Vander Vennen and Bernard Zylstra (Toronto: Wedge, 1979).

Douma, Jochem "Appendix: The Use of Scripture in Ethics." In *The Ten Commandments: Manual for the Christian Life*. Translated by Nelson D. Kloosterman. 355–90. Phillipsburg, NJ: P & R Publishing, 1996.

Dulles, Avery. "Infallibility: The Terminology." In *Teaching Authority & Infallibility in the Church, Lutherans and Catholicis in Dialogue VI*, edited by Paul C. Empie, T. Austin Murphy, and Joseph A. Burgess, Minneapolis: Augsburg Publishing House, 1978, 69-80.

———. "The Orthodox Imperative." *First Things* (2006): 31–35.

———. *Magisterium, Teacher and Guardian of the Faith*. Naples, FL: Sapientia Press, 2007.

Eberstadt, Mary. *Adam and Eve after the Pill, Revisited*. Foreword by Cardinal George Pell. San Francisco: Ignatius Press, 2023 (2012).

Echeverria, Eduardo. "Bavinck on the Family and Integral Human Development." *Journal of Markets and Morality* 16.1 (Spring 2013): 219–37

———. "Fr. James Martin, 'bridges,' and The Triumph of the Therapeutic Mentality." *Catholic World Report*. June 16, 2017. https://www.catholicworldreport.com/2017/06/16/fr-james-martin-s-j-and-the-triumph-of-the-therapeutic-mentality/.

———. "Guarino's Prolegomena of Systematic Theology," *Homiletics and Pastoral Review*, October 27, 2022.

———. "Living Truth for a Post-Christian World: The Message of Francis Schaeffer and Karol Wojtyla." *Religion & Liberty* 12, no. 6 (November/December 2002).

———. "Male and Female He Created Them: Ecumenical Reflections." *Homiletic & Pastoral Review*. December 23, 2020. Male and Female He Created Them: Ecumenical Reflections - Homiletic & Pastoral Review

———. "Mercy and Truth: Pastoral Care of Individuals in Spiritually and Morally Problematic Relationships." In *Clerical Sexual Misconduct: An Interdisciplinary Analysis.* Edited by Jane F. Adolphe and Ronald J. Rychlak. 365–81. Providence, Long Island: CLUNY Media, 2020.

———. "Nature and Grace: The Theological Foundations of Jacques Maritain"s Public Philosophy." *Journal of Markets & Morality* 4, no. 2 (2001): 240–68

———. "No, @JamesMartinSJ, the analogy between slavery and homosexuality does not hold." *Catholic World Report.* October 26, 2019. https://www.catholicworldreport.com/2019/10/26/no-jamesmartinsj-the-analogy-between-slavery-and-homosexuality-does-not-hold/.

———. "Solum Magisterium?" *Crisis Magazine,* September 15, 2023. https://www.crisismagazine.com/opinion/solum-magisterium.

———. "The Splendor of Truth in *Fides et Ratio*" *Quaestiones Disputatae.* 9, no. 1, (Fall 2018): 49–78.

———. "Vincent of Lérins: The Development of Christian Doctrine." In *The Faith Once For All Delivered: Doctrinal Authority in Catholic Theology,* edited by Kevin L. Flannery, 171–98. Steubenville, OH: Emmaus Academic, 2023.

———. *Berkouwer and Catholicism: Disputed Questions.* Boston/Leiden: Brill, 2013.

———. *Dialogue of Love: Confessions of an Evangelical Catholic Ecumenist* Eugene, OR: Wipf and Stock, 2010.

———. *Pope Francis: The Legacy of Vatican II.* Revised and expanded edition. Hobe Sound, FL: Lectio Publishing, 2019 [2015].

———. *Revelation, History, and Truth: A Hermeneutics of Dogma.* New York: Peter Lang Publishing, 2018.

———. *Roman Catholicism and Neo-Calvinism: Ecumenical and Polemical Engagements.* New York: Peter Lang Publishing, 2024.

———. *"In the Beginning..." A Theology of the Body.* Eugene, Oregon: Pickwick Publications, 2011.

Eijk, Willem Jacobus Cardinal. *De Band van de Liefde: Huwelijksmoraal and Seksuele Ethiek.* Utrecht: KokBoekencentrum Uitgevers, 2022.

Erickson, Millard. *Christian Theology.* 2nd edition. Grand Rapids, MI: Baker Academic, 1998 [1983].

Ernst, Harold E. "The Theological Notes and the Interpretation of Doctrine." *Theological Studies* 63 (2002): 813–25.

Farley, Margaret A. "Feminist Consciousness and the Interpretation of Scripture." In *From Christ to the World: Introductory Readings in Christian Ethics*, edited by Wayne G. Boulton, Thomas D. Kennedy, and Allen Verhey, 51–57. Grand Rapids, MI: Eerdmans, 1994.

———. "The Role of Experience in Moral Discernment." In *Changing Questions: Explorations in Christian Ethics*, edited by Jamie L. Manson, 47–68. Maryknoll, NY: Orbis Books, 2015.

———. *Just Love, A Framework for Christian Sexual Ethics.* New York: Continuum, 2006.

Finley, John D. "Metaphysics: A Note on Soul, Body, and Sexuality." In *Sexual Identity, The Harmony of Philosophy, Science, and Revelation.* Edited by John D. Finley. Steubenville, Ohio: Emmaus Road, 2022, 237-50.

Finnis, John. *"Historical Consciousness" and Theological Foundations.* The Etienne Gilson Series 14. Toronto: Pontifical Institute of Medieval Studies, 1992.

———. "Personal Integrity, Sexual Morality and Responsible Parenthood." In *Why Humanae Vitae Was Right: A Reader.* Edited by Janet E. Smith. 171–92. San Francisco: Ignatius Press, 1993.

Fisher, Jeff. "Reformed and Always Reforming." *The Banner.* September 30, 2024.

Francis with Fabio Marchese Ragona. *Life: My Story Through History.* Translated by Aubrey Botsford. Milano: HarperCollins Italia, 2024.

Francis. *Dilexit Nos.* October 24, 2024. Encyclical Letter, "On the Human and Divine Love of the Heart of Jesus Christ."

———. *Evangelii Gaudium.* No. 66. Nov 24, 2013.

Gadamer, Hans-Georg. *Truth and Method.* Second revised edition. Translated and revised by Joel Weinsheimer and Donald G. Marshall. New York: Continuum, 1994.

Gagnon, Robert A. J. "Are There Universally Valid Sex Precepts?" *Horizons in Biblical Theology* 24 (2002): 72–125.

———. "How Bad is Homosexual Practice According to Scripture and Does Scripture"s Indictment Apply to Committed Homosexual Unions?" 1–11. http://robgagnon.net/articles/HomosexHowBadIsIt.pdf.

———. "Is Homosexual Practice No Worse Than Any Other Sin?." January 7, 2015. http://www.robgagnon.net/articles/homosexAreAllSinsEqual.pdf.

———. "Scriptural Perspectives on Homosexuality and Sexual Identity."

———. "Sexual Orientation," email correspondence, July 8, 2005;

———. "What Should Faithful Lutherans in the ELCA Do?"

———. "What the Evidence *Really* Says about Scripture and Homosexual Practice: Five Issues."

———. "Why a New Translation of the Heidelberg Catechism is not Needed: And why Homosexualist Forces in the PCUSA Seek it." June 19, 2008. Why a New Translation of the Heidelberg Catechism Is Not Needed (robgagnon.net)

———. *The Bible and Homosexual Practice: Texts and Hermeneutics.* Nashville: Abingdon Press, 2001.

Garrigou-Lagrange, Réginald. *Thomistic Common Sense: The Philosophy of Being and the Development of Doctrine.* Translated by Matthew K. Minerd. Steubenville, OH: Emmaus Academic, 2021.

Gaudium et Spes. Vatican II. 7 December 1965.

George, Francis Cardinal. "A New Apologetics for a New Evangelization." *Theology Digest* 47, no. 4 (Winter 2000): 341–59.

———. "Catholic Faith and the Secular Academy." *Logos* 4, no. 4 (Fall 2001): 73–81.

———. "One Lord and One Church for One World." *Origins* 30, no. 34 (February 8, 2001): 541, 543–49.

———. "Public Morality in a Global Society: Catholics and Muslims in Dialogue." *Theology Digest* 49, no. 4 (Winter 2002): 319–33.

———. "The Culture in Which We Evangelize." Paper presented at Sacred Heart Major Seminary, St. John Conference Center, Plymouth, Mich., March 24–26, 2006.

———. "The Promotion of Missiological Studies in Seminaries." http://www.sedos.org/english/george_e.htm. "Law and Culture." *Ave Maria Law Review* 1, no. 1 (Spring 2003): 1–17.

———. "Contrasting Views of Marriage: The Need for a Defining Principle." *Public Discourse.* July 22, 2014. http://www.thepublicdiscourse.com/2014/07/13526/.

———. "Fr. James Martin, Friendship and Dialogue, and the Truth about Human Sexuality." *Public Discourse.* June 17, 2018. https://www.thepublicdiscourse.com/2018/06/21846/.

———. *The Clash of Orthodoxies: Law, Religion, and Morality in Crisis.* Wilmington, Del.: ISI Books, 2001.

Gereformeerde Kerk in the Netherlands, *God Met Ons, Over de Aard van het Schriftgezag,* [God with us: The Nature of Biblical Authority],

Giddens, Anthony. *The Transformation of Intimacy, Sexuality, Love & Eroticism in Modern Societies*. Stanford, CA: Stanford University Press, 1992.

Gilson, Etienne. *Elements of Christian Philosophy*, (Garden City, NY: Doubleday & Company, 1960).

———. *The Philosopher and Theology*. Translated by Ralph MacDonald, C.S.B. London: Sheed & Ward, 1939.

———. *The Spirit of Medieval Philosophy*. Gifford Lectures 1931–1932. Translated by A. H. C. Downes. New York: Scribners, 1940.

———. *Christianity and Philosophy*. Translated by Ralph MacDonald. London: Sheed & Ward, 1939.

Glas, Gerrit. "Homoseksualiteit en homo-ervaring." In *Open en kwetsbaar: Christelijk debat over homoseksualiteit*, edited by Ad de Bruijne, 19–30. Barneveld: De Vuurbaak, 2012.

Gondreau, Paul. "Thomas Aquinas on the Metaphysical Biology of Sexual Difference." *Pro Ecclesia* 30, no. 2 (2021), 177–215.

Grabill, Stephen J. *Rediscovering the Natural Law in Reformed Theological Ethics*. Grand Rapids: Eerdmans, 2006.

Grisez, Germain. "On Interpreting Dogmas." *Communio: International Catholic Review* 17 (1990): 120–26.

———. *The Way of the Lord Jesus*. Vol. 1: *Christian Moral Principles*. Chicago, IL: Franciscan Herald Press, 1983. https://www.twotlj.org/G-1-V-1.html.

———. *The Way of the Lord Jesus*. Vol. 2: *Living a Christian Life*. Quincy, IL: Franciscan Herald Press, 1993.

Guardini, Romano. *The End of the Modern World*. Wilmington, Del.: ISI Books, 2001. Originally published as *Das Ende der Neuzeit* in 1950.

———. *Wahrheit des Denkens und Wahrheit des Tuns*. Edited by J. Messerschmid. Third edition. Paderborn, 1980.

Guarino, G. Thomas, Msgr. *Foundations of Systematic Theology*. New York: T&T Clark, 2005.

———. *Vincent of Lérins and the Development of Christian Doctrine*. Grand Rapids, MI: Baker Academic, 2013.

———. *Vattimo and Theology*. London: T&T Clark, 2009.

Gustafson, James M. "Theological Bases." In *Protestant and Roman Catholic Ethics*, 95–37. Chicago: University of Chicago Press, 1978.

Habermas, Jürgen. "Religion in the Public Sphere" (public lecture, University of San Diego, March 4, 2005), *European Journal of Philosophy* 14:1, 1–25. http://www.sandiego.edu/pdf/pdf_library/habermaslecture031105_c939cceb2ab087bdfc6df291ec0fc3fa.pdf.

———, and Joseph Cardinal Ratzinger. "Pre-political Foundations of the Democratic Constitutional State." In *Dialectics of Secularization: On Reason and Religion*, ed. with foreword Florian Schuller, trans. Brian McNeil, C.R.V. (San Francisco: Ignatius Press, 2006).

Harvey, Van A. "The Pathos of Liberal Theology." *Journal of Religion* Vol. 56, no. 4 (October 1976): 382–91.

Hays, Richard B. *The Moral Vision of the New Testament: Community, Cross, New Creation—A Contemporary Introduction to New Testament Ethics*. San Francisco: HarperSanFrancisco, 1996.

Heinbeck, Raeburne S. *Theology and Meaning, Critique of Metatheological Scepticism*. London: George Allen and Unwin Ltd., 1969.

Helm, Paul. "Revealed Propositions and Timeless Truths." *Religious Studies* 8 (1972): 127–36

———. "Against Ideological Apologetics." *Reformation 21*. February 2007.

———. "Created Body and Soul." *The Gospel Coalition*. https://www.thegospelcoalition.org/essay/created-body-soul/.

———. "Why be Objective?" In *Objective Knowledge: A Christian Perspective*. Edited by Paul Helm. 29–40. Leicester, England: InterVarsity Press, 1987.

———. *Faith, Form, and Fashion: Classical Reformed Theology and its Postmodern Critics*. Eugene, OR: Cascade Books, 2014.

———. *The Divine Revelation*. London: Marshall Morgan & Scott, 1982.

Heslam, Peter S. *Creating a Christian Worldview: Abraham Kuyper's Lectures on Calvinism*. Grand Rapids: Eerdmans, 1998.

Hittinger, Russell. *The First Grace: Rediscovering the Natural Law in a Post-Christian World*. Wilmington, Del.: ISI Books, 2003.

Hoitenga, Dewey J., Jr. *John Calvin and the Will: A Critique and Corrective*. Grand Rapids: Baker, 1997.

Holwerda, David E. "Jesus and the Law: A Question of Fulfillment." In *Jesus and Israel: One Covenant or Two?*, 113–46. Grand Rapids, MI: Eerdmans, 1995.

Homosexualitatis problema (1986), Letter to the Bishops of the Catholic Church on the Pastoral Care of Homosexual Persons. http://www.vatican.va/roman_curia/congregations/cfaith/documents/rc_con_cfaith_doc_19861001_homosexual-persons_en.html.

Hughes, W. D., O.P. "The Infusion of Virtues." Appendix 3 in *Summa Theologiae*, vol. 23, *Virtue*, by St. Thomas Aquinas, 247–48. New York: McGraw-Hill, 1975.

Human_sexuality_report_2021.pdf (crcna.org)

Husserl, Edmund. *Experience and Judgment*. Translated by James S. Churchill and Karl Ameriks. Evanston, Ill.: Northwestern University Press, 1973.

International Theological Commission. "Faith and Inculturation," October 1988. In *Catholicism and Secularization in America*, edited by David L. Schindler. Huntington, Ind.: Our Sunday Visitor, 1990.

———. "Select Themes of Ecclesiology on the Occasion of the Eighth Anniversary of the Closing of the Second Vatican Council." In *International Theological Commission: Texts and Documents 1969–1985*. San Francisco: Ignatius, 1989.

Ioannes XXIII, "Allocutio habita d. 11 oct. 1962, in initio Concilii," 54. *Acta Apostolicae Sedis* [1962],

John Paul II. "A Deep Commitment to Authentic Christian Living." In *The Whole Truth about Man*. Edited by James V. Schall, S.J., 84–91. Boston: St. Paul Editions, 1981.

———. "Discorso Di Giovanni Paolo II Ai Partecipanti Al Congresso Internazionale Di Teologia Morale," §1. http://w2.vatican.va/content/john-paul-ii/it/speeches/1986/april/documents/hf_jp-ii_spe_19860410_teologia-morale.html.

———. "On the Occasion of Meeting with the Exponents of Non-Christian Religions." February 5, 1986, Madras, India. http://www.vatican.va/content/john-paul-ii/en/speeches/1986/february/documents/hf_jp-ii_spe_19860205_religioni-non-cristiane.html.

———. *Ecclesia in Europa*. 2003 Post-Synodal Apostolic Exhortation.

———. *Evangelium Vitae*, Encyclical Letter, March 25, 1995.

———. *Fides et Ratio*.1998 Encyclical Letter.

———. Letter instituting the Pontifical Council for Culture, May 20, 1982, AAS LXXIV (1982), 683–88, as cited in *Towards a Pastoral Approach to Culture*, Pontifical Council for Culture, 1999.

———. *Make Room for the Mystery: Visit of John Paul II to the USA*, 1995. Boston: St. Paul Books & Media.

———. *Springtime of Evangelization*. The Complete Texts of the Holy Father's 1998 ad Limina Addresses to the Bishops of the United States. Edited and translated by Fr. Thomas D. Williams, L.C. San Francisco: Ignatius Press, 1999.

———. *Ut Unum Sint*, 1995 Encyclical Letter.

———. "A Deep Commitment to Authentic Christian Living." In *The Whole Truth about Man*, edited by James V. Schall, S. J. 84–91. Boston: St. Paul Editions, 1981.

———. "Canonization of Edith Stein and Homily," Sunday, 11 October 2998, §6.

———. "Dialogue between Cultures for a Civilization of Love and Peace." *Origins* 30, no. 8 (January 4, 2001).

———. "Discorso Di Giovanni Paolo II Ai Partecipanti Al Congresso Internazionale Di Teologia Morale." §1. http://w2.vatican.va/content/john-paul-ii/it/speeches/1986/april/documents/hf_jp-ii_spe_19860410_teologia-morale.html.

———. "Homily of the Enthronement Mass," October 22, 1978. *L'Osservatore Romano*.

———. "Method and Doctrine of St. Thomas in Dialogue with Modern Culture." In *The Whole Truth about Man*, edited by James V. Schall, S.J. Boston: Daughters of St. Paul, 1981.

———. Apostolic Letter, November 10, 1994. *Tertio Millennio Adveniente*.

———. Apostolic Letter. *Mulieris Dignittatem: On the Dignity and Vocation of Women*. 1988.

———. *Dominum et Vivificantem*, Encyclical, 1986.

———. *Ecclesia in Africa*, 1995 Post-Synodal Apostolic Exhortation, §§59–61.

———. *Centesimus Annus*. Encyclical Letter, May 1, 1991

———. *Familiaris Consortio*, http://w2.vatican.va/content/john-paul-ii/en/apost_exhortations/documents/hf_jp-ii_exh_19811122_familiaris-consortio.html.

———. Letter instituting the Pontifical Council for Culture, May 20, 1982. *AAS LXXIV* (1982): 683–88. Cited in *Towards a Pastoral Approach to Culture*, Pontificial Council for Culture, 1999.

———. *Man and Woman He Created Them: A Theology of the Body.* Boston, MA: Pauline Books & Media, 2006.

———. *Memory and Identity, Conversations at the Dawn of a Millennium.* New York: Rizzoli, 2005.

———. *Reconcilatio et Paenitentia.* Apostolic Exhortation, December 2, 1984. http://w2.vatican.va/content/john-paul-ii/en/apost_ exhortations/documents/hf_jp-ii_exh_02121984_reconciliatio-et-paenitentia.html.

———. *Springtime of Evangelization: The Complete Texts of the Holy Father's 1998 ad Limina Addresses to the Bishops of the United States.* Edited and introduced by Fr. Thomas D. Williams, L.C. San Francisco: Ignatius Press, 1999.

———. *Veritatis Splendor.* http://w2.vatican.va/content/john-paul-ii/en/encyclicals/documents/hf_jp-ii_enc_06081993_veritatis-splendor.html#%2445.

John XXIII, *Gaudet Mater Ecclesia.* Allocution on the Occasion of the Solemn Inauguration of the Second Ecumenical Council *Gaudet Mater Ecclesia.* October 11, 1962. Translated by Joseph Komonchak. http://www.saint-mike.org/library/papal_library/johnxxiii/opening_speech_vaticanii.html. Latin text: "Allocutio habita d. 11 oct. 1962, in initio Concilii." *Acta Apostolicae Sedis* 54 (1962). http://www.vatican.va/holy_father/john_xxiii/ speeches/1962/documents/ hf_j-xxiii_spe_19621011_opening-council_lt.html.

Johnston, Rebekah. "Marriage and the Metaphysics of Bodily Union: Framing the Same-Sex Marriage Debate." *Social Theory and Practice.* Vol. 39, No. 2 (April 2013): 288–312.

"Joint Declaration on 'Diversity of Gender and Sexuality." *A Norwegian Christian Ecumenical Project 2024*. Online: felleskristen.no

Jones, Stanton L. "Sexual Orientation and Reason: On the Implications of False Beliefs about Homosexuality." Also published as "Same-Sex Science, The Social Science Cannot Settle the Moral Status of Homosexuality." *First Things*. February 2012. https://www.firstthings.com/article/2012/02/same-sex science

Kasper, Walter Cardinal. *The Gospel of the Family*. Translated by William Madges. New York/Mahwah, NJ: Paulist Press, 2014.

Kuby, Gabriele. *The Global Sexual Revolution, Destruction of Freedom in the Name of Freedom*. Foreword by Robert Spaemann. Translated by James Patrick Kirchner. Kettering, OH: Angelico Press, 2012.

Kuyper, Abraham. "Common Grace," exerpted in *Abraham Kuyper, A Centennial Reader*, edited by James Bratt, 165–201. Grand Rapids: Eerdmans, 1998.

———. *Lectures on Calvinism*. 1898 Princeton University Stone Lectures. Grand Rapids, MI: Eerdmans, 1931.

———. *Pro Rege: Living Under Christ's Kingship*. Abraham Kuyper. Vol. 2: *The Kingship of Christ in Its Operation*. Edited by John Kok with Nelson D. Kloosterman. Translated by Albert Gootjes. Collected Works in Public Theology. Grand Rapids, MI / Bellingham, WA: Acton Institute / Lexham Press, 2017.

———. *Wisdom & Wonder, Common Grace in Science & Art*. Edited by Jordan J. Ballor and Stephen J. Grabill. Translated by Nelson D. Kloosterman. Grand Rapids, MI: Christian's Library Press, 2011.

Kwasniewski, Peter. *Treasuring the Goods of Marriage in a Throwaway Society*. Manchester, NH: Sophia Press, 2023.

Lawler, Ronald, O. F. M. Cap. *What is and what ought to be: The Dialectic of Experience, Theology, and Church*, 84.

———, Joseph Boyle, Jr., and William E. May. *Catholic Sexual Ethics, A Summary, Explanation and Defense*. Second Edition. Huntington, IN: Our Sunday Visitor, 1998.

Lee, Patrick. "The Human Body and Sexuality in the Teaching of Pope John Paul II." In *John Paul II's Contribution to Catholic Bioethics*, edited by Christopher Tollefsen, 107-20. Dordrecht, Netherlands: Springer, 2004.

———, and Robert P. George. "Sex and the Body." In *Body-Self Dualism in Contemporary Ethics and Politics*, 176–217. New York: Cambridge University Press, 2008.

http://www.patrickleebioethics.com/jp2_on_sex_and_the_body.pdf

Letter to the Bishops of the Catholic Church on the Pastoral Care of Homosexual Persons (vatican.va), §6.

Levering, "Knowing What is "Natural": Thomas Aquinas and Luke Timothy Johnson on Romans 1-2." In *Logos* 12 (2009), 117-142

Lindbeck, George A. "Response to Bruce Marshall," *The Thomist* 53 (1989): 403–406.

———. *Infallibility*. The 1972 Pere Marquette Theology Lecture. Milwaukee, WI: Marquette University Press, 1972.

———. "The Infallibility Debate." In *The Infallibility Debate*, edited by John J. Kirvan, 107–152. New York: Paulist Press, 1971.

Lonergan, Bernard J. F., S.J. "The Dehellenization of Dogma." In *Bernard J. F. Lonergan, A Second Collection*, edited by William F. J. Ryan, S. J. et al. 11-32. Philadelphia: The Westminster Press, 1974.

———. *Method in Theology*. New York: Herder and Herder, 1972.

Luijpen, Wilhelmus. *Existential Phenomenology*. Fourth impression. Translated from the Dutch edition. Pittsburgh, PA: Duquesne University Press, 1965 [1959].

MacIntyre, Alasdair. "The Fate of Theism." In *The Religious Significance of Atheism*. New York: Columbia University, 1969.

Malo, Antonio. *Transcending Gender Ideology: A Philosophy of Sexual Difference*. Translated by Alice Pavey. Foreword by John M. Rist. Washington, DC: Catholic University Press of America, 2020.

Mansini, Guy, and Lawrence J. Welch. "In Conformity to Christ." *First Things*, April 2006. https://www.firstthings.com/article/ 2006/04/in-conformity-to-christ.

Maritain, Jacques. "The Conquest of Freedom." In *The Education of Man: The Educational Philosophy of Jacques Maritain*, edited by Donald and Idella Gallagher, 159–79. Garden City, NY: Doubleday, 1962.

———. *Integral Humanism: Temporal and Spiritual Problems of a New Christendom*. Translated by Joseph Evans. 1936. Reprint, New York: Scribner's, 1968.

———. *Man and the State*. Translated by Doris C. Anson. Chicago: University of Chicago Press, 1951.

———. *On the Philosophy of History*. Edited by Joseph W. Evans. New York: Scribner's, 1957.

Martin, Francis. "Revelation as Disclosure: Creation." In *Wisdom and Holiness, Science and Scholarship: Essays in Honor of Matthew L. Lamb*, edited by M. Dauphinais and M. Levering, 205–247. Naples, Florida: Sapientia Press, 2007.

———. *The Feminist Question: Feminist Theology in the Light of the Christian Tradition*. Grand Rapids, MI: Eerdmans, 1994.

Martin, James. "What is the official church teaching on homosexuality? Responding to a commonly asked question." *America*, April 6, 2018. https://www.americamagazine.org/ faith/2018/04/06/what-official-church-teaching-homosexuality-responding-commonly-asked-question.

———. *Building a Bridge*. Revised and Expanded. New York: Harper-Collins, 2018 [2017].

———. Fr. Martin's tweet of May 2013 as cited by Michael O"Loughlin on *Fr. James Martin & Others Are #SayingSomethingPositive - New Ways Ministry*.

Martin, Ralph, and Peter Williamson, eds. *John Paul II and the New Evangelization*. Cincinnati: Servant Books, 2006.

Mascall, E. L. *The Openness of Being, Natural Theology Today*. The Gifford Lectures, 1970-71. London: Darton Longman & Todd, 1971.

Mavrodes, George I. *Revelation in Religious Belief*. Philadelphia: Temple University Press, 1988.

May, William E. et al. *Catholic Sexual Ethics. Catholic Sexual Ethics: A Summary, Explanation and Defense*, 2nd edition. Huntington, IN: Our Sunday Visitor, 1998.

McGrath, Alister E. *Intellectuals Don't Need God and other Modern Myths*. Grand Rapids: Zondervan, 1993.

McGreevy, John T. *Catholicism and American Freedom: A History*. New York: W. W. Norton, 2003.

Melina, Monsignor Livio. "Homosexual Inclination as an 'Objective Disorder': Reflections on Theological Anthropology." In *Living the Truth in Love: Pastoral Approaches to Same-Sex Attraction*, edited by Janet E. Smith and Father Paul Check, 129–40. San Francisco: Ignatius Press, 2015.

Morse, Jennifer Roback. *The Sexual State*. Charlotte, NC: Tan Books, 2018.

Mouw, Richard J. *He Shines in All That's Fair: Culture and Common Grace*. Stob Lectures. Grand Rapids: Eerdmans, 2001.

Müller, Cardinal Gerhard, with Franca Giansoldati. *Vatican Confidential: A Candid Conversation with Cardinal Gerhard Müller*. Translated by Nicholas Reitzug. Manchester, New Hampshire: Sophia Institute Press, 2023.

———. *True and False Reform: What it Means to Be a Catholic*. Translated by Susan Johnson. Steubenville, OH: Emmaus Academic, 2023.

Mullins, Patrick. *Zorgen voor een eigenwijze kudde: Een pastorale ethiek voor een missionaire kerk*. Zoetermeer: Uitgeverij Boekcentrum, 2015.

Murray, John Courtney. *We Hold These Truths: Catholic Reflections on the American Proposition*. New York: Sheed and Ward, 1960.

Newman, John Henry Cardinal. *An Essay on the Development of Christian Doctrine*. 6th ed. 1845. Reprint, Notre Dame: University of Notre Dame Press, 1989.

———. *Apologia Pro Vita Sua*. 1864. Reprint, New York: Random House, 1950.

Nichols, Aidan. "Integral Evangelization." *Josephinum Journal of Theology* 13, no. 1 (2006): 66–80.

———. "Rerelating Faith and Culture." In *Christendom Awake: On Reenergizing the Church in Culture*. Grand Rapids: Eerdmans, 1999.

———. "Reviving Doctrinal Consciousness." In *Christendom Awake: On Reenergizing the Church in Culture*. Grand Rapids, MI: Eerdmans, 1999.

———. *Christendom Awake: On Reenergizing the Church in Culture*. Grand Rapids, MI: Eerdmans, 1999.

———. *Epiphany: A Theological Introduction to Catholicism*. Collegeville, MN: Liturgical Press, 1996.

———. *From Hermes to Benedict XVI: Faith and Reason in Modern Catholic Thought*. Herefordshire: Gracewing, 2009.

———. *From Newman to Congar: The Idea of Doctrinal Development from the Victorians to the Second Vatican Council*. Edinburgh: T&T Clark, 1990.

———. *The Shape of Catholic Theology*. Collegeville, MN: The Liturgical Press, 1991.

Niebuhr, H. Richard. *Christ and Culture*. New York: Harper & Row, 1951.

O'Collins, Gerald, and Edward G. Farrugia, eds. *A Concise Dictionary of Theology*. New York: Paulist Press, 1991.

O'Donovan, Oliver. *Begotten or Made?* Landrum, SC: Davenant Press, 2022.

Ott, Ludwig. *Fundamentals of Dogma*. Edited by James Canon Bastible. Translated by Patrick Lynch. Fully revised and updated by Robert Fastiggi. London: Baronius Press, 2018 [1952].

Pannenberg, Wolfhart. "History and Meaning in Bernard Lonergan's approach to theological method." In *Looking at Lonergan's Method*, edited by Patrick Corcoran, SM, 88–100. Dublin: The Talbot Press, 1975.

Paul VI. *Evangelii Nuntiandi*, Apostolic Exhortation, 1975. Evangelii Nuntiandi (December 8, 1975) | Paul VI

———. *Donum Vitae*. Instruction on Respect for Human Life in is Origin and on the Dignity of Procreation; replies to certain questions of the Day, February 27, 1987. Congregation for the Doctrine of the Faith. Instruction on respect for human life (vatican.va).

———. *Humanae Vitae*. July 25, 1968. Vatican.va.

Pearcey, Nancy R. *Love Thy Body: Answering Hard Questions about Life and Sexuality*. Grand Rapids, MI: Baker Books, 2018.

Pegis, *St. Thomas and the Problem of the Soul in the Thirteenth Century*. Toronto, Ontario: Pontifical Institute of Mediaeval Studies, 1978 [1934].

Pelikan, Jaroslav. "Nature and Grace." In *The Christian Tradition: A History of the Development of Doctrine, vol. 1, The Emergence of the Catholic Tradition (100–600)*, 278–331. Chicago: University of Chicago Press, 1971.

Perry, Louise. *The Case Against the Sexual Revolution*. Cambridge: Polity, 2022.

Persona Humana (1975), Declaration on Certain Questions Concerning Sexual Ethics. http://www.vatican.va/roman_curia/congregations/cfaith/documents/rc_con_cfaith_doc_19751229_persona-humana_en.html.

Homosexualitatis problema (1986), Letter to the Bishops of the Catholic Church on the Pastoral Care of Homosexual Persons.

Pietersma, Henry. *Phenomenological Epistemology*. New York: Oxford University Press, 2000.

Pius XII. Allocution "Magnificate Dominum" (1954). Online: Pope Pius XII, Allocution "Magnificate Dominum" (1954)–Novus Ordo Watch.

Plantinga, Alvin. "On Christian Scholarship," http://www.veritas-ucsb.org/library/plantinga/ocs.html.

Polanyi, Michael. "Knowing and Being." In *Knowing and Being: Essays by Michael Polanyi*, edited by Marjorie Grene, 124–37. London: Routledge & Kegan Paul, 1969.

———. "Sense-Giving and Sense-Reading." in *Knowing and Being: Essays by Michael Polanyi*, edited by Marjorie Grene, 181–207. London: Routledge & Kegan Paul, 1969.

———. "The Logic of Tacit Inference." In *Knowing and Being: Essays by Michael Polanyi*, edited by Marjorie Grene, 138–58. London: Routledge & Kegan Paul, 1969.

———. *Personal Knowledge: Towards a Post-Critical Philosophy*. Gifford Lectures 1951–52. New York: Harper & Row, 1964 [1958].

———. *The Study of Man*. Chicago: University of Chicago Press, 1959.

———. *The Tacit Dimension*. Chicago: University of Chicago Press, 1966.

Pontifical Biblical Commission, *What is Man? A Journey through Biblical Anthropology*. Translated by Fearghus O"Fearghail and Adrian Graffy. London: Darton, Longman & Todd, 2021.

Pontifical Council for Culture. *Towards a Pastoral Approach to Culture*, May 23, 1999.

Pontifical Council for Justice and Peace, *Compendium of the Social Doctrine of the Church*. Libreria Editrice Vaticana, 2004. Chapter 4, Part 3, section b, §§171–84. http://www.vatican.va/roman_curia/pontifical_councils/justpeace/documents/rc_pc_justpeace_doc_20060526_compendio-dott-soc_en.html#The universal destination of goods and private property.

Pope, Stephen. "The Vatican's Blunt Instrument," *The Tablet* (August 9, 2003). https;//www.clgs.org/marriage/history_ pope.html.

Pottmeyer, Hermann J. "Tradition." In *Dictionary of Fundamental Theology*, edited by René Latourelle and Rino Fisichella, 1119–26. New York: Crossroad, 1994.

Pronk, Pim. *Against Nature? Types of Moral Argumentation regarding Homosexuality*. Grand Rapids, MI: Eerdmans, 1993.

Radcliffe, *What"s the Point of Being a Christian?* London: Burns & Oates, 2005.

Rahner, Karl. "Dogmatic Constitution on the Church: Chapter III, Articles 18–27." In *Commentary on the Documents of Vatican II*. 5 vols. Vol. 1, edited by Herbert Vorgrimler. Translated by Lalit Adophus, et al. New York: Herder & Herder, 1967–69.

———. "The Development of Dogma." In *Theological Investigations*. Vol. 1, translated by Cornelius Ernst, 39–77. Baltimore, MD: Helicon Press, 1961.

———, and Herbert Vorgrimler. *Theological Dictionary*. Edited by Cornelius Ernst. Translated by Richard Strachan. New York: Herder & Herder, 1965.

Ratzinger, Joseph Cardinal. "Doctrinal Commentary on the Concluding Formula of the *Professio fidei*." 1998.

———. "Doctrinal Note on Some Questions Regarding the Participation of Catholics in Political Life," Congregation for the Doctrine of the Faith, November 24, 2002, no. 4, http://www.vatican.va/roman_curia/congregations/cfaith/documents/rc_con_cfaith_doc_20.

———. "Faith, Philosophy and Theology." In *The Nature and Mission of Theology*, translated by Adrian Walker. San Francisco: Ignatius Press, 1995.

———. "Pluralism as a Problem for Church and Theology." In *Church, Ecumenism, & Politics*. San Francisco: Ignatius Press, 2008.

———. "Searching for Peace, Tensions and Dangers." In *Values in a Time of Upheaval*, 109–10.

———. "To Change or to Preserve? Political Visions and Political Praxis." In *Values in a Time of Upheaval*, translated by Brian McNeil, C.R.V., 11–29. New York: Crossroad, 2006.

———. "*What Is Truth?* The Significance of Religious and Ethical Values in a Pluralistic Society." In *Values in a Time of Upheaval*, 53–72.

———. "What Keeps the World Together, The Pre-political Moral Foundations of a Free State." In *Values in a Time of Upheaval*, 31–44.

———. *Caritas in Veritate*, §3. http://w2.vatican.va/content/benedict-xvi/en/encyclicals/documents/hf_ben-xvi_enc_20090629_caritas-in-veritate.html.

———. *Donum Veritatis*. On the Ecclesial Vocation of the Theologian. Congregation for the Doctrine of the Faith, May 24, 1990.

———. *Eschatology, Death and Eternal Life*. 2nd ed. Translated by Michael Waldstein. Edited by Aidan Nichols, OP. Washington, DC: Catholic University of America Press, 2007 [1977], 79–181.

———. "The Church's Teaching Authority—Faith—Morals." In Principles of Christian Morality, Translated by Graham Harrion, 45-73. San Francisco: Ignatius Press, 1986.

———. *Principles of Catholic Theology*, Translated by Sister Mary Francis McCarthy, S.N.D. San Francisco: Ignatius Press, 1987 [1982].

———. *The Spirit of the Liturgy*. Translated by John Saward. Dan Francisco: Ignatius, 2000.

———. *The Yes of Jesus Christ*. Translated by Robert Nowell. New York: Crossroad, 1991.

———. *Theological Highlights of Vatican II*, trans. Henry Traub, et al. (New York: Paulist Press, 1966.

———. *Truth and Tolerance: Christian Belief and World Religion*. Translated by Henry Taylor. San Francisco: Ignatius Press, 2004.

———. *Truth and Tolerance: Christian Belief and World Religions*. Translated by Henry Taylor. San Francisco: Ignatius Press, 2004.

———. Ratzinger, Joseph with Vittorio Messori. *The Ratzinger Report: An Exclusive Interview on the State of the Church*. Translated by Salvator Attanasio and Graham Harrison. San Francisco, CA: Ignatius Press, 1985.

———Ratzinger, Joseph's commentary on *Dei Verbum*, the dogmatic constitution on divine revelation

Reformed Ecumenical Council, Athens 1992. *Hermeneutics and Ethics*

Regnerus, Mark. *Cheap Sex: The Transformation of Men, Marriage, and Monogamy*. Oxford: Oxford University Press, 2017.

"Reflective Equilibrium." In *Stanford Encyclopedia of Philosophy*. Spring 2004 Edition.

Reilly, Robert R. *Making Gay Okay, How Rationalizing Homosexual Behavior Is Changing Everything*. San Francisco, CA: Ignatius Press, 2014.

———. *Making Gay Okay, How Rationalizing Homosexual Behavior is Changing Everything.* San Francisco: Ignatius Press, 2014.

Ridderbos, Herman. *Paul: An Outline of His Theology.* Translated by John Richard De Witt. Grand Rapids, MI: Eerdmans, 1975.

Rieff, Philip. *The Triumph of the Therapeutic.* Fortieth Anniversary Edition. Wilmington, Delaware: Intercollegiate Studies Institute, 2006.

Rist, John M. *What Is a Person? Realities, Constructs, Illusions.* Cambridge: Cambridge University Press, 2020.

Roberts, Christopher C. *Creation and Covenant, The Significance of Sexual Difference in the Moral Theology of Marriage.* New York: T&T Clark, 2007.

Rowland, Tracey. *Culture and the Thomist Tradition After Vatican II.* New York: Routledge, 2003.

Rubin, Lillian. *Erotic Wars: What Happened to the Sexual Revolution.* New York: HarperPerennial, 1990.

Schaeffer, Francis A. *The God Who is There.* Thirtieth anniversary edition. Downers Grove: InterVarsity Press, 1988.

Schilder, Klaas. *Christ and Culture.* Translated by G. van Rongen and W. Helder. Winnipeg: Premier, 1977. Originally published in 1932.

Schindler, David L. "Christology, Public Theology, and Thomism: de Lubac, Balthasar, and Murray." In *The Future of Thomism*, edited by Deal W. Hudson and Dennis William Moran, 247–64. Minneapolis: American Maritain Association, 1992.

Schockenhoff, Eberhard. "A Consistent Ethic of Life (with a Few Blemishes): Moral-Theological Remarks on *Evangelium Vitae* and on Some Protestant Questions about It." Edited by Reinhard Hütter and Theodor Dieter. 237–61. Grand Rapids, MI: Eerdmans, 1998.

———. *Natural Law and Human Dignity: Universal Ethics in an Historical World.* Translated by Brian McNeil. Washington, D.C.: Catholic University of America Press, 2003.

Second Vatican Council. *Apostolicam Actuositatem* [Decree on the Apostolate of Lay People], November 18, 1965.

———. *Lumen Gentium* [Dogmatic Constitution on the Church], November 21, 1964.

Seerveld, Calvin G. *A Christian Critique of Art and Literature*. Ontario: Association for Reformed Scientific Studies, 1964.

———. *How to Read the Bible to Hear God Speak*. Sioux Center, IA: Dordt College Press, 2003.

Sertillanges, A. G. *The Foundations of Thomistic Philosophy*. Translated from the French by Godfrey Anstruther. Providence, RI: CLUNY, 2020.

Shimron, Yonat Shimron. "Christian Reformed Church Brings LGBT Stance into Faith Statement." *Christianity Today*. June 15, 2022.

Smedes, Lewis. "The Bible and Ethics."

———. *Mere Morality*.

Smith, James K. A. "On 'Orthodox Christianity': some observations and a couple of questions," *Fors Claviga*, Friday, August 4, 2017. Online: Fors Clavigera: On "orthodox Christianity": some observations, and a couple of questions.

Sokolowski. *Eucharistic Presence*. Washington, DC: Catholic University Press of American, 1994.

———. *The God of Faith and Reason, Foundations of Christian Theology*. Washington, DC: Catholic University Press of American, 1995 [1982]/

Sprinkle, Preston. *People to Be Loved: Why Homosexuality is not Just an Issue*. Grand Rapids: Zondervan, 2015.

Stanford Encyclopedia of Philosophy. "Reflective Equilibrium." https://plato.stanford.edu/archives/spr2004/entries/reflective-equilibrium/.

Stob, Henry. "Calvin and Aquinas." In *Theological Reflections: Essays on Related Themes*, 126–30. Grand Rapids: Eerdmans, 1981.

———. "Observations on the Concept of the Antithesis." In *Perspectives on the Christian Reformed Church: Studies in Its History, Theology, and Ecumenicity*, edited by Peter De Klerk and Richard R. De Ridder Grand Rapids: Baker, 1983.

Stout, Jeffrey. "The Voice of Theology in Contemporary Culture." In *Religion and America: Spirituality in a Secular Age*, edited by Mary Douglas and Steven M. Tipton, 249–61. Boston: Beacon Press, 1983.

Stump, Eleonore. "Orthodoxy and Heresy." *Faith and Philosophy* 16, no. 2 (April 1999): 147–63.

Sullins, Paul. "The gay gene myth has been exploded." In *Mercatornet*, September 3, 2019. https://www.mercatornet.com/conjugality/view/the-gay-gene-myth-has-been-exploded/22824. Sullins" article is a commentary on the recent findings in a study of the genetic basis of homosexuality published in the journal Science: https://science.sciencemag.org/content/365/6456/eaat7693

Sullivan, Francis A. *Magisterium: Teaching Authority in the Catholic Church*. Eugene, OR: Wipf and Stock Publishers, 2002 [1983].

Swinburne, Richard. *Revelation*. Oxford: Clarendon Press, 1992.

Taylor, Charles. "Two Theories of Modernity." *Hastings Center Report* 25, no. 2 (March-April 1995): 24–33.

Thielicke, Helmut. *The Ethics of Sex*. Translated by John W. Doberstein. New York: Harper & Row, 1964.

Tracy, David. "A Hermeneutics of Orthodoxy." In *Christian Orthodoxy*. Edited by Felix Wilfred and Daniel F. Pilario. *Concilium* (2014/2), 71–81, 74–75.

———. *Plurality and Ambiguity: Hermeneutics, Religion, and Hope*. San Francisco: Harper & Row, 1987.

———. *The Blessed Rage for Order: The New Pluralism in Theology.* New York: The Seabury Press, 1975.

Trigg, Roger. *Rationality and Religion.* Oxford: Blackwell, 1998.

———. *Reality at Risk: A Defence of Realism in Philosophy and the Sciences.* Sussex: The Harvester Press, 1980.

Trueman, Carl. "The Battle for the Body." *First Things* (September 21, 2023). https://www.firstthings.com/web-exclusives/2023/09/the-battle-for-the-body.

———. *The Rise and Triumph of the Modern Self: Cultural Amnesia, Expressive Individualism, and the Road to Sexual Revolution.* Wheaton, IL: Crossway, 2020.

Turner, Philip. "Sex and the Single Life." *First Things* 33 (May 1993): 15–21.

USCCB. *Always Our Children, A Pastoral Message to Parents of Homosexual Children and Suggestions for Pastoral Ministers.* 1998.

van der Hoeven, Johan. "Na 50 Jaar: Philosophia Reformata—Philosophia Reformanda." *Philosophia Reformata* 51.1–2 (1986): 5–28.

van Genderen, J., and W. H. Velema. *Concise Reformed Dogmatics.* Edited by Ed M. van der Maas. Translated by Gerrit Bilkes. Phillipsburg, NJ: Presbyterian & Reformed, 2008.

Van Til, Henry R. *The Calvinistic Concept of Culture.* Grand Rapids: Baker Academic, 2001. Originally published in 1951.

Vanhoozer, Kevin. *Biblical Authority After Babel* (Grand Rapids, MI: Brazos Press, 2016

Vatican I, *Dei Filius,* Denzinger §2020

Vatican I. Dogmatic Constitution *Dei Filius* on the Catholic Faith, 1870.

Vatican II, *Apostolicam Actuositatem.*

Vatican II, Dogmatic Constitution, *Lumen Gentium* (1965), §25; "Profession of Faith," Congregation for the Doctrine of the Faith (1989); *Donum Veritatis,* Congregation for the Doctrine of the Faith (1990);

"Commentary on the Profession of Faith"s concluding paragraphs, Professio Fidei (1998). All of these documents may be found in appendices e–h, respectively, in Dulles, *Magisterium, Teacher and Guardian of the Faith*, 131–181

Vatican II. "Gaudium et Spes" (Pastoral Constitution on the Church in the Modern World). December 7, 1965.

Veenhof, Jan. "Nature and Grace in Bavinck." *Pro Rege* (June 2006): 10–31.

Verburg, Marcel E. *Herman Dooyeweerd: The Life and Work of a Christian Philosopher*. Translated and edited by Herbert Donald Morton and Harry Van Dyke. Jordan Station, Ontario: Paideia Press, 2015.

Via, Dan O., and Robert A. J. Gagnon. *Homosexuality and the Bible: Two Views*. Minneapolis: Fortress Press, 2003.

Vriesman, Rev. Aaron. "The Difficult Synod of 2023 and What it Says about the CRC," *The Banner*, July 28, 2023.

Webster, John. *Holiness*. Grand Rapids, MI: Eerdmans, 2003).

Weigel, George. *Witness to Hope: The Biography of Pope John Paul II*. New York: HarperCollins, 1999.

Welch, Lawrence J., and Guy Mansini. "In Conformity to Christ." *First Things*, April 2006. https://www.firstthings.com/article/2006/04/in-conformity-to-christ.

White, Thomas Joseph. *The Light of Christ, An Introduction to Catholicism*. Washington, DC: Catholic University of America Press, 2017.

Wojtyla, Karol. "Ethics and Moral Theology." In *Person and Community: Selected Essays*, translated by Theresa Sandok, 101–106. New York: Peter Lang, 1993.

———. "Ethics and Moral Theology" In *Person and Community: Selected Essays*, translated by Theresa Sandok, 101–106. New York: Peter Lang, 1993.

Bibliography

———. "On the Metaphysical and Phenomenological Basis of the Moral Norm." In *Person and Community: Selected Essays*, translated by Theresa Sandok, 73-94. New York: Peter Lang, 1993.

———. "Subjectivity and 'the Irreducible' in Man." In *Person and Act*, 536-45. Originally in *Analecta Husserliana* VII, "Subjectivity and 'the Irreducible' in Man," 107-14. This essay has been retranslated by Theresa Sandok, with a slightly altered title, "Subjectivity and the Irreducible in the Human Being," in *Person and Community*, 209-17.

———. "The Problem of Catholic Sexual Ethics." In *Person and Community: Selected Essays*, translated by Theresa Sandok, 279-99. New York: Peter Lang, 1993.

———. "The Problem of Experience in Ethics." In *Person and Community: Selected Essays.*, translated by Theresa Sandok, 107-127. New York: Peter Lang, 1993.

———. "The Problem of the Theory of Morality." In *Person and Community: Selected Essays*, translated by Theresa Sandok, 129-61. New York: Peter Lang, 1993.

———. "Thomistic Personalism," in *Person and Community*.

———. *Love and Responsibility*, Translation, Endnotes, and Foreword by Grzegorz Ignatik, New Translation. Boston: Pauline Books & Media, 2013 [1960].

———. *Man in the Field of Responsibility*. Translated by Kenneth W. Kemp and Zuzanna Maślanka Kieroń. South Bend, IN: St. Augustine's Press, 2011.

———. *Person and Community: Selected Essays*. Translated by Theresa Sandok. New York: Peter Lang, 1993.

———. *Person and Act and Related Essays*. Translated by Grzegorz Ignatik. (Washington, DC: Catholic University of American Press, 2021.

Wolters, Albert M. "Creation Order: A Historical Look at Our Heritage." In *An Ethos of Compassion and the Integrity of Creation*, edited by Brian J. Walsh, Hendrik Hart, and Robert E. Vander Vennen, 33-48. Lanham: University Press of America, 1995.

———. "What Is To Be Done? Toward a Neo-Calvinist Agenda." http://www.wrf.ca/comment/article.cfm?ID=142.

Wolterstorff, Nicholas "The Promise of Speech-act Theory for Biblical Interpretation." In *After Pentecost: Language and Biblical Interpretation*, edited by Craig Bartholomew, Colin Greene, and Karl Moeller, 73-90. Grand rapids, MI: Zondervan, 2001.

———. "Keeping Faith: Talks for the New Faculty at Calvin College." *Occasional Papers from Calvin College* 7, no. 1 (February 1989).

———. "Resuscitating the Author." In *Hermeneutics at the Crossroads*, edited by Kevin J. Vanhoozer, et al., 35-49. Bloomington and Indianapolis: Indiana University Press, 2006.

———. "Tertullian's Enduring Question." *The Cresset* (June/July 1999): 1-14.

———. "The Role of Religion in Decision and Discussion of Political Issues." In *Religion in the Public Square: The Place of Religious Convictions in Political Debate*, edited by Robert Audi and Nicholas Wolterstorff, 67-120. New York: Rowman & Littlefield, 1997.

———. *Divine Discourse, Philosophical Reflections on the Claim that God Speaks*. Cambridge: Cambridge University Press, 1995.

———. *Religion in the University*. New Haven: Yale University Press, 2019.

———. *Until Justice and Peace Embrace*. Grand Rapids: Eerdmans, 1983.

Wright, N. T. "N.T. Wright in Debate about Homosexuality 4." Live event at Sierra Retreat Center in Malibu, California, February 2009.

Zuidema, S. U. "Common Grace and Christian Action in Abraham Kuyper." In *Communication and Confrontation: A Philosophical Appraisal and Critique of Modern Society and Contemporary Thought*, 52–104. Toronto: Wedge, 1972.

Zuidervaart, Lambert. "Holistic Alethic Pluralism: A Reformational Research Program." *Philosophia Reformata* 81 (2016): 156–78.

Index

A

Allison, Gregory R., 408
Anscombe, Elizabeth, 300
Anthropology, 97-98, 126,
　129, 132-33, 135-36, 139,
　141, 145, 147, 149-52,
　154-56, 164, 168-69, 173,
　176, 182-83, 188, 194-95,
　206, 219, 284, 288, 290-
　91, 296, 320, 323, 330,
　333, 335, 337-38, 341-42,
　352, 355, 360-61, 370,
　386, 393-96, 398, 405-06,
　418, 420, 423, 429, 435,
　442-43, 449, 452-53, 496-
　97, 505-06
Aquinas, St. Thomas, 47, 151,
　153, 170, 175-77, 179-80,
　181, 183, 213, 232-33,
　312, 320-21, 333
Ashley, Benedict, OP, 240-41,
　244, 263
Augustine, 21, 213, 440

Authentic Freedom, 276, 403
Authenticity, 234, 317, 348
Autonomy, 64-5, 72, 207, 213,
　286, 353, 373

B

Balthasar, Hans Urs von, 59-
　60
Basil of Caesarea, 61
Bavinck, Herman, 9, 208-09,
　286, 364
Benedict XVI (see also
　Ratzinger), 6, 55, 62, 77-9,
　86, 265, 329, 399, 431,
　443, 457, 504

C

Call to Holiness, 281, 468–69,
　478
Cardinal Eijk, 95, 97, 99, 131,
　135-36, 138-42, 153-54,
　194, 198, 208, 212-13,

242-43, 267, 303, 305, 406, 410, 433, 463
Cardinal Ratzinger, 54, 89, 95, 102-03, 115, 333, 350, 397, 399, 401, 417-18, 443-47, 456-57, 495, 503-04
Caritas in Veritate, 399-400, 455
Catholic Social Teaching, 5, 19, 75
Chastity, 96-7, 99, 101, 105, 352, 427, 442, 448-49, 452-53, 455, 463, 465, 480-81
Christian Ethics, 126, 239, 251, 282, 346, 369, 444, 500
Christian revelation, 6, 64, 382
Complementarity, 97, 198, 207, 257, 309, 315, 407, 411-12, 452
Congregation for the Doctrine of the Faith, 207, 406-07
Conjugal Act, 289, 300

Conjugal Love, 96-7, 294, 296, 339, 341, 427, 452, 491
Conscience, 72, 77, 83, 146, 229, 237, 286, 434, 449, 460-61, 484-85
Contraceptive Mentality, 300
Culture of Life, 72-3, 75-6
Culture Wars, 205, 405

D

Dei Filius, 226, 362
Dignity of the Human Person, 80-1, 154, 231, 286, 355, 403
Dignity of the Person, 73, 84, 340, 343
Divine Persons, 304, 309, 316
doctrine of creation, 1, 219
Dooyeweerd, Herman, 1, 9, 25, 47, 126, 129, 131, 199, 213, 335
Dualism, 8, 10, 63-5, 132-33, 145, 148-50, 153, 185-86, 250, 284, 330, 410

E

eschatology, 15, 211
Evangelii Gaudium, 506
Evangelii Nuntiandi, 483
Evangelium Vitae, 72
Experience and Judgment, 126
Expressive Individualism, 286

F

Familiaris Consortio, 142, 319, 451
Farley, Margaret, 243, 327, 349, 374, 392, 500-01

G

Gaudium et Spes, 117, 138, 140, 211
Gender Identity, 141, 411
Gender Ideology, 126
Giddens, Anthony, 299, 301
Gift of Self, 24-5, 74, 97, 143, 288, 317, 355, 453
Gnosticism, 71, 80, 284

H

Homosexual Acts, 97, 242-43, 303-04, 412, 415, 418, 433, 436
Homosexualitatis problema, 207, 406-07, 413-15
human rights, 5-6, 79-80, 229-31, 256
Human Sexuality, 23, 100, 178, 209, 212, 214, 216, 218-19, 269, 289, 291, 297-98, 302, 310, 330, 354, 396, 405-06, 428, 480, 487

I

Incarnation, 7, 43, 65, 68-9, 73, 96, 175, 490
Integral Evangelization, 3-4, 489

J

Jesus Christ, 2, 12, 15-6, 25-8, 31, 33, 35-7, 43, 47, 52, 54-5, 57, 62-3, 69-70, 72-

3, 90, 118-19, 166, 218, 247, 257, 281, 326, 360-61, 365, 368, 379, 440, 447, 468-69, 473, 479, 488

Joseph Cardinal Ratzinger, 54, 95, 333, 495

K

Kuyper, Abraham, 9-10, 34, 48

L

Law of Gradualism (Gradualness), 274-75

Love and Responsibility, 318, 340

Lumen Gentium, 28

M

Man and Woman He Created Them: A Theology of the Body, 144, 195, 199, 205, 261, 332, 334, 336, 393, 406

Marriage, 1, 2, 71, 73, 79, 95-102, 104, 106, 131, 136-39, 143-44, 207, 214, 220-22, 234, 243, 255, 257, 259-60, 263, 266, 271, 289, 293-96, 298, 300, 302-08, 310, 313, 315-16, 327, 339-343, 352, 354, 360-61, 393-96, 409, 426, 435, 440, 442, 450, 452, 481, 490-91, 496-97

Materialistic Anthropology, 288, 290-91, 296, 337, 405

Moral Absolutes, 241, 282

Moral Judgment, 225, 241, 272, 282, 374, 459

Moral Life, 239, 245, 254, 260, 271, 285, 386, 389, 402, 450, 467, 480

Moral Norms, 95, 101, 218, 230-31, 235, 237, 241, 243, 260-61, 265, 269, 282, 327, 352, 357, 359, 361, 374, 459, 491, 497

Moral Realism, 282

Moral Relativism, 76, 359

moral revelation, 5

Index

Moral Theology, 126, 345-46, 369-70, 441, 500
Moral Truth, 6, 83-4, 101, 237, 266, 269, 276, 282-83, 324, 357, 403, 433, 459, 491
Morally Problematic, 278, 397, 400-01, 504-05

N

natural law, 5, 75, 77, 94, 97-8, 99, 126, 138, 175, 213, 215, 222, 229-32, 234-38, 260, 267, 272, 304, 329, 352, 356, 359-60, 388-92, 411-12, 427, 435, 453
Natural Moral Law, 6, 76, 98, 102, 104, 352
Nature and Grace, 2-3, 7-13, 36, 50, 65-7, 264-65, 312, 489
new evangelization, 3-4, 7, 17, 70-3, 91, 488

O

Objective Disorder, 414, 418, 421, 428
Objective Moral Order, 252, 411, 433, 505
Objective Truth, 72, 268, 347, 382, 488

P

Pastoral Care, 126, 278, 397, 399-401, 405, 504-05
Person and Act, 132, 181, 187, 193-94, 199, 203, 334, 336
Persona Humana, 406, 433
Personalism, 174-77, 179, 186-87
Personalistic Norm, 291-92, 325, 333
Phenomenology, 168, 188
Philosophical Ethics, 126, 345-46, 370, 500
Plantinga, Alvin, 286-87
Pluralism, 36, 487
Pontifical Biblical Commission, 453

Pontifical Council for Culture, 27
Purity, 60, 62, 94, 263, 443

R

Redemption, 1, 3, 6, 8, 12, 16-7, 26-7, 30, 32, 43, 47, 52, 57, 63, 66, 67-9, 166, 211, 221, 245, 261-62, 264-65, 279, 311-14, 316, 394, 406, 424, 436, 462, 464, 482-83, 488-89, 506
Relationality, 133, 219, 222, 296, 373
Relativism, 54-5, 76, 80, 330, 356, 359, 500
Renewal Movement, 209, 224, 283, 405

S

Sacrament of Marriage (see also Marriage), 144, 354, 396, 409
Same-Sex Attraction, 407, 411-12, 417-18, 465
Secularism, 71
Seksuele Ethiek, 406
Sexual Difference, 96, 136-7, 198, 284, 301, 309-13, 331, 393, 395, 409, 450, 488, 490, 496
Sexual Disenchantment, 288, 291, 302
Sexual Ethics, 73, 95, 98-9, 101, 106, 126, 131, 197, 212-13, 222, 243, 258, 318-19, 324, 326-27, 329-32, 352, 354, 357, 360, 372, 392, 396, 443, 454, 490-91, 496-97
Sexual Revolution, 126, 205, 208, 214-15, 223-24, 283, 296-99, 436, 497
sick reason, 90
Subjectivism, 76, 190, 193, 287, 292, 341, 374, 470, 476-77

T

Teaching Authority, 103, 109, 213, 448, 478,
Teleology, 322, 329, 384, 389

Theology of the Body (see *Man and Woman He Created Them*)
Tolerance, 82, 276
Total Self-Giving, 338
Truth and Love, 399, 447, 457, 504

U

Unitive and Procreative Ends, 329

V

Veritatis Splendor, 228, 361
Vincent of Lérins, 116, 226, 261, 269, 362-63

W

Western culture, 3-4, 72, 488
Witness to the Truth, 465, 472

www.ingramcontent.com/pod-product-compliance
Lightning Source LLC
Chambersburg PA
CBHW071400230426
43669CB00010B/1397